CHILDREN, PSYCHOLOGY, AND THE SCHOOLS

Research and Trends

CHILDREN, PSYCHOLOGY, AND THE SCHOOLS

Research and Trends

BRYANT FEATHER

Chicago State College

WALTER S. OLSON

Chicago Board of Education

SCOTT, FORESMAN AND COMPANY

Front cover photo by Hal A. Franklin II. High-school students are shown in the Hyde Park section of Chicago, waiting for morning classes to begin. In the background are some of the controversial mobile classrooms—known in Chicago as "Willis wagons" after former Chicago school superintendent Benjamin J. Willis.

Back cover photo by Bob Amft.

PREFACE

Teachers, parents, and students of psychology have at least one interest in common: children. Consequently, they need to know something about the results of psychological research relating to children. No science — certainly not psychology — can be static; and in these days of unprecedented expansion of knowledge, it is more difficult than ever for a conscientious teacher to follow, even at a distance, the findings of the educational psychologists. Teachers must attempt it, nevertheless. For what is more important professionally than to understand children in order to prepare them for the increasingly complex problems that surely lie ahead?

Children, Psychology, and the Schools will acquaint concerned persons with some of the contemporary projects, interpretations, and trends in educational psychology. The titles of the nine parts of the book show the comprehensive range of the readings, many of which are original contributions not available elsewhere. We believe this book of readings can easily be adapted for use with most texts in courses on educational, child, adolescent, and abnormal psychology as well as in courses on delinquency and the family. The selections dealing with preschool programs, the special problems of subcultures, new approaches to self-control and discipline, and dropouts and delinquents as well as those that invite teachers and counselors to take critical looks at themselves may be especially timely and useful.

Parents of very young children and their teachers are more and more convinced that the proper preparation for school, whether at home or in the Head Start Program, may be the key to success in the subsequent school years. Hence, considerable attention is afforded this new field of preschool preparation in Part I. Because changes are occurring so rapidly in today's schools, special treatment is given in Part II to the setting in which learning is expected to take place — to the techniques being tried in tradition-bound areas such as reading, to a new medium of education, television, and to the discovery and nurture of creativity and talent. Part III deals with children who develop intensely complex psychological problems either because of maternal deprivation or because of a culturally different family background. It also discusses children with physical and mental handicaps and describes new classroom methods of handling the problems of such children. Part IV has an approach to discipline that is new, promising, and exciting; its basis combines religious, Freudian, and pragmatic elements. Part V is concerned with classroom behavior problems. Part VI considers the complex problems of the adolescent — his need for information, his search for means of communicating with his parents and the adult world, and his demand for appropriate sex education. Part VII takes a close look at today's dropouts and delinquents, and at the programs that help to prevent delinquency and dropping out of school. Trends and practices that enable teachers and counselors to gain a better understanding of themselves and of their jobs are presented in Part VIII. The psychology of testing and the use of test results receive extensive treatment in Part IX.

Special credit and appreciation are extended by the editors to Scott, Foresman's College Division, and especially to Miss Louise Howe. Special assistance by Miss Alice Krysher and Mr. Don Klemick is also acknowledged.

BRYANT FEATHER
WALTER S. OLSON

TABLE OF CONTENTS

V
APPLICATION OF LEARNING THEORY TO BEHAVIOR PROBLEMS

VI
REACHING FOR ADULTHOOD

VII
DROPOUTS AND DELINQUENTS

VIII
TEACHERS AND COUNSELORS

IX
TESTING

Part I

GETTING READY FOR SCHOOL

The entire future success and happiness of a child, both in school and in life thereafter, may be determined or greatly influenced by the preparation that is made for his beginning school. The attitude of the family during the years prior to the first year of kindergarten is often subtly revealed to a child by things that are said in the home about school, teachers, and education in general. The absence or presence of books, records, even conversation itself, will influence feelings about school and education and its worth and ultimate value.

Children learn most from imitation during these formative years and much of their socialization and interpersonal relationships will be, or should be, well developed before they ever enter schools. Those children who are not developed are disadvantaged and may take years to catch up, even if there has been no lasting traumatic damage to the personality structure.

All of the principles of conditioning should be applied to the very young child. Parents should begin to plan for that first day of school well in advance, actually months or years ahead of the child's date of entry. "Beginning school" should not be a one day traumatic event, but rather the culmination of a long period of preparation. Children should be exposed to school buildings, school personnel, and procedures at an early date. They should be made to feel that going to school is a natural, important, and an exciting step in the growing up process.

In instances of deprivation because of economic, social, or other forces, a variety of experimental techniques have been and are being tried to enrich the experience and training offered in the home, and to correct or resolve any conflict or damage that may have already been done. It seems that a child diagnosed and treated prior to five years of age has a good chance of overcoming any disadvantage that may have existed and of being able to compete with other children.

So much importance is attached to the readiness and preparation of children for formal education of late, that the government and others have developed special programs to meet the needs of those deprived children. Long before "Head Start," nursery schools and prekindergarten programs had become vital parts of many communities and families. Since special preparation and conditioning were found to be of psychological import to some children, it was felt that its benefits should be offered to all children.

In some instances children are ready for the formal school experience well ahead of others, and there is a growing practice for such precocious children to be entered into government or private nursery schools or "Head Start" programs. There is always the problem of determining the readiness and need for such programs prior to starting traditional kindergarten and there is still a great need for scientific tests which evaluate "readiness" for education outside the home. Progress is rapidly being made, but there is still no one sure method to know when a child is ready for school.

The availability of several kinds of programs makes the choice more complicated for parents of children who are ready to begin school at an early age. Some government supervision and checking affords a minimum of assurance to parents that the program that they are considering has at least reached and maintained the standards established by the state which include the physical plant, the teaching and administrative staff, the program of study and activity, the selection of students, and the safety and health precautions.

No matter which program he may enter, there is none as important as his home conditioning. And there can be no doubt that "getting ready for school" is vital to a child's growth and to the lifelong effects of his education.

Helen Bradley

"HEAD START" IN EDUCATION AND LIFE

For some time psychologists and educators have been considering various plans for preparing a child for his first school experience. It was obvious to many, for a number of reasons, that children were not being adequately prepared to begin school, even at the kindergarten level.

We now have developed an exciting and successful plan for preschool preparation, called "Head Start," directed and operated by Miss Helen Bradley in Chicago.

Well-established psychological principles have been applied to the problems. The family is involved, the child's needs are met, and training for each child begins at whatever level is necessary. Exposure to new experiences is arranged, and opportunities for expression both formally and informally are provided.

Without a doubt, the experiences of the Head Start Program, not only as reported by Miss Bradley, but also by others throughout the United States, will be further evaluated and refined, and ultimately they will become part of the formal, government educational program.

Interest in and concern for the care and education of young children is not new. The importance of the early years of a child as the ideal starting point in his education has long been recognized. Almost every society has made some provisions for the care of young children of mothers whose circumstances forced them to be away from home. In some countries it was considered essential for factories to provide some type of preschool care and training for children of mothers in their employ. The work of Maria Montessori is well known; the work and programs of the infant schools in Europe have been detailed and publicized. The nursery school program in London may well have been the "parent" of nursery schools today. These programs, as well, were designed to deal with the communities—mainly urban.

The thinking of leaders in the field of education, and studies of how children learn have pointed to the all-important preschool years as pivotal in the child's development. Everyone is acquainted with the quotation attributed to Dr. Parker, highlighting the importance of early education. When an anxious mother came to him expressing concern for her child, Dr. Parker asked the age of the child. When told that the child was five, his

reply was classic: "Mother, you are already five years too late."

Yet much of the attention to early childhood education has been a form of lip service with little public support for programs of a formal nature. There have been day care centers for the poor; nursery schools generally have been tuition schools which catered to the so-called middle class. Public education in many states did not—and does not —provide for kindergarten programs. Money was unavailable. Such programs were expensive; economies were effected at the lower end of the scale. This area was generally considered the responsibility of the home.

Teen-agers have been in the news and in the spotlight of education for the past few decades as never before. Deep concern has been registered for the dropout; the juvenile delinquent made headlines. Then came Sputnik, and with it a new focus upon the entire educational system of the United States—and the achievement of students. Next came the controversy of "Why Johnny Can't Read." The elementary school became the center of attention, particularly the primary grades.

As a result of this renewed emphasis upon

areas of human development, significant were the findings of research providing evidence of the need for emphasis on preschool education. The studies of Bloom and others highlighted the potential for education of the young – the very young child in particular. Early childhood education was again being reviewed. The social and economic problems which have increased since World War II and the Korean conflict have focused attention and concern upon resolution and correction of the problems which have arisen in our society. The search is underway for causes. The need for remediation and, more importantly *prevention*, are the concerns of leaders. Political, social, educational leaders – all are united in the search.

It is recognized that the mobility of population, the trend away from rural areas, the rapid growth of cities, and the accompanying problems have caused dramatic changes in our country. Automation has replaced large numbers of skilled and unskilled workers. The problems of the nation's poor have become so numerous that they cannot be overlooked. The War on Poverty has been announced. The needs of the disadvantaged and concerns for children have converged in education today – in both public and private systems. Money became available, not only for elementary and secondary education but for preschool and prekindergarten children, with particular concern for programs for the culturally disadvantaged or so-called deprived pupils.

In 1965 the Head Start Program began. Primarily a government funded program, Head Start is a program involving not only the children but also parents and communities. Because Head Start was designed to be a comprehensive educational program, intensive and extensive social and psychological as well as medical services were provided in addition to the program in the classroom. Health programs were not limited to the routine inspections and diagnostic aspects of examination. Follow-up and referrals of families to appropriate agencies for treatment and assistance are important aspects of the entire health and social service component.

The general objective of the Head Start Program is to provide a climate, an environment in which a child may develop his innate ability and realize his real potential as a person at his own level of development. Basically, all children have the same potentialities and the same problems. The disadvantaged child for whom Head Start is designed has extra problems. A good preschool program takes into account the deficiencies of the deprived home and accordingly the program is designed to do the jobs which are normally assumed by parents in middle-class homes. Head Start calls for a cooperative effort to involve parents and communities in order to evaluate a child's abilities and deficiencies, meet and satisfy the needs of children who are severely deprived of the very basic elements of childhood: love, outlet, security, experience. All resources have been marshalled to improve the total environment of the child.

The curriculum covers language arts, communication, and simple nature experiences and was based on exposure to experiences, taking part, successes, mastery and involvement. The students explored: they used equipment and toys which were carefully selected and designed for specific purposes. There were some toys they had never known before. The children expressed themselves: they painted, they sang, they danced, they listened, they heard stories, they talked, they became acquainted and associated with other children of their own age, they learned to share, and they learned to get along with one another. The children enjoyed books: they told stories, they dramatized episodes, they engaged in "Let's pretend with a purpose," and they role-played. The children took trips: they went to the zoo and the park, they toured their neighborhoods, they visited the fire station and post office, they planted flowers, and they celebrated birthdays. The children experienced success: they learned about themselves, their skills, their abilities, and their limitations.

Class size was limited to twenty children working under the direction of a fully qualified teacher and two teacher aides. Assisting the teacher were auxiliary staff members: a curriculum consultant and a social service team which was composed of a teacher-nurse, a parent coordinator, an adjustment teacher. Under the guidance of this team, the preschoolers used the classroom and the out-of-doors as a learning laboratory. Significantly, the children reacted to the learning experience with all the fervor of the small child experiencing for the first time the wonder of life. In response, the teaching team, spurred by the flexibility of the program and the depth of the needs of the students, became even more creative in meeting the students' needs.

Parent involvement was of maximum importance to the Head Start Program if the total impact of child development and community responsibilities was to be realized. Parent organizations were formed in each center during the first week of the program. These parent organizations helped to plan activities and programs to meet the particular center's needs. The Community Action Program entailed unified activities of civic, business, and local people which were aimed specifically toward developing a consciousness of community pride in appearance, and establishing a core of individuals to work diligently and systematically toward this goal.

Recognition of the importance of the family unit in the development of the child was basic in planning the program. Parents were involved; now involvement of the entire community became a vital component of each center's program.

A variety of programs, experiences, and activities to serve the needs and interests of parents was cooperatively planned by parent coordinators and the parents of preschool children. These programs were comprehensive in scope, involving objectives which were designed:

– to develop a more positive self-image for parents (described as a spirit of "self-help" to replace patterns of apathy and dependence)

– to actively involve parents and community in the school life of the children and thus to bring about a closer understanding of the program's goals

– to provide educational experiences for parents in an effort to help them better understand the physical, emotional, and educational needs of their children

– to help parents become acquainted with their city and the educational, cultural, and recreational opportunities it offers

– to provide opportunities for intracultural exchange resulting in increased understanding between the various ethnic groups of Chicago and the contribution each group makes to the total fabric of society

– to bring home, school, and community closer together with all working toward the goal of the best possible education for preschool children.

Large group meetings for purposes of parent education and organizational business, small group meetings to discuss particular problems shared by parents, committee meetings to implement parent activities, individual conferences, educational tours, and workshops were geared toward attaining maximum involvement and participation of parents in the developmental and educational program for their children. Recognition of mutual concerns encouraged parent commitment and established the parents as important members of the Head Start team.

Parents need to be involved in school programs. The poem "Children Learn What They Live" points up the importance of the home and the environment.

If a child lives with criticism,
   He learns to condemn.
If a child lives with hostility,
   He learns to fight.

If a child lives with ridicule,
  He learns to be shy.
If a child lives with tolerance,
  He learns to be patient.
If a child lives with encouragement,
  He learns confidence.
If a child lives with praise,
  He learns to appreciate.
If a child lives with fairness,
  He learns justice.
If a child lives with security,
  He learns to have faith.
If a child lives with approval,
  He learns to like himself.
If a child lives with acceptance and friendship,
  He learns to find love in the world.
                              —*Anonymous*

The Community Action and Beautification programs mobilized all forces—pupils, parents, teachers, civic leaders, and local business owners—to improve the total environment of the child.

Community participation was the means of achieving vital and meaningful goals which included:

—extending the basic values of the preschool program to the community
—improving community surroundings
—involving both parents and teen-agers in community renewal
—achieving better neighborhoods.

Daily contacts were made with local merchants, community leaders, and neighborhood clubs. Mornings, afternoons, evenings, and weekends were filled with meetings designed to develop pride and leadership in the local community. Efforts were made to foster understanding and to develop respect for the cultures of all ethnic groups involved in the program. An action program enlisted the support and cooperation of all residents.

Neighborhood parades which advertised beautification aspects of the preschool program also served to mobilize community resources. Unsightly lots were cleared of debris to make way for play areas for young children and communication areas for parents. Civic leaders and merchants contributed to the establishment of facilities and of equipment which provided an extension of the preschool program to formerly undeveloped lots in the area.

Beautification of property was realized as thousands of children and their parents planted flowers, painted fences, cleaned alleys, and disposed of garbage. Beautification activities became a daily practice.

Specialized personnel in the Community Action Program established classes in home economics for mothers and shop work for fathers. General directions and suggestions for electrical repair were provided for parents who must budget time and income to provide for their needy families. Parents were transported to and from classes by Head Start personnel. Buses were engaged for this purpose where feasible and possible.

Pride was the appeal and lasting achievement the goal. Dedication was the driving force as principals, teachers, public officials, merchants, agencies, parents, and residents joined forces to assist those in need to find ways of helping themselves.

This is an exhilarating time for preschool education, but the recent focus of educators on early childhood education, and the consequent rush to implement programs for preschool learning, have left little time for evaluation. We have made some discoveries, however, and have reinforced some old beliefs in these first years of Head Start and pre-primary education. We realize that

—children need to live for today; to be accepted as children; to be given a childhood
—parents must be involved in the child's learning
—children have individual differences and differing levels of development at any given age—each is unique and needs to be provided for individually

—children need help to develop better, positive self-image

—early childhood is the best time to develop self-image

—early childhood is the best time to develop concept formation and language development

—dealing with deprived young children is not baby-sitting, nor is it kindergarten

—the school must establish the value of cultural exchange and respect for religious differences in educating the child—understanding must be gained of the child's total environment

—there must be a continuation and follow-up and follow-through for all children through the grades. Curricula need to be revised in the kindergarten and primary grades.

From the vantage point of working with preschool children and families, the question comes frequently to mind: How can we assess the true value of Head Start preschool experience? Surely, at this stage, it would be difficult to assess the value of a single child's emergence from fearful shyness to absorption in a group . . . difficult to weigh the value of a program in which a child can cry because he does not want to go home at the close of the preschool day . . . difficult to gauge the subtleties of inner change that cause a child to ask, "Why can't I go to school on Saturdays?" How does one measure the faith and enthusiasm of teachers summed up in one parent's remark, "When I am preparing my child for school, she sings all the while"? And what of the remark of another parent concerning the teacher attitude that is reflected throughout the program: *"My boy likes school because you like him."*

We assess by experience, observation, and evaluation. For the child who gropes to understand, the great need is to help him to realize himself and something of the world around him. What we have striven to do for that child in the past—as always—is to give him a sense of himself through the medium of our basic hard work and belief in this program. We already know that teachers have reported significant changes in the behavior of children. We cannot yet know the long-range effects of those changes which only time will adequately reveal.

It is our hope, perhaps an idealistic one, that a real childhood as expressed in this selection from Francis Thompson would be the heritage of every child:

Know you what it is to be a child? It is to have a spirit yet streaming from the waters of baptism; it is to believe in love; to believe in loveliness; to believe in belief. It is to be so little that the elves can reach to whisper in your ear; it is to turn pumpkins into coaches and mice into horses, lowness into loftiness, and nothing into everything. And for each child its fairy godmother in its own soul; it is to live in a nutshell and count yourself the king of infinite space.

David P. Weikart

PRESCHOOL PROGRAMS: PRELIMINARY FINDINGS

Mental retardation among the disadvantaged raises psychological problems which have long been researched by specialists in the area of early child development. Today principles are being applied to meet the obvious needs of this particular segment of the population.

Because of the great variation in the socioeconomic group in the country and the differences in child rearing, it can only be expected that there would be a variety of unique problems among the disadvantaged group. Certainly the preschool age group is one to which the greatest amount of attention should be directed in view of the recognized psychiatric fact that the most important developmental years, physically and psychologically, are the years one to five.

The article points out that much work had been done by nursery and prenursery schools for years, but now with the additional emphasis from federal funds, past experience can be reviewed, retested, and modified in view of new knowledge. Also, experimental programs can be tried and the research indicates that there are many new and promising practices that have not been used which may produce rewarding benefits to this age group and to society in general.

On the final day of the 1961 annual convention of the American Association on Mental Deficiency, a panel of child development experts presented a series of papers on the educational problems of the disadvantaged child. The consensus of the panel was that a preschool intervention program might be what was needed to correct the intellectual deficits with which disadvantaged children start out in school.

When this group met, such thinking was largely speculative. The panel little anticipated what was to come: the massive adoption of preschool intervention as a nationwide answer to the educational problems of the disadvantaged child. Yet in 1965 more than 500,000 four- and five-year-olds attended six to eight weeks of preschool financed by more than $90,000,000 of federal funds, and Operation Head Start had moved into the national conscience as a national "good."

It is generally agreed that intervention before the disadvantaged child attends regular school is the most promising area for action. Bloom (1964) pointed out in his summary of the research on child development that the period before four years of age is the time of greatest intellectual growth and is therefore the optimal time for training. Scott (1962), working with animals, developed the concept of "critical period." Observing the effect of various kinds of deprivation, such as isolation, on lambs and puppies, he concluded that timing was a crucial factor in early environmental conditions and hypothesized that various kinds of experiences

have a major effect when they occur at one period in time but not when they occur at another period. "Organization can be strongly modified only when active processes of organization are going on." Krech (1960), Rosenzweig (1964), Bennett (1964), and others have successfully identified and measured physiological changes in the brain that relate directly to early experiences in carefully controlled studies with laboratory rats.

Pasamanick & Knoblock (1961) have documented the impact of deprivation most vividly in their study of infant development. Employing samples of Negro and White infants selected for equal birth weights and absence of defects or premature birth, and using the Gesell Development Scale, they found no significant difference between the two groups at 40 weeks of age; the White babies obtained a developmental quotient of 105.4 and the Negro babies a DQ of 104.5. At age 3, the first 300 of the original 1,000 children studied were retested and a highly significant difference was found. The development quotient of the White children rose to 110.9, while the DQ of the Negro children fell to 97.4. Bayley (1965) found no differences between 1 to 15-month-old Negro and White babies nor between boys and girls, first-born and later born, or babies from different cultural backgrounds and geographical locations.

Abridged from *The Journal of Special Education*, Vol. 1, No. 2. Winter 1967. Reprinted by permission of the author and the publisher, *The Journal of Special Education*, 443 S. Gulph Road, King of Prussia, Pa., 19406.

In view of research evidence such as the above, then, preschool intervention between 10 months and age 5 ought to prevent or correct the cognitive deficits found in disadvantaged children. What results support this conclusion?

Preschools are not virgin territory. They are inhabited, traditionally, by successful and intelligent middle-class children and taught by university-trained teachers. The teaching methods traditionally employed are child-centered and permissive. Sears & Dowley (1963, p. 814) characterize these methods as " . . . watching and waiting for the child's needs to emerge and determine the timing of different activities. . . ." The specific aims of the traditional nursery program are seen as (p. 822): (a) meeting organic needs and establishing routine habits; (b) developing motor skills and confidence; (c) developing manipulatory skills; (d) developing control and restraint; (e) developing appropriate behavior; (f) psycho-sexual development; (g) language development; (h) intellectual development.

Research on programs with these traditional curriculum goals has produced varied results. Reviews of the literature by Fuller (1960), Sears & Dowley (1963), and Swift (1964) indicate that for middle-class children, on the whole, there is no difference on any characteristic or dimension between control and experimental groups by the time the groups reach the third grade. There are indications, however, from the early and extensive work of Skeels (1966), Skodak (1949), and others at the Iowa Child Welfare station and from Kirk's (1958) more recent study with mentally handicapped children that children who are labelled as culturally deprived may be directly and permanently aided by preschool experiences. Recent reviews by Robinson (1966) and Fowler (1966) also support cautious optimism in respect to such improvements.

With this background we come to the present and a major wave of studies focused entirely on disadvantaged preschool children.

THE RESEARCH

The current research can be categorized by the specific disadvantaged population studied, by the range of services provided, and by the program or curriculum methods used in the treatment phase of the project. Unfortunately, many current projects are either short-term programs without planned follow-up or are still in progress, so that long-term data on effectiveness of intervention are not available. For critical evaluation, most studies include social, emotional, and cognitive factors. A few have planned for the use of standardized achievement tests as long-term criteria.

The various populations under study are Northern Negro in great city slum areas and metropolitan fringe cities, Southern Negro, Northern White, and institutionalized mentally retarded.

The project services range from simple short-term programs with limited objectives to ambitious programs aiming at a total impact. A typical short-term project would be one of these: a several-days-a-week nursery, a six-to-eight-week summer preschool, or a concentrated reading-readiness program. A total impact project would include all of these: at least two years of preschool experience, carefully planned parent education programs, regular home visits by teachers and social workers, and medical services.

For the purposes of this review, various projects will be summarized and grouped on the basis of their specific curriculum orientation. It is this orientation, rather than the over-all project services rendered, that seems to determine the results.

Three different basic preschool teaching methods are used, which can be summarized as follows:

1. *Traditional nursery school methods.* "Watching and waiting for the child's needs to emerge and determine the timing of different activities." The primary goals are for social, emotional, and motor development.

2. *Structured nursery school methods.*

Carefully sequenced presentations of teacher-planned activities according to a specific developmental theory. The primary goals are cognitive and language development. Traditional nursery school materials and activities are frequently employed, but used to achieve pre-determined goals.

3. *Task-oriented nursery school methods.* Carefully sequenced presentations of teacher-planned program activities to accomplish specific predetermined goals such as reading, arithmetic, or logical thinking. New, specifically designed, task-related activities and materials are employed; those of the traditional nursery school are not.

The primary instrument for assessing the effectiveness of intervention programs has been the Stanford-Binet Intelligence Scale. While the instrument has been criticized as being too culture-bound to be an effective test of intelligence for disadvantaged children, no major scale has been available to effectively replace it with younger children. In addition, its predictive validity correlations with academic success in school and later job attainment remain unimpeachable.

The critical results from intervention programs are not those associated with IQ change, of course, but with improvement in achievement. Unfortunately, there is very little research information relevant to this problem, as most studies have not investigated long-term effects of early stimulation programs.

The following section of this paper presents examples of each of the three intervention methods along with the available statistical data. Where possible, the Stanford-Binet Intelligence Scale is used as the immediate dependent variable or criterion of effectiveness, and achievement tests are used as the intermediate dependent variable.

PROGRAMS EMPLOYING TRADITIONAL
NURSERY SCHOOL METHODS

Four programs will be discussed: (a) Alpern's Community Center Project; (b) Henderson's Preschool and Primary Education Project; (c) Strodtbeck's Reading Readiness Project; (d) Operation Head Start.

It is inaccurate to classify all of these programs as traditional nursery schools. Many new and varied techniques have been employed. The projects are presented in a rough continuum from those using the most to those using the least traditional methods.

Alpern's Community Center Project

Overview of Project and Program. Alpern (1966) evaluated an enrichment program for socially disadvantaged children sponsored by a community house which for many years has operated nursery school programs. Two groups of four-year-olds with 22 children in each group were formed before the start of school in the fall of 1964. The groups were matched for sex, intelligence and "readiness" as measured by the Metropolitan Readiness Test, Form R. The curriculum goals of the school were to: (a) increase the children's language skills, (b) develop positive attitudes toward the concepts of teacher, learning, and school, and (c) increase knowledge of middle-class values and experiences. The experimental group attended nursery school three times a week with an average attendance of 72 sessions. The control group did not have this experience.

Results. The first year results were: (a) There were no differences in intelligence between the groups at the time of initial or second testing, (b) Both groups made significant gains in all three readiness measures from initial to second testing, and (c) There were no significant differences between the groups in any of the readiness tests. A follow-up is to be undertaken.

Henderson's Preschool and
Primary Education Project

Overview of Project. The Ford Foundation has sponsored several major preschool experimental programs. The Preschool and Primary Education Project of the Council for Human Services in Pennsylvania (Henderson, 1965) is an illustration of these. The project has two components: short-term summer schools and year-round programs that serve over 1,000 children. Included, too, are parent education programs with educational visits to the home by teachers as often as twice a month and/or direct case service by trained social workers. The administrative control is widely diffused to each participating school district, and only the data collection is centralized at the project's headquarters in Harrisburg, Pa. The project is still underway.

The year-round program differed from the summer program in its greater stress on language development and in its more ordered and sequential introduction of new materials and experiences to the children. The actual curriculum and methods, however, were the responsibility of each individual teacher. To ascertain the focus the teachers gave to their individual programs, they were each asked to list the main accomplishments of the summer:

1. About two thirds of the teachers listed the main accomplishments of the program as either social, emotional, or motoric.

2. Fewer than one quarter listed the main accomplishments as intellectual (for example, cognition and language).

3. Half of the teachers did not list any cognitive or language accomplishments for the summer program.

4. Almost all of the teachers perceived the key learning problems to be of a social nature.

Results. The results of the summer project on standardized tests include data on the Illinois Test of Psycholinguistic Abilities (ITPA) and the Peabody Picture Vocabulary Test (PPVT). The Stanford-Binet Intelligence Scale was not employed. For those children who attended the summer preschool project augmented by a year of parent education

and assistance from teachers and social workers, no significant differences between the experimental and control groups on the PPVT IQ and the ITPA Language Quotient were found.

The results of the year-round program are not much different. Measured after a year of preschool and three months of kindergarten, the experimental group was found to have a significantly higher PPVT score than its control group. The groups were not significantly different on the ITPA Language Quotient. A second group to have preschool experience was also compared with a control group. This time no significant differences were found between experimental and control groups on either PPVT or ITPA IQ.

At the entrance into first grade, experimental and control children were compared on the Metropolitan Readiness Test. The results indicate the experimental and control children are about equally "ready" for first grade instruction since no significant differences were found.

Strodtbeck's Reading Readiness Project

Overview of Project. Strodtbeck (1963) initiated a reading-readiness nursery program for four-year-old Negro children. It was felt that the preschool relationship with the family could be used to improve the child's later school adjustment and the mother's understanding of the educative process. The research design called for a continuing series of groups (about N-10 in each) to participate in a 13-week reading-readiness program. Testing was done three months before the child's entrance into the nursery, at entrance, and at end of nursery. This method used each child as his own control by testing three months before treatment.

Program. The program had various goals depending upon the methods and orientation of the different teachers in charge. This project is one of the few where two basic styles of curriculum were employed. Groups I and

II (N-15) experienced a program described as "mothering while teaching." The teachers observed the children and noted the natural leadership in the group-teaching intervention centered about the spontaneously generated activity of the children. The teachers prided themselves on the development of maturity in the children's peer relations. These methods are those traditional to nursery schools.

Groups III, IV, and V experienced a different, more controlled teaching style. The teachers closely supervised free play activities and demonstrated to the children how to carry out the activities and projects. Verbal participation was greatly encouraged and emphasis was placed upon the noon day meal. The method closely parallels those of projects reported in the next section.

Results. The study is one of the few research projects which permit a tentative comparison for teaching methods on several replicated samples. There is a clear difference of 4.3 IQ points (significance level not available) between the attainment of the children in the readiness program taught by traditional methods and the readiness program taught by a somewhat structured method, in favor of those taught by the structured method.

Operation Head Start

Overview of Project. Operation Head Start was a massive federal program involving more than 500,000 children. While research was built into the program, much of the project study did not employ control groups. The project included six to eight weeks of preschool, parent involvement, medical services to children, and nutrition programs. The teachers for the project were not required to be certified preschool teachers, but all attended at least a week of paid orientation at universities and colleges throughout the country.

Program. While traditional-style nursery school methods seem to have been used in most programs, the general fervor with which the project was implemented produced many innovations.

Results. Allegato (1966), in reviewing data released by the Head Start Headquarters, quotes Richmond, director of the project for the Office of Economic Opportunity, as saying that Head Starters gained an average of nine points in IQ (probably the PPVT). He also said that they were more proficient in learning, had more intellectual curiosity, and were better adjusted to the classroom. "Standard tests showed significant gains in the educational achievements and mental ability of Head Start children all across the country."

Sigel, however, in a personal communication, commented on the Merrill-Palmer findings in the Detroit Head Start groups. After one month of kindergarten in regular Detroit programs, there were no differences on the PPVT between those children who had attended Head Start and those from the same environment who had not. While these findings cannot be generalized to all 561,000 Head Starters, the implications are strong that eight weeks of summer school and four weeks of regular school *both* produce change in participating children.

Discussion. Qualitative evaluation was included in most of the project reports. Nearly all reports contained an enthusiastic section discussing the general response of the children to the program. "He didn't talk for six weeks and now listen to him!" is a typical comment. Asking questions, use of new language, and, of course, social, emotional, and motor development, were also remarked upon by the teachers.

On the standardized tests, where carefully controlled research has been employed, the results are consistent. The total outcome of all projects using the so-called traditional methods of nursery school education with a disadvantaged population is that there are no statistically significant differences on standardized intelligence tests or achievement measures. Long-term follow-up data are not available. The absence of differences between groups may be altered by later growth by experimental groups or increased deficits in control groups. At this time no specific theoretical position can be substantiated.

PROGRAMS EMPLOYING STRUCTURED NURSERY SCHOOL METHODS

Two such programs will be described briefly: (a) *Gray and Klaus's Early Training Project*; (b) *Deutsch's Preschool and Early Elementary Education.*

While these projects depart radically in some ways from the concerns of the traditional nursery school, the basic teacher-child relationship is preserved, with its focus on social adjustment, peer relations, good work habits, etc. The structure is derived from the programs' clearly-stated goals for specific cognitive and language development.

Gray and Klaus's Early Training Project

Overview of Project. One of the early studies in the current series was initiated by Gray and Klaus (1965) in Murfreesboro, Tenn. The Early Training Project involved carefully selected experimental and control groups of Negro children. One experimental group (N-20) had three summers of preschool experience and a second group (N-20) two summers of preschool experience of ten weeks each summer before entering regular first grade. Both groups were visited in their homes by a project visitor each week throughout the year between preschool experiences. A local community control group (N-20) was established as well as a distal control group (N-27) in a nearby community. Follow-up is still in progress.

Program. The curriculum was specifically designed to prevent the accumulation of deficits generally thought to occur in the development of disadvantaged children. The

curriculum procedures were based upon a review of the literature on differences in social class, in child-rearing practices, in motivational patterns, in language, and in perceptual and cognitive development. Two classes of variables were employed in the day-to-day programing. The first class comprised attitudes toward achievement, especially as related to the kinds of activities expected in school, persistence, ability to delay gratification, and interest in typical school materials. The second class comprised aptitudes necessary for achievement, especially as related to perceptual and cognitive development and to language.

Results. The project was evaluated by several intelligence and achievement tests. Over the two-year period, the experimental groups gained an average of 7 IQ points while the control group lost an average of 5 IQ points. The difference in final scores is statistically significant. While the results of only two testing periods are given, a total of five Stanford-Binet or Wechsler Intelligence Scale tests were administered between 1962 and 1964.

The project reports that on first grade screening tests, the experimental children did "conspicuously" better than the controls. No statistical data are given.

Deutsch's Preschool and Early Elementary Education Project

Overview of Project. The Institute for Developmental Studies of New York City under the direction of Deutsch (1965) has instituted a series of intensive and far-reaching studies on the preschool and early elementary education of disadvantaged children. The experiments on the preschool level involve a complex design of special treatments of varying lengths. The effects of both one- and two-year preschool programs are being tested, as well as the impact of specially designed kindergarten through third grade classes. The information available at this time involves youngsters in experimental groups who have participated in special classes at age 4 and then have moved into specially enriched kindergarten programs. The control children did not participate in preschool and entered kindergarten directly. Most of the children are Negro. The project is still in progress.

Program. The program has been described as having no single philosophic system or theory behind it (Deutsch, 1965). The approach is seen as flexible and exploratory. "Eclectic combinations of the developmental and educational theories advanced by such workers as Piaget, Hunt, Bruner, Montessori, Jensen among others" (p. 58) is the Annual Report's description of the classroom curriculum development efforts. The physical space of the classroom is ordered to help build the child's concepts of order and space. Efforts are made to enhance the child's self concept through the use of Negro dolls, stories involving Negro children, and photographs of the child himself. Language development is encouraged through classroom activities designed to elicit verbal responses. Auto-instructional devices have been developed and are employed at all program levels. These include the Listening Center with tape-recorded lessons and stories and the use of the Bell and Howell Language Master.

Attention is given to training in auditory and visual discrimination. The activities involved in the training also serve as a means of teaching concepts and imparting knowledge. Extensive supervision is provided for teachers of the experimental groups.

Results. Goldstein (1965) presented the results on two groups of children who had participated in the pre-kindergarten program. For Group I, the net gain in the two years is 5.0 IQ points for the experimental group as contrasted with a loss of 7.0 IQ points for the control group. The second experimental group demonstrates a similar pattern, though

the control group did not lose as much over the one-year period for which the data are available. The post-test score differences between the groups are statistically significant in all cases.

Large amounts of other data have been collected by the Institute, including that from the PPVT, the ITPA, and the Columbia Mental Maturity Scale. No information on achievement data are available at this time.

PROGRAMS EMPLOYING TASK-ORIENTED PRESCHOOL METHODS

Unlike the programs outlined above, projects have not been widely instituted. While other programs seek to remedy the developmental deficiencies of disadvantaged children through adjusted or enriched natural environments, the task-oriented preschool method attempts to achieve the same goals through artificially contrived procedures. Cazden (1966) calls these "non-natural" treatments.

Most of these programs have very direct goals. There is no climbing apparatus, no doll corner with social-dramatic play, and no juice time with one cookie on normal days and two when visitors are present. There are things to be mastered and the program is directly focused on the task at hand.

Perhaps the most highly developed task-oriented curriculum is that of Bereiter (1965, 1966) at the University of Illinois.

Overview of the Project. The project involves 15 disadvantaged four-year-old children in attendance at a University of Illinois preschool. The ITPA is employed as well as specially developed academic measures of the children's progress. There are three 20-minute sessions a morning, each devoted to the direct teaching of language, reading, and arithmetic. Each of these periods is separated by 30 minutes of refreshments, singing, and a shorter period of relatively unstructured play activity. "Each subject has its own teacher, who works with each of three groups of children in turn, as in a high school" (Bereiter, 1965, p. 3). All three subjects are taught at one time with the groups of children rotating from teacher to teacher.

Program. The curriculum is academically oriented, based on two premises: (a) Mere enrichment of experience is not enough to enable the culturally deprived child to overcome his backwardness in the skills necessary for later academic success. (b) Training in the formal, structural aspects of language will have more value in the improvement of academic aptitude than will training directed toward facilitating social communication.

The curriculum uses direct instruction to achieve the specific goal of developing the information processes necessary for thinking.

The language program is organized to help the child acquire grammatical statement patterns and an understanding of the logical organization of these patterns. Precise pronunciation, a critical requirement, receives considerable emphasis. The child's language is regarded as being basically nonlogical and lacking in the formal properties necessary for organized thought. The teaching method for the language program derives from the techniques of modern oral methods of teaching foreign languages. "Pattern drill" is the basic technique employed.

The arithmetic and reading programs also use these methods with rules taught through the patterning of language. In arithmetic the emphasis is upon learning statement forms, such as $2 + 0 = 2$ (identity). The teaching of arithmetic operations places emphasis on the formal meaning and not on concrete objects generally used as a basis for arithmetic education. Reading instruction follows the same pattern, with emphasis upon a maximum amount of experience in the explicit handling of rules and statements. In teaching, "We demanded the children's attention by continual questioning; we demanded that they look and respond, with or without understanding" (Bereiter, 1965, p. 26). After the basic rules about words are learned, the chil-

dren progress to phonic blending, etc., and then on to formal reading.

The task-oriented approach is best summarized by Bereiter in his comment, "Full participation of all children in the learning tasks is treated as a requirement to which the children must conform (much like the handwashing requirement in the conventional nursery school" (1965, p.4).

Results. Results are not fully available at this time. Basically the project reports excellent success in obtaining the cooperation of the children, growth in general intellectual ability, and academic development.

Discussion. Data from the projects discussed in this paper lead to a number of tentative conclusions about effective educational programing for disadvantaged children.

TRADITIONAL VERSUS STRUCTURED METHODS

The selection of adequate criteria by which to judge effective programing has always been difficult in education (Ryans, 1960). The general debate in the nursery education field has tended to be that one must choose between a cognitive and language development program structured by teacher planning and a program that promotes the socio-emotional growth of the child and is structured by the child's expressed needs. Two sets of criteria have been proposed to assess curriculum effectiveness. For the first type of program, standardized achievement and intelligence tests have assumed prime importance. For the second type, the teacher's qualitative assessments of the child's social and emotional growth are used. Each position, and with some justification, sees little value in the other's criteria of success.

It appears from the data presented in this paper that those programs which aspire to the development of improved socio-emotional adjustment by the child do obtain that goal. It appears that programs which intend to produce cognitive and language development obtain the same goal of socio-emotional growth and produce the desired intellectual development as well. The extensive Henderson study in Pennsylvania points up very clearly that preschool teachers, left unsupervised, will focus on the child's social and emotional growth. This focus will produce no significant change in intellectual development. The Perry Project, the Deutsch projects, the Strodtbeck II groups, Dawe's program, and others all report the same kinds of social and emotional growth and record impressive success with intervention in intellectual development. The Perry Project also finds significant differences in later academic achievement.

The conclusion is that preschool projects with the disadvantaged child must provide planned teacher action according to a specific developmental theory in which the primary goals are cognitive and language development. It seems that good social and emotional adjustment are an essential condition for such development, but focus on adjustment alone does not automatically produce the desired intellectual growth.

WHEN SHOULD PRESCHOOL INTERVENTION OCCUR?

The timing of preschool experience has been viewed as critical. Bloom (1964) has predicted that 50 per cent of the intelligence measured at age 17 is developed by age 4. He also suggests that a conservative estimate of the effect of extreme environments on intelligence is about 20 IQ points (1964, p. 89). Pasamanick & Knoblock (1961), however, document the occurrence of deprivation by age 3. It is reasonable to assume that:

1. The experiences provided by the environment to the disadvantaged child are inadequate for continued normal development after age 1.

2. The process of deprivation is probably insidious in that it deprives the child of key experiences necessary to establish the foundation for future development before the effects of the deprivation process are noticeable through performance tests.

From this viewpoint, all projects reported in this paper are remedial rather than preventive in that the services are offered after the deprivation has occurred. Several new projects are underway exploring the gap between age 1 and age 3. Projects by Caldwell at the University of Syracuse and Schaefer at the National Institute of Mental Health represent two of these. Data are not available from these at this time.

HOW STABLE ARE OBTAINED RESULTS?

A major point to be noted in considering projects is that after the first year's initial spurt in obtained IQ, there is a tendency for a drop the second year. This drop occurs whether the child is enrolled in a second year of a structured preschool or in a regular school. If a drop does not occur, no further rise is especially evident. Fowler (1966) attributed this second year drop to diffuse programing on the part of projects that find the phenomenon.

The basic problem may be that the education of the disadvantaged child passes through a number of stages that force different programing goals upon the teacher. The readiness to accept these stages varies greatly from teacher to teacher and project to project. For example, Riessman (1964) identified two crucial stages in teaching the disadvantaged. The first stage is simply to achieve some form of contact and communication with the child to win his attention and confidence. The second is to develop an educational program. Riessman points out that many teachers and programs feel they have succeeded when the goals of the first stage are attained and fail to move on to the second.

Looking at this point of view and the data beginning to be available from preschools, it is possible to suggest a natural evolution of preschool programs.

Stage One: Silence. During this stage the child is brought into contact with the environment of the preschool and the adults who operate the program. Just talk! Say anything! In Riessman's terms, the goal is the establishment of rapport with the child. This goal is suspiciously like that of the traditional nursery school curriculum. No real cognitive growth occurs, since the program is not oriented toward cognition and language development. The emphasis is upon expression of self and adjustment. This stage seems to be the focus of the teachers in the Henderson project, a good many Head Start programs and other general intervention programs. These are the projects that basically registered no long-term and few short-term gains in intellectual or achievement growth. This stage is necessary and absolutely essential if the second stage is to be undertaken. Once contact has occurred, education may begin.

Stage Two: "Des god damn peaches am burning!" This now-famous quote from *Life* magazine's article on the Deutsch project illustrates the goal of the second stage. A "set" for learning, problem solving, and language growth is produced. Excitement with new things in new situations alerts the child mentally and prepares him for learning. Rapid short-term intellectual growth or an increased mental alertness results. Dawe obtained 14.2 points of IQ change in only 50 hours of instruction. Perry Project has obtained up to 20 points in eight months. The stimulation through exposure to new language and demands for critical thinking combine to produce in the child a new capacity for problem solving and alertness to the outside world. An obvious outcome is an increased ability to respond to problems presented by adults in their demand for language and attention and to handle situations such as intelligence tests more efficiently.

Stage Three: "These god damn peaches are burning!" Now alert, the child is ready to learn to participate in the full educational process that Riessman identifies. The rapport

stage is fairly easy for good teachers to achieve. The development of a "set" or "alertness" for learning can be created with a well-defined and teacher-planned curriculum. The completion of the third stage, however — long-term and systematic educational programing — is what is essential but generally missing. Perry Project, Kirk's study, Deutsch's programs have all grappled with this problem. The girl must learn to transform her ghetto speech into educationally functional language. The "god damn" can stay because we're broad-minded, but without the correct verb form the girl may be permanently handicapped in logical thinking.

It is the difficulty in implementing this third stage that seems to set the limits to the child's growth potential. We simply do not know what to do in order to speed up the development process and continue the growth rate. The problem sets a practical limit of eight months on preschool intervention programs. That is as long as is necessary to complete stage two and place the child at a new level of functioning. It may be that Bloom (1964) is right when he suggests that a 10-point change is all that is possible during early childhood, since that is the magnitude of the change that is being obtained in most programs.

Perhaps it may be concluded that the question isn't, "How stable are the obtained results?" but, "Why are they so stable?"

CURRENT DIRECTIONS IN PROGRAM DEVELOPMENT

There is increasing interest in the task-oriented approach to preschool education. Bereiter (1966) goes directly to the teaching of language, arithmetic, and reading. Gotkin (1966) has produced a series of activities designed to teach reading. Blatt (1966) has employed O. K. Moore's responsive environment to introduce reading at the preschool age. It may be, however, that these approaches are too specific to permit broad development of intellectual skills.

Many preschool teachers have turned to the early work of Montessori, McMillan, and others (see Braun, 1964). The outcome of these attempts is not known as yet, but the general observation seems to be that they are too narrow for current needs.

Basic cognitive and language skills have received increasing attention. A good example is Cazden's (1966) summary of the key areas and problems of language development of the disadvantaged child. Deutsch and his co-workers have been involved in the development of many specific methods that have wide application. The tape recorder listening center is a good example. Smilanski (1964) has suggested many practical ideas, especially the use of social-dramatic play.

Perhaps the most promising efforts, however, are the efforts to apply broad theories of intellectual growth and development to the preschool curriculum (Garrison, 1966). Sigel (1964) and Almy (1966) have suggested methods of utilizing Piaget's concepts. Bruner (1966) has suggested specific methods and outlined immediate goals. Guilford (1966) has designed a model to facilitate the teaching of cognitive processes. These efforts, collectively and individually, may hold the solutions to the development of adequate programs to accomplish the basic tasks of preschool education.

CONCLUSION

It may be premature, but the debate between the so-called traditional and structured curriculum methods seems to be over. The tradi-tional nursery school methods, so effective in fulfilling stage one of the educational process, are ineffective in accomplishing the basic goals of preschool intervention with the disadvantaged child. Programs should now pass rapidly through the first two stages outlined above and arrive at stage three, which is where the basic problems are. Additional research in the field is needed to explore the effectiveness of various curriculum methods and devices rather than the problem of preschool versus no preschool experience. Based upon the population sample, the control group's growth pattern and even the pattern of the experimental group's growth with known curricula are predictable. Certainly the Skeels (1966) follow-up study places the long-term results on the side of any style of intervention, especially when the control groups remain in deprived environments.

While the timing of intervention apparently can be very flexible, much work needs to be done in exploring the use of the period between age 1 and age 3 for a preventive program. The use of teachers as tutors and educational consultants to disadvantaged families with preschool children on a long-term basis might prove to be effective.

The doors to preschool education for disadvantaged children are open, and funds are available for financing such education. Teachers and researchers concerned with early child development must turn to the serious study and implementation of sound cognitive development theories if the expected results in accelerated child growth are to be obtained.

David P. Weikart

A LONGITUDINAL STUDY OF DISADVANTAGED PRESCHOOL CHILDREN

Scientists have long recognized that longitudinal study is the best technique for evaluating programs or testing theories. The design of Dr. Weikart's study is one of the best and the work has been done carefully and is well documented. It concerns itself with all aspects of the development and life of the disadvantaged child: intellectual growth, academic learning, and social adjustment. It recognizes that the problems involved are complex and extremely difficult to isolate for independent study and evaluation. However, by using two large samples, carefully equated, reliable results have been obtained.

The positive and exciting finding is that preschool experience can alter intelligence – a controversial theory but if the findings can be positive a most exciting breakthrough might occur in manipulating the future educational patterns of children. As one might expect, preschool experience was found to alter school behavior and achievement for some children. Modestly, Dr. Weikart points out that this is not the only answer, that there are many other approaches which should be operating simultaneously to bring about changes in learning behavior, but this is an additional possible approach for bringing about desirable results.

Preschool intervention programing has been widely hailed as an effective technique for preventing the developmental deficits agreed to be common among culturally disadvantaged children. The basis for the interest in such programing is that early childhood seems to be the most promising time for effecting desired improvement in intellectual growth, establishing the basis for academic learning, and assisting social adjustment in general. While the theoretical basis would seem to point to an unusual potential for success in preschool education, the research results in the field have been disappointing. Historically, reviews of the research report few if any differences between groups of children attending or not attending preschool by the time the groups reach third grade. Although results from the Perry Preschool Project with disadvantaged children are still preliminary, sufficient data are available to draw tentative conclusions. The results are not as encouraging as some might have hoped nor as bleak as some might have predicted.

This paper will report the longitudinal findings on the initial pilot group "Wave 0," who enrolled in the project in the fall of 1967. While complex data are available from a wide variety of assessment procedures, the information presented will be on intellectual growth as measured by the Stanford-Binet Intelligence Scale, on achievement patterns as assessed by the California Achievement Test, and on school behavior as rated by the

Pupil Behavior Inventory and the Ypsilanti Rating Scale. The last section of the paper will report some initial findings regarding children from the experimental group who are high achievers as compared to those who are low achievers three years after completion of their participation in the project.

THE PERRY PRESCHOOL PROJECT

Overview of the Project

The Perry Preschool Project is an experiment to assess the longitudinal effects of a two-year preschool program designed to compensate for the mental retardation which is associated with cultural deprivation. The program consists of a cognitively oriented preschool and home visits to involve mothers in the educative process. The project has been in operation since September 1962, and is scheduled for completion in December 1967. More complete details can be found in other reports of the project.

The population from which each year's sample is selected is Negro, culturally deprived, and diagnosed as mentally retarded. Control and experimental groups are equated for mean cultural-deprivation rating and mean Stanford-Binet IQ. Other measures include the Leiter International Performance Scale, the Peabody Picture Vocabulary Test, the Illinois Test of Psycholinguistic Abilities, Parental Attitude Research Instrument (Radix Adaptation), and various school measures such as achievement tests, teacher ratings, and attendance records.

The preschool program is a permissive but teacher-structured one to guide the youngsters toward increased cognitive development. Heavier emphasis is placed on verbal stimulation and interaction, dramatic play, and field trips than on social behavior and other traditional concerns of nursery schools.

Weekly home visits provide each family with an opportunity for personal contact with one of the child's teachers. The mother is encouraged to participate in the actual instruction of her child, thereby increasing her understanding of school, teachers, and the educative process. The teacher's demonstration of child-management techniques indirectly teaches the mother alternative ways of handling children.

Group meetings for the mothers and fathers of preschool children provide opportunities for exchanging problems relating to children. This group approach serves to reinforce the changes in individual parents' views concerning the education of children.

The Project involves a series of replications to obtain sufficient numbers for longitudinal study. Since youngsters attend preschool for two years, a new pair of three-year-old experimental and control groups is added each year to previous samples. The various groups who participate in the project are designated as "Waves." Wave 0 and Wave 1 started preschool in the fall of 1962. At that time, the Wave 0 children were four years old. The Wave 0 youngsters have spent a year each in the nursery, kindergarten, first and second grade and are now in third grade. Wave 1 and all subsequent Waves have had two years of preschool. Wave 5 started the program in the fall of 1967. This report will discuss only Wave 0.

The Population

Ypsilanti and the surrounding township form a community of 50,000 persons on the fringe of the metropolitan Detroit area. Within 10 miles are two major state universities, the University of Michigan and Eastern Michigan University, five major hospitals, many industrial plants, and the usual small service businesses. The community has the lowest tax base of any unit in the county. As housing is cheaper in Ypsilanti than in surrounding communities and as the city has the only public housing in the county, many working-class families have settled in the city though they may work elsewhere.

About 25 per cent of the Ypsilanti population is Negro with few in the middle class or above. Because of traditional housing patterns, almost all of these Negroes live in the southwest section of the city, where, for the most part, their children attend Perry School. Because of the major problems faced in the education of lower-class Negro children, it was determined to locate the project in the Perry area.

Selection of the Yearly Samples

To reach the total preschool population in the Perry School area, the school-census information is reviewed in the fall of each year to locate the families who have not been surveyed in the spring. Interviews are held with these families, and data pertaining to socioeconomic status collected. From these data, a cultural deprivation (C. D.) rating is calculated.*

1. The father's occupation on a 4-point scale (or the mother's occupation if there was no father in the home). (One point for unskilled, 4 points for skilled work.)
2. Average number of years of education completed by the mother and the father (or by the mother only, if no father was in the home).
3. Density in the home (number of rooms/ number of people), multiplied by 1/2 to give this ratio a 1/2 weight.

*This C. D. index is an adaptation of the one used by Martin Deutsch of the Institute of Developmental Research in New York City.

Each component is divided by its standard deviation to equate the different distributions. The cultural deprivation ratings of the families with children of appropriate ages ranged between 5.3 and 16.8, and a cut-off point of 11 is used as the upper limit.

The next procedure is to administer the Stanford-Binet Intelligence Scale to the children with a C.D. rating below 11. Only those children who are evaluated by the examining psychologist as educably mentally retarded, with no major organic involvement, are considered eligible for the preschool program. The obtained scores are regarded as a function of cultural deprivation and, as such, indicate those children needing assistance.

The specific sample of each wave of the Perry Preschool Project is defined as three-year-old children living within the boundary of the Perry School district, coming from culturally deprived families, and testing in the range of "educably mentally retarded."

The experimental and control groups are matched initially on two selection criteria: cultural deprivation and mental retardation. Two additional factors, sex ratio and percentage of working mothers, are also balanced when possible. Descriptive data on the experimental and control groups of Wave 0 can be found in Table 1. The project has experienced little difficulty in gaining cooperation of parents whose children have been selected to participate in the project.

The Instructional Program

In establishing the project the only requirements outlined for the instructional program were that it be designed to compensate for and prevent further cognitive deficits and that it operate five days a week three hours per day. The Project does not attempt to assess different methods of educational intervention. Wave 0, 1, and 2 experienced a gradually evolving program with an instructional method that can best be described as "verbal bombardment." In this method, the teacher maintains a steady stream of questions and comments to draw the child's attention to aspects of his environment. This "bombardment" does not necessarily demand answers on the part of the children. It is continued when rewarding a child for good performance, when disciplining him, and when presenting academic

TABLE 1

CHARACTERISTICS OF WAVE 0 AT THE TIME OF ENTRANCE: September 1962

Characteristics	Experimental	Control
Size of Sample	13	15
Mean Stanford-Binet IQ	78.4	75.0
Mean Cultural Deprivation Rating	8.5	8.2
Per Cent of Boys	62	60
Per Cent of Working Mothers	8	20

TABLE 2

STANFORD-BINET INTELLIGENCE SCALE   Wave 0 Data

Time of Comparison	Experimental	Control	Difference	Significance
	(N−13)	(N−15)		
Fall, 1962 Entrance into preschool	78.4	75.0	3.4	n.s.
Spring, 1963 Completion of one year in preschool	91.1	82.2	8.9	.01
Spring, 1964 Completion of kindergarten	88.9	84.6	4.3	n.s.
Spring, 1965 Completion of first grade	90.7	84.6	6.1	n.s.
Spring, 1966 Completion of second grade	85.5	83.9	1.6	n.s.

material. The complexity of the language is increased as the child's verbal ability develops. An observer in preschool receives the impression that the teacher is acting like a middle-class mother interacting with her young children.

Wave 3 and succeeding Waves of the project are experiencing a somewhat different program. A program based upon Piaget's cognitive development theory has been implemented. The instructional program can be best described as an effort to firmly establish the precursors essential for the child's development of an adequate foundation to permit the growth of language and logical thought.

FINDINGS

There are three areas that preschools must demonstrate ability to affect in the general development of children. These are intellectual growth, academic achievement, and school behavior. It is critical that the effects of preschool programing be observable several years after the experience and that they be measured by instruments that are at least systematic if not standardized. It may be too much to expect that a single preschool experience for eight weeks or even two years affect the course of all future development. Yet, it is essential that there be some measurable impact. Immediate, good reports from teachers and parents are not sufficient evidence upon which to justify massive preschool programs.

Intelligence Test Results

Table 2 represents testing results on the Stanford-Binet Intelligence Scale for the Wave 0 experimental group and their controls over a four year period. At the start of preschool there was no statistically significant difference between the group selected to receive preschool stimulation and those who were to remain at home without the program. By the end of one year of preschool, the experimental group had a 12.7 IQ gain (78.4 to 91.1). The control group had gained, without preschool, 7.2 IQ points (75.0 to 82.2). This difference in group means is statistically significant. However, at the end of kindergarten and again at the end of first grade, the difference in group means does not reach statistical significance as the experimental group decreases several IQ points and the control group gains several more points. By the end of the second grade, the trend is complete and the experimental group is almost identical in measured intelligence with the control group (85.5 vs. 83.9).

While the data are not presented here, the measured intellectual growth pattern followed by Wave 0 is being closely paralleled by each succeeding replication of this initial study.

Achievement Data

With this strong indication that intelligence test performance by children from limited environments attending regular schools will *not* be modified permanently by preschool experience, it is critical that the achievement patterns of preschool trained children be compared with those of a non-preschool group. A consistent series of studies has found that, at the end of the kindergarten year, achievement on reading readiness tests and teacher rating of reading readiness show no statistically significant differences between control and experimental groups (Henderson, 1965; Kirk, 1958). Indeed, Alpern (1966) even found that at the end of *preschool* there was no difference in reading readiness. More important to studies of preschool effectiveness are the achievement results in elementary grades for those youngsters who have participated in programs as compared to those who did not. Table 3 gives the information on two years of achievement scores from the California Achievement Tests administered at the end of first and

second grades from the Perry Preschool Project.

The startling finding is that the experimental group is able to profit from regular school instruction and obtain a highly significant achievement superiority over the control group. This finding is even more striking when Table 2 is reviewed and it is recalled that the actual measured intellectual level is the same for both groups.

These data, then, suggest that preschool experiences for children from disadvantaged homes will not greatly change the measured intellectual level, but may provide the foundation necessary to produce improved academic achievement. With preschool, groups of children from limited environments may be able to better utilize the general intellectual ability they have in a school setting.

School Behavior Data

Information on school and social behavior has been the most elusive of data on preschool effectiveness. While nearly all preschool projects report that participating children are "more open" as a result of their experience, follow up information is seldom available.

Two social rating scales have been employed in the Perry Project. The first, the Pupil Behavior Inventory, was developed by Vinter and others (1966) of the school of social work, University of Michigan, for appraising classroom behavior of junior high delinquent boys. It was designed to measure behavioral and attitudinal factors which affect the degree of success a pupil will have in achieving educational goals. The scale is completed by teachers who rate 34 different school related items on a five point scale for each child. The original scale has been found to be adequate and has been used without revision for the purposes of the project. Five factor scores are obtained: Classroom conduct, Academic motivation and performance, Socio-emotional state, Dependence upon teacher, and Personal behavior.

TABLE 3

CALIFORNIA ACHIEVEMENT TESTS
WAVE 0 DATA   MEAN PERCENTILE RANK

Spring, 1965 Completion of first grade	Experimental	Control	Difference	Significance
Reading	30	8	22	.05
Arithmetic	10	3	7	.05
Language Skills	39	16	23	.05
Total	22	5	17	.05

Spring, 1966 Completion of second grade	Experimental	Control	Difference	Significance
Reading	23	4	19	.05
Arithmetic	17	5	12	.05
Language Skills	20	3	17	n.s.
Total	18	3	15	.05

Table 4 presents the ratings of the experimental and control groups from kindergarten through second grade. Three trends may be observed. The first trend is that only one of the five factors is statistically significant at each grade level, academic motivation in kindergarten, socio-emotional state in first grade, and personal behavior in second grade. Second, and more important, is that except for the teacher dependency factor, all mean ratings favor the experimental group on all factors each year. Third, children who have attended preschool are consistently seen by teachers as being equal or slightly more dependent upon teacher aid than children who have not had preschool, indicating little difference in teacher-child relations in spite of greater experience in school by experimental children.

A second rating scale, the Ypsilanti Rating Scale, was developed to permit teachers to make more global ratings of child development. This scale includes four factors: Academic potential, Social development, Verbal skill, and Emotional adjustment.

Table 5 presents the information from this

TABLE 4

PUPIL BEHAVIOR INVENTORY
WAVE 0 DATA

Factors	Experimental	Control	Difference	Significance
SPRING, 1964 KINDERGARTEN				
Classroom Conduct	3.737	3.666	.071	n.s.
Academic Motivation	3.385	2.667	.718	.05
Socio-Emotional State	3.723	3.537	.166	n.s.
Teacher Dependence	3.269	3.557	.288	n.s.
Personal Behavior	4.244	3.905	.339	n.s.
SPRING, 1965 FIRST GRADE				
Classroom Conduct	3.639	3.633	.006	n.s.
Academic Motivation	3.523	2.943	.580	n.s.
Socio-Emotional State	3.954	3.353	.601	.05
Teacher Dependence	3.500	3.233	.267	n.s.
Personal Behavior	4.333	4.092	.241	n.s.
SPRING, 1966 SECOND GRADE				
Classroom Conduct	3.804	3.434	.370	n.s.
Academic Motivation	3.273	2.682	.591	n.s.
Socio-Emotional State	3.969	3.557	.412	n.s.
Teacher Dependence	3.635	3.643	.008	n.s.
Personal Behavior	4.410	3.982	.428	.05

scale. While no significant differences are found in kindergarten or first grade, the experimental group is rated significantly better on three of the four factors in second grade. At all levels, the experimental group is rated higher than the control group on all factors. As on the Pupil Behavior Inventory, teachers assign children in the experimental group increasingly higher ratings at each grade level on social development while the ratings of the control group remain unchanged. Surprisingly, teachers do not rate the experimental group significantly higher in academic potential in spite of their better achievement on standardized tests.

On the whole, then, the results from teacher ratings of pupils for Wave 0 support the position that one year of preschool experience does make a difference in school behavior. In fact, the impact of preschool seems to be increasing each year instead of becoming less.

High and Low Achievement Groups

In the final analysis, the goal of most preschool projects is successful academic performance in school. With full recognition of the dangers involved in establishing groups after the data have been collected, Wave 0

TABLE 5

YPSILANTI RATING SCALE
WAVE 0 DATA

Factors	Experimental	Control	Difference	Significance
SPRING, 1964 KINDERGARTEN				
Academic Potential	13.85	11.38	2.47	n.s.
Social Development	12.77	12.07	.70	n.s.
Verbal Skill	4.54	3.64	.90	n.s.
Emotional Adjustment	8.31	7.57	.74	n.s.
SPRING, 1965 FIRST GRADE				
Academic Potential	13.50	10.13	3.37	n.s.
Social Development	14.08	12.40	1.68	n.s.
Verbal Skill	4.50	3.93	1.07	n.s.
Emotional Adjustment	10.50	9.40	1.10	n.s.
SPRING, 1966 SECOND GRADE				
Academic Potential	13.54	11.00	2.54	n.s.
Social Development	15.92	11.07	4.85	.01
Verbal Skill	5.08	3.64	1.44	.01
Emotional Adjustment	10.77	7.71	3.06	.01

experimental group children were divided into two subgroups based upon first and second grade achievement test scores. High achievers were defined as those children who obtained California Achievement Test total scores at or above the 12th percentile in both grades. Low achievers were defined as those children with total scores at or below the 5th percentile. The mean second grade percentile rating for the high achievers was the 37th percentile. The mean for the low achievers was the 2nd percentile. An examination of scores of children in the control group disclosed that none obtained a California total score high enough to be classified as a high achiever and that the group as a whole obtained a mean at the 3rd percentile level.

Table 6 presents the information on intelligence test scores for the high and low achievers from the experimental group. While there is an initial mean difference in Stanford-Binet IQ, both groups show a gain of about 14 points during the year of preschool. The difference between the groups is that in subsequent years the high achievers maintain and improve their Stanford-Binet performance while the low achievers gradually return to their initial level of performance. While final differences in IQ are substantial, they are not statistically significant for these small groups.

Review of the results on the Pupil Behavior Inventory and the Ypsilanti Rating Scale show distinct trends. The high achievers are consistently rated higher than are the low achievers although the differences are seldom statistically significant. Teachers rate high achievers significantly higher on academic motivation and potential than low achievers by second grade, however. This is in line with actual achievement profiles, of course, and may reflect a good achievement-good behavior-good achievement cycle.

Low achieving experimental children tend to occupy a position midway between high

achieving experimental children and the control group in general on the two behavior rating scales. The low achieving children test below the control group on the Stanford-Binet but are no different in achievement.

DISCUSSION

Preschool has been highly heralded as a major method of altering the patterns of intellectual growth, academic learning, and social adjustment of disadvantaged children. From these data, it would seem that the problems are more complex than initially thought. While the group of children who experienced a structured preschool did not

---

TABLE 6

STANFORD-BINET INTELLIGENCE SCALE
High and Low Achievers[a]   Wave 0 Data

Time of Testing	High Achievers	Low Achievers	Difference	Significance
	(N=5)	(N=5)		
Fall, 1962 Entrance into preschool	82.0	75.6	6.8	n.s.
Spring, 1963 Completion of one year in preschool	96.0	89.8	6.2	n.s.
Spring, 1964 Completion of kindergarten	99.2	80.8	18.4	.05
Spring, 1965 Completion of first grade	98.4	85.2	13.2	n.s.
Spring, 1966 Completion of second grade	98.2	78.8	19.4	.05[b]

[a]High achievers are defined as those who obtained a California Achievement Test total score above the 12th percentile level in both first and second grades. Low achievers are those whose scores were below 5th percentile in both grades.
[b]Analysis of covariance was performed to adjust for initial mean differences. Adjusted Spring, 1966, difference was 14.4, and it is not significant in this small sample.

---

record a permanent long term gain in intellectual ability when compared to a control group, it is evident that the experimental group is actually two distinct subgroups. When the subgroup that did produce academic achievement is examined, it is apparent that they obtained significant IQ growth in the year of preschool and consolidated that growth over the following three years. Further, they were able to profit from academic instruction offered by the elementary school, achieving only slightly below expectation for their intellectual level. Perhaps even more important, teachers rated them highest on various social-behavior factors such as academic motivation, personal behavior, etc. In short, preschool experience, as an educational therapy, "worked" with about half of the youngsters.

For the experimental subgroup that did not respond to preschool, the pattern is also clear. After an initial gain in functional ability, as measured by an IQ test, this subgroup reverted to its original level of functioning during the three year follow up period. The group was unable to profit from regular academic instruction, demonstrating little, if any, academic achievement. There were social changes, however, as teachers tended to rate this subgroup more favorably than the control children as a group.

When the control group is examined, it is clear that none of the children is able to profit from regular school instruction and that teachers rate their social behavior in less favorable terms than either of the experimental subgroups.

It is difficult to place the preliminary findings presented in this paper in the framework of other current preschool research studies until more long term follow up data are available. In general, all programs which employ a carefully structured preschool curriculum (Kohlberg, 1967; Sprigle, 1967; Weikart, 1967) report first year IQ gains of about 15 points, depending on the population served. These data are a far cry from those reported by Smilansky (1966) of an average IQ gain of 30 points for disadvantaged Israeli children in preschool projects of the Szold Institute. On the whole, however, these preliminary results should be cause for rejoicing. Any time education can point to a technique that offers a 50 per cent "cure" rate with mean gains of 16 IQ points of four year duration, almost average achievement for a two year period, and good social behavior ratings, we have something to be enthusiastic about. Yet these findings are based on a small pilot sample. Worse, yet, the experiment is in the process of being replicated not once but five times. This spring all Waves in the project will be tested again and more evidence as to whether these initial findings are representative will be forthcoming. It is not possible to make too many claims when the data which may refute these claims may be collected by my own staff.

Then too, several issues are raised as a result of these findings. One of the more important is, why was the curriculum effective with only half of the youngsters? An extended study of structured preschool curriculum methods is called for. Alternative efforts to reach children at an even earlier age would seem appropriate. Other preschool styles might be employed such as home teaching to involve the mother as a supporting aide to promote intellectual growth. Second, why were at least half of the children able to profit from the regular elementary school curriculum? It has become fashionable to say that the reason for the failure of Head Start children to achieve in kindergarten or first grade is the curriculum and teaching they encounter. Apparently this is not so. It is the training they received before they entered elementary school that is equally in error. Third, academic success precedes changes in behavior and motivational patterns. On the basis of standardized achievement tests the high-achieving group was differentiated from the low-achieving and control groups in first grade. But teachers did not recognize a difference in other areas until a year later.

David P. Weikart   27

The phase in preschool research as represented by the Perry Project was essential in the development of educational answers to massive deprivation faced by minority-group children. The initial evidence suggests that preschools can alter intelligence, school behavior and achievement for some children. Meaningful action to ameliorate the problems of disadvantaged children is possible. But preschools are not the sole solution. Other methods must be found so that more children can be reached. The goal is the identification of critical situations that produce or prevent adequate intellectual development. Preschools can contribute to that goal.

Jane Schwertfeger and David P. Weikart

THE NATURE OF PRESCHOOL BENEFITS

Experts agree that mental deficiency is one of the major concerns of society today. Every possible interdisciplinary approach to the solution of the problem should be considered and reviewed. The Ypsilanti study is an attempt to answer the controversy about the significance of preschool experience for disadvantaged children, particularly those who would often be labeled as mentally retarded.

Frequently psychologists have questioned the possibility of altering one's "intelligence," as evidenced by inquiry into the problem of "raising one's IQ." Many communities are even challenging the right of schools and psychologists to test the intelligence of school children. This has been questioned as an infringement on one's privacy, and law suits have been instigated to prohibit such testing.

Dr. Weikart's study in Ypsilanti establishes that school children not only profit from regular school instruction but that those children who had preschool experience, particularly if they were from disadvantaged homes, have the foundation necessary to produce improved academic achievement. Preschool experience is not a reflection on nor threat to the existing order of things but rather allows for the training of children handicapped by their environment so that they may be better able to utilize programs offered in the regular school setting.

Interestingly, the author points out existing weaknesses in our psychological and educational techniques for studying and evaluating younger children. He points up the need for experimentation in the use of new tests and techniques. Psychologists have long concerned themselves with "readiness" particularly as it applied to reading. Now, the focus of attention is on "readiness" for learning in general and for socialization. Again a new challenge is presented to educators and psychologists to determine techniques for evaluating readiness and also of assisting those who are not at their expected developmental readiness level. In reality, the need for research in this area is pointed up and presented as a challenge to future scholars.

Using preschool education to reduce the effect of deprivation on patterns of learning and socialization goes back to the early 1930's, when it was suggested that a school experience could help prevent the decelerating development of orphanage children.

The outcome was an unfortunate long-term controversy over the significance of preschool experiences for disadvantaged chil-

Adapted from *The Michigan Education Journal*, Vol. 34, March 1967, 18-28. Reprinted by permission of the authors.
Editors' Note: This article includes some materials from the preceding article by David P. Weikart.

dren. In general, it was suggested that early education may be a crucial experience for certain children but for the majority, an advantage but not essential.

In 1961, on the last day of the annual convention of the American Association on Mental Deficiency, a panel of developmental psychologists presented a series of papers on the educational problems of the disadvantaged child. The general consensus of the panel was that a preschool program might be able to correct the deficiencies with which such children start school. The panel also felt that through appropriate preschool programing, the child might be better able to profit from regular school attendance.

At that time, such thinking regarding preschool was mere speculation. The panel little anticipated the massive adoption of preschool intervention as a technique to resolve one of the nation's major education problems: the education of the disadvantaged child. Yet in 1965 more than 500,000 four- and five-year-olds attended six to eight weeks of preschool financed by more than $90 million in federal funds. This performance was repeated in the summer of 1966 and Operation Head Start has now moved into the national conscience as a national "good."

There is little precedent for such massive and rapid growth of a new form of education. Without a doubt, preschool programing represents a commitment by a broad segment of the population to help lower-class children. Yet the informed and cautious observer is not overly enthusiastic about such unrestrained commitment. It may represent too much too soon. Preschools can hardly be the sole solution for the educational problems produced by a myriad of social conditions. Current knowledge about the possibility of change and appropriate curriculum for disadvantaged children is still too uncertain.

Two areas that preschools must demonstrate ability to affect are intellectual growth and achievement performance. It is critical that these effects of preschool programing be observable several years after the experience and that they be measured by standardized methods.

Many studies have demonstrated the ability to obtain short-term changes in intellectual performance as measured by such standardized tests as the Stanford-Binet Intelligence Scale. Dawe (1942) conducted a short-term training program for orphanage children.

In the 50 hours of training sessions for the experimental children, she stressed those factors known at that time to relate to superior language development. Even though the contact with each child was limited and occurred within a three-month period, the experimental group obtained a 14.2 IQ gain (80.6 to 94.8). The control children, who experienced no substantial change in their environment, recorded a 2.0 IQ loss (81.5 to 79.5). The difference in final IQ scores is statistically significant. Dawe, unfortunately, did not follow up her groups beyond the final testing.

A similar study is reported by Kirk (1958). Two important aspects were included in his study. First, groups were drawn from youngsters living in their homes as well as from those living in institutions. Second, a follow-up testing was completed a year after enrollment in regular public schools. Of considerable importance are two implications from this study. The first is that limited environments such as those found in institutions fail to adequately support intellectual growth. In short, intellectual growth is not automatic and is subject to change. Second is an indication of the potential impact school attendance can have upon intellectual growth. The impact is so great that in terms of measured intelligence, the control group, which did not participate in preschool, closed the gap with the experimental group after only one year of regular school experience. These two findings are tied closely together.

PROGRESS DOCUMENTED

Intellectual growth is the function of experience within an environment where information and stimulation are available and provided when needed. Where such support for intellectual growth is minimal, it does not occur at an acceptable rate.

The Perry Preschool Project in Ypsilanti documents the progress of disadvantaged children in an environment where the deprivation is not as extensive. The intelligence test data are similar to those obtained by Kirk but a more extensive follow-up is available. Table 1 gives testing results on the Stanford-Binet Intelligence Scale for the pilot group of preschool children and their controls over a four-year period.

At the start of preschool there was no statistically significant difference between the group (13 pupils) which was to receive the preschool stimulation and those (15 pupils) who were to remain at home without the program. By the end of one year of preschool, the experimental group had a 12.7 IQ gain (78.4 to 91.1). The control group had gained, without preschool, 7.2 IQ points (75.0 to

82.2). This difference in group means is statistically significant.

At the end of kindergarten and again at the end of first grade, the difference in group means declined in its statistical significance. By the end of the second grade, a trend was complete and the pilot group was almost identical in measured intelligence to the control group (85.5 vs. 83.9).

With this strong indication that intelligence test performance by children from limited environments attending regular schools will *not* be modified permanently by preschool experience, it is critical that the achievement patterns of preschool trained children be compared with those of the non-preschool group. A consistent series of studies have shown that at the end of the kindergarten year, achievement on reading readiness tests and teacher rating of reading readiness of their pupils show no statistically significant differences between control and experimental groups (Henderson, 1965; Kirk,

---

TABLE 1

WEIKART: PERRY PRESCHOOL PROJECT　　　　Stanford-Binet Intelligence Scale Wave 0 Data

Time of Comparison	Experimental	Control	Difference	Significance
Fall, 1962 Entrance into preschool	78.4	75.0	3.4	n.s.
Spring, 1963 Completion of one year (in preschool)	91.1	82.2	8.9	0.1
Spring, 1964 Completion of kindergarten	88.9	84.6	4.3	n.s.
Spring, 1965 Completion of first grade	90.7	84.6	6.1	n.s.
Spring, 1966 Completion of second grade	85.5	83.9	1.6	n.s.

TABLE 2

WEIKART: PERRY PRESCHOOL PROJECT
California Achievement Tests

Wave 0 Data Mean Percentile Rank

Spring, 1965, Completion of first grade	Experimental	Control	Difference	Significance
Reading	30	8	22	.05
Arithmetic	10	3	7	.05
Language Skills	39	16	23	.05
Total	22	5	17	.05

Spring, 1966, Completion of second grade	Experimental	Control	Difference	Significance
Reading	23	4	19	.05
Arithmetic	17	5	12	.05
Language Skills	20	3	17	n.s.
Total	18	3	15	.05

1958; Weikart, 1964). Indeed, Alpern (1966) even found that at the end of *preschool* there was no difference in reading readiness.

More important to preschool effectiveness studies are the achievement results at higher grade levels of those youngsters who have participated in the program as compared to those who have not. Table 2 gives the information on two years of achievement scores from the California Achievement Tests administered at the end of first and second grades from the Perry Preschool Project.

The startling finding is that the experimental group is able to profit from regular school instruction and obtain a highly significant achievement superiority over the control group. This finding is even more striking when Table 1 is reviewed and it is recalled

that the actual measured intellectual level is the same for both groups.

These data, then, suggest that preschool experiences for children from disadvantaged homes will not greatly change the measured intellectual level, but may provide the foundation necessary to produce improved academic achievement. With preschool, the child from a limited environment may be better able to utilize the general intellectual ability he has in a school setting.

Although those who work with young children feel that improved social skills should be one of the most significant areas of benefit, this goal has not been supported by actual research data. This may be true for several reasons:

1) Measuring social behavior change in

young children is among the most difficult of research tasks because the instruments now available are designed for older children or adults.

2) Experts have difficulty agreeing on what constitutes ideal social behavior.

3) Social behavior is influenced by more than the school experience and the isolation of critical experiences has been difficult.

Studies done with normal children suggest that children who attend preschool are more socially outgoing, have better use of social techniques, and greater maturity and independence (Ezekiel 1931; Joel, 1939; Vitz, 1961). About an equal number of studies indicate contrasting evidence (Walsh, 1931; Jersild and Fite, 1939; Brown and Hunt, 1961).

Studies with socially disadvantaged children support change in social skill. Kirk (1958) concludes that on measures of social adjustment, children in his experimental group were superior to controls on social items on the California Test of Personality, had better peer relations during play, were rated by teachers as more socially mature, and were given positive social choices more often by peers on sociometric tests.

The lack of data about social-skill development seems to come from a paucity of studies rather than from negative findings. Also, whether or not improved development continues may depend upon additional school experiences.

READINESS TO LEARN

Some dramatic and lasting changes in life style appear to come about because preschool experience prepares the child to take advantage of a new environment. The major contribution of the school experience may be to make the child ready for a series of stimulating opportunities. Placement of orphaned children in homes for adoption is an outstanding example.

Skeel's study (1966) dramatically docu-

ments this point. The study is a follow-up on children exposed to different life experiences in infancy and early childhood. Experimental children tested as mentally retarded were exposed to a radical shift in care, a preschool experience, and adoption. The control group, initially higher in intelligence, was kept in a relatively non-stimulating orphanage environment. The two groups later showed definite contrasts in educational and occupational level and family adjustment, with the experimental group looking best.

Weikart (1966) suggests that after an appropriate school experience, the disadvantaged child is more ready to learn and able to participate in an educational experience. Many times this, plus his increased development and adjustment, are enough to put him into learning settings which continue to stimulate him. The child becomes available for regular rather than remedial education.

Medicine, dentistry, and psychiatry suggest that early identification and correction of physical and emotional defects have been major contributions of programs such as Operation Head Start, the Dearborn Study (1966), and the Jones Preschool Project (1966). The role of the preschool in health problems has suggested possibilities that are as yet untapped.

A major problem in evaluating the effect of programs is that preschool education has been recommended and criticized as an antidote for problems of the education of the disadvantaged — with little definition as to what such an experience includes. The haste in program implementation, the naïveté of the sponsoring groups, and severe lack of appropriately trained personnel have led to a multitude of good, poor, and indifferent programs.

The lack of success in application of "tried" though not necessarily "true" methods has led to a wasteful controversy between the old and new curriculum experts. In addition a major problem is that it is difficult, in spite of the best plans, to control curriculum in such a diffuse operation as a preschool.

There seem to be three kinds of teaching programs, as follows:

1) A program which concentrates primarily upon the social-emotional development of the child. It most often is characterized by child-centered and child-led experiences, permissiveness, decreased teacher intervention, and a de-emphasis on cognitive learning.

2) A program which concentrates upon intellectual and language development along with consideration of social and emotional development. Such programs are characterized by active teacher sequencing of activities and action, heavy use of the natural environment in planned and incidental learning, and consideration of individual needs.

3) A program, characterized by a strong intellectual push, often to the exclusion of consideration of social or emotional development. Readiness is considered as the product of direct experiences provided by the teachers. Such programs give little or no attention to individualized teaching and often concentrate on and have faith in a particular methodology.

It is premature to say which of these programs produce desired results. It appears that programs which aspire to improved socio-emotional adjustment serve that goal and programs which aspire to cognitive and language change serve that goal. Programs attempting to do both also work, according to their goals. Projects to date have described the teaching curriculum, but none have controlled and documented the actual experience. This needs to be done.

It appears that the learning goals need to be carefully defined for individuals, a curriculum planned and carried out, and then observed and documented. There is a strong need to be open and experimental with methodology. What is known about individual differences and patterns of development suggests that it will not be possible to rely upon narrowly prescribed programs or to push too far beyond developmental limitations of each child. There is still a need to fit the learning program into context with the child's environment and development. Only longitudinal studies are going to indicate how lasting are the effects.

It is expecting too much that a brief exposure to a special school experience permanently will alter all future performance. Preschool has shown that, when carefully designed, it can obtain changes in certain significant areas. The challenge is for kindergarten and elementary programs to take advantage of the changed skills.

Part II

THE SCHOOLS TODAY

The environment *in which learning occurs has long concerned psychologists, educators, and parents. Years of research and experimentation have pointed up the need for more consideration to be given to the physical plant called the "school." Architects have given careful attention to the findings of the experts and today are beginning to build the type of buildings that will be conducive to learning and the development of productive and happy lives. Special attention is being given to light, sound, atmosphere, aesthetics, and functional equipment; exciting motivational results are being obtained. Many of the innovations can be adapted to the home as well as to the school.*

Specialists interested and aware of group dynamics and the interaction of individuals are contributing much to improving the class arrangements and organization. *The question of hetero- versus homogeneous grouping of students is still an unknown area and additional experimentation and research is needed.*

One of the most dramatic changes in schools today is in the technique of teaching reading. New materials are being used based on a revolutionary new approach — success should come before failure. This is an idea so simple and logical in itself that it apparently was not considered a key factor in motivating children to read and to want to learn. The introduction of new programs based on proven psychological principles should be carefully investigated, and integrated into the curriculums. Another such innovation is the use of television instruction on both a public and closed circuit basis. It is proving functional and feasible despite some dismal failures. A workable and greatly improved technique is evolving.

In our schools today, a greater recognition of creativity and *a growing emphasis on the development of talent is being encouraged. The technique of recognizing talent is still not perfected and many of the tests and methods of the past are being reevaluated. The attempt, in itself, to single out creative children is a great step forward for the traditional school system.*

Lawrence B. Perkins

WORKPLACE FOR LEARNING

The environment in which learning occurs has always been of importance to educators. Cooperative planning between the school psychologist and architect insures the application of various psychological principles which might be influential in the school surroundings. In the following article, Mr. Perkins discusses the practical and realistic new developments in the field of school buildings optimal for learning. He is well aware that the psychological "set" or attitude of the student begins as he approaches the school building. Hence, it is desirable to create a positive view toward what is to happen when he enters the building. Perkins stresses that the physical surroundings can be an important stimulus to learning because of the curiosity innate in healthy children who are gregarious by nature and eager for new experiences. The first visit to a school by the newly enrolled child may begin the conditioning of his attitude toward education for years to come – hence the special significance of the building and the room involved in this first experience.

Inside the building, provision must be made for activity and movement since psychologists know that a child requires physical activity, variety and change as well as freedom of movement and expression in order to be healthy and ready to learn.

Mr. Perkins emphasizes the fact that adequate light is required for perception; such light adds to the child's feeling of fun and pleasure, which is psychologically apt. Scientific lighting provides control over this stimulant; it is used to create and maintain a desired mood, as well as the proper conditions for seeing. The purely aesthetic sense is also valued and nurtured in the new type of school building. Research of the past several years has pointed out and analyzed the emotional reactions of children to various colors. Mr. Perkins comments on this research; he also discusses the use of the rich colors of the outdoors and of nature as well as the use of artificial color within the building.

In psychology much concern is directed toward the authoritarian figure who, in the schools, is usually considered to be the administrator. To help students better identify with the administrator and members of his staff in order to work and learn better, the architect attempts to make school offices seem less foreboding and less threatening. By wise treatment of the office space one lessens the threat of authority, increases respect for efficiency, and helps to create the image of an understanding, cooperative, well-organized, and hardworking executive.

Since methods of teaching, approaching, stimulating, and motivating each youngster must vary from child to child, and from teacher to teacher, the architect today needs to design and organize the classroom to accommodate this many-avenued approach. Flexibility and adaptability are the key words to describe the new classroom; cheer and imagination are incorporated in its planning. This is particularly true, Mr. Perkins points out, in special rooms such as the gym, library, auditorium, laboratories, and cafeteria. In the cafeteria the child has many socializing experiences and learns social customs and mores. His experiences in this cafeteria area are related to and may affect his attitude toward nutrition which, in turn, has profound physical and psychological effects.

In order that a room may provide an atmosphere conducive to eager learning, the architect needs to be aware of the growth and development expectancy of children in each grade level, and he must make certain that the room, equipment, and furniture are properly scaled to size. Since we expect today that the training in schools will include the learning of responsibility, orderliness, and efficiency, the school building must provide experience and equipment that promote these qualities through provision of lockers, closets, storage space, and teaching tools.

In his discussion of both indoor and outdoor physical equipment, Mr. Perkins shows great awareness not only of visual stimuli but also of tactual stimuli, of the need to touch and manipulate various forms and materials. All these things offer varied ways to stimulate children's imagination and creativity.

The architect's goal should be to apply psychological principles to his own specialty in order to create a setting in which learning can best occur. Mr. Perkins might have added that the same psychological principles should be applied by parents in the home.

The school building must be a setting which makes more effective the work or play goings-on in and around it. It must contribute to, and intensify the appropriate mood for, each activity—be it exhilarating or serene—and it must do this intentionally.

This is well understood and accepted in music. Beethoven knew exactly how he wanted his audience to feel when he wrote his *Ninth Symphony*. Although he was too deaf to hear it himself, he succeeded in so practicing his art that for generations people have felt the exaltation he planned for them.

The serenity of a Corot landscape is no mere record of observed light and color. Only an unusual person can look long at such a painting without sharing its serenity. Nor is this less true in literature or sculpture. Think what Poe could do to transmit a mood—or Rodin. These responses are real, and it is the obligation of the artist to draw them forth, whatever his art may be.

ARCHITECTURE

The awe and spiritual elevation which some of the noble Gothic cathedrals inspire is no accident, nor is the gaiety of the Petit Trianon. It is for their success as works of art that they are remembered and kept alive.

We do not mean to say, of course, that the school building is to be designed as a self-conscious "work of art" but, if architecture is to serve the cause of learning through the school building, it is the duty of the architect to study the needs and functions of each school, and to arrange the elements of his design so that they best serve these needs and functions. The architect must fashion a tool for the teacher. He must provide the physical facilities for the complex task of developing minds and personalities. Then, and most important, he must create the atmosphere, the environment that contributes most to the full growth of each child's mental, physical, and spiritual potentials.

One of the major problems the school designer must consider is the "first impression" his building gives. Those of us who began our education in one of those big, ugly, fortress-like school buildings remember that First Day as a frightening experience. The grim face of the building was awesome; it was bullying. Here was a witches' castle, a place of fierce teachers and cruel older children. However "scientifically-planned" these buildings may have been, the best provided little in the way of a welcome or an appetizing introduction to education for the young newcomer. But just how can a school building be made to say "welcome"? First, both school building and approach should be designed with just that in mind. Open-armed and friendly, they greet the student without overwhelming him. They blend with the landscape and harmonize with the world, so that the approaching student knows the school as part of something familiar, something friendly. Too, the walls open with glass, so he sees what is going on inside; instead of being awed by the unknown he is

Adapted with permission from Lawrence B. Perkins, *Workplace For Learning*, Reinhold Publishing Co., a subsidiary of Chapman-Reinhold, Inc., New York, 1957.

Lawrence B. Perkins   37

made eager to see more and to become part of the world within the school.

Seeing, approaching, entering, and becoming part of a school are not separate steps. Going toward, and going into a school are one. You see the building from a distance, then you see into the building, then you are in the building—without being made conscious of a defined entry. Thus, "going to school" is a gradual, natural action, and when we say the school is part of the world around it, the phrase is more than figurative.

All entrances to school buildings are designed to be disarming—a natural progression from the outdoors—to welcome the student, to put him at ease. But they attempt more than this. Through open planning and glass partitions, they show him the activity in inside rooms. The lobby leads the student visually to the building's life. It suggests that he go on, that he take part. And it can serve as a social gathering place, and as a showcase for school activities.

Flowing from entrance and lobby, the corridor is the school's thoroughfare. But shouldn't it be a pleasant avenue, not a forbidding tunnel? Physically, the corridor is a space for people moving from room to room. Psychologically, it can be a place for refreshment of the mind, for unwinding and relaxation, and for pleasant socializing. And the more the corridor is opened visually to the world around it, the better it does its psychological job. The sunlight that pours through the glass walls can brighten, warm, and unify the rooms that feed off the corridor.

Corridors bathe the school in sunlight, and give the students a thrilling command of the countryside. A bright atmosphere can be brought to the most functional parts of the building, even the stairway.

The principal's office doesn't have to be an ogre's den. It can and should express the friendly, guiding authority that at once controls and assists the student. If they prefer, the school's administrators can be accessible, and still have visual control of the school from their offices. In any event, the adminis-tration offices are related to, and made an evident part of, the school's life by partitions you can see through.

If there is one thing that educators—and school architects—can agree on, it is that there is more than one way to teach. The "way" may be the single-street method, direct from teacher to student. Or it may be the "many-avenued" approach, giving the student the opportunity to learn by working alone and with other students, as well as from teacher and textbook. Or it may be a combination of these and other methods.

Whatever the educational philosophy, however, two facts are clear. First, that the student can learn much from his environment, from the world around him. And second, that the school structure can do much to express and implement whatever teaching methods are followed. Nowhere else in the school is this as evident as in the classroom.

Traditional classroom design, with its rigidly-arranged seating, high-silled windows on the left, and authoritarian location of the teacher, was based on several assumptions: That all students were right-handed. That daylight beamed on just a few rows was enough for the whole room. That neither teacher nor students should ever move into groups, or change location. That teacher-to-student lectures, recitations, and at-desk study were the sole activities in the classroom. That the world around the classroom had nothing to teach the student. Of course, some, if not all, of these assumptions are still debated.

Today's classroom design is based on other principles, most basic of which is flexibility — flexibility to keep pace with changing concepts of education's role in society, and of the teacher's role in the learning process. Also, the classroom must reflect the teaching methods of the school; it must be an efficient tool and a suitable atmosphere for education, regardless of the educational approaches used.

So we open the classroom on both sides to daylight. We give both right-handed and left-handed students adequate lighting in all parts of the room. We use movable seating, so students can work individually, in groups, or as a class, depending on the teaching plan of that day or of the school. We provide space and facilities for individual and group project work when the program calls for it. And, most important, we open the classroom to the world outside, whether the environment around the school is a wooded glen or a busy city street. We make the world a part of every student's curriculum. In short, we seek to break the traditional rectangular, five-rowed classroom from its mind confining pattern.

Free the classroom of its traditional design straitjacket, and students become individuals, rather than rows of faces. "Group-academic" teaching can be informal, and can benefit from cheerful lighting. Open planning and glass-topped partitions help the student feel a part of the larger school community. He senses his relationship to other students in other rooms. And, looking outdoors, he feels the mind-freeing and eye-resting experience of a limitless classroom, he learns from the changing scenes of the outdoor world. The classroom should provide space and facilities for every activity the school program calls for. Whether the student is to learn by working alone, with a small group of classmates, or with the whole class, the space, the tools, and the mood must be right. Rooms and furniture scaled to child-size, and usable, colorful materials provide an atmosphere conducive to eager learning.

Many of today's elementary school teaching programs seek to acquaint the student early in his school life with the miracles of natural science, and with the basic principles of a technical world. To carry out this idea the classroom facilities must foreshadow those of the high school and university. The elementary classroom work alcove is the seed of the high school laboratory and college science building.

More than one avenue—this is the key to one of today's theories of education. It recognizes that children are individuals who respond in different ways to the same stimulus. Thus, the student learns from teacher, textbook, and sources all around him. From the class grocery store "play," he has another viewpoint on arithmetic, economics, and perhaps agricultural geography. Acting a role in a school Indian village, he feels other cultures and other times, and can better measure his own. Watching plants grow, small animals behave, days and seasons pass, he grows intimate with the world. What John learns best from an arithmetic book, Mary may not see until she counts change in the "grocery store." So that both John and Mary may learn subtraction and become fully developed individuals, the classroom must be a versatile teaching tool. Ask any teacher about basic requirements for classroom and school design. Storage space ranks high on the list. Lockers in corridors or clothes hooks and storage spaces in classrooms for each student help to develop the sense of responsibility that goes with orderly possession. These facilities, as well as classroom toilets, drinking fountains, and sinks, are all teaching tools.

Lighting can make the classroom come alive. But it must be treated as something more than so many foot-candles, evenly distributed. For classroom lighting is more art than science. Naturally, the first job is to provide proper seeing conditions, but this is not the only goal. Lighting must also contribute to the mood for learning, to the psychological well-being of the student. It must be a stimulant. Bland, coldly uniform, "scientifically-planned" lighting usually has the opposite effect: it bores and depresses. A clue to the best answer can perhaps be found in the lighting of the fields and forests, where the eye evolved. So, too, the classroom can have a lighting that changes, that is a shifting interplay of opposites—warm and cool, light and shadow, soft and hard, level light and accent light. This will give the interest and stimulation that make the classroom a place to enjoy, an agreeable place to work and learn. And it should be added that this natural lighting is in no way an obstacle to the use of audiovisual teaching equipment — not as long as there are window shades or drapes.

The recipe for a pleasing classroom atmosphere, one that stimulates and encourages learning, is at best nebulous. At least two additional ingredients, however, can be pinpointed: the fresh, ever-changing outdoor scene, and bright color. Make the outdoors part of the classroom and paint the walls, ceilings, or fixtures in vivid primary colors, and you have done much to make the classroom a friendly, *workable* place.

The first step of a child's educational life must, above all, be an easy one. This means a kindergarten room that welcomes, encourages, becomes a friend. In design terms, it calls for a room and furnishings scaled for small bodies and young minds. It calls for spaces within the room that are large enough for a wide range of activity, varied and interesting enough to entice the child and hold his attention. The kindergarten should have a generous view of nature . . . and it should be made easy to enter. The feeling of intimacy, warmth, and informality is nowhere more important than in the kindergarten. Friendly materials, varied textures, gay color, and again, the outdoor scene all contribute to this mood. Space, both occupied and felt, is indispensable to the effective kindergarten program.

In the school playroom or gymnasium, there must be room to play, and often room to watch. There must be room to store equipment, also space for lockers and shower rooms. There should be an open, invigorating atmosphere. Glass walls can add a feeling of infinite space to the limited number of square feet the room encloses. They also bathe the room in daylight, for an alert mood. To be avoided, however, are the glare and extreme contrast from improper balance of glass and solid wall areas. To gain a high ceiling without a sense of oppression, arched trusses can often be used to do their func-

tional job and bring even more space to the openness of the room. Finally, this must be a versatile room — a room for dances, band practicing, and PTA teas, as well as basketball games. There is a logical limit, however. Flat floor, lack of eye-directing lines, acoustical and scheduling problems most often make the gym-auditorium room an unhappy compromise. The auditorium has been called a place of climax. It is the school's gathering place, a place for exciting group experiences. For these, it needs a dignity and an uplifting quality. It should be designed for focusing of attention, for an atmosphere which can be controlled and chosen. Still, it must not lose the intimate quality which serves to bring audience and performers closer together. Thus, completely artificial lighting, warm, friendly materials plus cooler colors, and seats that curve around the stage help the audience identify itself with the action. And the audience interacts on itself, because there are no barriers within the audience or between audience and performers.

It is one thing to house books, and another to make reading a delightful experience. The well-designed school library should do both. The intellectual heart of the school, this room should be quiet, but not stifling. It should be relaxed, but not sleepy. It should encourage concentration without being a slavedriver. In short, the library is a place to make reading a pleasant, enriching experience. The library room should provide spaces for both individual concentrated study, and informal, relaxed group reading. Intimate groupings and furniture scaled to its users enhance the friendly mood of the successful library. The fine arts are finding their place in school architecture with growing insistence, and in no more welcome place than in the library. The library is just one place where painting or sculpture can enrich the learning environment.

Lunchtimes at school can be important learning times, too, for the student. The lunchroom serves a broader purpose than mere caloric intake. Dining with his classmates, the student develops socially, learns that manners and consideration can be more than mere artificial rules. Thus, the school cafeteria should create an atmosphere that encourages relaxed, but reasonably well-mannered, conduct. It is as much a teaching facility as the classroom. The cafeteria can also do multiple duty as a playroom, study hall, music room, social room, or place for meetings.

There are some days during every school year when the outdoors is itself the classroom. The class goes outdoors, to *see* and *hear* the blue jay and the thrush, to *touch* the bark of the willow, to come into actual contact with the world around. This can be done by placing the classroom so that it *feels* as if it is a part of the surrounding land, by identifying an outdoor area for the room and for the school, and sometimes by giving each room its own door to the area.

Entering the school, there are no barriers from the outdoors; inside the school, the outdoor scene is in constant view. Now, leaving the building, the transition from indoors to outdoors is gradual, almost imperceptible. The student was never completely separated from the outdoor world, so he never feels trapped in the building, never feels "unchained" when he leaves. His school "plant" is an interesting site, itself part of the world, and only partly roofed. The architect who designs a school building cannot think only in terms of shelter, or blueprints, or brick and stone and steel. He must think about the individuals who will use the building. He must think about the job the building should help to do: the full development of all of each student's potentials. If the architect keeps these things in mind, he may be able to contribute in some small way to the achievement of the educator's goals – by creating a building that is a tool for the teacher and an expression of the school's educational approach – by creating an atmosphere, a mood, to aid the student in every learning task set before him – by making the school a place the student looks forward to entering, and one he regrets leaving – by helping the student feel the unity of his classroom with other classrooms, and with the world. And if he does all this successfully, he will have done what every artist and educator wants. He will have created a beautiful building. For a beautiful building is one that is sensitive to the emotional needs of the humans who use it, one that serves the physical functions set for it, and one that has been designed with an understanding of the materials and building methods it requires. In terms of years of use and of effectiveness in doing its job, this building would be the most economical that could be designed. Buildings do not fall down; they are torn down. Ugly buildings are torn down long before their physical usefulness has ended. The more beautiful will last longer, be loved and cared for – and the beauty will make the greatest contribution to the job of education. To design for learning is to seek fitness, order, and beauty, and to place them in the service of those who learn, as well as of those who teach.

Herbert A. Thelen

WHAT'S NEW IN GROUPING?

Herbert A. Thelen has suggested a rather revolutionary plan for regrouping students in schools and reorganizing the curriculum – not just the program but practically the entire school, including the teacher. Refreshing and exciting is this idea of grouping children for educational purposes into mixed age groupings with cross sections of our socioeconomic structure in each group.

Mr. Thelen's suggestion is somewhat reminiscent of the ancient Greek educational practice of allowing students to group themselves around teachers from whom they could most readily learn. Children and teachers need to be matched so that a meaningful and productive relationship can take place. Motivation to learn and a permissive atmosphere are prerequisites to a successful implementation of Mr. Thelen's plan. New research is needed concerning grouping and interpersonal dynamics in every situation in which a number of individuals are brought together, whether in a school, community, or home setting. Teachers should profit more from the work of specialists in group dynamics and social psychology, and they should apply their findings to the classroom and the entire school.

Grouping determines what the mix of abilities, races, occupational plans, sexes, ages, and cultural backgrounds in a classroom will be. Since people have different ideas about what kind of mix is desirable (to them), they differ on how grouping should be done—that is, on the basis for deciding which children should be together or separate.

Admiral Rickover, for example, doubted that "the best interest of all our children" would be served by schools in which "the child with an IQ of 70 sits beside one of 170, and where the morally weak child freely associates with the child who has been carefully raised to distinguish between right and wrong and to conduct himself responsibly." Similar questions have been raised about seating Negroes next to whites, and in our grandfathers' day about seating girls next to boys.

Segregation or separation has also been advocated on the basis of previous achievement (marks or tests); speed of learning (following teacher's commands, completing assignments); ability in general (as in "streaming" in England) or in particular (as in James B. Conant's advocacy of a separate set of groupings for each major academic subject). I have seen friends put together in classes, and also seen friends separated. Elective classes like the school band produce grouping on the basis of interest. Physically handicapped pupils may be put together or distributed throughout classes.

The most popular basis of grouping at present is by ability (tracks) and by school subject. There are highly able, less able, and disabled children when it comes to each school subject. So, say some, let's sort children out by ability, put those of similar ability together, and do right by each group. This is homogeneous ability grouping. It has been advocated on and off for fifty years. It is currently riding high. It has been researched in several hundred studies, a few of which (notably those by Borg, Drews, Passow and associates) were done well. The conclusion is that homogeneous and heterogeneous (mixed) grouping by ability work about equally well as measured by typical measures of achievement. Certainly neither has a consistent advantage over the other. As far as school achievement is concerned, the case for homogeneous ability grouping is clearly *not* supported.

CRITICAL ELEMENTS

But let's look at the arguments in more detail because they throw considerable light on what is involved in making decisions on grouping. The common-sense hunch in favor of ability-grouping often errs. Some of the reasons have to do with the teacher, some with the group, and some with individuals in the group.

As Harold G. Shane of Indiana University has pointed out, probably the most important factor in ability grouping is whether or not the teacher believes in it. Because the teacher wields well-nigh absolute power in the

From *The PTA Magazine*, Vol. 62. September 1967, 22-25. Reprinted by permission.

classroom and is the judge of success and failure, his beliefs are self-proving when it comes to what (or who) will succeed or fail. Many teachers have strong reservations about segregation by ability. Some feel it is a sinister and unprofessional device for ignoring individual differences.

A second major consideration is that the teacher, given a very able or disabled group, often does not know what to do with it. Yet the whole educational justification for ability grouping is that one could do special things for the selected group that he could not do if the abilities were all mixed up. In general the popular notion is that more able kids should be challenged and less able kids should be loved and/or drilled.

Challenging the bright kid means things like pouring on the work, throwing him on his own, assuming he is highly interested in the subject. Yet no study shows that bright kids are necessarily more work-oriented, more self-directing or self-reliant, or more interested in school subjects than the less bright. When it comes to less able kids, the teacher's conception of love is likely to threaten the child. Emphasis on drill (fundamentals) is felt as a "get tough" attitude and a genuine deprivation of the most interesting parts of the course. In effect the teacher tends to stereotype the group and then proceeds to try to manipulate it (challenge, love, and/or drill) according to his stereotype. More often than not both the stereotype and the manipulation are in error.

PUTTING IQ IN ITS PLACE

Turning now to the homogeneous group itself, an odd fact, one that flies in the face of common sense, is that *homogeneous ability groups are not homogeneous with respect to the factors that matter most in teaching and learning.* If you compare 100 bright (high IQ) kids you will find that the average scores on achievement tests are higher for the bright than the dull. But if you take any one bright kid, you will find that he may have a high achievement score or a low one. It can be shown that IQ explains only about one quarter of the differences in achievement between two individuals — leaving three quarters to be explained by interest, attitude toward school, identification with the teacher, feelings of acceptance in the group, and so on. This means that *all* the kids in a bright group would do well only if the teacher could take account of a tremendous range of factors other than IQ. *These other* factors will be just as heterogeneous in a homogeneous ability group as in a normal, unselected group.

Now what has this to do with grouping? If you are trying to group kids to learn more — as distinguished from merely scoring higher on an achievement test — then the basis for grouping ought to have something to do with ability to engage with profit in learning activities. Most teachers of first grade, for example, would probably consider that the ability to *sit still* has more to do with learning than IQ. At higher levels, things like tolerance of frustration, optimism, sense of humor, ability to compartmentalize, acquiescence, femininity, and liking for the teacher are probably at least as important as IQ in determining what the various children will learn from classroom experience.

Finally, there is the individual child himself. Any way of grouping that restricts the range of attitude, verbal fluency, cultural backgrounds, and other differences also restricts the kinds of help individuals can get from each other. Kids form their own friendships, and these are terribly important to learning because they provide the child with the machinery for dealing with his private stresses and anxieties. In short, they enable him to maintain or enhance his sense of adequacy in the classroom, which is by nature complex, bureaucratic, and nonvoluntary. Depending on the child's personality and on the teacher's management of the classroom, this greater adequacy can be in the service of better or worse participation in learning activities and hence of more or less learning. But maintaining one's sense of

Herbert A. Thelen   43

adequacy is of higher priority than learning the things that the teacher, more or less arbitrarily, may insist upon.

It is better strategy, then, with most children, to redirect friendship groups than to deny their need. The voluntary friendship associations of children—the associations that have most to do with adequacy—have little or nothing to do with IQ, however. In a Ph.D. study just completed at the University of Chicago, it was found that kids with high IQ's tend to choose kids with low IQ's as their leisure-time companions and vice versa.

In the face of all this knowledge—demonstrated only recently, to be sure, but long suspected by educators—why do parents and the public feel so passionately that ability grouping is good? The brutal truth is not far to seek, and if you want to read all about it, study the report *Grouping in Education* (Wiley, 1966), prepared by an international conference of experts at the Hamburg UNESCO Institute of Education.

The fact is that throughout the world schools have not one mission, but two. The task of teaching arithmetic, social studies, and other subjects is one mission. The other is to induct children into the larger society, or, more specifically, to indoctrinate them and prepare them for their place within the society. There is some relationship between the two missions, but the latter is far more important to parents. And when the two come into conflict, it is the determining one. In short, in a homogeneous ability group, the child may not learn more academic content and skills, but he can be much more easily indoctrinated into a particular social position. For such groups are also social-economic groupings. In the British studies, for example, 70 per cent of the children in the top group of three ability groupings are also in the top social-economic stratum. The relationship is even closer for the lower ability groups.

Recently I met with some parents who were insisting on ability grouping for their *first-grade* children. What they were really asking the teachers to do is what they themselves are most eager to do: teach their bright kids to expect to attend a good college, become professionals, live in the suburbs, develop the right taste in women, wine, and religion. And the parents who did not come to that meeting—and who do not come to any meetings at school—are the ones whose children are to be segregated and taught that there will be no place for them in the productive society, that their future is to be that of marginal welfare clients. They are to be taught these things through the continual experience of school failure until they are old enough to drop out. But nobody has yet succeeded in showing how to get them to resign themselves to this subhuman fate.

A MATTER OF CONSCIENCE

As things now stand, the sort of parents who read a magazine like this are beginning to be aware of an extraordinarily difficult choice: They feel they have to choose between ensuring that their children succeed in terms of middle-class social criteria and helping American society resolve the social crises that threaten its very survival.

This is a hard choice in conscience, but when the chips are down, there isn't much contest. The effort to sweep the whole thing under the rug by pretending the issue is academic achievement provided the out for several decades. But present facts do not support that argument. And even the parent who may be willing to jeopardize his child's position (or at least the parent's fantasies about it) feels the sacrifice might be in vain. He has no assurance that eliminating social-economic segregation in favor of heterogeneous classes would in fact help the lower group. In other words, eliminating an evil does not always guarantee that good will replace it. And from what I have seen of many schools, I sympathize with this doubt.

There is, of course, a way out. That way is drastic alteration of schools. This will not be brought about easily, for the movers and shakers in education are by no means clear on what the better practices would be. Even if they were, the task of bringing the changes about is staggering. Nevertheless I shall sketch practices that could resolve the basic conflict.

First, we must toss out social-economic groupings, and replace them with unselected classes. For elementary schools the classes should be neighborhood cross sections. For high schools the classes should be community cross sections. And most classes should be formed from a three-year range of ages, not from the present fifth grade, eighth grade, and so on. Then we have to figure out methods of instruction that capitalize on diversity of ability and background—the feature of American society we like to boast about around the world.

Now, some questions on heterogeneous groups: How do we form them? Can they work effectively? What common purpose or attitude or orientation will unite a group? Many studies of groups and some recent experiments provide clues.

The classroom group should be selected for a particular teacher—that is, each teacher should be given the students he can best teach. Our studies show that the students a teacher can reach (meaning, probably, the ones who can in some way identify with him) tend to be quite heterogeneous with regard to IQ, ability measures, and backgrounds. It is the common identification with the teacher that unites the group. In fact, in our studies the most important feature of these "teachable" groups is their greater solidarity or cohesiveness. Such heterogeneous groups can work effectively and learn as much as homogeneous ability groups, although the extent of their superiority depends on how the teacher teaches.

The teacher must engage the children in activities that seem purposive, worthwhile, even exciting to them. Under these conditions they will learn more, remember it better, and use their knowledge in a wider range of situations now and later—and this, of course, is why we have schools, with their emphasis on knowledge as a way to adequacy. For activities to be sensible to a child (or to an adult, for that matter), he must understand what is expected, what the rewards will be, why they matter to him. To achieve this calls for two things.

In planning activities, some knowledge of individual children must be taken into account. By all odds the simplest way to get this knowledge is through listening intently to children as they participate in making some of the decisions about the activity. It will be found that no one activity is equally appropriate for all the kids at any one time (this is true in homogeneous groups too).

Hence, although the group at any one time may have a common general purpose (for example, to learn how redskins provided their food), several quite different learning activities will be required to encompass, and capitalize on, the range of student readinesses, motivations, and abilities. This suggests using projects blocked out with the whole class but undertaken by small groups. At this point troublesome problems of organization and supervision arise. Since management and supervision are likely to be too complex for one teacher, we will have a teaching team. Fortunately there has been abundant experience with team teaching. Many schemes are possible, but I would suggest two teachers with three or four semitrained associates, who might be parents recruited from the social-economic strata of the pupils. Together the team would probably deal with a class of forty or fifty.

UNITY AND DIVERSITY

The class will operate as a whole group for legislative purposes such as clarifying the common purpose for projects and making its own rules for managing its small society. It will operate in a variety of subgroupings specially composed for different subpurposes, such as carrying out particular projects or holding ten- to fifteen-person seminars for discussions. It might have four- or five-man leaderless "bright idea" groups. It will frequently dissolve for individual work, with desks facing the wall and social interaction ruled out of order.

There will be both formal and informal arrangements for students to help each other, both within project committees and with skill-type assignments. This practice can be arranged quite simply by giving assignments to groups, not individuals: "By next Monday, I expect everyone in the class to know the times table up through the sevens. It is your responsibility to see that you all do. I will give you twenty minutes right now to start drilling each other." Having kids help each other is a tremendous, virtually untapped teaching resource. It demonstrably benefits the children who teach and those who are taught.

The practices outlined here will require teachers to change their views of curriculum, evaluation, lesson planning, and their professional role. Ultimately they will have to take seriously the idea that education is developed through the process of *inquiry* and that the process of inquiry in turn provides a way of coping realistically with the classroom world of teachers, subjects, pupils, parents' expectations, and neighborhood life. But teachers can learn, and a good way to stimulate learning is to confront a carefully chosen team of teachers with a large heterogeneous group of students.

So there you have it: Decisions on grouping, as the international committee discovered, depend on educational objectives and methods. For wise decisions we need community discussion and increasing awareness of the facts of today's world as they impinge on the lives of the many communities of children to be educated.

Wilma J. Pyle

THE TEACHING OF READING

In this exciting new approach to the perennial problem of teaching children to read, Dr. Pyle has applied a basic psychological principle to a vital and necessary job. Since much learning presupposes an ability to read, it is absolutely fundamental that every child learn this skill as soon as possible, and that it have positive rather than negative connotation and meaning for the child. Dr. Pyle bases her technique on the idea that success and pleasure must precede failure and its accompanying frustrations and pain. Since children vary greatly in their ability to learn visually, she finds that it is best to add auditory learning to the written word, and that the content be interesting to the learner and be related to his previous experience and background.

In addition to having both visual and aural attraction for the children, her experimental plan appealed to their need for independence and self-determination. It aided greatly in developing a positive self-concept. By avoiding ego-damaging failure at the outset, negative attitudes toward reading were prevented.

The results were so amazing and rewarding that a major publisher of reading texts and materials has introduced a whole new series of texts and records based on Dr. Pyle's findings.

In recent years there has been increased emphasis on providing for individual differences in the reading curriculum and in reading instruction. This emphasis has derived from the premise that it is the responsibility of the schools to offer an effective education for all children with their varying interests, abilities, and socioeconomic and cultural backgrounds. It has been commonly accepted that every child has a right to have the opportunity for meaningful experiences in reading in which his interests and abilities are fully taken into account.

Success in reading is necessary in the very beginning of reading instruction. Only when children begin to experience success and self-confidence in reading can they progress from the level of listening and liking books to the level of becoming independent readers, whether the reading program is primarily the basal or individualized approach. There is a dire need in the first-grade reading program to provide challenging and interesting reading activities that can enable a child to build and maintain a high level of self-motivation and a positive self-concept. In an attempt to meet this need, the writer designed a reading innovation for the first-grade level to augment the basal reading program as well as to serve as a catalyst in creating interest in reading and purpose for learning reading skills.

THE PROBLEM

The purpose of this study was to explore the possibilities of developing interest in reading, creating positive attitudes toward reading, improving reading skills, and extending experiences in reading through the use of an expanded reading "diet" for first-grade children. This was accomplished through the use of fifty selected trade books and corresponding recordings. Such an experimental procedure was designed to give the child an opportunity to select books which appealed to his interests, enabling him to fol' ow the text and illustrations both visually and aurally. This reading innovation was intended to be an addition to the regular reading program that was suggested by the school system, not as a substitute for it.

DESIGN AND PROCEDURE

The method of study involved a control group having the opportunity to use fifty phono-

graph recordings of selected trade books and six portable phonographs equipped with headphones. The experimental group had the opportunity to use identical phonograph recordings and equipment, plus the use of fifty trade books which corresponded to the phonograph recordings. The study was conducted in the Waterford Village School, Waterford Township, Michigan.

In order to deal accurately with questions about how the sample of the main study was to be selected, its representativeness, and its adequacy, a pilot study was conducted. According to the findings of the pilot study, a minimum sample size of thirty-three children was adequate for the main study in order to estimate the population mean of all first graders in the Waterford Township Public Schools, with the desired precision which was to the nearest 15 per cent with 95 per cent confidence.

The sixty-seven first-grade children who remained enrolled from the beginning (October) to the conclusion (June) of the study, comprised the sample for the main study. The sixty-seven children were randomly assigned to two classrooms. The control group was composed of thirty-four first-grade children — fifteen girls and nineteen boys. The experimental group consisted of thirty-three children — thirteen girls and twenty boys. The average chronological age of the children in the control group was six years and six months, and in the experimental group, six years and four months.

For the purposes of this study, each of the first-grade teachers agreed to follow the same reading instructional patterns and to devote equal daily time to reading instruction. Both teachers adhered closely to the use of the basal readers in the Ginn series of preprimers, primers, first-grade readers, and the accompanying workbook materials. Both followed the suggested supplementary activities in the teacher's manual for the basal series. Regular weekly library periods were provided for each group.

It was pointed out to the teachers that they

were not responsible for instructing the children in the use of trade books and phonographs. The agreed-upon plan was to let the children select their own records and books to use silently and individually in addition to regular reading instruction. Slower children were given equal opportunity to use the materials even if they did not complete their work. Each child had the opportunity to hear at least one record a day if he so desired. The investigator requested that the teacher of the control group not have library copies of the corresponding trade books in the room library.

Five instruments were used for gathering data in this study to determine any growth or differences in the two first-grade groups.

(1) The Harrison-Stroud Reading Readiness Profiles (Administered at the beginning of the study).

(2) The California Reading Achievement Tests (Administered at the conclusion of the study).

(3) Reading Interest and Attitude Schedule — Part I (Administered at the beginning of the study).

(4) Reading Interest and Attitude Schedule — Part II (Administered at the conclusion of the study).

(5) Schedule for Parents (Administered at the conclusion of the study).

The Fisher test was used to statistically analyze the data collected from the two standardized tests, the Harrison-Stroud Reading Readiness Profiles and the California Reading Achievement Tests. The data from the three Schedules constructed by the investigator were tabulated and interpreted. All the observations made of the children's reading behavior and patterns were compiled.

FINDINGS

At the outset of the study, the children in both the control group and the experimental group expressed a high positive interest in reading. More children in the control group told of having books and magazines at home and of having parents who liked to read than did the children in the experimental group. Both groups expressed a high interest in having someone read to them and strongly preferred to be read to rather than to read by themselves.

At the conclusion of the study, it was quite evident that more positive change had taken place in the experimental group than in the control group regarding interests and attitudes. The children in the experimental group expressed more interest and independence in reading. More children in the experimental group told that their families had books or magazines at home, that they themselves owned some books at home, that their parents liked to read, and that their parents read to them than did the children in the control group. Fewer children in the experimental group liked to be read to and more strongly preferred to read by themselves than did the children in the control group.

In the beginning of the study, the control and experimental groups were significantly alike in reading readiness with respect to using symbols, making visual discriminations with attention span controlled, using the context, and making auditory discriminations.

At the conclusion of the study, the control and experimental groups were significantly different with respect to reading achievement. The experimental group achieved a grade placement of 3.74 on reading vocabulary and 3.44 on reading comprehension, while the control group achieved a grade placement of 2.72 on reading vocabulary and 2.28 on reading comprehension.

There was a difference between the control and experimental group in terms of the frequency with which the trade books and recordings were used, as well as in terms of the patterns of use of these materials. The children in the control group used the recordings less frequently than the children in the experimental group used the combination of recordings and corresponding trade books. Initially, both groups had a high interest in using the trade books and/or recordings. By January, however, midway through the study, this interest had diminished in both groups. The level of interest in the control group continued to drop consistently from January until the end of the study. Different patterns of story selectivity were evident in the two groups. In general, the experimental group exhibited broader selectivity and a greater interest in the stories by the end of the study.

There was a difference between the control and experimental groups in their use of the Ginn basal reading series. More of the children in the experimental group progressed more rapidly and completed the books at an earlier date than did the children in the control group.

The sample of parents of the children in the control group who were interviewed generally expressed a favorable attitude toward the recordings. Many of them stated that their children wished they had the corresponding trade books in their classroom. The parents of the children in the experimental group who were interviewed were highly interested and enthusiastic about their children's responses and attitudes concerning the trade books and corresponding recordings. In general, the sample of parents of the experimental group strongly indicated that this reading innovation had directly helped their children to read better and to be more interested in books and school. Many parents of the experimental group who had older children stated that they wished that their older children had had this kind of exposure to trade books and corresponding recordings.

CONCLUSIONS

It is concluded from this study that trade books used in combination with their corresponding recordings do have a positive effect upon and a place in the first-grade reading program. This conclusion is based upon the following reasons:

(1) It was evident that the use of trade books in this study was most effective in creating interest in reading.

(2) A more positive attitude toward the school's reading program was expressed by parents of the children in the experimental group than was expressed by parents of children in the control group.

(3) The availability of trade books and recordings apparently provided an incentive for children to want books of their own and indirectly created more enthusiasm for reading in the home.

(4) The children who used a combination of trade books and recordings developed more self-direction in reading and became more experienced in the process of self-selection in reading materials. The process of self-selection allowed each child to realize more fully his reading potential. Each child was enabled to experience some degree of success which enhanced his self-concept and, in turn, inspired the desire to learn to read. Thus, at the conclusion of the study, there was a marked preference by members of the experimental group to read by themselves, while members of the control group were much less enthusiastic about reading independently.

(5) The use of trade books with the recordings appears to have provided an incentive to read and, consequently, a purpose in learning reading skills. Trade books, used in this designated way, reinforced the basal reading program. On the whole, the children in the experimental program progressed more rapidly in the Ginn basal reading series than those in the control group. At the close of the study, the children in the experimental group evidenced an average of one grade placement higher in total reading achievement than did the children in the control group.

(6) The combination of trade books and recordings in the classroom of the experimental group enabled those children to maintain interest, as well as to progress independently in some aspects of learning

to read. This provided more time for the teacher to carry out individualized instruction needed by some children.

(7) The combination of trade books and recordings have provided for individual differences in reading interests and abilities. The books used ranged from first-grade through fourth-grade reading ability and/or interest level. Self-pacing was possible, allowing the slower learners to repeat their experience with a particular book and record as often as they desired. It also provided rapid learners with the experience of a larger variety of and increasingly more difficult reading materials.

James J. Zigerell

TV AND OUR CHILDREN IN SCHOOL

Our government has been founded on the principle that education should be made available and free to all citizens. A new medium has long been needed to complement this principle. Television offers such an opportunity to expand the range of school contact and bring teaching into every home.

However, educators felt that by using educational television, many of the basic psychological principles would be violated and that the total results would be less effective than the quality of learning which was supposedly occurring in the traditional, live classroom. Questions of motivation, participation, interaction, and evaluation had to be considered. The following article points out that there are still many unsolved problems in television teaching but that they are being approached realistically and solved gradually.

As one might expect, there has been considerable resistance to television teaching. Teachers particularly, resist the change. Anything that might appear to be a threat to their position, their status, or their security is looked on with disfavor, or at least with great question and concern. However, as these fears are allayed, general acceptance of television teaching is coming about and many colleges now give graduate and undergraduate credit as well as high school credit for television work. Many modifications of the uses of television teaching are practical, particularly for homebound children, and also for students who need additional work because of absence or because of their slow learning pattern. Psychologically the program seems sound, but it needs further evaluation and experimentation.

School television is destined to survive both the assaults of its promoters and its detractors. Instructional television — usually called ITV — seems to be entering a phase during which its rich potential can be tapped. By now it is apparent that ITV is not the big medicine that will solve the problems plaguing education as a result of inadequate financing, lack of space, and dwindling numbers of qualified teachers.

Learning by Television, the 1966 Ford Foundation report written by Judith Murphy and Ronald Gross, although welcomed by many readers as confirming their conviction that ITV is and has been a colossal flop, did succeed in clearing the air. Its warnings that instructional television occupies "a marginal position in American education" and that "instructional television's success as a tool for educational innovation and improvement hangs in the balance" have excited — in some circles, at least — a good deal of self-criticism, which is a healthy development.

Despite the disenchantment of some well-wishers, ITV is here to stay. The medium itself is too powerful to be ignored, even by the most conservative of school people. Here from *Changing Times*, the influential Kiplinger magazine, is an indication of how informed opinion is going outside the schools:

TV, it has been obvious to many educators, could be an exciting way to widen the horizons of students. A live event might be watched—say a space shot or a congressional hearing—and then discussed in class. Students might produce a play and then see it on video tape and analyze it. An experiment performed at a college lab by an outstanding scientist could be transmitted to hundreds of high school classrooms; details seen under a microscope in the classroom might be enlarged so that all could see and discuss them.

Right now, some 10,000,000 elementary and secondary students get a portion of their studies through ITV. About 600,000 college students have access to it. And as new stations are built, just about all youngsters in the country will have it available to them.[1]

The Kiplinger editors are aware of the findings of *Learning by Television* and go on to say:

Yet, in spite of all this exciting promise, in spite of the millions of dollars that have been spent on it and the several years that it has had to take hold, instructional television has been a major disappointment. How come? Two main reasons: Schools haven't bothered to tie it into their regular curriculums; and the TV programs that are available for instructional use are, with a few exceptions, pretty dull. The most conspicuous result of television teaching, says a recent report, is that [it] "has displayed in public what had . . . gone on behind too many closed classroom doors—uninspired teaching."[2]

This sentiment is shared by many of the best-intentioned teachers and school administrators. Instructional television presently occupies a somewhat uneasy position in the school world. As an instructional medium it remains outside the main instructional currents, having as yet only marginal use. Yet it is recognized by those who have approached it critically and with open minds as the most promising of all the newer media. Reasonable champions of ITV—as opposed to the promoters and hucksters—are disappointed that it has had so little impact on the school program.

Perhaps at this very juncture Marshall McLuhan should be allowed his word. He seems to be reminding us that almost without our being aware of it a remarkable change has taken place in the sensory environment in which communication and learning take place. The change is from the "linear" or step-by-step involvement of the bookish experience to a multi-sensory immersion in the new media. As he puts it in his widely discussed *Understanding Media*:

Whether there will be TV in every classroom is a small matter. The revolution has already taken place at home. TV has changed our sense lives and our mental processes. It has created a taste for all experience in depth that affects language teaching as much as car styles. Since TV, nobody is happy with a mere book knowledge of French or English poetry. The unanimous cry now is, "Let's talk French," and "Let the bard be heard."[3]

Finally, to bring these preliminary remarks to a close, let us look at a comment by an investigator of the uses of closed-circuit TV—a comment in which the case for ITV is put as a logistical necessity. Professor Leslie

1. "Computerized Classrooms Are Almost Here," A *Changing Times Reprint*. Published by the Kiplinger Organization.
2. *Ibid.*
3. McLuhan, Marshall, *Understanding Media* (Signet Books, New York, 1966), p. 289.

Greenhill, a psychologist at the Pennsylvania State University, writes in his introduction to a U.S. Office of Education publication entitled *Research in Instructional Television and Film*:

. . . television has excellent distributive powers. It can extend instruction (good or bad) to many places simultaneously. It is, therefore, an excellent means of extending teachers and above-average teaching resources to larger numbers of students than would be possible under direct instruction. . . . To the extent that the television teacher is more experienced than available classroom teachers and has better instructional resources than might be available to the average classroom teacher, it is possible that televised instruction can be superior to direct teaching. Some of the findings favoring televised instruction can possibly be accounted for by differences in the abilities of the teachers in comparison situations rather than by the influence of television *per se*.[4]

This hard-nosed, common sense statement complements McLuhan's vatic utterance. The use of TV in the school is an environmental as well as a logical neccessity.

All in all, we seem to be on the threshold of really exciting developments in instructional TV. There is an excellent chance that production techniques can soon be improved through resources to be made available when recommendations of the Carnegie Commission on Educational Television are implemented in the Public Broadcasting Law recently enacted by Congress. Some ITV production will be undertaken nationally or regionally, rather than on a piecemeal basis, when the regional production centers envisioned by the Commission are in operation. This development will supply much-needed impetus, as long as we remind ourselves of an associated risk. Production can become centralized in the way that commer-

cial TV production is centralized. The result: slick packaging and innocuous content.

The one really significant recommendation of *Public Television*, the report of the Carnegie Commission published in 1967, has to do, however, with a matter broader than production resources. It urges sponsorship of "extensive and innovative studies intended to develop better insights into the use of television in formal and informal education." And especially challenging to all convinced of the potential of TV in instruction is the following statement:

Even the claims made for instructional television by its most passionate defenders are in their essence defeatist. It is maintained that students learn as well from television as by conventional means, or that television can educate more cheaply. *Such statements scarcely intimate that there is a powerful new medium of communication capable of making its own impression upon the process of education.*[5]

All authorities on the subject are agreed that instructional television can serve basic educational needs. Among these needs in the lower grades is the need for improved instruction. This can be met in part by ITV. Another need involves opening the classroom to the world beyond. This can be served through instructional and commercial TV. By serving both these needs, TV can enrich learning experiences for youngsters and make classroom goings-on relevant to the buzzing world on the outside. Then too, it can no longer be doubted that children learn as well by television as they do by conventional methods.

Most teachers who have given TV a fair chance in their classrooms are quick to applaud instructional programming in science,

4. Ried, J. Christopher, and Donald MacLennan, *Research in Instructional Television and Film* (Washington, D.C., U.S. Government Printing Office, 1967), p. 4.
5. "The Report and Recommendations of the Carnegie Commission on Educational Television," *Public Television; A Program For Action* (New York, Bantam Books, 1967).

art, music, and literature currently available. A few of the series distributed on a national basis have the kind of production finish school children associate with commercial TV after countless hours spent watching at home. Skillful production, however, is not an end in itself, but is a means to an instructional goal. Thus, Robert Smith, the teacher of the popular "Wordsmith" series, distributed to schools through the country by the National Center for School and College Television, uses the resources of the TV studio to arouse his pupils' interest in English vocabulary. A gifted teacher, he is aware that learning presupposes the active involvement of the learner. Therefore, with the help of TV directors and producers, he and his viewers in the intermediate grades play games— flashing words on attractive placards and inserting them into a "machine" that breaks words into parts. He uses these visual aids to encourage his young viewer to learn by discovery: the pupil "discovers" that he really knows the meaning of a prefix in a strange-looking word and has a clue to its meaning.

Another successful series for intermediate grades, John Rugg's "Geography," produced by the Denver Public Schools and distributed to schools throughout the country by the Great Plains Instructional Library, makes the question of how our planet depends on water a lively one. Some of the lessons have the urgency and excitement of a TV documentary. Yet a momentary theatrical fillip is not the objective. The lesson is designed to be an integral part of a classroom's instructional program, with the teacher encouraged—and expected—to build upon the content of each TV lesson.

These two examples suggest several of the dimensions that instructional television can lend to the classroom. The TV lessons, based on sound instructional principles and supported by imaginative studio production, have a structure and finish the busy classroom teacher cannot possibly bring to a conventional lesson plan. The programs strike the observer as sound because they supply

what Professor William Clark Trow has labeled "customer satisfaction."[6]

Part of the satisfaction comes from imaginative employment of production devices –e.g., in the geography series, the use of a "talking" animated droplet of water. Here is the multi-sensory impact that McLuhan tells us the child has come to expect. At least, through these devices the attention of the child is fully engaged.

In addition, successful series like the two just mentioned, capture the attention of young viewers through the skill and personality of the teacher. The teacher who is so-so in the classroom is so-so on television, a consideration which leads some practitioners of instructional television—especially outside the U.S.—to advocate the use of professional actors working from a script prepared by a team of teachers. Unfortunately, the flaw in this procedure—aside from considerations of cost—advisable as it may be from the standpoint of achieving professional polish of delivery and pacing, is that it deprives the youngster of the prime virtue of television as a means of distributing instruction: the one-to-one contact between teacher and pupil. The teaching performance is a quasi-dramatic, rather than a dramatic, performance. It invites active participation, rather than empathy. The teacher is not striving to create the illusion of the Hollywood film or the TV situation series. He is desirous of awakening young minds and jogging them into an act of discovery, no matter how modest in scope. If his task were no more than to serve as a dispenser of information or a source of diversion in a long school day, perhaps there would be ample warrant for the employment of professional announcers or actors in instructional series. But in the geography series discussed, the teacher tries to order and control his material and employ visual and quasi-dramatic devices in such a way as to lead the attentive child to discover

6. See "Teachers and Television," *Psychology in the Schools*," July 1967.

for himself the dependence of our planet on its water supply. Or visitors who observe primary and intermediate grade children viewing TV lessons in Spanish or French are often struck by the way pupils and television teachers are *en rapport*. For the children the lesson is not a representation of action that takes place, or took place, somewhere else. Rather, it is an event actually taking place in their midst. Hands shoot up excitedly when the TV teacher asks a question. When told to do so, the children repeat phrases and sentences as if the TV teacher were walking up and down between the rows of seats.

All this, of course, will not of necessity lead to learning any more effective than that resulting from conventional instruction. It does make learning more enjoyable. But does this mean that only instructional television materials produced in fairly elaborate studio facilities with professionally trained production personnel can be effective? By no means. There is abundant evidence that closed-circuit presentations done with only a minimum of equipment can be effective, provided the teacher is gifted and the lesson is well structured. The fact remains that the pupil, if his attention is engaged, will regard the face on the TV screen as "my teacher."

Closed-circuit television produced within the school, when intelligently used, can greatly enrich the classroom experience of the child. First of all, it enables the school to extend the talents of gifted teachers to more pupils than would normally be possible. Second and equally important, it encourages the creative employment of team-teaching efforts. Think only of the possibilities of creating exciting and foolproof demonstrations of elementary scientific principles, demonstrations beyond the capacities of many teachers, and certainly beyond the time and resources at their disposal.

Yet all that has just been said about the glowing possibilities of making learning richer and more pleasurable for children hinges upon one element: the attitude of the classroom teacher. A television lesson is something that must be built upon and made part of a larger learning situation. Ideally, it supplies an opportunity for classroom teacher and pupils to share in a joint act of learning, with the teacher in the position of guide, rather than as purveyor of information. The children's appetite for the lesson should be whetted by discussions before the telecast. The teacher's attitude of keen attention and anticipation in the course of the telecast will rub off on the children. Activities and discussion following the lesson will make children regard television as more than a break in the day's routine.

OPENING THE CLASSROOM TO THE WORLD

For far too long in American education a mystique has surrounded the enclosure called the classroom. There the teacher is sole monarch, with the outside world shut out. Pupils dutifully read aseptic social studies texts while the commercial television networks are covering significant political events in the nation's capital. The television set, one of which, it can safely be predicted, will soon be in every classroom in the nation, is an electronic window to the wide world. Soon with satellites orbiting in both hemispheres, events in London or Tokyo can be viewed in remote rural classrooms of the U.S. and form the basis of today's lesson in current events.

For too many of our children what happens in school has little relevance to what happens on the outside. This does not mean that the traditional kind of curriculum, sequential and articulated, should be abandoned in favor of one improvised on the basis of events as they occur. It does mean, however, that the classroom teacher must stop thinking of herself as the exclusive source of information and the sole determiner of what is to be learned. Television, whether instructional or commercial, gives the classroom a point of contact with the "real" world, thus making the school less of the artificially lighted and heated greenhouse. As proponents of television never tire of pointing out, the one advantage TV has, say, over film, is its immediacy. The happening can be immediately captured – and stored for later reuse on videotape.

It is tempting to dream of the school of the future. Closed-circuit facilities within the school, area schools hooked together by a microwave network, large libraries of videotaped materials that can be called upon immediately by the teacher for group viewing, or by the pupil for individual viewing in a study area – all these things make the present-day school setting seem impoverished indeed. For tomorrow's children, TV will be more than a diversion or an electronic storefront for the salesman. It will, indeed, be an extension of the sensorium.

LEARNING VIA TELEVISION

Inevitably, everyone who listens to a recital of the merits of making television instruction a part of a school's program asks: but how well do children learn by television?

Certainly it can be answered immediately that there is no evidence that children cannot learn by television. The U.S. Office of Education's *Research in Instructional Television and Film*, cited earlier, summarizes several hundred investigations of both the effectivenesss of learning by television and the attitude of pupils and teachers toward television as a medium of instruction. Much of the investigation involves comparisons of the performance of pupils receiving instruction on TV with that of pupils receiving instruction in the conventional way. Professor Greenhill, in the introduction to the survey, summarizes the research as follows: "The vast majority of these studies has revealed 'no significant differences' in measured performance between students who were instructed via television and those who were taught directly." He also notes that "the studies are uneven in quality," a fact that becomes clear almost immediately to anyone who reads through the abstracts.

As for pupil attitude toward television, Murphy and Gross' *Learning by Television* summarizes surveys conducted by the research organization commissioned by the Ford Foundation. Extensive interviews revealed that pupils in the elementary and high schools are largely in favor of television instruction.

Without doubt, one can conclude that children do learn by television and *like* to learn by television. To put it another way: TV viewing in the classroom can be both profitable and pleasant – a conclusion suggesting the mountains laboring to produce a mouse. We need hardly plow through long pages of trivial and inconsequential research to discover that children like TV or can learn from it. They come to school already having learned a good deal from television in the home. They come to school associating fun with television viewing. The fact that the survey of attitudes just cited shows that as the student moves up the academic ladder, his approval of instructional television tends to turn to disfavor indicates that schools are not exploiting an initial advantage.

Students of instructional TV like Professor Greenhill and the Ford surveyors, Murphy and Gross, suggest that the right questions are not asked by investigators. Greenhill, for example, points out that conclusions purporting to assess the instructional effectiveness of the medium are often statements about the effectiveness of a certain teacher or the level of sophistication of his pupils, rather than statements about the potential of the medium. It should also be emphasized that conclusions as to pupil performance derive, as a rule, from measurement of performance in conventional tests of information or skill. An alert pupil who reads a chapter in a geography textbook on the continents and their formation may do as well on the conventional kind of test as the student of comparable ability who has had classroom instruction to supplement the text. Still no one would argue that classroom instruction is valueless. It has a dimension all its own and imparts experiences not measurable by the conventional instruments. Cannot this be said of instructional television? When creatively employed, it has a dimension all its own that cannot be measured by an English achievement test.

Again, surveys of pupil and teacher attitudes must be approached with caution. The authors of *Learning by Television* discuss a study of classroom teachers' attitudes toward Midwest Airborne programming conducted by psychologists Egon Guba and Clinton Snyder. The two investigators found that teachers were disappointed that the medium had not brought improvement to the school program. But the investigators found that:

This result seemed to be related to several factors: the teachers generally had no training in the use of TV in the classroom;

their roles were little changed by the introduction of televised instruction, since for the most part it was used only once a day; and patterns of use in the classroom tended to be dictated by agents or circumstances beyond the teacher's control. ("We were interrupted by the telelesson," complained one teacher.) From these teachers' descriptions, the effect of television on their classes was no more beneficial than the weekly assembly film of an earlier generation.[7]

It seems at times that children learn and enjoy learning by television, despite the abuses to which the medium is subjected. Luckily, TV is too potent a medium and too promising a medium from the instructional point of view to go the way of last year's assortment of audiovisual devices.

Keith Bailey

CREATIVITY AND CHILDREN

Do you have a gifted child? Many parents have considered this question at some time in the development of their child. Often there is a question – not only in the parents' mind but also in the mind of the teacher – as to whether a child is "special." People are always hopeful of having a budding genius, and often this may be the case.

Psychology, for years, has spent time in connection with other academic disciplines, exploring the discovery, nurture, and development of talent or creativity, whether it is intellectual or in a special field such as art, music, or drama. We have not always recognized this as a search for talent. Studies dating back to the work by Dael Wolfe have shown that probably half of the human resources in the United States are never developed.

For a long time Mr. Bailey, an artist and a scholar, has been exploring the problem of discovering talent and creativity. His writing concerning creativity and children is based on original work of Freud and Jung as well as other psychologists. In addition, he treats the subject from the standpoint of a teacher and a parent. He seems to indicate that there is a degree of creativity or latent talent in all individuals which can and should be nurtured for the welfare of the individual as well as for society in general.

Every human being is unique, special, one of a kind – an individual. If we believe this honestly and sincerely, then it must concern us greatly that our schools for the most part only give lip service to this philosophy. In-

stead of recognizing the uniqueness of each child and organizing schools and life to foster this characteristic, schools are doing just

7. Murphy, J., and Ronald Gross, "Learning by Television" (New York, The Fund for the Advancement of Education, 1966.)

the opposite by their demands for conformity, by their establishment of goals about which the student has nothing to say, and by their everlasting concern for facts and data (many of which will be disproved before the child even finishes his formal education). This "closed" system of education will not develop the creative adults that our world so badly needs.

What is creativity? Can we give tests that will measure it? What can we do to foster creativity? Basically, creativity is finding new solutions to problems by reorganizing our past experiences to produce new ideas, being unafraid to fail, realizing that there is more than one possible solution to any problem or situation. The creative child is usually fluent, original, and independent. Not all children are capable of such behavior, but we all are unique and thus capable of contributing our "creative" thoughts to the solution of the world's problems, provided our environmental conditions are structured to foster this capacity within us.

Psychological research indicates that people tend to respond in fixed ways, whether the response occurs immediately after the stimulus or whether it follows a complicated set of symbols and choices. An individual tends to react in accordance with the previous experience which he has received through his various psychological faculties and/or as a result of his culture. The creative process has enabled him to free himself from the limits and pattern of usual responses.

Creativity tends to meet a longing or a search for a new object or for a new state of experience or of existence which often is not easily found or easily attainable.

According to Freud, creativity originates in conflicts, which spring from the more fundamental biological drives; creativity consists of attempts to solve such conflicts. Childhood experiences are very important, and personal experiences often explain the peculiar characteristics of the creative work. The role of sexuality in creativity is always prominent, Freud believes. He traces the creative person's desire to know the unknown back to the child's sexual curiosity. According to Freud, the child's inquiring over sexual matters has three possible outcomes: the first is "energetic repression," which is favored by educational and religious inhibitions. The second outcome occurs when sexual investigation is not totally repressed, but is coped with by thought processes or by compulsive defenses; this transformation occurs when the intellectual development is sufficiently strong. In the third outcome, which is the "most rare and most perfect type," sexual curiosity is sublimated into that curiosity which leads to creativity. Freud was primarily concerned with the importance and relevance of motivation in creativity, not with the essence of creativity itself.

Motivation, conscious or unconscious, is important, but it is hard to believe that the phenomenon of creativity can be reduced to a motivational mechanism. A more urgent problem is to determine why and how a few gifted men are able to transform the effect of their early or late personal experiences into creative productivity.

Jung points out that creativity cannot be seen merely as the result of personal life experiences; it transcends the personal experience and originates in the "collective unconscious." This Jung feels is the depository of the archetypes: primordial experiences which have reputedly occurred in the course of generations. The archetypes may surpass man's understanding; they may be many-sided, demonic, and grotesque. Jung feels that the creative person is at the mercy of this re-emerging content. Schachtel (1959) felt that every individual should be "open to the world" and have a variety of experiences. He felt the quality of the encounter (experience) that leads to creative experience consists primarily in the "openness" during the encounter and in the repeated and varied approaches to the object, in the free and open play of attention, thought, feeling, and perception. He advocated exposing children to as many and varied experiences as possible to encourage them to approach life with an open, vital awareness.

Many teachers have had the experience of having the "arts" used as the dumping grounds, or baby-sitting service for the school system. Perhaps you have heard teachers say: "Oh! send————to music; he is too dumb to read." Or again, "Jim's sure a good artist and it's a good thing, because he's poor in everything else. . . ." Both of these statements are products of another myth: that intelligence and creativity are separate abilities. On the contrary, factual evidence all seems to indicate that creativity is actually a unique way of using one's intelligence. To adapt successfully, uniquely, and effectively to the exigencies of one's changing environment is both intelligent and creative.

The best nursery and kindergarten teachers that this author has observed and studied have been exceptional in their concern for uniqueness and have recognized the individuality of each child. This in turn places little or no pressure upon the child to meet adult standards. In their classes, learning is approached as something exciting. Each child is encouraged to react in his own way and the children's reactions vary from childish to exceptionally mature. However, this kind of teaching may break down under the constant administrative and social pressure for conformity. It seems that the longer the child is in school, the greater are the pressures to fall into line, and this endangers his individuality. Though the kindergarten teacher is in the most important position to nurture creativity, often this teacher is lowest in status and prestige with respect to other teachers and the school administration. It makes one wonder just how smart we really are.

The workings of the creative mind imply certain personality characteristics. The creative person is occupied with problems, rather than with himself; he is deeply interested in self-goals rather than with those established or dictated by schools or society. Adults often find this threatening. He likes to figure things out for himself and to work on his own ideas and projects; for this reason, he needs freedom and variety of expression. This self-sufficiency is frequently hard for adults to accept and/or tolerate. To be creative, the child must keep his sense of awe, wonder, curiosity, and hope. He must have the ability to see ordinary happenings in a new light and to interpret them with new meanings. Adults find it hard to realize that age is merely a state of mind. The creative child must have purpose and goals; he must have the capacity to concentrate completely on a task, yet he must also be flexible and spontaneous; he must be willing to try a new approach if an old one, or one that he has tried before does not work. Too often schools say or imply that there is only *one* way, the right way – the teacher's way.

Does all this sound as if the creative person is difficult, nonconforming, temperamental, and egocentric? Well, he may be all these things, since schools and society force him to be so in order to keep his creativity from being killed off or lost. Society gives lip service to his individual differences, but seldom fulfills this commitment. It does not create a favorable climate in which creativity can and will flourish. Studies of creative adults and creative children point to certain child-rearing practices which tend to nourish the child's innovative capacity. Creative children tend to come from democratic families – democratic in philosophy, organization, and operation. These are families in which the children are encouraged to make decisions, allowed to take some responsibility for their own destinies; each child is honored and rewarded for his own uniqueness and, as a result, creativity emerges. The parents in such families show faith in their children's ability to make decisions; they value the honesty and courage of their creative child and this, in turn, encourages the autonomy and personal strength necessary to think new and creative thoughts, to do creative things. This opportunity afforded the child to follow his own inclinations and interests will develop the problem-centeredness and perseverance necessary to the creative act.

Can schools help the parents' effort to foster and nurture creativity? Of course, if they are willing to become concerned with questions and matters that stimulate children instead of handing them answers. Memorizing lists of facts, filling notebooks with teachers' comments, copying models, and parroting texts—all this leaves no room for creativity. When the teacher alone does all the planning, the child is left to respond only to her direction. The result is authoritarianism, however pleasant or well-meaning the teacher may be. Creativity cannot flourish unless the individual shares in his own destiny; he must help set the goals *with* the teacher. Our schools need to provide programs rich in experiences, experimentation, and exploration so that the children will have material for new ideas and can learn to seek new answers and be encouraged to do so. Daily routines may be necessary to a degree, for they do meet the needs of both teacher and student. But they should be extremely flexible to allow the pursuits of ideas and the completion of both individual and group projects. Attempting new answers entails risk, and children will not take risks if they feel that the results may mean failure. Failure has become a very negative and painful word; teachers need to be able to accept mistakes as honest attempts at learning and synthesis, to recognize that creation rarely occurs without false starts and many, many revisions. Teachers must offer opportunity for success and dispel fear of failure. Children need acceptance of their honest attempts to succeed.

The rights of the individual and respect for his uniqueness should be the foundation of all education. All must have respect for the others, be they children or adults. Creativity, like learning, is a process, a growing process. Given the capacity, society, families, and schools need only provide the setting and emotional atmosphere, and the child will develop his own creative capacity to its fullest.

Leonard J. Simutis

PSYCHOLOGY AND MUSICAL TALENT

Parents, and all individuals connected with youth and their welfare, are always asking the question: Is my child a talented musician? Not only must they ask the question but they also have an obligation to discover the answer. Psychologists and musicians have been searching for an answer to the question for years, an answer that would be easily arrived at and offer reasonably reliable evidence of such talent at an early age.

Dr. Simutis discusses at length the studies that have been made in this area and reports on the various existing tests which determine whether a child has a talent that can be developed with training. How this talent is expressed and developed is another matter of concern and is related to the question of aptitude, and to exposure and experience offered by a child's environment which will stimulate him to varying degrees of musical proficiency.

Early discovery and nurture of musical talent is important, and the responsibility is both the parents' and the schools'. Exposure to a great variety of music and to the many musical instruments during the child's formative years should bring out any real potential. Then the schools must provide both motivation and means for developing it. It is assumed that talent which is developed and utilized will make a person happier, give him a sense of accomplishment, and satisfy many of his psychological needs as well as offer him the possibility of a professional career in music.

The field of music has been subjected to scientific scrutiny by many kinds of scholars. Physicists, physiologists, sociologists, and psychologists have focused their attention on those aspects of their field that relate to music. A number of books have been published which treat music in its relationship to psychology. The approaches utilized by various authors have been sociological, philosophical, cultural, theoretical and even laboratory-oriented. Each author has presented what he considers the essential subject matter of a psychology of music along with its problems and possible solutions. Often there is little agreement as to what constitutes a psychology of music, and terminology related to musical talent is often interpreted in different ways.

During the nineteenth century, Helmholtz and Stumpf experimented with the perception of single and combined tones and with consonance and dissonance. Both men were concerned with the acoustical elements and their relationship to hearing. Carl Seashore's study *The Psychology of Musical Talent*, published in 1919, is considered the starting point for the psychology of music. In it, Seashore presented his system of evaluating musical talents known as the *Measures of Musical Talent*, the first known examination designed to discover latent musical talent.

In 1937, James L. Mursell brought together and interpreted a vast amount of research material from both English and foreign sources dealing with the psychology of music. *The Psychology of Music*, published in 1937, along with one written by C. Diseren and H. Fine that same year were the first books published since 1919 that were related to the subject. During the same decade psychology of music books by Carl Seashore (1938) and Max Schoen (1940) were published. After another lapse of time, two more books, published in 1953, appeared on the subject. One was a translation from the German of *Introduction to the Psychology of Music* by G. Revesz and the other, *An Objective Psychology of Music* by Robert Lundin.

A second edition of the latter book was published in 1967. In 1958, *The Social Psychology of Music* by Paul R. Farnsworth was published. Most of these psychology of music books concern themselves with the physical dimensions and problems of sound, musical talent and ability, and the measurement of musical aptitude or talent. The latter books incorporate problems related to industrial and therapeutic uses of music.

The area of talent is of special interest to the teacher and parent. The music psychologists allot considerable portions to the topic but do not always agree with the usage of terminology related to talent. Ability, power, gift, natural endowment, aptitude, capacity, skill, and musicality are terms variously used in some association with the term "talent." Most music psychologists limit themselves to the terms "musicality," "musicalability," "musical aptitude," "musical capacity," and "musical talent" whenever they discuss this specific area.

MUSICALITY

James L. Mursell believes that there is a mental function existing in human nature which can be labeled "musicality."[1] He defines musicality as "responsiveness to the tonal and rhythmic patterns which are the substance of the art of music." Mursell also believes that musicality is almost universal among the human species and may also be present among subhuman species. In the human species musicality is revealed at a very early age beginning with responses to lullabies. Mursell warns that the concept of musicality must not be confused with the concept of talent because the "relationship is simply that individuals clearly differ in their innate sensitivity to musical stimuli."

Max Schoen relates musicality to musical reception and musical talent to musical performance.[2] According to Schoen, one may

1. Mursell, James L., *The Psychology of Music*. New York: W. W. Norton & Co., Inc., 1937.
2. Schoen, Max, *The Psychology of Music*. New York: The Ronald Press Co., 1940.

perform in a way that is technically superior without possessing musicality. Another person may possess musicality by being receptive, sensitive and appreciative of music but may be unable to perform. Ideally, one should possess musicality and the ability to perform.

Revesz brings musicality into the realm of aesthetics, or the beautiful in music.[3] He considers this to be the heart of the matter and gives a factual definition of the terms and then describes a musical person. According to Revesz musicality is "the need and capacity to understand and to experience the autonomous effects of music and to appraise musical utterances on the score of their objective quality (aesthetic content)." The mental conquest of music as art would characterize a musical person and not the emotion, enthusiasm, love of music or warm interest in it. Such a person would possess a deep understanding of musical forms, the structure or movement plans of a composition. He would possess a finely developed sense of style and music processes of thought and would experience the musical composition as though he were creating it. He would be able to judge and evaluate artistic qualities of musical compositions. Revesz believes that musicality is an inborn property that requires development which could irradiate an individual and become a characteristic trait of a person's personality. This is a description of the highest form of musicality and various levels or degrees would be possible down to unmusicality, or an unmusical person.

MUSICAL ABILITY

Robert W. Lundin[4] describes musical abilities as acquired skills learned to various degrees of proficiency. These skills could be the ability to distinguish between two pitches or intervals, to harmonize, to sing at sight, or to perform on a musical instrument. Paul Farnsworth focuses his attention on the term "ability" and believes that it is the broadest

and safest term because it suggests the power to act.[5] He believes that ability "is always the resultant of the interplay of heredity and environment." The physical structure of a person can limit or facilitate achievement – the environment can inhibit or aid. Musical abilities do not seem to be inherited any more or less than other abilities.

Carl Seashore, who devised the first music test in 1919, believes that there are six abilities utilized in hearing musical tones: pitch, loudness, rhythm, time, timbre, and tonal memory. A controversy ensued surrounding the validity of the Seashore tests. Mursell believed that there existed a general factor of musicality referred to as the omnibus theory by Seashore. This Gestalt point of view sees things in terms of wholes whereby the whole is greater than the sum of the parts. In other words, musicality is more than a sum of special sensory abilities. Seashore's point of view in contrast to the Mursell omnibus theory is referred to as the theory of specifics. Seashore denied that there is a general factor of musical behavior. He believes that musicality is the combination of a number of separate and possibly unrelated abilities. Max Schoen has a variant of the theory of specifics which emphasizes the affective and intellectual side of the musical mind.[6]

MUSICAL APTITUDE AND CAPACITY

Aptitude in music is usually defined as the capacity (or potential) for musical achievement. It is the inborn capacity that enables a person to realize and develop specific or general capacities, properties, or behavior. Mursell cautions that "we must avoid thinking of aptitudes as faculties or unitary mental

3. Revesz, G., *Introduction to the Psychology of Music.* Translated from the German by G. I. C. De Courcy. Norman: University of Oklahoma Press, 1954.
4. Lundin, Robert W., *An Objective Psychology of Music.* New York: The Ronald Press Co., 1953. (2nd rev. ed. 1967).
5. Farnsworth, Paul R., *The Social Psychology of Music.* New York: The Dryden Press, 1958.
6. Schoen, Max, ed. *Effects of Music: A Series of Essays.* Freeport; N.Y.: Books for Libraries, 1927.

entities." He believes that they should be considered as dynamic trends of the entire personality. A viewpoint as expressed by Revesz in his *Introduction to the Psychology of Music:*

> Aptitude signifies merely natural propensity, a potential ability by means of which certain properties, capacities, and productive powers may be realized through the operation of environmental factors and the systematic training of the personality.

For Revesz aptitudes are undefined, not sharply differentiated and they would manifest themselves primarily in the form of direction of interest and "in a marked educability and a rapid progress in the field indicated by the aptitude." Aptitude would indicate fitness for performance, and talent would indicate "capacities far above the average in a special field of human activity."

There are many interpretations regarding the concept of aptitude and as to whether the term should be limited to specific fields. Probably the best summary of the aptitude concept can be stated by regarding aptitude as a capacity to learn.

MUSICAL TALENT

An answer to the problem of finding a suitable definition for what we mean by "musical talent" might be found by comparing the term to "mechanical aptitude." General usage seems to confine the word "talent" to artistic, musical, and perhaps literary endeavors. General usage may refer to other endeavors as "mechanical aptitude." There probably isn't any reason for confining the term to these connections. Since we are dealing with common usage, one may be led to believe that talents and aptitudes really do not have different psychological functions.

Some psychologists distinguish between musical talent and musicality. This group of psychologists believes that musical talent refers to a capacity for musical performance, and that being musically receptive is musicality. A person could appreciate, be sensitive to, and have a feeling for music without being capable of performing. Another person could be a superior performer and not possess a sensitivity to music. He would possess a talent for performing but would not possess musicality. The ideal, of course, would be the possession of both traits. Then again, some psychologists will include musicality as a part of talent.

If the terminology related to ability, capacity, aptitude, talent, and musicality is difficult to distinguish and define, the discovery, encouragement, and development of musically talented and capable persons reveals its own problems and difficulties.

THE DISCOVERY, ENCOURAGEMENT, AND DEVELOPMENT OF MUSICAL TALENT

The discovery of musical talent can be accomplished through three different means: tests of musical ability (or aptitude); developmental program of general music at the elementary-school level; and private music lessons coupled with the interest of parents.

Tests are available that make a serious attempt to predict musical success. The assumption is that if a person can receive a good score he should profit from training in musical performance. These tests of musical talent, ability, and aptitude are ordinarily administered in a classroom situation by a music educator or psychologist. The available tests will not be described but will be listed chronologically by date of first publication. Descriptions can be found in the newer psychology of music books.[7]

A high test score may not guarantee musical success, but a low score should identify those whose chances for success are doubtful. In other words, the music tests may be more useful for predicting failure than success. A great need exists for personnel who could administer the tests and give realistic appraisals regarding the possibilities of musical success. The mechanical test results should be coupled with the human approach of a guidance counselor with knowledge of

7. See Bibliography on page 319.

music and its problems. More research is needed in the music testing field. Some authors consider the music tests to be inadequate, unreliable, and invalid as predictors of future musical success. However, most music talent tests will usually indicate whether a person has the capacity, aptitude, and ability to pursue either a career in music or the study of an instrument as an avocation. A solution may be to administer the available music tests by qualified personnel at the elementary-school level when musical talent should be and could be discovered.

There is probably no better way for a child to reveal his musical inclinations than to allow him a real chance to discover music and to discover himself musically. One of the aims of school music, especially in the elementary grades, is to offer a child various musical experiences in a developmental program. A vital sequence of general music should actually foster talent. It would and could open up the world of music to the child. Musical awareness and musical initiative would be stimulated. Constructive musical choices and discoveries would be encouraged, and varied experiences of success with music would be brought to him. In other words, the discovery of talent largely depends upon the right kind of experience and contact. Use of rich, appealing, aesthetically significant material should be taught with artistic feeling and human sympathy. The school music curriculum should first encourage talent and then reveal it.

As soon as a parent or teacher has discovered a child with an aptitude or ability for music, the trait should be encouraged. The child must also have the will to pursue the discipline that is required in the development of the specific skills peculiar to the art of music. Along with the will, the child should have the physical requirements necessary for the performance of a specific instrument. Heredity will determine the physical qualifications and environment. The family atmosphere should be one that will be conducive to the aesthetic and emotional requirements of the musical art. It certainly

helps if the parents realize the value of a musical background, especially if they themselves were given the opportunities of musical study.

A new technique or method of training violinists should be mentioned because of the influence this technique could exert in the field of music study. Shimichi Suzuki has been able to train children as young as three years of age to imitate performances by the world's great violinists. He believes and stresses the fact that a child begins to learn as soon as he is alive. His technique is to expose the child to recordings of the great violinists by repeating a composition until it becomes known to the child. When the child is old enough to hold a small violin he is instructed in the simplest techniques of the instrument. Usually, groups of children learn to play these compositions before they learn how to read the musical score. They are able to produce fine music after learning the music by the rote method. The elimination of exercises reduces boredom and the music they learn is aesthetically pleasing. The part played by parents is quite important. A parent (usually the mother) is expected to practice and learn along with the child. This should encourage the child to learn. The intention of this new technique is to give young children the opportunity, pleasure, and enjoyment of performing good music together without the anxieties and discouragement that sometimes is found in private study.

Musical talent is not always easy to discover. It is vital that the talented child be discovered as early as possible. The available standardized tests of musical aptitude or ability should be helpful but reliance should be given to subjective means as a definite aid in the identification of a musically talented child. Competent musicians should be able to discover musically talented children by testing and observing. Once the talented child has been identified his talent should be encouraged by his teachers, his parents, and by his peer group. Development will take place if there is an interest in music and the will to persevere by the musically talented child.

Leonard J. Simutis 63

Part III

CHILDREN WITH SPECIAL PROBLEMS

Accepting the idea that all children are entitled to an education and that schools are created and maintained for the welfare of every child points to the great range of responsibility the schools must bear in providing educational opportunities for all kinds of students. The ordinary school cannot handle every child regardless of his physical or mental handicaps. There are many students who require special educational programs, and psychologists along with other specialists are called on to develop programs that might prevent psychological problems from occurring in those students who have educational handicaps based on mental handicaps and the resulting adjustment problems.

Children that have mental handicaps are being more accurately diagnosed, and treatment has been extended, on a long-term basis, to include family and parents who often need guidance as well.

Students with adjustment problems often come from orphaned or broken family situations in which the security of family life is lacking and no reinforcement occurs. There can be no doubt that the role of the home and family has an important relation to the students' performance and initial adjustment to school. Today the father-figure is absent from many homes, and the frequency of divorce confronts children with the need to adjust to stepparents or placement in foster homes or in institutions. As a result, the development of the children's personality and their psychosexual development are often disturbed.

Sociologists and educators must study the effect of the changing family structure and its role in society as well as personality development in relation to education. The problem of educating institutional children is a difficult one since non-functioning parents are most harmful to the child's adjustment to school. The non-traditional family organization is part of today's world, and programs must be developed which allow satisfactory growth and maturation of these children into happy and productive persons.

Because of the mobility of society today and because of our general acceptance of an urban pattern of life, we are forced also to deal with the psychological needs of minority groups that are found in every large city. It makes little difference whether such groups are Negroes, Puerto Ricans, Mexicans, American Indians, or others; they encounter similar problems and need professional help and understanding; often they require supportive therapy as well. Since ghettos with minority groups are a part of our current way of life, we are now discovering better ways to understand the children of these groups so that we can work with them, their parents, and the whole community in which they live. The aggressive violence of young people today is intensified by the fact that many of them belong to minority groups and are confronted by the pressures and complexities of adjusting to a new culture. We must find solutions to the current rash of riots and outbreaks in schools and colleges which threaten to destroy our society and its culture.

The needs of disadvantaged children who enter our schools must not only be accommodated by programs in the system, but administered by sensitive and genuinely interested persons who believe in equalizing the educational opportunities of those who are in need of special attention.

Whether the child is physically or mentally handicapped, or part of an inadequate family background, or being raised in the ghettos of our cities, the human concern shown by educators and professionals in related fields often has the greatest effect on persons who might otherwise suffer severe frustration and personality damages if neglected or left behind in a hostile environment.

Rudolph R. Deyle

THE EFFECTS OF MATERNAL DEPRIVATION AND INSTITUTIONALIZATION: A Study of Attitudes

Much of the emphasis in education and research has been on the effect of the family on the child. It is common knowledge that for a normal and healthy development of the child, both physically and psychologically, the ideal environment is that of the home with both parents present. When for a variety of reasons it is necessary for the child to be reared in an institutional setting, everything possible should be done to make certain that the child develops a normal and functioning personality. To help understand both the problems which face administrators, and the effects of raising children outside of the family setting, Dr. Deyle presents the following report.

From the conclusions of this article, one may gain new insights into the psychological principles used in institutions which might be applied to the home and school setting.

INTRODUCTION

The many negative consequences of separating a child from his parents and placing him within an institution have been well documented by numerous studies over the years. However, these studies have generally failed to provide experimental validation of their findings, with their conclusions usually having been drawn from clinical observation. Although the value of such observation is not to be denied (many of the relationships inferred by the writer in this paper are similarly based upon clinical observation) there are more objective methods of assessing some of the variables operating within the institutional environment.

The purpose of this paper is to review some of the negative consequences of institutionalization upon children; to attempt to relate some of these consequences to various aspects of the institutional environment—drawing heavily upon the writer's experiences in working with the institutionalized children and the child-caring staff; and to provide some objective evaluation of the existing attitudes of the staff and children within an institution for dependent children.

Specifically, the writer will attempt to obtain some verification of the following hypotheses:

1) It is possible to determine whether the institutionalized child has a positive or negative attitude toward his environment.

2) Attitudes of institutionalized children can be changed through manipulation or change within the institutional environment.

3) There will be a close correspondence between the institutionalized child's attitudes toward his institutional environment and the attitudes of the child-caring staff toward that same environment.

There is felt to be considerable value in investigating these hypotheses. It is generally accepted that attitudes have both affective and response characteristics. Early definitions characteristically defined attitude as a tendency to respond in a particular way to some psychological object (Allport, 1935; Nelson, 1939). Therefore, knowing whether an individual's attitudes toward a particular psychological object are either positive or negative should provide some predictability to that individual's behavior. As attitudes are felt to be learned—with much of this learning being based on the individual's experiences—one might postulate that the institutionalized child's attitudes will have a close correspondence to the negative or positive experiences provided for him in the institution. Therefore, knowing whether the child has positive or negative attitudes toward his institutional environment will provide the institution with an estimation of the quality of their program.

The second hypothesis has value in that demonstrating that attitudes can be altered through a change within the environment will provide evidence to the institutional staff of the necessity for a continuing evaluation of the environment provided for the children together with the possibility of incorporating positive elements and eliminating negative ones.

Verification of the third hypothesis will hopefully suggest to the institutional staff the magnitude of their influence upon the children they care for. Correspondence between the attitudes of the children and staff will point out the need for the staff to critically evaluate their own attitudes.

REVIEW OF THE RELATED LITERATURE

The review of the literature includes those studies which have focused on the negative consequences of maternal deprivation and institutionalization together with the clinical observations of the writer.

The Institutionalized Child—Who Is He?

Some clues to the identity of the type of child requiring institutionalization have been provided by the names of the institutions themselves: "Orphanage," "Foundling Home," "Home for the Friendless," etc. The orphan is the unwanted and deserted child, one who is too disturbed to remain in his own home or whose parent or parents are too disturbed to care for him; the child whose home has been broken by death, divorce, or desertion; the child with mental or physical handicaps who needs specialized care that cannot be provided in his home.

This paper is primarily concerned about the dependent child—the child who comes to the institution because of the disintegration of his home due to death, divorce, desertion,

mental illness, or conflicts between the parents. Although many of the reported studies are about the very young child who is institutionalized at birth or shortly thereafter because of unwed parents or illness, the majority of the writer's experiences have been with children who are institutionalized after approximately the first three years of age. It is this age child that is less likely to be adopted; for whom a foster home may not be found; and who may remain in the institution until 17, 18, or 19 years of age. It is not unusual for many of these children to spend from 7 to 14 years within the institution. At the time of institutionalization they are not psychotic, mentally retarded, or delinquent.

Types of Institutions

Institutions are essentially of three types: (1) Institutions that primarily provide long-term custodial care. They provide shelter, administer to the child's physical needs, and place maximum emphasis on the child's compliance and conformity with the general routine of the institution. (2) Institutions that attempt to provide shorter term care, with emphasis on the individual needs of the child. (3) The third type of institution is the one that provides specialized service to a particular group of children—the emotionally disturbed, delinquent, or the mentally retarded (Gula, 1958).

This paper primarily focuses on children who have been placed in institutions of the custodial type. Bettelheim and Sylvester (1948) describe a custodial institution in which a rigid, comprehensive, and impersonal regime allowed no room for individual decisions on the part of the children, demanding only their compliance. This was felt to lead to emotional apathy, lack of spontaneity, and an incapacity for active adjustment to events which were commonplace to noninstitutionalized children.

In the many studies dealing with "institutionalization," relatively few of them have been sufficiently descriptive of the institutional environment to permit adequate assessment of the particular variables found there. However, in general, the institutional environment has been described as lacking in sensory, emotional, and social stimulation – together with providing minimal opportunity for the acquisition of learning. Very little auditory or visual stimulation is provided the infant and he is given minimal opportunity to explore his environment. Little affective stimulation is given the child with there being a lack of variability in the feeling tone experienced by the infant in his interactions with others. The adult-child ratio in the majority of the institutions in the studies reported in this paper averaged about one adult to ten children, providing minimal interaction between them. It was also characteristic that there was not one consistent caretaker, but rather many, providing little opportunity for the child to find gratification from one person consistently. Daily routines in the institutions tended to adhere to rigid schedules with little or no consideration being given to individual differences and needs.

Effects of Institutionalization on the Child

Writers in this area have usually related the detrimental effects of institutionalization to the various kinds of deprivation experienced by the child. In the majority of the studies there has been little distinction between the terms "maternal" and "psychological" deprivation, with these being essentially interchangeable. Goldfarb (1945) writes of the consequences of the psychological deprivation felt by the infant in the institution:

> There is a cumulative evidence that an extensive period of deprivation of babies in an infant institution is profoundly detrimental to their psychological growth. There is also evidence that the pernicious effects of the early experience persist even in the face of careful placement in selected foster homes, casework supervision and, in some cases, psychiatric treatment. The extreme deprivation experience of the institutional children has apparently resulted in a quasiconstitutional fixation on the most primitive levels of conceptual and emotional behavior.

Rhodes and Matthews (1957) reported what they felt were the "indices of maternal deprivation in young children" as experienced through extended institutionalization: weight loss and physical deterioration without apparent physical basis; fixed smile without appropriate stimulation; excessive preoccupation with the self and a failure to react to normal external stimulation; reaction with anger or unusual excitement if the child's preoccupation or isolated activity is interrupted by another.

Bakwin (1942) elaborated on the negative effects of extended hospitalization of infants. Although receiving an adequate diet, the infants failed to gain properly. He found that they were listless, apathetic, appeared unhappy, and seldom smiled or babbled spontaneously. Their appetites were poor and they slept less than infants who were in their own home. Defecation was more frequent and infections of the respiratory tract often persisted for months, whereas the usual term for the infection, if the infant were at home, would have been one or two days. Within a few days after returning the hospitalized infant to his home, the foregoing behavior disappeared and there was a prompt gain in weight. In all of these reported studies, the authors are essentially talking about the infant's reactions to maternal deprivation. Ribble (1944) reported on the reactions of marasmic infants who were in the nutrition ward of a city hospital. "Foster mothers" were experimentally introduced to provide personal care for the infants with the result that appetite, alertness, and reflex responsiveness were markedly improved.

The writer has had the opportunity to observe the behavior of a large group of infants in a hospital setting – age of the children ranging from a few months to several years. Although hygienic conditions were excellent, staff was well trained and supplemented with numerous volunteers who functioned as did the foster mothers described by Ribble, essentially all of the foregoing effects of institutionalization were observed in the children.

The capacity of the infant to radically alter the pattern of behavior observed while in the institution and to make rapid strides forward in catching up both physically and emotionally with an expected norm of development was observed by the writer when he and his wife brought a nine-month-old infant girl into their home as a foster child. The infant had remained all nine months in the institutional setting and had experienced some additional trauma as surgery was performed at approximately eight months of age to correct a birth defect. Before placement, the child was described by the staff of the institution as being an extremely content and happy child. Reportedly, she never cried, played contentedly with toys given her, ate what she was expected to, and was of a cheerful disposition. At first meeting, she was observed to be alert, unsmiling, passive, and readily permitted handling by women. She displayed a fear reaction to men, possibly because unpleasant examinations, injections, and in her case an operation were all performed by male physicians. It was later learned that she had experienced respiratory infections and, shortly after entering the writer's home, required medical attention because of a continuation of this type of infection.

At the time of placement, the infant was extremely passive and made minimal attempts to act on her environment. She was unable to sit by herself, had not learned how to crawl, and in general had poor muscle coordination. When wishing to move from one place to another she propelled herself by rolling. She displayed minimal irritation to frustration but frequently when sleeping would scream out in terror, sob uncontrollably, and when wakening would display intense fear and avoidance reactions to the person attempting to comfort her. Whatever "memories" triggered off these reactions must have been of a severely traumatic nature—possibly memories of the surgery.

Her progress in the new environment was rapid. By the second day she was pulling herself to a sitting position by grasping the writer's fingers and within a week could remain in that position unaided. By the end of two weeks, she was crawling and able to pull herself to a standing position. She became increasingly active and intensified her efforts to manipulate the environment around her. She cried more readily when frustrated, displayed temper, and would babble and laugh when playing with other members of the family. Her avoidance of males quickly disappeared and the fear reactions that she had displayed when sleeping decreased rapidly and eventually ceased. During the months that followed she rapidly acquired new skills (catching up as it were) and has continued to display a normal rate of growth and development in all areas. The stimulation and love provided by foster parents and two older foster brothers appear to have readily overcome the physical and emotional consequences of her previous institutional experiences. She was subsequently adopted into the writer's family.

Later Effects of Early Institutionalization

Rogers (1961) expresses the premise that self-acceptance, in the broadest sense, is essential to general personality development and especially to effective interpersonal relationships. If the individual is to find self-acceptance then he must first find acceptance by another. However, it is just this intimate, continual acceptance from another that is lacking in the life of the institutionalized child.

Crow and Crow (1962) indicate that depriving the child of normal or comparatively normal parental care from the very beginning of life is generally more devastating to the physical and emotional development of the child than if institutionalization occurs after a relatively normal infancy. From the writer's experiences with both types of children, he feels that the individual's current and subsequent adjustment is primarily dependent upon the adequacy of the environment in which he finds himself – whether it be in infancy, childhood, or later – whether it be in institution, foster or natural home.

Intellectual Retardation as a Result of Institutionalization

Spitz (1945, 1946) and Fisher (1952, 1953) found that the degree of intellectual retardation appeared related to the length of time the child had been institutionalized – the longer the term of institutionalization, the greater the degree of retardation. However, later studies by Rheingold (1956) and Rheingold and Bayley (1959) did not find this relationship – possibly because they reported on institutions that had attempted to provide individualized stimulation and a consistent relationship between a parental figure and the infant.

In observing the I. Q. scores of the approximately 700 children in each of the larger institutions to which the writer has access, he found a pronounced skewing of the distribution of I. Q.'s towards the lower end of the normal curve. A far greater proportion of the children fell below I. Q. of 90 than above 110. However, the evaluative instrument has usually been a group Otis test, and typically if an individual test such as the Stanford-Binet or WISC were administered to one of those children scoring poorly on the Otis, a significant increase of from 5 to 20 I. Q. points was found. The institutionalized child's failure to do well on the group type test appears most closely related to poor reading skills (majority of children in these institutions read at least two grade levels below their current placement), apathy, and a failure to grasp what we expect of them.

The reported studies on intellectual retar-

dation of the institutional children were perceived as talking about current intellectual functioning rather than intellectual potential. Current functioning does fluctuate greatly, depending upon the type of evaluative instrument used and the motivational and experiential state of the child. The marked degree to which a child's current intellectual functioning can change – or possibly the accuracy with which the potential can be measured is well known to those who attempt to measure intelligence. A case-in-point is that of a child who was admitted to an institution for the mentally retarded following testing by the writer. He had scored in the Mentally Defective range on the Stanford-Binet and both his observed and reported behavior was that of a retarded child. Following placement, at about two year intervals, the writer again tested the child, using the S-B for the second testing and the WISC for the third. There was a marked positive change in I. Q. score on the second testing and on the third test he scored well within the average range. Reported and observed behavior reflected a similar positive change. The child was placed in a regular school and continued to function within the Average range. Although, admittedly, this is an atypical case, the writer feels that it provides an example of how a child can be helped to utilize more fully his intellectual potential if provided with appropriate stimulation and guidance in an environment which is able to help him gratify his basic needs.

Effects of Institutionalization on Personality Growth

Effects of deprivation other than intellectual retardation are reported by many authors as being the consequence of institutionalization. Levy (1937) found that children who had been deprived of maternal love and care during infancy demonstrated shallow affect and various "neurotic symptoms." These symptoms were felt to have resulted from deficient social relationships and the children continued to manifest consistent difficulties in establishing appropriate relationships with others.

Milton (1957) feels that it is essential that the child be provided with stable early relationships, for it is through such stability that the child establishes clear concepts of himself and others. Through the support and acceptance of loving parents, he becomes able to share this love with others.

Bowlby (1952) presents in considerable detail the consequences of a child's being separated for extended periods of time from the mother and the security of the home environment. The most severe consequences were observed in those children who had experienced such deprivation from the age of approximately 3 to 30 months. The deprivation appeared to result in emotional retardation and subsequent curtailed development; marked difficulties in interpersonal relationships and in affectional responsiveness; retarded speech and in some cases retarded physical growth; apathetic response to stimulation from the environment.

Three kinds of maternal deprivation were described—no mother figure during the infant's first years; separation from the mother figure for a matter of months early in the child's life; or a shift from one mother figure to another. The longer the period of separation and/or the greater the intensity of the isolation and deprivation experienced by the child, the greater the resultant deterioration.

Studies and observations of those children who have experienced severe maternal deprivation during their early life have revealed that almost always, the result is retardation in physical, intellectual, and social functioning. Symptoms of physical and mental illness may appear and many such children appear to have been permanently damaged.

The adult adjustment of individuals who have experienced maternal deprivation as infants and children presents difficulties which contribute to the overall problem in this area. Such adults, as parents, have been found less able to care properly for their own children. Bowlby (1952) states:

The origin of adults being unable to make effective family relationships is not infrequently itself the result of their having been deprived of a normal home life in their own childhood. Thus . . . a self-perpetuating social circle in which children who are deprived of a normal home life grow up into parents unable to provide a normal home life for their children, thus leading to another generation of adults unable to do the same for others.

Similar findings are reported in the comparative studies by Harlow and Harlow (1962). They found that female monkeys who had been poorly mothered became poor mothers themselves. The female monkeys who were reared without mothers of their own—with either no substitute or with cloth surrogates—did not make maternal responses to their own infants and consistently rejected the infant's attempts to make contact with them. These mothers were also labeled as being extremely aggressive towards other monkeys and with only one exception did they exhibit what was felt to be normal sexual behavior.

The writer learned in talking with personnel at one institution that many of the girls who were once there as infants return to the institution as unwed mothers and repeat the sequence of events for their children to which they were subjected. Although the proportion is small and not statistically significant—many of the children with whom the writer has had contact in the child-caring institutions have parents, one of whom or both, were former residents of the institution.

It is also not unusual to find the houseparent or cottage mother of the children in the religious institution to be a nun who was herself raised at the institution.

Further Developmental Consequences of Institutionalization

Language. Studies by Rheingold and Bayley (1959); Rheingold, Gewirtz, and Ross (1959); Fisher (1952) and Goldfarb (1945) all found that language development in the institutionalized child was consistently retarded. For the development of speech, Berelson and Steiner (1964) report the following as being important:

> The number of adults in daily contact with the child (children who associate mainly with adults acquire language more rapidly than children whose primary association is with other children); amount of exposure to and stimulation by verbal materials; and number of playmates.

They found that institutionalized children were slower in language development than children in the lowest socioeconomic homes and that the speech handicap was likely to be permanent.

Conscience. Sears, Maccoby, and Levin (1957) state that the greater the love-oriented control of the child, the stronger the development of guilt when he misbehaves. Withdrawal of love when combined with warmth for the child are effective in producing a strong conscience. Excessive parental punishment, lack of warmth, or failure of the child to identify with the parent result in an inadequate conscience development. Inconsistencies between parental behavior and teachings and a lack of consistency in the moral values taught, also effect a less than adequate development of conscience.

The lack of warmth from the parental figures in the institutional setting; the inconsistencies which are likely to be found both in the teaching and between the teaching and behavior of the many figures interacting with the child may be hypothesized as being the basis for the slow development and subsequent weakness of the institutional child's conscience.

Although one might expect that there would be less inconsistency in and less distance between the teachings and behavior of the parental figures in institutions staffed by personnel of a religious order, the writer has not found this to be the case. Such inconsistencies are not only verbalized by the children seen in treatment—with the offending adult usually being viewed as undeserving of respect and obedience—but are readily observed in the daily interactions between the children and the staff. Invariably it is these staff members who not only find it difficult to control their children but whose children present behavioral problems in all areas of their functioning.

Punishment. Sears et al. (1953) found that "harsh physical punishment was associated with high childhood aggressiveness [and] the development of feeding problems." As Hilgard (1951) points out, there is a tendency for old behavior patterns to be re-enacted. Therefore, parents are likely to rear their children in the same manner as they were reared although there may not be any awareness that they are doing so. The harsh and sometimes brutal punishment administered to institutionalized children may be viewed as a re-enactment of the treatment experienced by the cottage parent in their own home or possibly in the same institution when they were a child. The consequence is the perpetuation of a vicious circle.

Development of Independence. Sears et al. (1953) reported that rigidity in feeding schedules and excessive pressures in efforts to wean the infant tend to foster dependency in early childhood years. The more rejection experienced by the child—the more dependent he becomes. If prematurely forced towards independence—the more anxious he is about independence in adult life. Minimal nurturance or satisfaction obtained during the early years of infant dependency may result in either minor dependence on others or excessive generalized dependency. Overprotection and excessive permissiveness result in excessive dependency or in rebellious and defiant behavior.

Development of Ambition, Drive for Achievement. McClelland et al. (1953) gave the contributing factors in the development of ambition and drive for achievement in the child. Early encouragement and reward, together with good identification with parents, produce high achievement needs. The more reasonable the demands, the more the child will persist. The relationship with the mother is very important, yet independence should be rewarded. Demonstrations of affection and early parental demands for achievement also produce strong subsequent drives for success. Excessive restrictions and over-protection of parents prohibit the child's striving toward independent achievement.

Almost without exception, the custodial type institution provides the opposite of that which would result in the development of adequate language, a strong conscience, appropriate behavior patterns, mature independence, and the development of ambition and drive for achievement. For comprehensive overviews of all the research in this area, up to the time of their reviews, reference is made to Whitmer, Yarrow, Ainsworth, and Glaser (1962) and Yarrow (1964).

Why Does Institutionalization Result in Deprivation?

The writer contends that it is not the separation from home and family, the isolation from "mother," that is the basic deprivation. With the majority of the children in the institutions, the home environment, the relationship with parents and siblings have already provided the basic elements of deprivation. But removal from the home does not remove the deprivation; rather, by placing the child in a custodial type institution, the basic deprivation is intensified and perpetuated. In working with these institutions, the writer has become increasingly aware that the institution does not remain a source of gratification and security for the child. Instead, the institutional staff forms a symbiotic relationship with the children, becoming dependent on them. It would seem that staff members obtain *their* primary gratification

and security from the children. Staff members of these institutions are in reality institutionalized in much the same manner as the children. They manifest the same type of problems as the institutional child. Intense rivalry and suspiciousness exist between staff members, and the children under their care are constantly used as a means of acting out against each other. Staff residents are extremely dependent, have great difficulty in establishing constructive relationships with others, tend to remain isolated within the community, and tend to be profoundly unhappy and dissatisfied. Unable to communicate effectively with each other, staff members resist the help of others in attempts to find solutions to their problems and readily project the blame for their difficulties onto others.

When these institutions fail so devastatingly to meet the basic needs of their own staff, it is impossible that they could do other than intensify and perpetuate the deprivational experiences of the children they have in their care.

Who Else Contributes to the Child's Deprivation?

The reported studies and my own observations would lead one to assume that the institution is the sole offender in depriving the child. In reality, all agencies concerned with the care of children have not only contributed markedly to the type of institution the dependent child is confronted with, but consistently contribute in their own way to intensifying the child's deprivation. Case loads carried by social workers are of such magnitude that frequently the child is fortunate if he is seen yearly. Yet this is the individual who must act as the primary source of communication between the child, his family, the court, and all the various units concerned with the continued welfare of the child. The writer recently interviewed a young woman who had been institutionalized for 16 years and who had never seen a case worker during this time. Two years ago, a brother who had been with her in placement for 12 years was placed in a foster home and subsequently disappeared from her life. She had never been informed where he had gone. It is not unusual for a child to be moved from the institution to a foster home or the reverse with no preparation of the child and with no previous meeting between the parties involved. As a consequence, a great many of such placements are traumatic, necessitate removal and replacement, with the same procedure usually occurring.

Another factor which studies on institutionalized children have usually ignored is the selection factor manifested by those agencies and individuals which seek institutionalization rather than foster home or adoption of the child. If the infant is perceived as bright, responsive, attractive, and without quite evident physical defects—foster home and/or adoption is usually sought and found. Consequently, one might hypothesize that the majority of those children who eventually experience long-term institutionalization are those who for some reason were originally perceived as less likely candidates for a more favorable kind of placement.

Guidance centers, placement agencies, and courts have typically taken the child from his family with minimal efforts or none at all expended to rehabilitate the family and to return the child. Until such time as all those involved in the study and care of children are willing to take a realistic look at how they are perpetuating the deprivation of the institutionalized child, it is doubtful if effective ways can be found to prevent its continuance.

DESIGN AND APPLICATION OF
THE RESEARCH MATERIALS

In the preparation of the research materials, the assumption is made that an individual's attitudes will be reflected in his statements about a psychological object. Thurstone's definition of attitude was selected for use in this project: "The degree of positive or negative affect associated with some psychological object" (Thurstone, 1946, p. 41).

An open-ended, sentence completion form was constructed by the writer for administration to the high school students within a large Catholic residential institution for dependent children. The items selected for the sentence completion form were subjectively chosen by the writer but were based on areas that tended to elicit affect associated statements from the children (Appendix I).

The sentence completion form was administered to all of the high school students (N = 148) during one of their regular school study periods. They were informed that the form was part of a project being conducted by the writer and they were assured that what they wrote would not be viewed by the staff within the institution.

Following administration, the forms were collected and reviewed by the writer. Five of the sentences (Numbers 5, 14, 22, 25, and 27) were selected as producing affect laden statements. Fifty of the completed forms were randomly selected from the high school students and submitted to two judges for their assessment of the statements as being either positive or negative. The judges were Ph.D. level clinical psychologists who had one or more years of experience in working with institutionalized children. Specifically, the judges were asked to judge each of the five statements from each child as being either a positive (+) or negative (−) statement according to the following criteria:

1) Read each statement and check it on your scoring sheet as being either a positive (+) or negative (−) statement.

2) Any statement which is considered to be a statement of fact and has no positive or negative element— score +. (ex. "I am a boy." "Daily Mass is required at the Home.")

3) If an item has been left blank— score it negative.

4) Statements of the following type should be scored accordingly: "Good but . . ." (followed by a negative element— score mi-

nus). "Bad but . . . ." (followed by a positive element — score positive).

Following scoring, each form was algebraically summed with the form being given either a positive or a negative total score. The separate ratings of the two judges were then compared for percentage of agreement between them. A high percentage of agreement between the two judges would support the hypothesis that the children's attitudes towards the institutional environment could be assessed as either positive or negative using this procedure.

The hypothesis that the children's attitudes could be altered through change within the institutional environment was investigated in the following manner. Two years after the initial administration of the sentence completion form, the form was readministered to all of the high school students within the institution. Twenty-five subjects were randomly selected from the sophomore class (first administration) with their forms being scored according to the foregoing criteria and then compared with the sentence completion forms obtained from these same children while in the senior class (second administration).

This particular high school class was chosen as over a two year period, several specific environmental changes had occurred for them: change of dormitories and cottage mother; association with new teachers in the classroom; and greater responsibilities in their job assignments. Another element which could influence attitude change and which is not necessarily related to a change within the institutional environment, is the seniors' anticipation of impending graduation and leaving the institution.

The forms from the first and second administration were scored (using the five sentences already noted) and compared using chi square for correlated data. A significant chi square would support the hypothesis that attitude change in the institutionalized child can be brought about through changes within the institutional environment.

In working with the children and staff of the institution over a period of several years, the writer became aware of the marked similarity of their attitudes towards various aspects within the institutional environment. An attempt was made to determine if this similarity could be more objectively assessed. For this purpose, a questionnaire for the religious staff of the institution was prepared by the writer (Appendix II). The form was administered to all of the religious staff with their responses being summarized and classified according to their content. The attitudes expressed by the staff were then compared with the attitudes expressed by the children (as obtained by the two administrations of the sentence completion forms).

The questionnaire for the religious staff was given to fifty-four nuns and priests on the staff at the institution. Sixty-three per cent of those receiving the questionnaire attempted to answer it. Twelve per cent of those returning the questionnaires failed to complete that portion of the questionnaire pertaining to the self. This portion of the questionnaire was admittedly the most difficult section and reflected a problem experienced by many on the staff — of being unwilling to critically evaluate their own attitudes.

Content of the returned questionnaires was summarized and categories selected according to those aspects of the institutional environment toward which attitudes were expressed. Two or more of the returned questionnaires had to focus on an aspect of the institution as being either positive or negative for it to be considered as a significant aspect. As each questionnaire was filled out independently by the individual staff member, and as there was no preselection relative to what particular aspects they should consider — two individuals independently focusing on a particular aspect was felt to warrant its consideration as an important element within the institutional environment.

The percentage of individuals focusing on a particular aspect of the environment was computed and a comparison made between the attitudes of the staff and those of the children. Although the measure used to compare the attitudes of these two groups was quite subjective and a gross measure, clear similarities in attitude were evident.

RESULTS AND DISCUSSION

Scoring of the sentence completion forms by the two judges (original administration of the forms) indicated 94 per cent agreement between their ratings. The hypothesis that it is possible to determine whether the institutionalized child has a positive or negative attitude toward his institutional environment was supported.

Using the same criteria for scoring, two separate sentence completion forms (administered to the same child with a pre- and post-test design over a two year interval) were statistically compared using chi square for correlated data (Siegel, 1956). A chi square of 4.0 was obtained ($p = .05$). This significant difference between the two sets of scores was in the direction of negative to positive, indicating a positive change in the children's attitudes towards the institutional environment. Surveying the content of the individual statements indicated a more positive feeling towards the cottage mother, the teacher, the self, and the institution as a whole. There was no change on the statements concerning daily Mass with the majority of the children expressing negative attitudes toward this aspect of their environment. As there had been a change in dormitories, cottage mothers, and some teachers over this two year period, the change in attitude is attributed to these changes within the child's environment. The hypothesis that attitude change would accompany environmental change was supported.

Determining the relationship between the attitudes of the staff and children was accomplished as follows: 1) The most frequently expressed positive and negative attitudes by the children on the administrations of the sentence completion form were totaled and ranked in order according to percentage of frequency. (Ex. The most frequently expressed negative attitude of the one hundred forty-eight high school children was towards daily Mass attendance. The second most frequently expressed negative attitude was towards the cottage mother. The third . . . et cetera.) This procedure was followed in ranking the expressed attitudes of the staff, the rank being determined by the percentage of staff personnel centering on that particular aspect as being positive or negative. These rankings are given in Appendix III. Comparison of the two rankings reveals marked similarity — especially in that area where the staff considered those aspects of the institution which were least beneficial for themselves.

The close correspondence between the attitudes of the children and the staff towards the institutional environment supported the third hypothesis.

It is important to note that a closer correspondence existed between the staff's perception of what was most and least beneficial for themselves and the children's perceptions, than between what the staff felt was most and least beneficial for the children and the children's perceptions.

This finding is felt to indicate a lack of realistic awareness on the part of the staff of those aspects which are truly beneficial or detrimental to the children in their institution. It is further indicated that if the staff members are able to make a careful self-evaluation concerning their reactions to the institutional environment, they will have a clearer understanding of those aspects of the environment which need to be changed, not only for their benefit, but for the benefit of the children.

The marked similarity between the attitudes of the staff and children suggests the proposition that the children have many of the attitudes they do as a consequence of the attitudes of the staff. Accepting the premise that the children learn from the adult models in their environment (attitudes and behavior reflective of their attitudes) the foregoing proposition is certainly tenable. Therefore, it is expected that a positive change in the staff's attitudes toward the institution would result in a similar positive change in the children's attitudes.

The results of this study are felt to have the following implications and possibilities of future research:

1) The attitudes of institutionalized children and of the institutional staff towards their institutional environment can be assessed as being either positive or negative. However, the development of an empirical attitude scale which would permit quantification and measurement of the intensity of these attitudes is needed.

2) Demonstration that the institutionalized child's attitudes towards his environment can be changed through environmental manipulation suggests that a critical evaluation be made of the existing environment with the negative elements being eliminated where possible.

This aspect will be extremely difficult to accomplish in many institutions. Not only are some staff members reluctant to critically evaluate their environment, but they are usually unable to incorporate change when negative aspects are detected. The basis for this difficulty is felt to be the authority structure within the institution, which dictates that change in institutional policy can only be effected by the one individual who has the least amount of association with the children and the staff, and therefore minimal awareness of those aspects within the institutional environment which are beneficial or detrimental.

3) The attitudes of the children and the staff within the institution and the similarity between these emphasizes the need for critical evaluation of the institutional environment. Not only do the institutional policies, expectations, and procedures relative to the children and staff appear to be in need of revision, but also the need for a general staff re-education and training program relative to the care of the institutionalized children.

Although the institution considered in this study is currently undergoing slow, positive change, those aspects in greatest need of revision cannot change if the individual who decides the institutional policy does not agree to the need for such change.

Lillian Dimitroff

CONCEPT OF SELF AND TEACHING CULTURALLY DIFFERENT PEOPLE

Dr. Dimitroff has taken a sound psychological focus for her research on culturally different people – the concept of self. It is obvious that environment has traumatic effects on this concept, and children from culturally different families are apt to have serious psychological repercussions in their adjustment to the schoolroom. The role of family and parents in such environments is often different from that of the conventional school-age child.

Interestingly, the self-concept is more secure in a younger child and is altered only after a few years in school and exposure to more complex experiences of competition and achievement which threaten his level of confidence.

Dr. Dimitroff also takes a very realistic look at integration and the interracial situation and the problems which were found in such programs as Head Start and the Higher Horizons projects. She has also developed an experimental technique for improving instruction of culturally deprived children and offers specific, practical, and realistic tips to teachers of such programs. These conclusions are based on actual experience, as observed in the inner city schools, and as reported and discussed in the seminars of teachers and intern teachers working in the area.

A DESCRIPTION OF CULTURALLY DIFFERENT PEOPLE

Culturally different people are those who are not fully accepted in the mainstream of American life today. At the risk of labeling these people, one should remember that we are a culturally pluralistic nation which rather recently has come to recognize the concept of cultural pluralism as being as valid as the concept of the melting pot in describing our nation. Culturally different people have a distinct life style. Though separate from the American mainstream they are not without an Americanized culture of their own. The fact remains, however, that this distinct way of life seems more disadvantageous in meeting the demands of increasing urbanization and of competing in a technologically advanced economy. Generally speaking these people have crowded into the older parts of our major cities; their habitats are described as comprising a ghetto. The people are generally classified as belonging to the lowest socio-economic class whose style of living is not entirely devoid of positive aspects and is preferred by some people. In our major cities these people make up a considerable proportion of the population in comparison with those who could be considered middle class or upper class. At their present rate of increase, within a few years the proportion of these children enrolled in the public schools of our fourteen largest cities will increase to one in two pupils. The difficulties of teaching these children are well known.

THE EFFECTS OF A POOR CONCEPT OF SELF

Many reasons have been suggested to explain the learning problems of this segment of our school population. The fact that culturally different pupils have a poor self-concept is worth examining as one of the causes of learning difficulties inasmuch as there is a close relationship between negative self-concept and problems of learning.

A child's concept of self refers to his feeling of self-worth and competency. This self is the product of an individual's social experiences – a mirror of the interaction between the person and the society with which he has had contact. The self, moreover, is a continuum, rooted in the past and influencing behavior in the future. If the experiences of the past have been satisfying enough to build a foundation for a future, the motivation and drive to learn will be present because the self comprehends that his aspirations are within the realm of the possible. On the other hand, many culturally different people – especially Negroes – have developed a poor self-image both as a result of impoverished experiences in the home and deprivation in the community. Although an experience occurred in early childhood and is buried in the subconscious, it is, nevertheless, functioning. "The young child's identity arises partly from what is done to and for him and what he is told about himself . . ."[1] Extreme deprivation in the home has a numbing effect on the intellect of a child living in such an environment. In this type of home as in any other, the young child observes the techniques of dealing with others and their effectiveness in solving problems of daily living.

> As a child . . . begins to explore his small world, he may be continually blocked, scolded, and even punished for his curiosity and his impulsive activity, being told that he is bad and treated as unacceptable or rejected. From these verbalized statements about himself, often colored with strong parental feelings, the child begins to develop an image of the self . . . frequently with feelings of anxiety, shame, guilt, resentment and hostility.[2]

At present genetic aspects have yielded to environmental forces as the primary influence

1. Lawrence K. Frank, "Clues to Children's Identity," *Childhood Education*, XLII, (January, 1966), p. 276.
2. *Ibid.*, p. 277.

of our most challenging and baffling educational problem. "The more averse and demoralizing are his family life and his neighborhood, the more often his identity may be stunted or distorted."[3]

Such an experience emphasizes a child's observation of adult frustration, helplessness, dependency and even hopelessness. The small child internalizes these experiences especially as they apply to his mother; they become a part of his being; they are the preparation and background which he brings to the school. Although the child cannot or will not verbalize how he feels or thinks about himself, his play, coloring, drawing and spontaneous dramatizations communicate his *story about himself*. It behooves teachers to cultivate the sensitivity to the particular "story" which each child brings to the classroom, and with this understanding, to comprehend the educational *milieu* in which they will have to function; it is perhaps quite different from their expectations and preparational background.

A relatively small percentage of children with a culturally disadvantaged outlook succeed in school. Coming from a deprived background, generally speaking, the self which this child brings to school does not prepare him for learning in the usual manner. In the period when this individual should have experienced a satisfying development of his mental and emotional powers, the stupefying and destructive environmental effects have retarded his growth. Consequently, his defeat by school experiences and his bitter emotional reactions to overt as well as covert rebuffs have hardened his negative self-image which, in turn, slows the mastery of skills and content needed for success in our culture. The emotional impact of a culture foreign to that of his school and teachers sometimes can be so devastating to his self as to close the avenues of communication. "A child's life is more greatly affected by the way his emotions develop than by either his physical or mental development. Within rather wide limits, success and happiness in school, in his life work,

in his family relations, in his daily living depend much more on his emotional maturity than on his physical or mental maturity."[4] Each reaction, be it mental, physical, social, or emotional, leaves a person a slightly changed human being, and without a healthy means of communication, he is severely handicapped. His emotional maturity is largely a product of his ability to communicate.

Regardless of the race of the culturally different child, his environmental relationships have left him with a negative self-concept. This coupled with a mother-child communication system *lacking in range of* alternatives of thought, action, and cognitive meaning have crippled the child's ability to function in a school situation. Family relationships structure as well as communication and language shape the thought and cognitive styles of problem solving of the individual.[5]

The culturally different child comes to school with a restricted language background characterized by a limited vocabulary, sentence fragments, stereotyped expressions, short sentences, simple grammatical structure, lack of precision, and even substitution of gestures for words. Expectations about the nature of school and what takes place there have been unwittingly represented by the low-socio-economic mother in a manner which has not helped to prepare her child to profit from school. According to research conducted by Dr. Robert Hess of the University of Chicago this mother might give the following instructions: "Well John, it's time to go to school now. You must know how to behave. The first day at school you should be a good boy and should do just what the teacher tells you to do."[6]

3. *Loc. cit.*
4. J. Murray Lee and Dorris May Lee, *The Child and His Development*, (New York, 1967), p. 123.
5. Robert D. Hess and Virginia C. Shipman, "Early Experience and the Socialization of Cognitive Modes In Children," *Child Development*, XXXVIII, (December, 1965), p. 870.
6. *Ibid.*, p. 877.

In contrast, research by Dr. Hess revealed that the middle-class mother would instruct her child in the following manner:

First of all, I would remind her that she was going to school to learn, that her teacher would take my place, and that she would be expected to follow instructions. Also that her time was to be spent mostly in the classroom with other children, and that any questions or any problems that she might have she could consult with her teacher for assistance.[7]

Whereas the first mother represented the role of the child at school as compliant, passive and dependent upon authority, the second parent portrayed the classroom situation as a place to learn. She implied that the child's role would be an active one and that school *would be an extension* of the home experience. For the first child in this comparison, a poor self-image, a disorganized home, poor language background, constant noise, lack of systematic visual stimulation and poor nutrition militate against success at school.

A REVIEW OF PERTINENT RESEARCH

Although the bulk of research relating to aspects of concept of self and the instruction of culturally different children will be reviewed in this section, some studies will be referred to in other portions of this chapter because of their close relationship to subjects under consideration.

CONCEPT OF SELF AND THE FAMILY

As stated above, a child's self-picture stems from early sources and can cast a shadow over the remaining years of his life. The earliest sources of a child's self-picture are his contact with his mother and others in his family. "Once a child has his self-picture, he acts it out. . . . It determines not only his behavior but his mental health, future success, and happiness."[8]

This same point of view concerning the effects of early experiences is supported by a study conducted by James V. Mitchell, who ascertained that the crux of the parent-child relationship seems to be that the child's perception of what his parents are is determined by other people's estimate of the parents. This he considers to be more important than specific characteristics of home life.[9]

For a Negro child, especially, this could be a devastating observation, because he observes that his *parents are relegated* to an inferior position. The above point of view was supported by Mitchell's study of 145 female sophomores at a midwest university; his conclusion follows:

Self-acceptance is influenced appreciably by a satisfying and congenial family life while the development of anxiety and neurotic symptoms will more likely be occasioned by the subject's perception that she is failing to meet standards rather than any dissatisfaction with family life *per se*.[10]

This study confirmed the importance of family life, but for these subjects, injury to ego as a result of unsuccessful competition seemed the crucial factor in good adjustment to the school situation.

The matriarchal family organization, characteristic of many lower-class families, has often been blamed for a child's personality disorders and ultimate failure in school. Certainly, older children are not likely to develop the same self-concept in such an organization. Dodd's study, briefly described below, did not go far enough for conclusive evidence. He attempted to ascertain whether drawings of women made by children who live in a matriarchal society will be more

7. *Loc. cit.*
8. Katherine Roe, "Your Child's Self-Picture," *Childhood Education,* XXXVIII, (March, 1962), p. 333.
9. James V. Mitchell, "Self-Family Perceptions Related to Self Acceptance, Manifest Anxiety, Neuroticism," *The Journal of Educational Research,* LVI, (January, 1963), p. 236.
10. *Ibid.,* p. 242.

complete than their drawings of men, signifying a difference in relationship. The sample consisted of 103 culturally deprived, Negro children between the ages of four and one-half and five and one-half in Buffalo, New York. The results were that both boys and girls drew a greater number of more complete women than men.[11]

The fact that children at this age are very much attached to their mothers is obvious although this study is inconclusive and needs to be followed to its logical conclusion to ascertain whether results are different with older subjects, and whether a matriarchal family organization is *productive* of more personality disorders and learning difficulties than a patriarchal order. Martin Deutsch and Bert Brown investigated 543 urban children to ascertain the effects of the father's absence from the home. Children in father-absent families as compared with those from intact families scored significantly lower on standardized tests; this fact was even more marked at fifth grade level than in the primary grades. This would seem to suggest a negative cumulative effect of father absence.[12] This piece of research does not conclusively answer the question whether lower scores of children from father-absent homes are connected to poor self-image.

CONCEPT OF SELF AND CHILDREN'S ABILITY TO FUNCTION EFFECTIVELY

Beeman Phillips[13] felt there is a "progressive and age-related pattern of development of the self . . . and (it) is a factor in the accuracy of self-perception. As postulated above, older children would provide more accurate information in some types of research. The subjects were four classes of third grade pupils who were tested on a modification of Amatora's Children's Personality Scale to obtain self-ratings. Teacher ratings and peer ratings were also obtained. Findings indicated that sixth grade estimates were closer to reality and in nearer agreement with those of

teachers and peers than third grade estimates.[14] This study also disclosed that older children with more accurate self-perception may also feel that high academic aspirations may be futile if they belong to a culturally *disadvantaged group*. This feeling may be reinforced by statistics which show that as culturally disadvantaged boys and girls progress through school both their I.Q. and performance deteriorate.

For the culturally disadvantaged, the self-concept has been shown to deteriorate as the child gets older. "In self-concept are bound up one's hopes, fears, defenses, and self-esteem . . . the nucleus of personality."[15] For the younger child, the school is a secure and protective place. It is at the third grade level that the self-concept seems to take a precipitous drop; this is also the time when many culturally disadvantaged children begin to have really serious learning problems in school. Morse analyzed the responses of more than six hundred pupils in alternate grades from three through eleven to a Self-Esteem Inventory. The third grade responded in a significantly different manner; they showed a high self-regard. After this grade, results showed a significant decrease in concept of self which improved again in the eleventh grade. Even in this improved period, 44 per cent of the eleventh graders wished they were somebody else.[16]

These replies certainly indicate the degree of discouragement in both the elementary and secondary school. Just as important is the implicit suggestion to educators that the longer boys and girls are in school the less positive is the self-concept. The problem is to make school children educationally produc-

11. John M. Dodd and Robert R. Randall, "A Comparison of Negro Children's Drawings of a Man and a Woman," *The Journal of Negro Education*, XXXV, (Summer, 1966), p. 287.
12. Benjamin S. Bloom, Allison Davis, and Robert Hess, *Compensatory Education for Cultural Deprivation*, (New York, 1965), p. 104.
13. Beeman N. Phillips, "Age Changes in Accuracy of Self-Perceptions," *Child Development*, XXXIV, (December, 1963), p. 1041.
14. *Ibid.*, p. 1044.
15. William C. Morse, "Self-Concept in the School Setting," *Childhood Education*, XLI (December, 1964), p. 196.
16. *Ibid.*, p. 197.

tive instead of struggling with a sense of failure.

The law of this land is that schools shall be racially integrated. A pertinent piece of research by Webster and Kroger was concerned with ascertaining how integrated adolescent associations affected Negro concepts of self. In three integrated high schools in the San Francisco Bay area, over 300 Negro adolescents were tested with a questionnaire. The following information was sought:

1. Will Negro subjects with white friends score significantly higher on measures of personal independence than Negro subjects without white friends?

2. Will Negro subjects with white friends report significantly higher scores in respect to these points?

   a. Social competence: this referred to a subject's feelings of social competency, that is, how competent and comfortable he felt about his abilities to interact socially with others.

   b. Intellectual esteem: this focused on a subject's estimate and confidence in his intellectual ability.

   c. Physical esteem: this dealt with a subject's level of esteem for his physical attributes.

   d. Will total self-concept scores of Negro youths with white friends be higher than those without white friends?

3. Will Negro subjects with white friends report significantly higher scores in regard to levels of aspiration?

   a. Will vocational aspirations be higher?

   b. Will levels of expected vocational attainment be higher?

   c. Will perceptions of potential for later occupational attainment be higher?

4. Will Negro subjects with white friends predict for themselves significantly higher levels of future social acceptance by the total society?

5. Will Negro subjects with white friends score significantly lower in respect to ethnic concern or anxiety?

6. Will Negro subjects with white friends score significantly lower on a measure of group esteem, that is, display ethnocentrism?

7. Will Negro subjects reporting no white friendships state a significantly greater preference for associations with Negroes?

Results supported an affirmative answer to all the questions. An important exception, however, was the physical esteem dimension which did not produce any significantly different scores for the two groups. As in some other studies, the possession of Negroid features with a high level of visibility constitutes a reality for all Negroes regardless of their outlook or Caucasian friendships. Concerning the sixth question regarding feelings or anxiety over being a Negro, the scores reported for the two groups were not significantly different. Likewise, no significant difference was indicated by the two groups as to their levels of esteem for Negroes as a group, but the subjects without Caucasian friendships expressed a preference for associating with Negroes.[17]

Although the self-concept of Negroes as a group is lower than among Caucasians, obviously it is not uniformly so. Inasmuch as accepted attitudes and behaviors of any ethnic group exert a powerful influence upon its members, it would seem that the adolescents with white friendships displayed a higher degree of independence, inner strength, and self-concept than the average. In addition, the group with the higher self-concepts and the Caucasian friendships would naturally raise the level of its experiences, human contacts, and vocational goals. No doubt, their lives were thus enriched. Inasmuch as a positive self-concept contributes to optimum educational attainment, this group probably displayed higher academic achievement, although this was not a part of the Webster-Kroger conclusions.

17. Staten W. Webster and Marie N. Kroger, "A Comparative Study of Selected Perceptions and Feelings of Negro Adolescents with and Without White Friends in Integrated Urban High Schools," *The Journal of Negro Education*, XXXV, (Winter, 1966), pp. 55–61.

RELATIONSHIP BETWEEN CONCEPT OF SELF AND READING

Reading is a necessary skill for satisfactory educational progress, and research concerning the self in relation to the development of this skill is pertinent to the subject under consideration. There has been evidence for a period of years that there is a relationship between a poor self-concept and severe retardation in reading. The review of some of the research of the last decade supports this point of view. In an unpublished doctoral dissertation, L. Barber of the University of Michigan found that children accepted in remedial reading "displayed anxiety about self and relationships with people to a marked degree."[18]

In an unpublished doctoral study by D. D. Lumpkin at the University of Southern California in 1959, fifth grade overachievers and underachievers were matched in respect to chronological age, mental age, sex, and home background. The overachievers revealed significantly more positive self-concepts.[19]

R. F. Bodwin made a similar type of study of 100 pupils with reading disability, 100 with arithmetic disability and 100 with no educational disability. He found that the relationship between immature self-concepts and reading disability yielded a correlation of .72 at the third grade level and .62 at the sixth grade level.[20]

Research has also sought the relationship between self-concept and academic achievement. In Flint, Michigan, M. A. Bruck of Michigan State University measured the self-concept of 300 pupils using samples from the third through sixth grades and from the eleventh grade. This doctoral dissertation revealed a positive and significant relationship between self-concept and grade-point averages *at all grade levels* in which students were considered.[21] In 1960, D. E. Homachek at the University of Michigan School discovered that high achievement and intellectual self-images were related to reading age. Also in that year at Northern Texas

State College, L. C. Seay found changes in self-concept were positively associated with experiences in the remedial reading program.[22]

The objective of Wattenberg and Clifford was to determine which was the antecedent phenomenon, a poor self-concept or reading disability. Measures of mental ability and self-concept were obtained during the first semester of kindergarten of 185 children in two elementary schools in Detroit. Two and a half years later, measures of 128 children remaining in these schools were obtained of progress in reading and self-concept. Their hypotheses follow:

1. Measures and ratings of self-concept taken during the first semester of kindergarten will be predictive of later achievement in reading.

2. There will be low correlation between a mental test score and measures and ratings of self-concept.

3. The relationship between reading achievement and changes in measures of self-concept from kindergarten to second grade will be positive but low.

4. Evidence of ego strength will show a high positive correlation with achievement in reading.

5. Ratings of self-concept will display characteristics of defensive reactions; children verbalizing a high ratio of self-reference will show lower success in reading than those demonstrating little preoccupation with self-characteristics.[23]

Evaluation of data supported these hypotheses: the data indicated a definite link between competence and improvement of self-concept, and a decided correlation between kindergarten scores and later reading achievement. This study indicated that self-

---

18. See William W. Wattenberg and Clare Clifford, "Relation of Self-Concepts to Beginning Achievement in Reading," *Child Development*, XXXV, (June, 1964), p. 461.
19. *Loc. cit.*
20. *Loc. cit.*
21. *Loc. cit.*
22. *Ibid.*, p. 462.
23. *Ibid.*, pp. 463–464.

concept in kindergarten has greater influence in the development of reading skill than the reading experience has upon the self-concept.[24] The results of this study definitely indicated that measures and ratings of self-concept and ego strength in kindergarten were predictive of later reading achievement. Along with tests of mental ability, measures and ratings of self-concept seem to describe the child's potential more accurately than by tests alone. Definitely positive self-concepts were shown to be antecedents to and predictive of reading accomplishment and also correlation between feelings of competence and of personal worth was indicated.[25]

SELF-CONCEPT AND THE TEACHER

Understanding the importance of self-concept can assist teachers, counselors, and parents to achieve a deeper understanding and insight into a child's behavior and a better working relationship with children. Information is offered in the studies which follow:

Hugh V. Perkins in 1954–1955 investigated the effects of social-emotional climate; teacher participation in an in-service child study program; and acceptance by teachers and others of the self. The relationship between grade levels and changes in children's self-concepts was defined as an indication of *congruency* between self-*concept* and self-*ideal*. The findings follow:

1. Girls generally registered greater self-ideal congruency than boys, although all children revealed greater congruency between self and ideal-self with passage of time.

2. Greater congruency of self and ideal-self was revealed by children whose teachers are participating in a child study course and by sixth graders.

3. A lack of relationship between changes in children's self-ideal–self-congruency and

changes in their acceptance by peers was disclosed.

4. Children achieved increased self-ideal–self-congruency during a period of time that they were in attendance at school.[26]

The results of this study might be different if it were repeated now in a school attended largely by culturally different children.

Earl McCallon postulated that "self and ideal-self concepts are acquired through environmental influences . . . that variation in environment might facilitate or retard the movement toward . . . self-ideal–self-congruency."[27] The purpose of his study was to investigate the relationship between certain teacher characteristics and change in the congruency of children's perception of self and ideal-self. His sample consisted of 47 fifth and sixth grade teachers and their pupils. Results indicated a movement toward greater congruency of self-ideal–self-perception by the children in this study.[28] This researcher believed that teachers exert a strong influence on children's development and the perception of self-ideal–self-relationship.

There has been much research to find the personality characteristics which distinguish the effective teacher, but so far no one set of characteristics have been selected as the key which distinguishes the effective teacher. Seeing that self-awareness (how teacher appears to her pupils) is an important factor in teaching behavior, a teacher who has this quality is aware of her impact on the pupils.

The Wright-Sherman study sample consisted of 40 teachers and their pupils. The instruments used for this evaluation were the "Semantic Differential Evaluative Adjectives" and the "Leader-Tyrant Evaluative Statements." These instruments sampled the

24. *Ibid.*, p. 465.
25. *Ibid.*, p. 466.
26. Hugh V. Perkins, "Factors Influencing Change in Children's Self-Concepts," *Child Development*, XXIX, (June, 1958), p. 226.
27. Earl L. McCallon, "Teacher Characteristics and Their Relationship to Change in the Congruency of Children's Perceptions of Self and Ideal-Self," *Journal of Experimental Education*, XXXIV, (Summer, 1966), pp. 84–88.
28. *Ibid.*, p. 87.

past of the teachers as well as pupils' feelings towards and impressions of their teachers. The hypothesis was that teacher self-awareness is related to evaluation of childhood authority figures. Four authority figures were used: mother, father, best-liked teacher, and least-liked teacher. Multiple correlation coefficients between teachers' self-awareness and their evaluation of authority figures was .52 for girls and .62 for boys. The findings suggested that self-awareness among women teachers was contingent on the idealization of the mother rather than father and on a moderate rather than on an extreme evaluation of former teacher images. Lack of self-awareness increased with idealization of father.[29] Considering the importance of teacher self-awareness, in working with children in the classroom, one can only assume that the teacher's need for satisfaction and self-respect dictated a low self-awareness to protect the teacher's ego.

Dr. James C. Lafferty of the Wayne County, Michigan Schools found a way to improve the self-concepts of teachers as well as the classroom climate. Instructors showed improvement in mental health after participating in a consulting program which included improvement of skills and self-confidence and analysis of informational levels. The faculty were organized into small groups for discussion and self-study; this program lasted for a year. The results of this program showed positive changes in self-concepts in 50 per cent of the cases.[30]

Teacher training institutions, too, have shown concern with the self-concept of the teachers as well as of the pupil. The self-concepts of trainee-teachers in two cultures, namely, England and Jamaica, were compared. The method was to have the subjects write unstructured compositions on the topic. "I Myself; the Person I Am; the Person Others Think I Am; the Person I Would Like to Be." In addition, both groups were rated on tests of self-concept. These comparisons were stated:

1. Both male and female, Jamaican students, regardless of age, rated themselves significantly higher in respect to self-concept than English teacher-trainees.

2. English male students rated themselves at approximately the same level as English female students; however, Jamaican female students rated themselves higher than Jamaican men and appeared to be less self-accepting.

3. There were no important differences between the self-concept scores of English students of regular age and of more mature years. In contrast, the mature Jamaican students rated themselves lower than those of usual college age.[31]

Another investigation of the self-concept of student teachers was the Lantz study. The major purpose of his investigation was to explore the relationship between concept of self of women elementary student teachers and classroom emotional climate. The following variables in the form of a questionnaire were used as predictors:

1. Self-concept score which was the expressed attitude of an individual about himself to his classroom emotional climate rating.

2. "Self-Other Discrepancy" score which was the disparity between an individual's expressed attitudes about himself and his expressed attitudes toward most other elementary teachers.

3. "Self-ideal Discrepancy" score which was the disparity between an individual's expressed attitudes about the ideal teacher and how it was related to her classroom emotional climate rating.[32]

None of the variables used as predictors was capable of predicting classroom emo-

29. Benjamin Wright and Barbara Sherman, "Teachers' Self-Awareness and Their Evaluation of Childhood Authority Figures," *School Review*, LXXI, (Spring, 1963), pp. 80–84.
30. Samuel A. Moore, "The Teacher's Self-Image," *Overview*, II, (December, 1961), pp. 23–25.
31. A. S. Phillips, "The Self Concepts of Trainee-teachers in Two Sub-Cultures," *The British Journal of Educational Psychology*, XXX, (June, 1963), p. 154.
32. Donald L. Lantz, "Relationship Between Classroom Emotional Climate and Concepts of Self, Others, and Ideal Among Elem. Student Teachers," *Journal of Education Research*, LIX, (October, 1965), p. 80.

tional scores beyond chance. The only variable from which any prediction of classroom emotional climate could be made was the "Self-Other Discrepancy" score for the skeptical-distrustful scale. People who rated themselves thus received higher classroom emotional climate scores, possibly because they expressed their own personalities in their teaching.

The importance of these studies is the emphasis they place on a teacher's self-concept which determines her general behavior by what she perceives herself to be and which is the foundation of a harmonious personality. A teacher's personality is of prime importance to success in the classroom. Although important, it is very intangible.

SELF-CONCEPT AND LEARNING

A child's self-concept, his social anchorages, (an individual's ability to find his place in the social group) and his readiness are necessary components of learning. The purpose of this study was to ascertain the self-attitudes and social anchorages of a select group of 61 junior high school math and science students in grades 7, 8, and 9 from Iowa public schools. It was felt that the findings might possibly indicate what should be included and what should be omitted in the junior high school curriculum. The "Twenty-Statement Test" was administered during the last week of the eight-week summer session. The conclusion was that one could surmise that the self-attitudes revealed by the "Twenty-Statement Test" could be valuable in curriculum planning, counselling and guidance, and teacher preparation.[33]

Joseph Caliguri, an elementary school principal in Las Vegas, Nevada, used four open-ended questions to explore the self-concept of 425 intermediate grade children in a minority group area. Children responded freely about aggressive behavior or feelings. Pupils' perceptions about things that made them feel important tended to show low expectations of disadvantaged children concerning ego strength. The topics which follow show the order of values children expressed:[34]

Topics	Response
Getting Material Things	31%
Personality Considerations	35%
Academic Concerns	26%
Physical Features	4%
Making Friends	3%
Receiving Praise	1%

Undoubtedly the order of importance of the above topics indicates need of material things and desire for independence. The responses also indicated significant implications for educators:

1. A need for broadening school and community activities as a basis for resolution of personal and interpersonal problems in socially approved ways.

2. Prestige-building activities as a conscious part of the school program should be included to increase feelings of self-identity and self-esteem.[35] From this study there was evidence that behavior of these children was really not controlled by what pupils knew but by their feelings, that is, their concept of self.

Whether self-concept and school achievement have a close relationship to each other was investigated by Brookover. He sampled 1050 seventh grade students. His findings indicated a significant positive correlation between self-concept and performance in the academic role, relationship between self-concept and performance in specialized areas, and a correlation between the perceived evaluations of significant others and pupil performance.[36]

33. Leland Holt and Manford Sonstgard, "Relating Self-Conception to Curriculum Development," *The Journal of Educational Research*, LVIII, (April, 1965), p. 351.
34. Joseph Caliguri, "The Self-Concept of the Poverty Child," *The Journal of Negro Education*, XXXV, (Summer, 1966), pp. 280-282.
35. *Ibid.*, p. 282.
36. Wilbur B. Brookover and Shailer Thomas, "Self-Concept and School Achievement," *Sociology of Education*, XXXVII, (Spring, 1964), p. 278.

IMPORTANCE OF SELF-CONCEPT TO TRAINING CULTURALLY DIFFERENT PUPILS

The Culturally Different Child, Home, and School

"The child can only operate in terms of the way he sees himself . . . [he] withdraws or strikes out before the other person has a chance to establish a friendly feeling."[37] This description fits many culturally different children. The self is developed by the pattern prevailing in the culture. It develops in relation to what it feeds on, being selective in regard to what it perceives and chooses. The family plays a crucial role in the development of the self. Brazziel and Terrell found that when the family, along with the child and the school, participates in readiness activities, children's learning and learning potential is increased.

The results of a six-week readiness program which included Negro children and their parents produced these results:

1. At the end of six weeks the children in the experimental group tested at the fiftieth percentile of the Metropolitan Readiness Test, in contrast to the control group which tested at the fifteenth percentile.

2. After seven months the mean I.Q. of the experimental group was 106.5 as compared to a general expectation of 90.[38]

Jackson hypothesized that learning effectiveness can be impaired by membership in a socially deprived or a stressful family environment, or classroom conditions that create a threatening climate for learning. He postulated, moreover, that learning effectiveness is enhanced by positive attitudes toward school, realistic achievement goals, and feelings of self-confidence.[39]

Another student of these educational problems has expressed a view which also affects learning:

In a society in which mental inferiority, laziness, incompetency, and irresponsibility are part of the definition externally assigned to a group as in the case with the Negro, the group so defined will tend to confirm this definition.[40]

Confirmation of these expectations has occurred as a result of cultural and institutional forces in operation in our society which reward behavior conforming to this stereotype. For many years culturally disadvantaged people have accepted a given status in society which became a part of their own self-image. Acceptance of this status coupled with resultant life changes have lowered the motivational level of these people until many seem to be without any goals beyond daily survival. They have very low levels of aspiration, and these attitudes have become internalized for large segments of population. The result has been an overwhelming number of serious learning problems which have not yielded to the usual classroom methods of instruction. This serious problem has been compounded by the large numbers of culturally different children in our largest urban centers which are faced with a serious shortage of well-trained teachers.

The concept of self not only affects how children learn but also how they behave. The problem of the Negro male to earn a decent living and to occupy a respected position in the home and community is reflected in the behavior and learning problems of many Negro boys at school. In their attempt to maintain their self-image they emphasize physical prowess and rebellion. Thus, many renounce artistic, abstract, and intellectual activities. In view of this evidence of a poor self-concept of Negro school boys, it is not strange that there are usually more Negro girls in honor classes than boys.[41] Another factor

37. J. Murray Lee and Dorris M. Lee, *The Child and His Curriculum*, (New York, 1960), p. 31.
38. Bloom, Davis, and Hess, *op. cit.* p. 88.
39. Philip W. Jackson and Nina Strattner, "Meaningful Learning and Retention: Noncognitive Variables," *Review of Educational Research*, XXXIV, (December, 1964), pp. 513–527.
40. Ralph Hines, "Social Expectations and Cultural Deprivation," *Journal of Negro Education*, XXXIII, (Spring, 1964), p. 137.
41. Clemmont E. Vontress, "The Negro Personality Reconsidered," *The Journal of Negro Education*, XXXV, (Summer, 1966), p. 217.

relative to the problem is family background; a relatively small percentage of Negroes are not even one generation removed from poverty. The home has not been equipped with books and other cultural artifacts, and the school experience is often not stressed or looked upon as really desirable.

Other problems stemming from disadvantaged homes which find their way into the classroom are as follows: the selective inattention cultivated by children in order to survive in a noisy environment is later used to tune out the teacher. Aggressiveness combined with quickness has demonstrated to many slum children that they will be more successful in competition for a limited supply of material comforts. With such a background, these individuals develop into impulsive children. These are the hyperactive youngsters who rush out of their seats to get the attention of the teacher, to examine something in the classroom, or to follow some explorations of their own. Such a child has a very short attention span, experiences difficulty in concentrating or sitting long enough to learn skills necessary for school success. The nonvigorous child has learned to survive in his environment by being passive. In school he is withdrawn, lethargic, and very difficult to reach. Poor nutrition is responsible for many listless children in classrooms. Also, the paucity of toys in the home has caused a failure to develop manipulative skills. Even if these children came to the classroom with a good self-image, maintaining it would be difficult in the face of the problems mentioned above.

RAISING CONCEPT OF SELF AND MORE EFFECTIVE TEACHING OF CULTURALLY DIFFERENT PEOPLE

Improvement of Concept of Self

Improving concept of self is a lengthier and more difficult process than tearing it down. To produce such a change requires experiences which help the individual perceive the self in a more favorable light. Each involvement with the environment may mean assimilating something and surrendering something. The special problems of culturally different people are of a social, economic, and legal nature evolving from the cultural isolation of these groups. As stated before, the self largely determined by a background of accumulated experiences is selective in its perception of intake; if it perceives a hostile environment, it becomes almost impermeable. A prolonged unfavorable environment in which the self seeks to protect itself produces isolation with a diminished self as the least consequence.

Any program which purports to alleviate the present dilemma must approach it on a more inclusive front than the educational alone. The causes of deprivation must be sought and relieved. Minimally, any effective program must provide for economic escalation and for constructive interaction of individuals of culturally different groups within the larger social structure. New techniques must be explored for eliminating the barriers of communication which impede social action.[42] In order for culturally different people to learn, there must be a drive and a visible reward to people of their own group.

METHODS AND TECHNIQUES FOR IMPROVING THE INSTRUCTION OF CULTURALLY DIFFERENT CHILDREN

Learning is what the self perceives, accepts, reviews, synthesizes, interprets, and uses from the perceptual inputs before it at every waking moment. For this reason it is important that the teacher should arrange situations and provide experiences which are designed to help students see themselves as adequate and effective agents. For every child, the experience of success in some activity is important, but the Negro child needs continued opportunities to see himself and

42. Paul B. Warren, "Guidelines for the Future—An Educational Approach for the Culturally Disadvantaged," *The Journal of Negro Education*, XXXV, (Summer, 1966), p. 283.

his racial group in a realistically positive way from his earliest days through high school. There is a particular necessity for the Negro child to see examples of his own ethnic group who have made a success of their lives as a result of a good education. Dr. Sam Shepard of St. Louis has used young Negroes from McDonnell Aircraft Corp. to inspire higher levels of aspiration in Negro youth. To see Negro people who are successful in sports is not enough; sports do not emphasize the abstract levels of achievement. Schools attended by culturally different people have a great need for counselors who can fill in part of the gap of an inadequate home life. Giving a student the opportunity to talk about his problem and showing sympathetic interest make him feel he has a friend who is sincerely interested in him. Furthermore, if the problem is verbalized and viewed with perspective it is never as bad as it seemed originally. Nothing is more devastating than to feel one has a problem peculiar to himself; group therapy is, therefore, particularly helpful. A good counselling experience can truly give cuturally different youth an anchor.

Many teachers have had rewarding experiences with these young people. Here are a few tips to teachers of culturally different pupils:

1. Less teacher domination of a lesson with more guidance of children to find satisfying solutions.

2. More open-ended questions and more exploration of a number of answers rather than questioning for the "right" answer.

3. Less criticism of mistakes and failure and more utilization of mistakes as a part of learning.

4. Bibliotherapy can fill a need for vicarious experience because youngsters can read about and discuss people with similar conflicts, problems, and hardships.

5. Trips provide a needed background of experience to which reading and discussion can be related.

6. School projects providing status can supply these children with needed experiences as well as pride in accomplishment. Here are a few examples of such activities:

   a. Contests
   b. Assembly programs
   c. Bulletin boards
   d. Attractive classrooms

7. Guiding the child in making some object representative of school work which can be taken home to the parent will satisfy the pride of both child and parent.

8. Use of mirrors and pictures in elementary classrooms can improve self appearance as well as grooming habits. The child should be made to feel that his own image is the most important in the world and encouraged to take pride in it.

9. Directed listening can combat tuning out the teacher. Films, filmstrips, records, tape-recorded speeches, and live reports can be used with a listening guide sheet consisting of a skeleton outline to be completed as a student listens.

10. Scrambled outline related to familiar and well-structured material is a useful exercise for teaching relationships.

11. Negro children especially need to be made aware that this ethnic group has contributed to the history of this country from the very beginning. Such a project has been carried out at the Burns School in Chicago by student teacher Mrs. Helen Saunders of Chicago State College. This student teacher was very well informed on Negro history and wrote the materials presented to a seventh grade class. Pupils, parents, and teachers were pleased with these materials. Negroes and whites shared these feelings. When parents attending the culminating activities of the last unit were asked about their feelings concerning these materials, Negroes and whites expressed unanimous approval; moreover they felt that such material should be incorporated into the curriculum. At no time did the author observe any feeling other than pride when children were studying this material.

12. Role playing and dramatization pro-

vide understanding and gratification of children's desires to be admired and respected by their peers.

13. Raising the level of aspiration is important for children with a poor self-concept. Charles Reed, former student teacher at the Gregory School in Chicago, carried on such a project. Every week he asked his class, "What are you going to be?" Many of these children had poor adult models in the neighborhood and had not thought of an occupation. Each child had to describe what he wished to be. This exercise was very informative for the pupils, and it caused them to consider their aspirations, most important for their concepts of self.

14. Using concrete materials makes an educational experience meaningful to pupils who have difficulties with abstractions.

15. Linking lessons with making a living raises aspirations and supplies motivation.

16. Vicarious experience and less emphasis on abstractions can be provided by films, filmstrips, charts, cartoons, maps, globes, pictures, postcards, and stick figures.

17. The physical effort of writing a lesson helps many of these children concentrate and therefore retain more.

18. Introduce only one new difficulty at a time to prevent confusion and further deterioration of self-image.

19. Present small blocks of subject matter so that pupils find tasks within their reach and experience the satisfaction of completing a task.

20. Provide many simple practice exercises but allow plenty of time to complete them. These children are not speed oriented.

21. Hold frequent remedial drills; these pupils need repetition. Drills can be varied by making games of them. Having a little review just before lunch and before the end of the day is good reinforcement and good public relations, because children may tell their parents what they learned.

22. Use variety with frequent changes of activities to provide for short attention span.

23. Use graphs to record progress, so pupil can have the satisfaction of seeing the progress he is making.

24. Give much individual help to slow learners; a one-to-one relationship is very satisfying to this type of child's ego. The learning response in this kind of situation is frequently very good.

25. Work out special projects. The ego of any child is flattered by being a part of some special activity.

26. Provide a situation in which this child can succeed. Success improves the concept of self; a positive self-concept makes learning easier.

27. Use material from a child's environment, because it is more easily learned and retained.

28. Structure the activities in the classroom; the organization and predictability provide some emotional security to a child with a poor self-concept.

29. A warm personality is flattering to a child with a poor self-concept and makes it easy for him to identify with the adult. This is very supportive to a child. Juan Cruz, a former student teacher from Chicago State College, did a special project of teaching English to Puerto Rican children. His success with these children was due to his kind of personality, interest, and dedication which enabled these children to identify with him.

30. Last, I should like to urge teachers not to place implicit faith in I. Q. tests. For children of this type, tests are inaccurate; moreover, many of this world's most creative individuals would be eliminated by these tests.

Among the people who will have a great impact on the child's concept of self will be his teacher. Since this is the case, teacher training institutions should re-evaluate their efforts of contributing to a positive self-concept of teacher-trainees. In a study by Staines, more learning took place in classrooms in which the words and actions of the teacher were enhancing to the students.[43]

43. J. W. Staines, "The Self-Picture as a Factor in the Classroom," *British Journal of Educational Psychology*, XXXIII, (June, 1958), p. 108.

Indeed, teachers should periodically re-evaluate their behavior in terms of their effect on the self: what they say, how they say it, and the feelings which are communicated by facial expression and posture. A teacher in this type of school carries an additional load. In some ways working with children with a poor self-concept is a paradox: it is exhausting but yet it is satisfying. These people possess a warmth and an elemental strength, often found missing among more favored groups. The purpose of education is to produce more adequate people; a key to producing more adequate people is to improve their concept of self.

Juan S. Cruz and George R. Ricks

THE PUERTO RICAN CHILD

Material concerning a subcultural child is presented to draw attention to unique psychological problems of children whose parents belong to subcultures, whether they are Puerto Rican, Mexican, or others. With the mobility of today's society, the effects of relocating one's family in a setting that defines them as a minority group with strange mores is psychologically important; whether one moves from Puerto Rico to the heart of New York, or from the farm land of Mississippi to the inner city of Chicago. Again and again schools and social agencies as well as the church are faced with difficulties arising from cultural differences. These in turn may do serious psychological damage to the individuals involved. Usually in such instances society must deal not only with the child and the immediate repercussions from the relocation of a family, but also with the entire family's adjustment.

The great variety of differences between cultures is well illustrated by Mr. Cruz and Mr. Ricks. Individually, and in combination, there exists a complex of problems in the psychological adjustment of groups of persons of minority status at all ages. The authors indicate varying approaches to anticipating and solving the problems of cultural adjustment and point up the great need for understanding and research in this area.

The Puerto Rican child in the process of adjustment goes through many psychological changes as he grows up in the continental society. The most difficult phases of this adjustment deal with the process of identification. Since the youngster grows with a dual system of acculturation, he is in constant search for his identity. At home, he has been taught the values of his Puerto Rican culture, the extended family, respect for the adults, the acceptance of the "machado." The boys are expected to behave like men while in their teens; all of this cultural background tends to conflict with the culture that the youngster is exposed to in the regular classroom. It is expected that the youngster is taught in the regular classroom. It is expected that the youngsters make these choices between the two cultures at an early age.

The concept "Puerto Rican" among the youngsters tends to classify them as different, neither white nor Negro. This label makes the youngsters feel that they don't belong to either group. They are in constant search for their identity.

Many of the youngsters are aware of the lack of communication between themselves and their parents. They often state that they cannot communicate with their parents who still adhere to "the way that life is in the island," while the youngsters are learning a different set of values from their peers and the school.

The school represents another threat to the Puerto Rican in many ways. The Puerto Rican by nature is shy. When he is confronted in the school with the need to communicate in the English language, he tends to disassociate himself from the entire school environment. The practice of testing the Puerto Rican child in English is also detrimental to the child's personality. Children born and reared in the continental environment tend to be illiterate in both English and Spanish. Those that have migrated from rural areas in Puerto Rico are doubly handicapped because they were not taught how to read in Spanish and are unable to make the grammatical transition into learning how to read in English.

To understand this Puerto Rican child better, let us look at the cultural background from which he comes, and investigate some aspects of his adjustment to the mainland of the U.S.A.

Puerto Rico is a Caribbean, West Indies island, 35 miles wide and 100 miles long. It is a commonwealth,[1] associated with the United States of America, established in 1954. Its 2,850,000 residents represent a population density of some 714 persons per square mile as compared to a population density of some 57 persons per square mile in the United States.

Culturally, Puerto Rico has been affected greatly by sixty years of contact with the United States. While Iberian (Spanish) cultural heritage has been overshadowed in contemporary times, Puerto Rican national culture is primarily a blend of the culture of Spain and the United States; and is influenced but little by the indigenous Indian culture (Arawak) of the island. Thus, as compared with some other Latin American countries, Puerto Rico has been considered relatively weak in indigenous folk arts and aboriginal cultural traditions. For example, Indian culture is still meaningful in Mexico

and Peru, as is Afro-American culture in Brazil and Haiti. However, in Puerto Rico the Indians were absorbed or were killed off very early and the large population of African slaves (almost half of the population in the early 1860's) retained relatively little of the African cultural survivals that have enriched the cultures of other parts of the West Indies. Examples of the fusion of various cultures in Puerto Rico are quite obvious in aesthetic manifestations of the acculturative process. The "plena," a popular song and dance, represents a fusion of Iberian (Spanish) and African musical elements; while the Puerto Rican "decima" is a Spanish influenced folk-song poetry form.

Catholicism is the dominant formal religion among the population in Puerto Rico. Until recent times, the priests were largely foreign (the two bishops in Puerto Rico now are Puerto Ricans). Formerly the clergy seemed detached both from the national ambitions of the people and their daily life. Prior to United States sovereignty over the island (1898), the Catholic Church was a dominant force in political decisions; the island was closed to missionizing by Protestant sects. Although Catholicism now finds itself in direct competition with other sects, its impact is still deeply felt in the value system and patterns of behavior of the population. Its stress upon traditional relationships within the social structure gives it strong support from the upper and middle classes in urban areas. The emphasis and sanction on the dominant role of the household (dominant familial role of the father) lends similar support from culturally conservative small-scale farmers in rural areas where the family unit is the most important element in terms of productivity.

1. Puerto Rico is a self-governing commonwealth, associated with the United States of America through a voluntary compact. The compact is founded on Public Law 600. It is the result of a proposal by the people of Puerto Rico that the Congress of the United States provide for the organization of a government by the people of Puerto Rico under a constitution of their own adoption.

Protestant groups affect some fifteen per cent of the population. Indeed, Protestantism has gained considerable strength since its introduction to the island. Its major concentration seems to be in the towns and rural areas and membership chiefly among such faiths as the Evangelical Church, Seventh-Day Adventists, and the Pentecostal churches which tend to emphasize taboos on smoking, drinking, dancing, and sexual promiscuity. Their religious services stress singing to the accompaniment of the guitar and the drum.

Spiritualism, although generally ascribed to lower-class and rural people, appears to be quite prevalent among the middle and upper classes on the island. This belief in the ability of mediums to control causation by spirits, according to some scholars, occurs primarily among adherents to Catholicism rather than among Protestants. However, it serves mainly as a supplement rather than as an alternative to other religious beliefs.

Witchcraft also appears to serve as a supplement to Western religious forms. Although witchcraft is ascribed to the African-derived population in Puerto Rico, research by anthropologists indicates strong influences of witchcraft in culturally conservative areas where the population (Catholic and Protestant) is predominantly non-Negro. Indeed, field research has indicated less influence of spiritualism and black magic in all-Negro communities than in other communities.

The Puerto Rican family is in some ways similar to the family-type of peasant Europe. It is patriarchal and authoritarian, with the adult male commanding obedience and respect from all members of the family. However, the Puerto Rican family differs from the European type mainly in the prevalence of consensual or common-law marriage. It is estimated that one quarter of the marriages are of this type, and that as a result, about one third of the births are out of wedlock. However, the Puerto Rican's concern for family structure includes legal recognition for children born out of wedlock, and is reflected in the surnaming custom.

Although the original intent in naming a child was to denote legitimacy and lineage, parents in consensual or common-law marriage also tend to follow this practice. For children born out of wedlock, the usual practice was to register the child with the mother's family name only, but in several of the Latin American countries, this practice has been changed by law.

Among Spanish-speaking people, the child has the father's family name *and* the mother's family name attached to his given or baptismal name or names. Often it is desirable that his lineage be further indicated by adding the family name of an important grandfather or grandmother.

In Puerto Rico, the law requires that the names of both parents, married or not, must be recorded on the birth certificate. Provision is also made permitting the child born out of wedlock to use his father's family name. In any case, the continuation of the family name from one generation to the next is patrilinear.

Both the European peasant and the Puerto Rican exhibit concern for the virginity of female children and closely guard their associations with unrelated males. But while the European peasant generally arranged the marriage of his son or daughter to enhance his own condition, Puerto Rican marriages tend to be more a matter of early escape of the young daughter with a man whom her parents have not chosen. There is a pattern of hostility on the part of male members of a family toward would-be suitors. Hence, courtship is most frequently carried on through intermediaries and marriage is made possible by way of elopement of the young lady and her "novio." In spite of obstacles to marriage, the girl (especially among lower classes) of eighteen or nineteen is expected to have entered wedlock. Indeed, marriage at the age of thirteen and fourteen is not uncommon among peasant and lower-class Puerto Ricans. As a result, many individuals move directly from childhood to adult responsibility; the females have an early experience of childbearing and males an early responsibility for children.

The family situation in Puerto Rico is perhaps one of the stronger elements in the culture. Men might have children by a number of women, but they generally assume responsibility for all of them. Even with a relatively high degree of marriage breakups, there are always places in families for the children. The strong institution of godparents (the "compadre" and "comadre") for each child, provides a second set of parents who are ready to take over if the family of procreation in some way defaults (too many children, death, desertion, etc.). Children are neither resented nor neglected.

WHO ARE THE PUERTO RICAN MIGRANTS?

The concept "Puerto Rican" among the majority of mainlanders is that of an "immigrant" or "foreigner." This point of view is supported by the facts that (1) Puerto Rico is geographically separated from the mainland, (2) Puerto Rico is not a state, (3) there is a general ignorance of the meaning of the commonwealth relationship between Puerto Rico and the United States and (4) there is an apparent communication barrier created by the English and Spanish linguistic traditions among mainlanders and islanders.

However, Puerto Ricans are American citizens and as such are legally entitled to migrate to the mainland. There are two general types: (1) the urban Puerto Rican who generally moves from the cities of Puerto Rico to urban centers of the U.S.A.; and (2) the rural Puerto Rican who moves from the cane fields of Puerto Rico to perform seasonal labor on farms in the East and Midwest of the U.S.A.

Studies of Puerto Rican immigrants to the U.S.A. indicate that their main reason for leaving Puerto Rico is the desire for a better job. A Columbia University survey has shown that eighty-five per cent of the immigrants have quit jobs to come to the mainland, fifteen per cent had been unemployed at the time of migration, and seventy-one per cent had been fully employed for two years before migration.

Typically, for families with children, the father migrates first to find a job and living quarters. Then he brings over the rest of the family, often in stages. This results in a family that is divided between the continent and Puerto Rico and usually creates a situation in which one part of a family is "Americanized" and the other is not. A less typical but not uncommon pattern is the "fatherless" family in which the mother decides to go to the mainland where jobs are plentiful and a "better life" is offered for women and children. This latter fact partially explains statistics showing that more Puerto Rican mothers are employed here than in the commonwealth. The Cook County Department of Public Aid indicates that less than one per cent of its case load is of Puerto Rican families.

WHAT ARE SOME PROBLEMS OF ADJUSTMENT?

The normal Puerto Rican family structure undergoes serious change and stress in the new environment. Even in the case of a complete family, the husband-wife relationship is affected. Where the father is usually the main support of the family, he finds employment difficult or nonexistent, while the skills of the wife may bring home as much or more money than her husband.

In New York and Chicago, for example, it is often easier for women to get jobs in the needlework trades than for their husbands. Furthermore, when the woman earns more money than her husband, it may threaten his position as the head of the household and cause extreme tension in the family.

Parent-child relationships also feel the impact of stress and change. Since it is often the case that children have a better command of

English than the parents, they may assume a major responsibility in relations between the family and the "outside world." This may breed resentments or disagreements in the decisions which involve conflicts between the "old way" of thinking and the demands of the newer culture.

Traditionally, male children are given relative freedom in their youth. Outside of showing respect for the father, the male child is encouraged to discipline himself. Female children, however, are accorded entirely different treatment. They are carefully guarded with respect to relationships outside the family where their seclusion is related to sexual mores.

The result of the conflict between these indigenous culture patterns and the new standards of behavior and values has serious consequences. Like other children, Puerto Rican children tend to become as good or as bad as the children with whom they associate. Left to their own resources in the new environment, boys are frequently exposed to opportunities for falling into bad company, learning antisocial habits and developing patterns of disrespect and disobedience toward the illiterate and old-time parent. The girl is frequently seen to rebel against the restrictive patterns of staying at home and dating under the stifling conditions of a chaperon. The desire to emulate the behavior of their classmates sometimes results in deception on their part in order to gain their freedom. The settlement house or social center which encourages dancing, for example, may be seen as unwholesome by the parents. Yet, the girls may "steal" time to attend such activities.

Conservative Puerto Rican parents are subject to confusion and shock in the face of such situations. A feeling of inadequacy tends to result in several courses of action: (1) they "give up" their responsibility for the children and often desire that the child be taken over by some institution that will teach discipline and respect, (2) they exercise even tighter discipline and further alien-

ate or increase the emotional disturbance of the child, or (3) they may send the recalcitrant child back to stay with a relative in Puerto Rico until he is mature and learns to face responsibilities.

An additional difficulty in adjustment lies in the fact that the main task of child training is traditionally relegated to the mother. Outside of demanding respect and obedience, the father has little to do with children or management of the home. Indeed, such tasks are considered to be beneath male dignity. Left to her own resources, the Puerto Rican mother is often confused by the variety of patterns of child rearing she observes in her new cultural setting. Even though she may be amenable to change, she finds herself at a loss to choose a standard of discipline and behavior for her children.

WHAT ROLE DO SOCIAL AGENCIES PLAY?

Social agencies often find their programs and budgets inadequate to deal effectively with newcomers who are plagued with such problems as a divided family (culturally and geographically), a fatherless family, a low social-economic status, children in culture-conflict who have little or no command of the English language. Many newcomer families (Puerto Rican and others) embody all of these problems.

With the exception of Protestant sects (mostly store-front churches), social organizations of the grass-roots type are of relatively recent origin among Puerto Ricans in mainland U.S.A. In this respect, Puerto Ricans are similar to other Latin American populations; such organizations are rapidly increasing. The gap in organizational support and affiliation in the Puerto Rican community is filled by the Migration Division of the Department of Labor for the Commonwealth of Puerto Rico. This agency fills a role for Puerto Ricans similar to that which the NAACP and the Urban League fill for Negroes in the United States. It does not, however, assume leadership in community organizations, but provides professional services to stimulate and assist the development of grass-roots leaders. Among other functions this organization serves (1) as an employment agency, (2) as a source of orientation, information, and education for migrants, (3) as a public relations medium to correct misconceptions about Puerto Ricans, (4) to determine policy for the Puerto Rican community on problems of special interest, and (5) to develop community resources where they are acutely needed.

There are 38 Puerto Rican civic organizations in Chicago, each of which sends delegates to the advisory committee of the Migration Division. These are primarily self-help organizations; some have purchased property for general community and recreational use.

The probability is that language more than any other factor is the greatest handicap to the adjustment of Puerto Ricans in the U.S. Even the most unlettered migrant places a high value on education, but school is almost universally a frustrating experience because of the language barrier. Language also presents a problem for the adolescent male of maintaining self-dignity in his attempt to adjust to a new situation. For him it is embarrassing to speak English with an accent. Language too is most frequently a stumbling block to employment and full participation in the daily life of the larger community.

However, the Puerto Rican faces serious problems of adjustment not only related to the new language on his arrival in the States. The Puerto Rican must make adjustments to the weather which is more extreme—hot in the summer and very cold in the winter. The pace of daily life is rapid and no longer leisurely. Many a darker-skinned Puerto Rican who does not know discrimination as practiced in the States suddenly finds that his ability to make a living (or find a home) is frequently related to the color of his skin and not to ability or competence.

Although Puerto Ricans are attempting to adjust to a socio-cultural situation that is somewhat different from the one which earlier immigrant groups adopted, they seem to have chosen the approach of earlier immigrants. This is best seen in the activities of a core of young, educated Puerto Ricans in Chicago and New York. In New York, for example, ASPIRA, a group of Puerto Rican social workers, professionals, and teachers, have organized to work with students and their parents so that they will make the best possible use of educational opportunities. They run workshops in which they work out plans to get youth through high school or through college, give lectures on professional opportunities, look for money for scholarships, and try to reach parents and community organizations. These young Puerto Rican leaders also run an interesting annual conference which focuses on the concerns of the young people. They see the Puerto Ricans as following in the path of earlier ethnic groups which are regarded rather as models to be imitated than as targets for attack. The conference's emphasis is on the Puerto Rican potential for achievement rather than on the negative factors to be overcome, such as prejudice and discrimination.

THE PUERTO RICAN AND THE SCHOOLS

For Puerto Rican children and youth, school is perhaps the major factor influencing adjustment to the socio-cultural environment of the continental U.S.A. Traditionally, the school in Puerto Rico is considered the second home of the child, and the teacher is considered the second mother of the child. Thus, Puerto Ricans consider school an integral part of the daily life, according it great respect and many prerogatives in the handling of children. At the same time, however, they have expectations that the school will assume many responsibilities in the area of child welfare. The school enjoys the rights of corporal punishment, reprimand, and concern for the family background of the child. It also is charged with responsibility for identifying and referring children in need of medical aid, clothing, food, and so on to proper sources. This attitude toward school carries over in the Puerto Rican's experience on the mainland. Puerto Ricans will often send a sick child to school with the expectation that the principal or teacher will care for him. If the child fails to report to school, the teacher or principal must shown immediate concern for this absence. In view of his dominant role, all inquiries to the family should be directed to the father. As head of the family, he may not play the "heavy" role in matters of discipline, but it is he who normally represents the family at PTA meetings and other official matters. Even though a child may serve as his interpreter, the male adult remains the dominant factor.

It is most desirable that Puerto Rican pupils entering a school system feel they are understood in terms of their special background and needs. This implies that adjustment is a two-way process and focuses attention on what the school can do to improve and accelerate this adjustment.

It is of further importance that differences in cultural and social experience among Puerto Ricans be recognized. Among adults and pupils alike, four general categories may be delineated: (1) island-born, island-schooled, (2) island-born, exclusively mainland-schooled, (3) mainland-born, island-born parents, and (4) mainland-born, mainland-born parents.

As with other ethnic groups, one finds multi-problem families that might require special attention, especially while the family is adjusting to the new environment. Puerto Rican parents frequently do not respond to notices from the school or participate in school functions. When they do come, they are apt not to participate. This highlights the fact that such Puerto Rican parents should be dealt with as individuals.

The Puerto Rican child is generally sensitive in interpersonal and group situations. When faced with criticism or reprimand, a primary-grade child may run into a corner to cry rather than have conflict with an authority figure. Older children tend to withdraw into silence. This behavior grows out of a socialization process in which children are taught to respect adults and not talk back; they are also taught not to look at the face of an adult when speaking to him.

However, the Puerto Rican youngster with sophistication in mainland ways may present quite a different attitude. This is especially true of teen-agers who have been conditioned to the lifeways of slum areas in large cities. These youngsters are apt to rebel against the authority of parents, teachers, and even law-enforcement officers. Their behavior is frequently quite different from the docility exhibited by the youngster who has come directly from Puerto Rico.

WHEN DOES THE PUERTO RICAN PARENT COME TO SCHOOL?

When their children are performing in school assemblies, some parents are eager to help with the activity by sewing costumes. Others are willing to serve as school escorts, resource persons in the classroom (explaining how sugar is made, etc.) singing Spanish songs accompanied with guitars, or preparing and serving Puerto Rican dishes for classes with children of other backgrounds.

Mother's clubs conducted in Spanish, for mothers with children in kindergarten or primary grades, are particularly attractive when stress is laid on such practical matters as shopping trips to neighborhood stores (consumer education), knitting lessons, first aid, and instruction in nutrition. Adult evening schools are well attended when the teacher is bilingual. However, English classes for Puerto Rican mothers seem to be more successful when conducted during regular school hours.

The foregoing discussion may be regarded as a brief or rather superficial treatment of some features of Puerto Rican culture that seem to have relevance for the adjustment problems of migrants to the mainland. Nevertheless, it is well to keep in mind the fact that the culture of Puerto Ricans, as the culture of any people, is a dynamic phenomenon subject to rapid and sometimes intense change. The Puerto Rico of today is not the same as the Puerto Rico of ten, fifteen, or twenty years ago. The Puerto Rican living in mainland U.S.A. is not quite the same as the Puerto Rican who lives in Puerto Rico. While each may have an essentially similar cultural background, each is reacting to and interacting with a vastly different social and cultural environment. Thus, to understand the Puerto Rican, it is important to view his behavior from the viewpoint of an individual whose style of living is to some degree in conflict with his new environment.

A major purpose of this article is to highlight certain features of Puerto Rican culture and history as well as to point up contrasts between island and mainland culture that affect the process of cultural accommodation by Puerto Ricans in the United States. The adaptation of Puerto Ricans to mainland requirements is indeed not simple nor without stress; it has not been so for any group of people in the process of acculturation.

It is incumbent upon those who would assist in this process of cultural change to develop insights and understandings that will help to meliorate the degree of stress and conflict which is inevitable. Further study through reading, language skill, and first-hand knowledge of community life and problems (field trips and interpersonal relations with an open mind) is highly recommended to those who would enjoy an optimum measure of success in this effort.

Margaret Hall Powers, Samuel M. Schall, and Rosemary A. Welsch

UTILIZATION OF MEDICAL INFORMATION IN SCHOOL PLANNING FOR VISUALLY HANDICAPPED CHILDREN

Visually handicapped children have unique psychological problems and they require special understanding on the part of teachers, parents, friends, and themselves. As in the case of any child with a physical disability, the emphasis must be placed on the ways in which such a child is similar to other children rather than on the handicap and limitations it imposes. This article presents information concerning the utilization of medical information in school planning for visually handicapped children as an example of how one works with children with physical handicaps.

Effective planning for the placement of such children requires careful evaluation of all pertinent information. The authors use the Chicago Public Schools as an example of how this can be done well. In this system the child receives a complete evaluation: medical, psychological, sociological, and educational, and then a staff conference is held which jointly develops a plan for the child. In Chicago there is a program for the blind and for the partially seeing. Although visually handicapped students represent only a little over one in one thousand, they still need and deserve special psychological and educational attention and services.

Visually handicapped children are a challenge to the administrator of special education because of the careful evaluation required before appropriate educational planning can take place. Effective placement of a child depends upon a delicate balancing of medical, psychological, social, and educational information about him. The first step in evaluation is usually the securing of medical eye reports. In the Chicago Public Schools, as elsewhere, problems occur in securing adequate eye reports, in interpreting them, and in relating them to other available information about the child. In a community as large as Chicago sources of referrals for special placement and sources of eye reports are necessarily numerous, varied, and uneven in reliability.

CASE REFERRAL

The Bureau of Physically Handicapped Children receives referrals for consideration of special education services from a variety of sources: parents, ophthalmologists, other private physicians, optometrists, eye clinics, teachers, school nurses or psychologists, and other school personnel. More than half of the referrals of partially seeing children originate through the vision screening program of the school system itself. Regardless of the referral source the parents are required to have an eye report completed by the child's eye specialist on a special two sided form. The form was developed by the bureau and is provided to the parents upon request.

MEDICAL CRITERIA FOR PLACEMENT IN A SPECIAL PROGRAM

A review of the described eye reports is made by the consulting ophthalmologist of the Bureau of Physically Handicapped Children as a first step in screening and evaluation of referred cases. Medical attitudes have changed over the years and it is no longer believed that sight is saved by conserving it. Eye work is encouraged to increase proficiency in seeing. In thinking about a child's need for special placement or services in school, most importance is attached to what he can see with near vision. If he can read six or eight point type for near vision with comparative comfort, he may be able to achieve well in a regular classroom without special help, even if distant vision is only 20/100. Such vision would require front seat placement and a cooperative teacher but not necessarily special services, unless there are additional handicapping factors. On the other hand, a child who sees only ten point type for near and 20/50 or a little better for distance but who is slow learning may need special services at least on a temporary basis.

With blind children who have only light perception or less, there is no difficulty in deciding on placement. They clearly need a special class for the blind. However, if the child has somewhat more vision, ranging from finger counting up to 8/200, placement is more of a problem. Such a child may be a poor candidate for a class for the blind because he sees too much and may look at the braille dots instead of discerning them by touch. He will probably have to be placed in a class for partially seeing on a trial basis, with the possibility of a later transfer to a program for blind. If it is found that he is unable to see even 24 point type adequately, he will have to be transferred to a class for the blind in order to develop braille techniques as a major avenue of learning. In some of these marginal cases the medical prognosis may have to be an important consideration in placement, as between a blind or a partially seeing program.

Criteria for placement in a class for the blind are: light perception or less. Criteria for placement in a program for partially seeing are (a) near vision of 12 point or larger type with best corrected vision, and (b) distant vision in the better eye of less than 20/50 to

Abridged from *Exceptional Children*, Vol. 32, No. 1, September 1965, pages 5-11. Reprinted by permission of the authors and the publisher.

20/70 with best correction. No one diagnosis in itself, such as myopia, is considered a necessary criterion.

The following eye conditions may warrant temporary placement in a special program: (a) prolonged occlusion for amblyopia; (b) acute, irritated eye diseases during prolonged treatment; and (c) postoperative retinal detachment or other postoperative condition, upon the recommendation of the referring physician. Temporary special services may be required for children with such eye diseases as the following, which are believed to cause decreased vision temporarily but have a good prognosis: anterior chamber hemorrhage, trauma, iritis or uveitis, and acute phlyctenular or interstitial keratitis.

TOTAL EVALUATION, CASE STAFFING, AND PLANNING

Children whose eye reports show visual impairment warranting further consideration for special educational services are next scheduled for a psychological evaluation by one of the school psychologists who specializes in this type of case. The child also receives a complete health study, including a home visit, by the school nurse. The personnel of the child's present school submit a report of his academic and social adjustment. When all reports are gathered the case is discussed at a staff conference which includes the supervisor of the division of blind and partially seeing, the consulting ophthalmologist, a representative of the school nurse program, the coordinator of the vision screening program, and sometimes others.

Evaluation must be careful and must be multi-sided — medical, psychological, social, educational. Children with identical types and degrees of visual impairment may have quite different educational problems and needs because of nonmedical factors. Children with visual impairment range widely, not only in vision itself, but also in intelligence, work habits, academic achievement, cultural background, motivation, personality characteristics, emotional adjustment, the presence or absence of other physical problems or defects and in degree of parental understanding and interest. Year by year there is noted an increase in the number of visually handicapped children with multiple problems, particularly of central nervous system damage and mental retardation.

In evaluating a specific child's need for special educational services the staff must consider all of these variables, not the vision alone. After reviewing all the information gathered, the staff jointly develops a plan for the child. The plan includes a decision on the type of educational placement or service needed, identification of any special educational needs within that placement and identification of further medical, psychological, or social followup needed and how the followup can be accomplished.

ORGANIZATION AND SCOPE

It is the philosophy in the Chicago Public Schools that the most normal and effective place for a child to be educated is in the regular classroom of his neighborhood school. The child should be removed from the regular classroom only if his special needs cannot be met adequately there, even with the variety of possible special adjustments and modification which can be made by an interested and conscientious teacher and an imaginative principal. A child is removed from the regular classroom, therefore, only on a highly selective basis. Furthermore, even though placed in a special class, he is kept there only so long as he needs such highly specialized service. As soon as possible he is returned to his home school. With the blind there is little choice in placement. The special class is likely to be a permanent necessity. For the partially seeing, however, much greater selectivity in program is needed and is possible.

The first classes for blind children in the Chicago Public Schools were opened in 1900, Chicago being one of the first public school systems in the world to make this provision. Classes for partially seeing were first opened in 1913. The program has grown rapidly in Chicago to a scope indicated in Table 1. With only two exceptions, classes for the blind and for the partially seeing are located in different schools. This simplifies the task of orienting regular classroom teachers to the visually handicapped child who will be programed into their classes and avoids any educational interference between the two programs.

PROGRAM FOR THE BLIND

From Table 1 it can be noted that the number of blind is quite small as compared with the partially seeing. Facilities in the school system are adequate at present to accommodate all blind children from age three who

TABLE 1

ORGANIZATION AND SCOPE OF THE CHICAGO PUBLIC SCHOOL PROGRAM FOR VISUALLY HANDICAPPED CHILDREN

Program		Number of Schools Housing Special Centers	Number of Teachers	Number of Pupils
Program for the blind				
	Elementary school	6	19	107
	High school	3	4	43
	Total	9	23	150
Program for the partially seeing Special classes				
	Elementary school	21	32	307
	High school	7	7	118
	Total	28	39	425
Itinerant teacher service				
	Elementary school		11	115
	Total		50	540
Total combined program— blind and partially seeing[a]				
	Elementary school	25	62	529
	High school	9	11	161
	Total	34	73	690

[a]One high school and two elementary schools house classes for both the blind and partially seeing.

are educable, that is with IQ's above approximately 50. The blind constitute .03 of one per cent of the total enrollment of the school system, or approximately three in 10,000. It is of interest that there has been no significant increase in the total number of blind children in the Chicago schools in the past ten years, despite an increase of over 25 per cent in the general school enrollment over the same period.

Classes for the blind are located in regular elementary or high schools except for three classes of crippled blind children housed in a special school for physically handicapped. Every blind child is enrolled in a regular grade in the school and is programed to this grade from the special class for the types of activities and amounts of time which his individual needs require. Exceptions to this are educable mentally retarded blind children who are handled in a largely self-contained classroom designated as a multiply handicapped class. Blind children are eligible for transportation by school bus to and from their homes throughout their entire school career. However, increasing numbers of upper grade and high school pupils prefer to come and go independently, probably as a result of an increasing emphasis on orientation and mobility training.

PROGRAM FOR THE PARTIALLY SEEING

There are two types of programs for partially seeing pupils—a special class (resource room) program and an itinerant service program. Children with severe vision impairments, who need an intensive program of special teaching under the close supervision of an especially trained teacher, are placed in special classes for the partially seeing.

They are enrolled, however, as pupils in the appropriate grade of the school and extensively programed to that grade. Special classes are located in regular schools and widely dispersed throughout the city. No one school contains more than one or two such classes. Partially seeing children are transported by school bus until age ten, after which they are expected to use public transportation. Exceptions are made for children with multiple problems or in instances where transportation problems might present a hazard for the child. Early in 1960, the Chicago system instituted an itinerant teacher service for visually handicapped children with degrees of impaired vision at the lower limits of the range eligible for special education services. In this program the child remains in his home school and receives one or two visits per week or as often as needed from a teacher of the partially seeing. The special teacher provides enlarged print books and materials, gives the child special tutoring, and works closely with his regular teacher in regard to his adjustment and program. Experience with the itinerant program has shown that it is wise to be very selective in placing a child on this service instead of in a special class. Children can benefit from this service only if they have fairly satisfactory work habits, motivation, and school adjustment and only when conditions and attitudes in the specific school and classroom are favorable.

Partially seeing children now in special classes or receiving itinerant service constitute 0.1 of one per cent of the total school enrollment, or approximately one in 1,000. Since children on the waiting list for special service are not included in this figure, the actual incidence of partially seeing children needing special services would be slightly higher.

Margaret Hall Powers

THE PREVALENCE OF DEAFNESS IN SCHOOL AGE CHILDREN

The prevalence of children with physical disabilities in schools and in the community is of great concern to psychologists, educators, and parents. Each type of disability poses unique psychological problems at each stage of development of both the disability and the child's ability to cope with it.

Dr. Powers has reported on the prevalence of such children in the Chicago Public School system, and hopes that educators will recognize the important demand for services which attend the disabled child.

It is felt that society in general, as well as the psychologist and teacher, needs to be aware of these special issues and in turn to train professionals to deal with the particular problems posed by these children. Children with physical disabilities are different from other children, but the stress should be on the fact that such children are more like other so-called normal children than they are different from them. Emphasis should be placed today on this similarity rather than their total personality differences and to understand that only in their need to adjust to minor ways are they different. They are different, therefore, only in their adjustment to the demands of society and of life.

The prevalence of various disabilities in children is a matter of great importance to scientists, to members of many professions and to administrators of various kinds of services for the handicapped. Similarly the prevalence *rates* of various disabilities at any given time – the percentage of the population having the disability – is of extreme significance. Many aspects of educational and social planning have to be based upon estimates of change or lack of change in the prevalence rate of a disability over a period of years.

The program of special education for physically handicapped children in the Chicago Public Schools has been in existence for many years and provides a rich source of data for studying prevalence and prevalence rates among school age children in various disability categories. Because it is one of the largest school systems in the world prevalence data are based on large numbers and are relatively free from sampling errors. Moreover, since only one school system is involved, the degree of uniformity in case-finding and special class placement criteria and policy is greater than is usually found

when data from many sources are pooled. Pooled data usually involve different standards, different methods of selection and other uncontrolled variables.

Official figures were secured on the total elementary school enrollment (kindergarten through grade 8) and total high school enrollment (grades 9 through 12) in the entire Chicago Public School system for May of each year from 1954 to the present, a period of ten years inclusive. Data were tabulated on enrollment of deaf and hard of hearing, of blind and of physically handicapped (crippled and severely health handicapped) for the same month, May, for the same span of years. The prevalence rates for each year were calculated separately for the elementary school population and the high school population, as well as for the total school population. This was done for each of the three disability categories studied. These data are shown in Tables 1, 2 and 3.

Two unavoidable inaccuracies affecting

From *American Annals of the Deaf,* 1964. Reprinted by permission.

TABLE 1

ENROLLMENT OF DEAF CHILDREN IN THE CHICAGO PUBLIC SCHOOLS   1954–1964

Year	Elementary Schools			High Schools			Total		
	General membership (Kdg-Grade 8)	Deaf (Nursery-Grade 8)	Prevalence rate*	General membership (Grade 9-12)	Deaf (Grade 9-12)	Prevalence rate*	General membership (Kdg-Grade 12)	Deaf (Nursery-Grade 12)	Prevalence rate*
May, 1954	298,249	471	.158	85,876	108	.126	384,125	579	.151
May, 1955	309,501	470	.152	85,950	114	.133	395,451	584	.148
May, 1956	320,491	515	.161	85,787	114	.133	406,278	629	.155
May, 1957	330,823	540	.163	90,326	104	.115	421,149	644	.153
May, 1958	338,126	521	.154	94,839	104	.110	432,965	625	.144
May, 1959	348,605	537	.154	95,830	117	.122	444,435	654	.147
May, 1960	364,227	535	.147	94,856	113	.119	459,083	648	.141
May, 1961	375,686	584	.155	96,249	103	.107	471,935	687	.146
May, 1962	370,998	610	.164	102,664	115	.112	473,662	725	.153
May, 1963	383,432	651	.170	111,129	121	.109	494,561	772	.156
May, 1964	395,815	724	.183	116,458	108	.093	512,273	832	.162
Per cent of increase in 10 years							33.4%	43.7%	

*Per cent of general school membership. Figures express fractions of one percent.

Corrected figures for May, 1964:

Subtracting suburban deaf children (10 elementary and 8 high school), and deaf children under 5 years of age (64), since comparable children are not included in general membership figures, the corrected figures for May, 1964 are shown in the appropriate columns as follows:

	395,815	650	.164	116,458	100	.086	512,273	750	.146

TABLE 2

ENROLLMENT OF BLIND CHILDREN IN THE CHICAGO PUBLIC SCHOOLS   1954–1964

Year	Elementary Schools			High Schools			Total		
	General membership (Kdg-Grade 8)	Blind (Nursery-Grade 8)	Prevalence* rate	General membership (Grade 9-12)	Blind (Grade 9-12)	Prevalence* rate	General membership (Kdg-Grade 12)	Blind (Nursery-Grade 12)	Prevalence* rate
May, 1954	298,249	101	.034	85,876	20	.023	384,125	121	.032
May, 1955	309,501	95	.031	85,950	23	.027	395,451	118	.030
May, 1956	320,491	109	.034	85,787	20	.023	406,278	129	.032
May, 1957	330,823	119	.036	90,326	23	.025	421,149	142	.034
May, 1958	338,126	121	.036	94,839	24	.025	432,965	145	.033
May, 1959	348,605	129	.037	95,830	26	.027	444,435	155	.035
May, 1960	364,227	135	.037	94,856	30	.032	459,083	165	.036
May, 1961	375,686	118	.031	96,249	35	.036	471,935	153	.032
May, 1962	370,998	124	.033	102,664	29	.028	473,662	153	.032
May, 1963	383,432	122	.032	111,129	33	.030	494,561	155	.031
May, 1964	395,815	116	.029	116,458	42	.036	512,273	158	.031
Per cent of increase in 10 years							33.4%	30.6%	

*Per cent of general school membership. Figures express fractions of one percent.

Corrected figures for May, 1964:
Subtracting suburban blind children (1 elementary and 6 high school), and blind children under 5 years of age (7), since comparable children are not included in general membership figures, the corrected figures for May, 1964 are shown in the appropriate columns as follows:

	General membership (Kdg-Grade 8)	Blind (Nursery-Grade 8)	Prevalence* rate	General membership (Grade 9-12)	Blind (Grade 9-12)	Prevalence* rate	General membership (Kdg-Grade 12)	Blind (Nursery-Grade 12)	Prevalence* rate
	395,815	108	.027	116,458	37	.032	512,273	145	.028

Margaret Hall Powers   105

prevalence rate for all years listed in the tables need explanation. The Chicago Public Schools accept deaf, blind and severely crippled children at three years of age when the child's mental age is also up to three years. Children are not accepted in regular elementary school kindergartens until age five. Therefore, the figures for handicapped include a few preschool children whereas the general enrollment figures do not, thus increasing slightly the apparent prevalence rate of the handicapped.

Another factor also artificially increases the prevalence rates slightly. General memberships in Tables 1, 2 and 3 include only Chicago children, but figures for the handicapped include a few suburban children each year, in all three areas of disability. Retroactively only total data were available so preschool and suburban children could not be identified and eliminated in figuring prevalence rates. This correction could be made and was made, however, for the current year, 1964. Therefore at the bottom of Tables 1, 2 and 3 corrected figures for May, 1964 are given. The corrected prevalences and prevalence rates in Tables 1, 2 and 3 represent highly accurate and significant data on handicapped children.

Table 1 presents data on deaf and hard of hearing in special classes. The great majority of the elementary, high school and total memberships listed are profoundly deaf children. Only extremely hard of hearing children are placed in special classes and these are few in number. It is interesting to note in Table 1 that, in spite of a 43.7% increase in ten years in the number of deaf in the school system, the *prevalence rate* has remained remarkably constant over this period of time. It varies over a narrow range of from .141 to .162. The general membership of the school system has increased 33.4% in ten years but the deaf have increased at a slightly faster rate, 43.7%. The more thorough case-finding of the present as compared with ten years ago and a policy change in the direction of accepting for placement more multiply

handicapped deaf children as time goes on, probably account for the faster rate.

The lower percentage of deaf at the high school level than at the elementary probably results from the general over-ageness of deaf for their grades and the greater tendency of the deaf—for this reason and others—as compared with hearing students, to drop out of school before finishing high school.

Table 2 presents comparable data for blind children. Again, as with the deaf, prevalence rates have remained highly constant over a ten year period. The blind enrollment has increased in proportion to general school enrollment. It is anticipated that the incidence of blindness will drop sharply in the future, since retrolental fibroplasia, the cause of blindness in 60% of our present Chicago enrollment, has been brought under medical control. Comparison of Tables 1 and 2 will show that the prevalence rate for deafness is roughly five times that of blindness.

Table 3 presents enrollment data on children so severely physically handicapped by orthopedic and neurological disorders or by severe cardiopathy or other major health problems that they cannot be educated in regular schools and must be enrolled in special schools, with elaborate architectural and equipment adaptations and with provision of special therapy services. Of the total number thus enrolled approximately 33% are cerebral palsied, 21% are post poliomyelitis cases, 9% have congenital defects and deformities and 6.5% have extreme cardiac pathology. Other diagnoses occur with diminishing frequency.

In contrast to the deaf and the blind, the physically handicapped show a highly constant total enrollment over the ten year period in spite of the large increase in general school enrollment, resulting in a steadily falling prevalence rate. This decrease in the percentage of children in the school system who are placed in special schools has resulted from both medical and administrative reasons. Certain disabling conditions in children, notably poliomyelitis, are being elimi-

TABLE 3

ENROLLMENT OF PHYSICALLY HANDICAPPED CHILDREN IN THE CHICAGO PUBLIC SCHOOLS   1954–1964

Year	Elementary Schools			High Schools			Total		
	General membership (Kdg-Grade 8)	Physically handicapped (Nursery-Grade 8)	Prevalence rate*	General membership (Grade 9-12)	Physically handicapped (Grade 9-12)	Prevalence rate*	General membership (Kdg-Grade 12)	Physically handicapped (Nursery-Grade 12)	Prevalence rate*
May, 1954	298,249	1124	.377	85,876	244	.284	384,125	1368	.356
May, 1955	309,501	1159	.374	85,950	246	.286	395,451	1405	.355
May, 1956	320,491	1107	.345	85,787	264	.308	406,278	1371	.337
May, 1957	330,823	1170	.354	90,326	244	.270	421,149	1414	.336
May, 1958	338,126	1149	.340	94,839	248	.261	432,965	1397	.323
May, 1959	348,605	1183	.339	95,830	236	.246	444,435	1419	.319
May, 1960	364,227	1205	.331	94,856	220	.232	459,083	1425	.310
May, 1961	375,686	1203	.320	96,249	216	.224	471,935	1419	.301
May, 1962	370,998	1166	.314	102,664	213	.207	473,662	1379	.291
May, 1963	383,432	1144	.298	111,129	268	.241	494,561	1412	.286
May, 1964	395,815	1105	.279	116,458	307	.264	512,273	1412	.276
Per cent of increase in 10 years							33.4%	Essentially none	
	395,815	1045	.264	116,458	304	.261	512,273	1349	.263

*Per cent of general school membership. Figures express fractions of one per cent.

Corrected figures for May, 1964:
Subtracting suburban physically handicapped children (26 elementary and 3 high school), and physically handicapped children under 5 years of age (34), since comparable children are not included in general membership figures, the corrected figures for May, 1964 are shown in the appropriate columns as follows:

Margaret Hall Powers   107

TABLE 4

SCHOOL-AGE DEAF IN CHICAGO 1954–1964

Year	Chicago Public Schools		Archdiocese Schools		Combined School Systems		
	General enrollment (Kdg-Grade 12)	Deaf (Nursery-Grade 12)	General enrollment (Grades 1-12)**	Deaf***	General enrollment	Deaf	Prevalence rate*
May, 1954	384,125	579	262,805	75	646,930	654	.101
May, 1955	395,451	584	277,131	86	672,582	670	.100
May, 1956	406,278	629	289,051	98	695,329	727	.105
May, 1957	421,149	644	300,656	101	721,805	745	.103
May, 1958	432,965	625	313,802	106	746,767	731	.098
May, 1959	444,435	654	328,189	128	772,624	782	.101
May, 1960	459,083	648	336,197	134	795,280	782	.098
May, 1961	471,935	687	343,825	149	815,760	836	.102
May, 1962	473,662	725	350,974	141	824,636	866	.105
May, 1963	494,561	772	357,325	152	851,886	924	.108
Jan., 1964	523,289	820	364,628	165	887,917	985	.111
Per cent of increase in 10 years	36.2%	41.6%	38.7%	120%	37.3%	50.6%	

*Per cent of general school membership. Figures express fractions of one per cent.

**Some parochial elementary schools have kindergartens.

***Elementary school classes only until 1963; high school added 1963 and 1964. Figures include a few kindergarten deaf pupils.

Adjusted figures for January, 1964:

Subtracting 18 suburban and 64 children under age 5 from the Chicago deaf total, the remainder is 903.

Adding 28 non-attending Chicago school-age deaf and an estimated 10 Chicago school-age deaf attending the state residential school, the following figures result:

Estimated total school-age deaf children in Chicago   941

Combined school-age enrollment of public and parochial schools   887,917

Prevalence rate of deaf in combined enrollment   .106*

TABLE 5

ENROLLMENT IN EDUCATIONAL PROGRAMS FOR THE DEAF IN ILLINOIS 1954–1964

Year	Chicago Public Schools			Archdiocese of Chicago	Illinois School for the Deaf, Jacksonville	Day Classes in Public Schools in Illinois Outside Chicago			Out of School Deaf in Chicago	In Illinois
	Elem.	H. Sch.	Total			Elem.	H. Sch.	Total		
Spring, 1954	471	108	579	75	435			†		(1089)*†
Spring, 1955	470	114	584	86	418			†		(1088)*†
Spring, 1956	515	114	629	98	420			†		(1147)*†
Spring, 1957	540	104	644	101	400			†		(1145)*†
Spring, 1958	521	104	625	106	404			†		(1135)*†
Spring, 1959	537	117	654	128	406			†		(1188)*†
Spring, 1960	535	113	648	134	393	355	22	377		1552
Spring, 1961	584	103	687	149	394	398	25	423		1653
Spring, 1962	610	115	725	141	419	336	22	358		1643
Spring, 1963	651	121	772	152	435	381	28	409		1768
Jan., 1964	710	110	820	165	446	418	32	450	28	1909**

*Day classes outside Chicago not included.

**This total does not include Illinois deaf in non-public schools in Illinois or elsewhere except for the Archdiocese of Chicago, nor does it include non-attending school-age deaf children outside Chicago, figures which are not known but which would be negligible in any case.

†According to the January issues of the *American Annals of the Deaf* the enrollment for these classes outside of the city of Chicago were as follows:

1954......189	1957......209	
1955......179	1958......262	
1956......209	1959......217 -Ed.	

nated or reduced in severity as a result of medical research. Even more influential in reducing the percentage, however, is the gradually increasing care with which children are screened as to need for special educational placement and the increasing belief that all but the severely disabled should remain in regular schools.

In spite of the falling percentage of physically handicapped placed in special schools, this group remains almost twice as large as the deaf. In contrast to the deaf, where prevalence rates for elementary and high school students differ markedly, the blind and the physically handicapped show negligible differences between elementary and high school levels in regard to prevalence rate.

In order to get as complete a picture as possible of the total number of school age deaf in the city of Chicago data were secured on deaf enrollments and general enrollments for the past ten years in the schools of the Archdiocese of Chicago. These figures, summary figures for the Chicago Public Schools and combined figures for both school systems, are shown in Table 4. The two school systems provide the only classes for the deaf in Chicago. The adjusted figures below the Table come as close as it is possible to come to establishing the total number of school age deaf children in the city of Chicago. To the extent that Chicago is typical of the nation, estimates of school age deaf can be made for the nation as a whole by applying the prevalence rate to the total school age population of the nation.

Table 5 presents the most complete figures obtainable concerning school age deaf in the state of Illinois. A prevalence rate could not be calculated for Illinois because data were not available on the number of school age children in the state. It is to be hoped that all concerned with the deaf will keep increasingly accurate statistics on deaf children, including not only those enrolled in special schools and classes but also those not attending by reason of severe multiple problems or attending schools out of the state or attending facilities for other types of handicapped and, therefore, not counted as deaf. Only by accurate and complete record keeping will we be able eventually to establish a firm, dependable incidence and prevalence rate on deafness as a scientific basis for studying genuine trends and changes.

Frances A. Mullen

CRISIS IN THE EDUCATION OF THE HANDICAPPED

Parents and teachers who come in contact with children who exhibit learning difficulties are concerned as to whether they are confronted by a case of real mental handicap or by a deficiency of less serious nature which can be corrected through psychotherapy and/or educational-environmental manipulation. In cases of true mental handicaps — either on an educable mentally handicapped level or on a trainable mentally handicapped level — there is reason for serious concern. Much research has been done concerning the causes of such handicaps by physicians, biochemists, and geneticists. The education and training of handicapped individuals is now expected of the school as part of its total responsibility.

What can and should be done? Dr. Mullen reviews the current trend and points out the challenge of, and the need for, creative and imaginative planning for children with mental handicaps.

Programs of education for the retarded are proliferating in the schools of America at an accelerating rate. The momentum of the drive shows no signs of having reached its peak. Yet paradoxically research evidence has been quietly mounting for the past thirty years and more, suggesting that the special class format now almost universally used, is less than effective. Other research and isolated demonstration projects on innovative instructional techniques, are suggesting vividly the possibilities of other approaches, but the juggernaut demands for numerical expansion of facilities leave most school systems with little time or energy for anything but the production of more of the traditional type of class. Are we building toward a time not too many years away, when the winds of adversity blow even stronger on the schools, when the whole structure of special education for the mentally handicapped will collapse like an empty house of cards? The time is already late for the path of "progress" to take a drastic turn toward quality rather than quantity of services.

Psychology has long had a record of distinguished contribution to the diagnosis and treatment of mental retardation. In fact such work has constituted significant strands in the development of psychology as a whole. The Binet–Simon tests, forerunners of modern individual intelligence testing, were developed for the diagnosis of mentally defective children in France. The first psychological laboratory to offer services to the public schools of America, that of Lightner, founded in 1894 in Philadelphia, studied the mentally retarded. The Bureau of Child Study of the Chicago Public Schools, the first American school-based child guidance clinic, has spawned many educational innovations, including, in 1901, the initiation of a first class for the mentally retarded. Early studies of the learning of the retarded and attempts to develop sense training and other instructional techniques have influenced current experiments. Goddard's studies of the genetics and inheritance of mental deficiency near the turn of the century, discredited though the studies are today, opened a vein of inquiry into the relationships of nature and nurture. In the thirties the Skeels studies of the effect of environmental change on the intelligence of retarded infants created consternation in the psychological profession, but are today accepted as basic to modern child development theory.

Perhaps unfortunately, the special school classes for the group of children we now know as the educable mentally retarded, spread rather rapidly in the early decades of the century through the big cities of America, all too often becoming mere dumping grounds for problem youngsters of any description, ignored by school administrators and psychologists alike. The only concern seemed to be to get such children out of the hair of the regular teacher and principal, rather than to worry about what happened to him thereafter.

It was psychologists who helped to bring a fresh breath of hope and innovation in the thirties. For example, in Chicago, Dr. Grace Munson, with years of experience as a school psychologist when she became head of the school psychological services, initiated many reforms in teaching methods and programs for regular and handicapped children. In the "ungraded" EMH classrooms, she ruthlessly swept out the huge looms and substituted an intensive program of individualized instruction in reading and arithmetic. Her efforts proved that these youngsters could learn, effectively if slowly, if they were not shunted into unproductive, time-consuming activities. Unfortunately over the years, only the husks of her methods tended to be perpetuated. The classes later sometimes became silent rooms with overdependence on individualized instructional materials and paper and pencil tasks, something she had never intended. When another former school psychologist was given responsibility for the education of the mentally handicapped in 1948, she attempted to stimulate teachers to develop live, active classrooms, with much speech and activity, while maintaining the use of individualized teaching materials in the tool subjects for definite portions of the school day. Yearly evaluation of every pupil on academic achievement maintained considerable focus on those tool subjects. Oral language, and social adjustment and preparation for employment and family life were made priorities. Thus in many communities, psychologists worked with special educators for the improvement of programs of education of the retarded.

But in general, school psychologists, like the professionals in many other disciplines, whether medicine, social work, psychiatry, speech therapy, et al, tended to ignore the mentally deficient or to belittle work with the retarded as a waste of their valuable time and skills. As school psychology burgeoned after World War II, and especially after the Thayer Conference of 1953, the derogatory references to "routine psychometrics for special class placement" proliferated. Psychologists wanted to get out from under the load of examinations of the suspected retarded or the ordinary behavior problems, to the more exciting or newer fields of "therapy," counseling, consulting on the mental health of teachers; of differential diagnosis of brain injury, aphasia, perceptual disorders, autism, emotional disturbance. Some felt they should be involved in development of personnel policies for teachers and staff, or of sex education programs, or the improvement of the emotional and mental health climate of the total school. They worked on more effective techniques of consultation with administrators and teachers, and entered hundreds of other exciting avenues of research, demonstration, and service. All these are important challenges. It is no wonder that the retarded tended to be ignored, or resented when they could not be ignored because of state and local rules and policies.

But also, during the postwar years, the programs for the mentally retarded have grown beyond belief. The whole movement for the education of the "trainable" under public

school jurisdiction can almost be dated from that time. True, Minneapolis and some other cities had had such programs, but in 1948 the U.S. Office of Education found only approximately 1000 children across the entire United States in EMH classes in public schools. The parent groups concerned chiefly with the trainable or even more severely retarded grew with speed and momentum, a remarkable social phenomenon of the postwar years. In these 20 years they have secured legislation in every state and mushrooming services for the trainable in communities across the nation. Meanwhile the provisions for the educable mentally retarded in public school classes also multiplied three-fold between 1948 and 1963.

Upon the election of President Kennedy in 1962, the formation of the President's Panel on Mental Retardation brought the national government firmly and aggressively into the picture. On Capitol Hill, Congressman John E. Fogarty and other dedicated legislators spearheaded national legislative programs. With passionate support from across the country (more from the public than the professionals) they pushed through legislation that first brought money for research on the education of the retarded, then funds for the training of teachers and other needed professional workers, and now for instructional materials centers, regional research laboratories, and many innovative projects. NIMH supported much research in the field of mental deficiency, but the demand for a separate department of research on retardation eventually resulted in the formation of the National Institute of Child Health and Development (NICHD). Its general research on child development was expected to include heavy emphasis on the prevention and treatment of mental retardation. Vocational Rehabilitation laws were changed shortly after World War II to make the retarded eligible for these services. The Childrens Bureau greatly accelerated its services, reporting in June 1967 that approximately 140 mental retardation clinics across the nation were supported in whole or in part by Childrens Bureau funds. When the Elementary and Secondary Education Act of 1964 was passed, some particularly vocal senators wanted to amend it to make specific provision for innovative projects in the education of the handicapped school child, but relaxed on the assurance of the Office of Education that the handicapped were covered and would be included in programs approved. When the results of the first year's hasty implementation of Title I and the other provisions of this historic legislation began to filter in, it became clear that in practice, infinitesimal percentages of the newly available funds for the schools were going to improvement of services to the handicapped. Congress therefore passed the amendments of 1966 (Title 6 of ESEA) making specific allocations for the handicapped, including the mentally handicapped, and covertly expressing disapproval of the pre-

vious operation by establishing by law a Bureau for the Education of the Handicapped in OE — a rather unusual overriding of administrative authority by the legislative.

States also have increased their financial support of local public school programs for the retarded. There is some trend from permissive to mandatory state legislation. California has long *required* school districts to make provisions for the education of their handicapped children. In Illinois the mandatory legislation passed in 1965 set an effective date of 1969, and provided aid to school districts, local intermediate, and county, and to training programs for the needed professionals. As of 1967 at midstream, the schools were struggling toward the prescribed goal, but the task is tremendous. In the ten years prior to this legislation, in Illinois there had already been rapid growth in both trainable and educable pro-

TABLE 1

PUBLIC SCHOOL PROGRAMS FOR THE RETARDED IN ILLINOIS

		Actual Service 1956	1965	Estimated Need 1969
Pupils enrolled				
	Trainable	137	906	7000
	Educable	6715	15,123	70,000
Teachers				
	Trainable	N.R.	120	700
	Educable	N.R.	1148	4666
Districts.				
	Trainable	7	47	1496
	Educable	72	249	1496
Counties				
	Trainable	6	28	102
	Educable	40	74	102

grams (Table I) but in 1965 one fourth of Illinois' 102 counties still had no educational provisions for the handicapped and the unmet needs in all districts were still tremendous.

Assuming conservatively that two per cent of the population have an educable degree of mental handicap, and two-tenths of one per cent are "trainable," and that the population of Illinois in the age bracket three to twenty-one covered by this mandatory legislation will be at least 3,500,000 by 1969, the need for thousands of additional teachers and classrooms, and hundreds of psychologists is obvious.

Under such pressures from parents and public, from state legislatures and federal agencies, school districts across the nation are rapidly adding classes. While aware of the importance of standards, they are sometimes already settling for less than fully qualified personnel, and less than adequate housing. Most of all perhaps we should worry whether enough thought is being given to what is to be the nature of the program and what its goals and methods are to be.

During these same years, in warning to this rapid expansion, evidence has been mounting that the special education which American schools have been providing is of questionable effectiveness. Research studies, most of them hopefully designed to prove that EMH children do better in special than in regular classes, have appeared periodically at least since 1932; their results are almost uniformly negative or inconclusive. Kirk in 1964 summarized such studies, reporting on papers by Bennett 1932, Pertsch 1936, Cowen 1938, Blatt 1958, Cassidy and Stanton 1959, Elenbogen 1957, Thurstone 1959, Ainsworth 1959, Wrightstone 1959, Mullen and Itkin 1961. Criticism of many of these studies centers on the selective bias that sometimes determines that the more difficult multiply handicapped, or disturbed EMH child is the one who is placed in the special class as opposed to the retention in the regular grades of the more amenable or less handicapped

child. Some of the studies discussed used a variety of devices in attempts to control this factor, but the doubt remained. Apparently EMH children do as well academically in the regular grades as in a special class, possibly a little better. Such findings are almost universal in the literature. The evidence for superior adjustment and personality growth in the special class is more varied, with some positive outcomes, but by no means conclusive proof. Colleagues of Kirk therefore set out to put the record straight, or to get a definitive answer, by a better-controlled four-year study in an Illinois school system which had not previously had EMH classes. All primary children were examined and those eligible for an EMH program under existing standards of the state of Illinois were identified. Sixty of these, selected at random, were placed in special classes under well-trained teachers, with a well-prepared program of instruction. Another random sixty remained in the regular school program. While the study is still under analysis, it appears that the results are as inconclusive as those of previous studies.

Special educators have long ignored this mass of data, pointing to the fallacies of design, the lack of instruments for measuring the most important outcomes, and the imperfection of the instruments available for evaluating the limited outcomes we do attempt to measure. Each school system has so many success stories, each administrator and teacher sees so many children who appear to them to have made dramatic changes when given the advantages of a good special class, that they have been perhaps unable to accept these findings – quite possibly quite rightly.

Actually the important findings of such studies, is not that the kids do as well in the regular grades, but that they do not do as well as might be expected in either placement under present procedures. Records of many EMH classes suggest that few of the pupils even when they have had long years under good special teachers, attain the reading and arithmetic potentials predicted by their IQ's and mental ages. Dunn summarized fourteen studies of reading of EMH pupils, eleven of which showed reading achievement below M.A. expectancy. The average IQ in many EMH programs is about 75, suggesting at age 16 a mental age of a little over 11 years, and therefore an expectancy of achievement at sixth-grade level. Yet those responsible for EMH programs are frequently happy if half their EMH pupils of high-school age (not just the ones who go on to the usually highly selected high-school EMH classes) read at fourth grade or above, and tend to brag of the occasional pupils who attain sixth grade literacy. Perhaps this is as it should be. One announced goal of most EMH programs is social and economic competence. Many of these pupils, when they become adults, make adequate community adjustments and disappear into the general population. Community surveys are usually unable to identify anything like as many EMH individuals after age fourteen, as in the ten to fourteen year age group. Follow-up studies of the vocational and community adjustment of former special class pupils are numerous but far from complete or definitive. They suggest that the graduates of EMH classes do as well in social and economic adjustment in the community as their age mates from equivalent social backgrounds.

Innovations in school services to the retarded are being tried out, in formal research and demonstration projects, and in ongoing school programs. Some of these may be stimulated by soul searching derived from chagrin at the results of previous studies. More profitably, probably, the increase in such forward-looking research and demonstration can be attributed to the federal funds made available for research and for the training of professional personnel, and the growth of university programs, which have provided opportunities for interested and concerned professionals to devote themselves to the problems of retardation. In any case, there is

almost a flood of reports of such projects in the literature. Unfortunately the programs in many otherwise excellent school systems show little response.

Among the research studies are important experimentation on instructional methods. Learning theory and the principles of conditioned behavior change are being applied in controlled settings. There are studies on computerized learning programs, on the Initial Teaching Alphabet, on Montessori methods, Frostig methods, Strauss methods, on phonics, on work experience programs. In the school settings, emphasis has been on the importance of early special education, taking a leaf from Kirk's dramatic success in working with three, four, and five year old EMH children. Other emphasis is on expansion upward to the older age groups, with secondary school, work experience, and cooperative employment projects.

Related is the surge of interest in the culturally deprived, for the slums of our big cities all show concentrations of pupils diagnosed as mentally retarded. Psychologists are spending much energy developing ingenious procedures for differential diagnosis between mental retardation and brain injury, or between mental retardation and emotional disturbance. Yet these may be of relatively small social significance compared to differential diagnosis between mental retardation and cultural deprivation. What school psychologist in the light of today's evidence would be brave enough to say that he was not classifying as mentally retarded some, perhaps considerable numbers of, children who were "really" culturally deprived, with innate potential for average or superior intellectual success?

Even in the explosive area of integration versus segregation of special education facilities for the retarded, we see some slight evidence that the research reports have been read. In Newton, Massachusetts, for example, in the fall of 1967, when a class of boys who had been in a segregated EMH class the previous year was transferred to a new building designed for an experimental "non-graded" school, the boys were distributed in appropriate teachers' groups with non-handicapped children. The special teacher was transferred along with the boys and given a resource room. He provides services and support as needed by the boys and by the teachers with whom they are now placed, and in addition has time to render tutoring and other services to some non-handicapped pupils. Since the program had been in operation less than two months at the time the writer conferred with the staff, the results are unknown, but optimism prevailed.

The frequent complete segregation of public school classes for the trainable children, in separate school buildings, or in community centers operated by some other agency, deserves study. In many school systems, including Chicago, such classes have been maintained within regular school buildings without difficulties, and with increased understanding on the part of other pupils and teachers of the nature of mental handicap. Perhaps one of the most important by-products is that a considerable number of teachers and pupils come to realize personally and warmly that such children are members of the human race after all—something that too many of our citizens appear not to understand. The pattern across the nation, however, appears to be much more frequently an unquestioning acceptance of the need for separate facilities, and their value. Some of these separate programs do indeed show most excellent results, as at the Nightingale School in Long Beach, California, and many other American and New Zealand schools the author has had the privilege of visiting. Nevertheless long-term comparative studies of the progress and adjustment of trainable children in segregated and non-segregated studies would seem indicated.

In summary, then, the mental retardation programs of the schools present a terrific challenge to the education profession, and to the ancillary professions of school psychology, school medicine, and school social work.

There is need for great ingenuity and professional insight. Far more effective measures of school outcomes, especially the less quantifiable and more basic outcomes, must be developed. Far better instruments for differentiating between "pure" cultural handicap and "innate" mental deficiency, if there are such entities, and much better understanding of their complex interrelationships, are called for. Or perhaps on this diagnostic front, the real need is to forget labels and categories and develop the detailed diagnostic instruments that will give educators real help in determining what kind of education a kid needs today. More effective theories and methods of instruction probably will emerge from research focusing on a child's assets rather than his handicaps. As the schools attempt to apply new curricula, new methods, and new organizational patterns whose value is suggested by more controlled laboratory-type research, the school psychologist should be able to help effectively in the development of built-in evaluative schemes. Evaluation of ongoing practical school programs presents different problems and far more complex ones, than evaluation in controlled settings.

There is nothing routine about this challenge. It is a challenge to creative ability and imaginative planning. It implies hard-nosed research on existing programs, freewheeling new approaches to presently unsolved problems, backed by equally thoughtful evaluative criteria. It requires the guts to fight apathy, to challenge the status quo, to stick to a problem that will not yield to quick and easy solutions, to face discouragements and failures.

The headlong growth of services to the retarded provides a ferment in which change and improvement may find fertile soil—or in which quality may be lost in the sheer struggle for expansion. The professionals who accept the challenge of mental retardation in the years immediately ahead may well find great personal satisfaction in work in this exciting milieu.

William C. Morse

DIAGNOSIS OF LEARNING PROBLEMS WITH IMPLICATIONS FOR REMEDIATION IN THE CLASSROOM SETTING

As a result of society's demand that the school serve all children with any trainable degree of intelligence (usually above an IQ of 50), more and more students are required to attend school who might not otherwise be there. These children have special learning problems, and teachers are finding it progressively more difficult to rely on traditional methods of teaching. Although children are never excluded from school because of inadequacies and seldom excluded from school because of delinquency, some may be transferred to special schools or to special programs within a school.

The broad scope of the etiology of learning problems is stressed by Dr. Morse in his paper, "Diagnosis of Learning Problems with Implications for Remediation in the Classroom Setting." He warns that there is no short cut to understanding and resolving the issues of children with learning problems. The self-concept of the child facing developmental challenges varies with the groupings in which he finds himself. Dr. Morse reemphasizes the need for a complete diagnostic work-up by professionals in all areas: medical, psychological, sociological, and educational, and says this should be done during the on-going educational remediation. Children just do not "stand still" while professionals make their studies.

There are many varied and complex reasons why children do not learn in our tradition-bound schools of the past. New psychological approaches and principles must be found and implemented. Motivational problems abound and many still are left undiscovered or at least unsolved. Children with seriously impaired potential for learning require special consideration. Dr. Morse reports Dr. Rabinovitch's classification of children under the heading of dyslexia, which is characterized by an inability to deal with symbol learning – letters, words, sounds, and numbers as symbols in all areas – but he finds it most noticeable in reading.

In his conclusion Dr. Morse points out: "Educational programs often have to be largely individualized. . . ." This is supported by basic psychological principles and current psychological teaching and research which stress individual differences and the need for society to recognize them and adjust to them.

The present topic deals with children's learning problems which obviously implies a broad scope of etiology. Learning, as here used, has to do with the academic skills and knowledge as well as adjustment.

Let me say at the outset, I know of no valid shortcut to the complexity which is evident in children who have as a major symptom, or manifestation, learning problems. Nor do I know of any bargain-counter remediation. New names do not new solutions make. Why we shy away from a consideration of what is euphemistically termed the "whole child" in his natural environment escapes me. Those fixated on the inner nature paid so little attention to the day-by-day difficulties of developing actual behavior changes in these children that they are in danger of becoming prophets speaking mainly only to each other. Well-adjusted academic failures have no place. In their stead have come those who would lead us around by the nose of symptoms as if nothing else were germane. Even a long nose is not half a child. The youngster with learning problems is *first of all a child* with developmental challenges, with an emotional life and with an array of responses. He is not a hollow organism comprised of a symptomatic shell. He has a self-concept and is regulated by self-esteem.

Just as the children are complex, the classroom settings where these children are taught are seldom unidimensional. Most pupils are multiply handicapped and effective programs are consequently multiply faceted. It may be unfortunate, as one of my colleagues implies, but the fact is, teachers are human beings continuously emitting many cues, some assortments of which may be confusing. Teachers do get into the system. If rats learn mazes faster when the experimenter *thinks* the rats he is running are bright rats, than when he thinks he is running dull rats, there is no *doubt* but that the values of the teacher will produce certain interactions which are of prime concern.

Faced with a complex task where success is most difficult and beset by authorities who usually see the situation with professional myopia, it is little surprise that the teacher has become the most critical element in the whole process. Perhaps even the overtones in the way he introduces a child to a teaching machine may be as determinant as the machine's own operation. One special educator, after examining differential techniques, suggests that the only common variable is the remediator's belief in whatever the process he is using. Coming from the land of flying saucers, I realize credulity knows no bounds. It has been said that nothing has a greater hold on the human mind than nonsense fortified with technicalities. It is also easy to forget it is the child who must learn if there is to be a change. What we do as teachers functions only in what it causes the child to do. Theories are not in themselves productive: it is via their impact on the child's responses.

Classes mean grouping children. Since all children contain more than one dimension, groups will be mixtures. For example, the brain-injured child with higher-than-average overall intelligence often develops most successful ways of manipulating and controlling adults. These are fixated and rigid; in fact, they are the very essence of the ego structure. The skill with which this child is able to avoid confrontation with potential failure may be a harder matter to deal with than the actual disability. Or, the accumulative significance of minimal damage and lower class deprivation may be the squared power of either alone.

The selective factor used for putting certain children together may not be the factor most operative when they are together. Thus, one child with minimal neurological damage may find his competitive failure acute in the presence of a like-diagnosed peer who himself is unaroused since he is resigned to failing. The like profiles are lost in the dominance of new group-generated forces. The overall approach to this by many educators has been the pretence of abolishing group life. Ignoring group phenomena does not eliminate it. I have seen children "ungrouped" by booths who drilled holes to peek at their colleagues in the next compartment. Redl has pointed out that even in a one-to-one interview, the child has his group identifications right with him and part of the time in speaking to the individual child you are actually talking to those you have forgotten are there, his peers. Thus it is with children and their group life and it comprises a huge segment of pupil involvement. In our planning we should never forget that classes have a group life and teachers are group leaders. While it is possible to modulate the intensity of group aspects, it is not possible to eliminate them. Actually small size classrooms have a way of intensifying and focusing group interactions. The same amount of behavior may take place but in a restricted arena. A mild antagonism becomes a vendetta. The cavalier attitude of many experts when it comes to group aspects of classrooms leaves the teacher cold. While we are giving detailed ideas of how to spend an hour helping George, the teacher's mind is picturing the other six in their typical antics. It isn't that the teachers don't listen. It is just the interference of the noisy reality. A choice sometimes has to be made. Less time spent in tutorial may be superior to longer, unmanaged group exposure.

PATTERNS IN LEARNING PROBLEMS

We remember that rather than any simple syndrome, multiplicity is characteristic of children. Nevertheless, the matter of differential diagnosis is the key to remediation efforts. In examining the history of children who have been passed on from agency to agency in search of help, it has been evident that early diagnoses are frequently piecemeal and inadequate, resulting in wasted effort and confusion. A first step is study by competent experts of the several disciplines, *medical, psychological, sociological,* and *educational.* Otherwise hours are spent doing one thing when another is called for, or doing a single operation when several are needed in tandem. In my own opinion, the diagnostic effort must have two seldom applied extensions. The first is, no diagnosis should stand as an arbitrary solution. It is the best hunch, with varying certainty, leading to possible procedures. In difficult cases, the lack of reliability of the neurological and psychological evidence for prediction of specific remedial procedures is well known. Thus, reevaluation starts the very moment when actual work with the child begins. Second, the linkage between the problem as assessed and the service available has to be made more explicit. At the present time it seems likely that there may be more than one way to help many children. The diagnosis, if cast in terms of prognosis and related resources, would lead us to a symbiotic relationship between the problem and available resources. It has been particularly evident that a skillful teacher will come up with an astute series of observations after working awhile with a child. These observations are often more telling than our test results from the practical standpoint. Some may be a consequence of the teacher's behavior or the setting which brings out certain pupil responses. Whatever the cause, they are the essentials which must be incorporated rather than resorting to a "chart" which was really an educated guess. The tendency to disengage the diagnostic processes from the ongoing educational remediation constitutes one of the basic professional problems we face. There are reasons for this which we cannot deal with here, *but we need more diagnosis on the hoof.*

With the teacher, the group aspects, and prediagnostic aspects in mind as a backdrop, let us look briefly at the problems as they appear to the educational consumer of these diagnostic efforts.* Here we must think in terms of the educational format and classrooms. As Rhodes has said, we will run out of children before we run out of special categories. But, as a practical matter, we have to put them in packages. In our own experience, the following conditions are of prime concern and cut across typical diagnostic syndromes when educators consider learning problems.

Group 1. Children with unacceptable behavior manifestations but with potential for reasonably normal academic achievement.

(*Subgroup A*). First there are some disturbed children without academic learning problems, children who have behavior difficulties that are not yet pervasive. Somehow their school behavior and achievement is intact, but they present problems in other spheres of life. School may, in fact, be a compensating area and the youngster functions well here but finds the family or neighborhood a difficult situation. Until there is a manifestation in the schoolwork, these children may be overlooked though other signs of disturbance may be apparent. Here the overall screening and diagnostic aspects are very important.

*These are adopted from an analysis made for a report to Senator Sander Levin by Sam Davis, William Morse, and Ralph Rabinovitch, 1966.

(*Subgroup B*). Other children have achievement intact, but school behavior problems. Sooner or later, if the external press is severe, the various sectors merge and displacement of the problem into the school is common. This has been particularly evident in adolescents where even most stressful home situations may be too dangerous to react against openly and school takes the punishment. Some of these children act out in school and are a discipline problem but are no learning problem in the academic sense. They may not study or hand in assignments and the like, which will infuriate the education domain and produce intriguing side battles. Often they behave in such a manner as to put their whole future in jeopardy. Again, at adolescence, the developmental problems may precipitate educational failure. Lichter's work on neurotic responses to the school situation is important. Obviously, the school program for such children should be as unprovocative as possible, which is no easy task! The help the child needs, however, is in resolving other than school conflicts. Often the "behavior in the school" segment of his problem can be utilized to work back to generating conditions through active interview methods such as Life Space Interviewing. In addition to a more active style of counseling and therapy, considerable promise is suggested by group work in schools where these matters of behavior are the content for discussion. Work with the generating family situation may be the preferred method, but is often impossible for schools.

(*Subgroup C*). Children who have behavior difficulties confound the use of their normal potential for reasonable academic accomplishment. Inadequacies are evident now in the behavior and achievement spheres. There are also certain youngsters who get poor grades but are actually learning quite well on the criterion of objective test data. They have low "school survival" potential because they usually interfere with the learning of others, or seem to produce so little on classroom required tasks. They make teaching a most vexing experience and an omnipresent management battle. Some actively campaign against the system while others use more sophisticated resistance methods or even sit passive and inert. Although passivity may be tolerated, any of the others will cause trouble with a really conscientious, achievement-bound educational program. There are certain schizophrenic children who can and do learn quite well. But bizarre and idiosyncratic styles are difficult to accommodate in the group setting. Even some brain-injured children, otherwise able to learn in a regular school are affected by the stimulation of a large classroom. Others who have potential are diagnosed neurotic where anxiety reduces the ability to concentrate and relate properly to adult or peer. Still others are not limited in potential but have suffered severe neglect and respond with primitive and aggressive behavior, and react as if every request were a rejection. The goal is to encourage their learning potential.

There is a large group, which, having the intellectual ability to learn, at the same time shows deep motivational dispositions against schooling. There is no allegiance to the educational scene and its demands. Some of the more thoughtful students are found in the special group of activists who are campaigning against the educational establishment. They find their schooling a poor substitute for education. Here the change may be needed in the system, not the pupil. The system may be deficient in its staff attitudes, methods, curriculum, or achievement neurosis may be at the root.

At every age, from kindergarten through college, there are other school-alienated pupils who want "out." Many show obvious signs; they have concrete gratification needs, they are hard to keep still, low in attention to school tasks, and eager for enjoyment wherever they can find it. At adolescence they have already joined the materialistic society around them and are intense about "wheels," fun, and excitement. Add the frustration of low access to resources, and delinquency may be a solution. Patience is not a common trait, and much time has been wasted trying to make them into college-bound idealists or educational conformists. Drastic revisions in the educational program are required to provide both psychological and vocational adjustments for these problem pupils.

A special motivational problem is found in children with ego lacunae. These are children who verbally want to learn but are still pleasure-bound and have no habits of follow-through. They expect maximum rewards on minimum effort. School learning requires consistent diligence and a few moments of effort exhaust them. They are of longtime development, and we have found the family pattern as the source. Helping these "willing" children has proven most difficult. Their families do not see the need of helping since they deny their role. Careful grading of tasks is essential, and long-term programs are required.

There are also students who feign stupidity as a product of a family role and identification with non-academic fathers. Their difficulties are barely perceptible, and must be traced back to the family background. Often, they simply do not benefit from instruction.

Those with long-term value defects, the sociopath and the psychopath, whether delinquent or not, are often the children most nominated by the teacher for special programs. The continual monitoring they require, the ease with which they slip into misbehavior, and their ability to convert interventions to their own ends predicate the need for special class help. If one gets them early enough and follows Quay's proposals, many of them can show improvement. Teachers often get discouraged when they regress as they do, for the patterning is never smooth.

Clearly, in this group, measured or judged potential for academic achievement is not to be equated with expectation for such accomplishment. The educational obligation is to bring them within the pale of accepted behavior, not to make them all scholars. On the other hand, many will, with help, begin to function within reasonable limits for the ordinary academic channels. It has been our experience, however, that the access to the problem may limit intervention possibilities which we can use. It must be clear that each child requires careful appraisal. The self-concept and the motivational system must be examined in detail. There will be a broad range of programmatic effort called for, and certain mixtures will explode, but I see no other answer than to work each through with planning and support.

Group 2. These are children with ascertained or implied impaired potential for learning when they reach school. While it is clear by now that one seldom finds a happy, integrated non-achiever, there are many children whose capabilities are simply limited.

(Subgroup A). First there are the significantly deprived students. While there is an enduring debate over the impact of early childhood experiences on the child's performance in school, there is little question that many children are faced with limitations which, without a significant educational commitment, will be nonreversible and destroy their educational careers. In the most extreme cases are the children described by Bertha Riese in *Heal the Hurt Child.*[*]

There is extensive current attention being given to the so-called deprived pupil, though massive needs have produced great disorganization at all levels of these programs. In the author's own work, we have found it necessary to point to the specific psychological impact of at least five aspects of the problem: the background of economic deprivation; an early interest in the child on the part

[*]See Bertha Riese, *Heal the Hurt Child,* (Chicago: U. of Chicago Press, 1962).

of educators; adequate models for the child's training; educational predecessors for example and direction; and the cultivation of hope. The effort must include a total socialization experience with concentrated attention to understanding the best methods of learning and accomplishment.

(*Subgroup B*). Children with neurological defects are the last category to be mentioned, and this is one of special interest.

It is at once fascinating and disturbing to realize what has happened in the field of education of the so-called minimally brain damaged. Even the name itself is a matter for debate and dissension; at the same time, there are vigorous advocates of almost every technique from crawling to training of the mind. The only agreement I find is that males are the chosen group. A recent publication in this area is as close to a collection of prejudices as to verified practice. Public discussion is usually polite but corridor conversation is closer to assassination.

I have pondered the reasons for this because I have been most confused by the divergencies and polarization which characterize the field. Some is due, of course, to charismatic advocates, and certainly it is important to be motivated and enthusiastic though not deluded. It would seem the basic reason is the confounding complexity of the condition itself, with combination descriptive-analytic labels from developmental lag and perceptual difficulty to brain lesion. Any condition which generates so much difficulty fosters diligent efforts at remediation. The desire to help the less fortunate is a very strong motivation. The hope for a miracle cure is evident.

When objective and serious workers discuss their differences both in diagnosis and remediation, it sometimes appears that the Hawthorne effect produced by conviction may be the single constraint. However, others have suggested a more subtle force. Intake selection often begins to narrow the clientele range and certain subtypes of chil-

dren are seen more often than others. One learning disabilities center finds a change when the adjacent child guidance clinic closes its waiting list, for example. Some report a run on one or another syndrome for a period of time, hyperkinetic, or speech defects, etc.

Another issue is "selective looking" based upon prior assumptions. Most of the serious cases have various stigmata, and one can find considerable of what one looks for, be it anxiety or motor ineffectiveness. We are more prone to discuss what assessments we used than what were omitted and seldom does the work-up extend over the several days required to cover the many areas.

The psychologist's profession is to test, the physician to diagnose and prescribe, and the teacher to foster learning. One of the difficulties from the educator's point of view is the hiatus between the assessments on one hand, and the reeducation efforts on the other. Of course, the tests must have utility, and some expect them to relate, but often it is a mirage.

Bateman's excellent paper in the February 1966 *Review of Educational Research* covers the significant current concepts regarding this group. She defines the learning disorders as "those deviations in the learning processes which are associated with an educationally significant discrepancy between apparent capacity for language or cognitive behavior and actual level of language or cognitive performance. Even within this broad description, language must be understood as including vocal and motor expressive behaviors as well as the reception and manipulation of symbols."

Characteristics attributed to these children cover a wide range of stigmata. The general finding is that, as a group, they differ significantly from normal children in various measures but there is almost always overlap with normals reported in the curves. Also, few researchers have looked for children with disabilities in tested functions but no resulting achievement lags. The important point to note is that learning disability can be produced by many malfunctions and the individual patterns found in one child may be quite at odds with one found in another.

Deficiencies commonly found are in visual and auditory discrimination, dominance, memory, information storage and retrieval, and the ability to integrate a variety of experiences. They are low in ability to abstract the significant element from common experiences, nor can they generalize adequately. Again, no single etiological factor characterized reading disability. To quote Bateman, "The likelihood that there is one true cause or even description is remote." If there is no one cause, it also follows that one cannot expect a single course of remediation.

Rabinovitch considers these symptoms under the heading of dyslexia characterized by inability to deal with symbol learning, letters, words, sounds, and numbers in all areas, but feels it is most noticeable in reading. He estimates the percentage of school pupils who have serious disability of this nature at about 2 per cent. The verbal IQ on the WISC averages more than 20 points lower than the performance. Time, size, number and direction abstractions are learned only with great difficulty.

Now, whatever the neurological limitation, general or specific, the inability to make normal progress is a source of consternation to parents and teachers and the consequence is a damaged self-concept which accompanies the disability. As Rappaport points out, only if the environment is prophylactic will the child develop reasonable self-esteem since mastery, the key to security, is otherwise not forthcoming. The child does not stimulate typical parental or teacher responses. Rappaport states that he has never seen one who was not victorious in a battle with an adult who did not understand him by using various forms of "you can't make me." Still, it is well to remember the evidence that while the average risk will be greater, they can develop reasonable security and this, in school, involves both academic and emotional aspects.

It is increasingly obvious that there are several channels or approaches to educational work with this learning disability group. Part of the method differences are no doubt an outgrowth of the age of the child, particular performance problems and the severity of the disability to say nothing of theoretical biases. A very pertinent question is whether or not gains are sustained, and Bateman raises doubts about this after reviewing the findings. Continued support seems required. All of us are more interested in reporting quick success than long-term failures. We need a special grant program for failures to get more of it out into the open. Educational approaches differ.

A good many experts emphasize total body integration and self-image functioning or maturational stimulation. There are complex theories about these matters ranging from developmental lags to lesions. As we know, the sequence of training may be rigidly prescribed, although there will be differences in the sequences from one to another expert. Two things should be mentioned in this connection. One is, a child who lacks adequate mobility and space orientation, should be helped to acquire these skills in their own right. Second, whether eye-hand coordination in ball catching, for example, is the coordinator of reading, is an open question. The recent work of Robbins should at least help us keep an open mind. This is not the old chestnut of transfer of training, however; it is essentially the matter of developmental sequencing or as some claim the "stimulation of neurologic maturation" necessary to reading. We have classes devoted to such exercises. We never know the actual progress from the "exercise" because of the maturational lags aspect. Also body confidence yields self-security and nets better responses from others.

Perceptual training is an example of a remedial emphasis related to specific deficit, and many drills have been proposed. The question here is the issue of transfer of training — if one learns to make certain discriminations will this be available as a generalized skill in reading? Can we train his attention? Is there a skill of figure-ground discrimination? It should be noted that direct practice on the actual symbols (F vs. T and P), for example, is of a different order, and does not have to carry the burden of transfer. The fact of the matter is that the correlation between these functions is often +.60. This implies that there is often widespread total malfunction. It constitutes the desired elements in themselves. Smith tends to emphasize the former. Frostig speaks of the second, but appears to do both; again, derived gains may not be from supposed reasons. Mann and Phillips soundly criticize the fractional theory for special education.

Another approach is teaching around the limitation. If there is a weakness in a modality, one tries to use others. While multiple sensory approaches are most common, one could think in terms of assets (if there were any) and select processes designed to serve that end.

Medication as a primary or adjunct intervention is not being discussed except to say that those of us who are not physicians often hope for panaceas; sometimes it happens while other times it doesn't. The difficulty of finding the right drug and right dosage is obvious.

Our own attempts have involved all of these procedures at one time or another, and seldom has any neat plan worked. Many times no plan has worked. The teacher frustration is intense, and I could indicate by cases. Progress is slow and final results low in many cases. The other day we were planning high-school support for several who have been in special classes both in elementary and junior high. Dyslexic students of high-school age use films, recordings and discussion to learn, but the major problem is fitting them into the economy someplace. This is a personal counseling and specific training issue especially vexing with these youngsters.

When one thinks of the classroom, we have found less succor in theory than in a kind of eclectic pragmatism. The steps outlined by Bryant and the Albany Learning Disabilities Center have been good guideposts. The only cardinal premise *is not to give a pupil that which he cannot do.* Never overload. Bryant also believes that any session which results in predominately incorrect responses is a mistake. The work begins further back than the point of failure as revealed by diagnostic teaching. This diagnostic teaching has been of more real use than diagnostic testing. The specific task is defined by the unknown which must be mastered in doses within the limit of ability. This means going far back and working on the simplest elements in serious cases. If it is a matter of discrimination, then each of the elements to be discriminated is first overlearned by itself. Only the most gradual introduction of complexity is permitted. When the child becomes confused, the work returns to a position of certainty. The mechanics include every conceivable stratagem with multiple sensory aspects, card reading machines and individualized drills, as well as the usual prepared types of things from Smith, Frostig and others.

CONCLUSION

Finally a few generalizations. One of the problems in grouping is the intensity of the symptom expression, whatever it may be. The more severe cases will take more input than a typical public school can afford.

It seems advisable to separate out the severe learning disabilities who will have slow progress and most likely limited recovery. These will be extensive, high investment, long-term programs. When the evidence is fairly clear that special remedial techniques are not required as is the case for many disturbed but achieving children, we would face this fact and get on with interventions which do bear down on behavior. These range from traditional therapy to structuring and even sometimes exclusion as an educational pressure. At the present time interventions obviously range from the traditional approaches to many which emphasize a more behavioral methodology. Whatever we use does not excuse us from relationships between teacher and pupil which are supportive, pleasant and concerned.

In methods, there are probably many procedures which will have usefulness. There are many ways to meet dilemmas, individual therapy, Smith's programmed manual for parents, group processes, and teacher consultation.

Regardless of the etiology, if the acting out is not brought into reasonable control, it is improbable that any educational program in depth will be possible. Support is required to achieve a reasonable decorum, though in my mind, not compulsively rigid patterning. There will be outbursts from time to time unless we apply repressive tactics. Why be afraid of crises which we have finally learned are really teaching opportunities?

Educational programs often have to be largely individualized. All types of self-tutoring and materials should be available. Teachers are seldom given reasonable time for this aspect of their work, which is so critical and time consuming. But let us not have only individual experiences. We need group life as well for them.

It is unlikely that any child will be without emotional difficulties, even if his primary limitation is in the neurological area. All programs should be staffed with the resources for individual work as well as more traditional psycho-educational efforts. But we should not lose sight of the fact that achievement, even if it be most modest, may be the most significant therapeutic approach we can have, and in many instances it may be in itself sufficient, though this is not always the case. One would be most hesitant to recommend therapy to make a nonlearner happy with this state when there are accomplishments he might make.

Part IV

SELF-CONTROL AND DISCIPLINE

No single area of behavior concerns parents, teachers, or psychologists more than that of dealing with self-control. Parents have the primary responsibility to produce an individual capable of determining his own actions, controlling his own behavior, and running his own life in a way satisfying and rewarding to himself. They are aided by teachers, clergymen, and professionals in a variety of fields.

Followers of Freud have developed a theory of behavior and personality that traces the growth and maturation of an individual from the birth of an unsophisticated, biologically oriented animal through infancy, childhood, and adolescence into adulthood. During this cycle of growth, one develops and learns controls and basic judgment. With proper guidance, children begin to seek answers to their questions of "why" — why things happen, why they feel as they do, why there are rules and policies. They test and question authority and society in general. They strive to work out a way of life to meet their particular needs and circumstances.

In the process of this growth, a child often comes into conflict with his parents, other adults, his peers, even with himself. As these problems and conflicts occur, the child is frequently faced with disciplinary measures applied by authoritary figures in society as a means of enforcing external controls, of teaching desired behavior, and/or of reinforcing a child's own desires for internalized controls and self-judgments.

Authorities cannot agree on the best methods of "discipline." Various psychological principles are used to explain conflicting theories and practices; research attempts to find the best techniques. The answer is probably that there is no one perfect method but rather a variety of methods which have to be selected and adjusted to various situations and types of individuals. Discipline as such should become decreasingly necessary with age and maturation; externalized discipline should gradually become internalized.

In today's society, much attention is being given to the use of physical force as a means of discipline. Parents continue to ask whether they should spank their children; laws are often needed to prevent or discourage "child abuse," which, in many instances, is an extreme form of physical discipline that can do serious damage to a child when applied in an emotional state by an adult. There are many more effective means of showing disapproval than beatings, and the damage done to the psyche by such cruel, extreme, and usually irrational acts may have lasting traumatic effects. Most research seems to indicate that reward and praise is much more effective than physical forms of discipline in bringing about desired change and growth in a child.

It is to this end, the betterment and growth of the individual, that all discipline should be directed.

Father Francis Chiaramonte

THE FALLACY OF THE SUPEREGO

In the following article, Father Chiaramonte makes a comparison of the psychologist's and theologian's views of the superego and of the conscience. He points up the ambiguities in considering these two words synonymously, and discusses the different philosophic principles on which the two ideas are based. He concludes with an appreciation of the theologian's interpretation of conscience because it presents a more positive idea of human nature.

For psychologists, the concepts of id, ego, and superego are familiar. But for parents and teachers, these ideas may be less commonly known, though very relevant in dealing with children during the years in which the Oedipus complex must be resolved, and reasonable and satisfactory adjustments to life outside of the family must be made. Educators and parents who are aware of the psychological mechanisms which order and evaluate our actions cannot help but be better equipped to deal with the serious blocks that may develop from frustrations and conflicts in a child's growth.

Some psychologists equate the superego and conscience because they feel that both control man's adjustment to the rules of society independent of any basic, absolute rules.

After seriously studying what theologians say about conscience, other psychologists question the validity of this practice. Even though these scientists genuinely agree with the Freudian description of the superego, their concept of conscience is essentially different. For instance, they discern conscience as an innate absolute force over which man has no control: conscience keeps urging man toward objective good. While the first group asserts that the superego and conscience are a product of man, the second group feels that only the superego is. The latter group perceives conscience as an uncreated possession of man.

At a glance, some persons might think this difference of opinion to be somewhat superficial and academic. However, a candid study of each concept points up notable differences between them which are sufficiently profound to affect the ethical core and moral fiber of humanity itself. A counterbalance indicates the difference between an absolute standard of values, independent of enviromental forces to which

man is bound by virtue of his humanity; as opposed to a relative set of values formed by environmental forces to which man is conformed as a social being.

However, before anyone can make a responsible decision in this matter, he must clearly understand what Freud meant when he spoke of conscience and the superego; as well as what the theologians mean when they treat the matter of conscience. In this article I will briefly outline the historical development of both concepts; thereby presenting the reader facts from which he can judge whether or not the two terms should be equated. In turn this consideration will advance the scholar to further consideration and research, concerning absolute or relative norms of behavior.

As a medical practitioner Freud specialized in the treatment and care of patients, especially women, with nervous disorders. Consequently, the psychoanalytical theory Freud fathered is primarily the descriptions and conclusions he gleaned from his clinical observations of patients. In general, we can summarize the Freudian theory of the function and formation of the superego, by stating that the dynamic force of the id drives the organism in the direction of wish-fulfillment and tension reduction. In turn, the ego, in its search to enhance the organism must substitute real goals for the hallucinating goals of the id; instead, however, it is pushed into substituting moralistic goals for realistic ones by the superego. What moralistic goals the superego approves or rejects depends entirely upon the organism's environment.

Freud's theory about the formation of the superego is quite clear and definitive. The superego is the embodiment in the child of fundamental ideas, values, and morals of his society. It is the final stage of personality development: primarily, rooted in the Oedipus complex; secondarily, influenced by environmental forces.

On the other hand, when Freud begins to theorize about conscience itself, he is nebulous and ambiguous. For example, he says the "Ego ideal rules as conscience over the ego."[1] In this passage he is evidently identifying superego and conscience so he is justified when he uses the terms interchangeably. On the other hand, when Freud says: "Normal conscience is the impersonal form of the superego,"[2] he seems to indicate that conscience is derived from the superego. Further, he speaks of "conscience as a function of the superego," while simultaneously insisting that conscience is subordinate to the superego, as a slave is to his master.[3] Consequently, one finds it almost impossible to decide from his theory of conscience, Freud's pertinent meaning.

One notes that there is no ambiguity when Freud *describes* conscience as he observed it. His description is lucid and concise. Using mentally-ill persons, especially compulsive neurotics, to study conscience with its resultant guilt feelings, Freud describes conscience as a psychic phenomenon which speaks with absolute categorical certainty and authority, from which there is no appeal. Conscience needs no outside criterion to prove its judgments. It warns that certain transgressions will be punished by guilt feelings as well as produce guilt feelings once the trans-

gressions have been committed. Conscience makes the individual feel responsible for his actions. This sense of responsibility, coupled with a transgression or thought of a transgression, makes an individual deeply aware of his guilt. In turn, this guilt complex can lead to despair or mental illness.

In his attempt to explain human behavior, Freud invented the superego, an internal dynamic force created in man by society. To the theologians, this concept is completely unacceptable. For them, conscience is innate, uncreated, and governs society.

In a study of conscience, it is the theologian's task to concentrate on that deep force within every person which drives him to seek out what he understands to be good. Every human being experiences this force as something more basic than his own good will, more important than himself. This force is never silenced when resisted by a stubborn or unreasonable man. He sees it as binding even when trying to evade it. This is the phenomenon, uncovered by reason and experience, that the theologian sets out to explain.

This same phenomenon, at times, is graphically depicted in Sacred Scripture, a tool of the theologian. The Old Testament depicts the Israelites seeing God active in their life by moving them to do His will through their conscience. For instance, in the Book of Wisdom (XVII.10) one finds men sick with apprehension due to their bad conscience. Again, in II Kings (XXIV.10) "But now the count of Israel had been made, David's heart reproached him." To the Israelites, the guilt and discomfort they felt was the voice of God speaking to them urging them to mend their ways.

In later biblical history, Paul of Tarsus refers to conscience as an inner absolute teacher that binds one to follow the law of

1. Vandervelt, Rev. James J. and Odenwalk, Robert P., *Psychiatry and Catholicism*, McGraw-Hill Book Company, New York, 1957, p. 139
2. *Loc. cit.*
3. *Loc. cit.*

God as seen in nature (I Cor. VIII). Paul continues to identify conscience with right reasoning, so that anyone acting contrary to what reason tells him to be correct, is to be reproached.

Theologically, the discussion of conscience centered around an explanation of the uncreated dynamic imperative force, or predisposition in man, that assures an individual moral response in a concrete situation. Bernard Haring in *The Law of Christ*, gives a thoroughly concise and accurate account of the historical development of the theory of conscience.

Theologians, such as Albert, the Great, and Thomas Aquinas, spoke of an innate dwelling in man of the highest moral principles, "habitus primorum principorum." These principles are immediately evident to the intellect. For example, "Good is to be done and evil avoided," is an innate principle immediately evident and morally meaningful to man. The intellect, after recognizing these principles and understanding their truth, must present them to the will for choice. The human will, from its creation, contains within itself a predetermination towards good as perceived by the intellect. From this moment on, it is a simple matter of a syllogism. Certain innate principles are immediately evident to the intellect. Upon the presence of a stimulus, the decision of conscience is the conclusion of a syllogism. For example:

Avoid evil   (innate principle)
Stealing is evil   (stimulus)
Therefore, avoid stealing (conclusion of conscience)

The will had no choice except to consent to the syllogism; since the will by nature was predetermined by what is good. This does not preclude the fact that a person is free to go against the dictates of conscience, if he so desires. In such instances, he chooses against his conscience because he sees evil under the aspect of good. In the example cited, a man chooses to steal because he sees good in it for himself even though ultimately he knows the act of stealing is fundamentally wrong.

Conscience, according to the above theory, is an innate self-evident series of principles immediately evident to the intellect which present man with a series of "oughts" to guide his actions throughout life.

On the other hand, Alexander of Hales, Bonaventure, and Henry of Ghent, minimized human reason's role in conscience and extolled the human will. They admitted that reason is capable of arriving at a knowledge of good, but this knowledge *has* no driving force towards good, and thereby *proves* ineffective. The dynamic force comes from the human will which is innately created to love. This innate urge to love what is good is the dynamic force behind man's moral acts.

A recent and more comprehensive theory of conscience aims at a synthesis of the two previous theories. This theory considers conscience to be a "spiritual instinct for self-preservation arising from the urge for complete unity and harmony."[4]

Man is made in the likeness of the Trinity: the Father, the Son, and the Holy Spirit — three persons infinitely and harmoniously united into one Divine Essence. The human soul with its two separate operations — intellect and free will — is seen as the reflective created image of the Divine Trinity. The soul with all its qualities strives towards the same peace, unity, and harmony that exist in the triune nature of God. The instruments of unity are: the intellect, which naturally seeks the truth; and the will, which naturally yearns for the true good.

Unlike the Divine Essence, the soul is finite, and therefore, imperfect. Consequently, the finite nature of the intellect and will permits them to become separated in activity. The will can permit itself to follow a

4. Haring, Rev. Bernard, *The Law of Christ*, Vol. I, Newman Press, Westminster, 1963, p. 143.

"mirage" of good that, in turn, breaks its harmony with the intellect. In direct reversal, the intellect can rationalize an apparent good.

At this point, the spiritual instinct for complete unity and harmony intervenes. Whenever a split occurs between the intellect and will, man is deeply wounded. The wound is in the form of guilt feelings which beg for the restoration of harmony within the individual. In this theory, conscience is that dynamic force which drives man to maintain unity and harmony within the profound depths of his soul.

Permit me to add one note of caution. The unity and harmony sought between the intellect and will is not the *mere* alignment of these two psychic powers. What is sought is their harmonious alignment within the limits determined by human dignity. For man, although not physically forced to do so, is morally bound to act according to his human nature. Any conscious act to the contrary is degrading and makes him less a man.

For example, an animal could easily be provoked to maul or kill a human being. Such animal conduct evokes in a man emotions of fear and anger but never condemnation. We feel this behavior is natural to an animal and therefore he is not culpable. We realize that environmental forces assembled in a predetermined pattern stimulated the animal's hostile behavior beyond its control. It *had* to follow the drive according to its animal nature. On the other hand, we do not accept this behavior to be normal in man. We condemn men who kill other men even if they are provoked to murder. We instinctively realize and accept the fact that man's nature forbids him to act like a mere animal. Man is bound, not physically like animals, but morally, to act according to his human nature. Hence, we do not permit man to justify his behavior according to some phantasy of human nature. When this happens, he rationalizes and chooses a mirage of good over real good as dictated by his human nature, thereby shattering the unity and peace between his intel-

lect and will. Guilt feelings, in this instance, conscience, arise and prod him towards the psychic unity for which he was created. Consequently a mere alignment of the psychic powers is insufficient for man. An alignment commensurate with the depths of human nature is demanded.

Unfortunately, if Freud meant to identify the superego with conscience (there is evidence to this effect), one must point out that he erred in at least three areas: methodology, theology, and philosophy.

Freud attempted to abstract from the mentally ill, especially compulsive neurotics, principles to describe a healthy conscience. There is no doubt that this method contributed to the discovery of such essential elements of conscience as: ultimate authority, ability to warn against transgressions, plus potential to produce guilt feelings and anxiety. More importantly, however, Freudian theory to explain these phenomena is scientifically unfounded. According to Freud, there is a conflict between the instinctual drives and the repressing force within man. It is out of this conflict that man's conscience develops. This theory might very well apply to a "sick" conscience, but Freud had no real scientific basis to theorize about a healthy, normal conscience, using solely the observations taken from a sick, neurotic conscience. He was as erroneous in comparative judgment as a doctor would be who uses only his observations of a cancerous liver to explain the function of a healthy liver. Freud further neglected to explain how a pathological conscience, which is experienced as such in the case of the neurotics, is experienced as something meaningful (as a drive towards enhancement of the organism) in the case of a healthy person.

Further, where philosophers and theologians respected the human dignity of man, by emulating his highest qualities, intellect and will, to explain the phenomenon of conscience, Freud dwelt on man's lowest instincts – the id. Theologians have always granted that a conscience could be distorted, consciously or unconsciously, by man's lower instincts; yet they have always insisted that these urgings were distinct from conscience and had no part in its formation.

One of the significant and fundamental differences that emerges from the two concepts of conscience centers around the question of absolute and relative norms of morality. Theologians throughout history have insisted upon the existence of an objective morality, independent of the whims of man and society, identified variously as the Eternal Law, Natural Law, or Human Nature depending upon the theologian's point of view. Freud, on the other hand, never admitted an objective moral norm. He felt this gave conscience a too-exalted position. Instead, he insisted man created his own conscience by adjusting his asocial driving forces (the id) to society. Parental authority played the major role in forming the superego. What Freud neglected to explain, however, was the binding force of conscience that is felt in the depths of personality, even when this judgment of conscience contradicts parental authority and revolts against environmental conditioning. How can the superego (conscience) rise above its own conditioning forces? Unfortunately, by trying to prove that man creates his own conscience, Freud unwittingly sheds light on conscience, as an uncreated existing force over which mankind has no control.

Theologians traditionally distinguish between a lax, doubtful, and correct conscience. A lax conscience is an erroneous one which judges gravely sinful actions to be harmless. The person encouraging such a conscience is a law unto himself, justifying his actions by rationalization: e.g., such a person might approve of lying to someone who had lied to him. A doubtful conscience leaves the person undecided as to the morality of his actions: e.g., after weighing all the evidence a doctor might still not be able to decide whether or not he should operate. A correct conscience leads one to make a judgment commensurate with objective norms of morality. Freud treats almost exclusively the guilt feelings conscience generates. One feels that Freud identifies conscience with guilt. In such a case, he is dealing with only one kind of theological judgment—the lax conscience. Acting with such a conscience, an individual convinces himself by empty reasons, that a serious act is relatively harmless; thereby, bringing upon himself guilt feelings. Freud, at the same time, neglects to treat a correct and doubtful conscience, which further points up the fact that what he means by the superego is not what the theologians mean by conscience. Freud incorrectly equates a lax conscience with all forms of conscience.

Freud partially agrees with the theologians when he emphasizes the warning function of conscience. Theologians agree that it is the function of conscience to alert the person pondering a certain action which he knows to be wrong, to the possible mental anguish that he may experience, if the warning is neglected.

In conclusion, I believe that after a thorough comparative study of both the Freudian and theological concepts of conscience, it is not valid to equate the two terms. They are two distinct and deeply different concepts. Where Freud insists that man creates and controls his own conscience, theologians see conscience as an innate driving force towards objective good and truth, over which man has no control. Where Freud uses the id to theorize about the *cause* of conscience, theologians turn to man's highest and most distinctive qualities, the intellect and will to theorize about the *workings* of conscience. The cause is seen as innately implanted by the creator. Where Freud debases conscience and personality with the Oedipus complex, the theologians elevate it with the human intellect and will. Where Freud sees conscience driving man in the direction of subjective values and cultural ideals, theologians see it moving man in the direction of an objective omnipotent good, superior to himself and society.

William C. Morse

THE MENTAL HYGIENE VIEWPOINT ON SCHOOL DISCIPLINE

Discipline in the school, home, and community is becoming an increasingly serious problem. More frequently we read and hear of crises in the schools which require serious attention on the part of educators and parents.

Dr. Morse points out the lag in the development and application of sound psychological principles to the question of discipline. A new, more practical approach is needed. He prefers the case-analysis approach in diagnosing the most effective means of controlling behavior. In advocating an interpretive approach, Morse stays away from the merely punitive effects of discipline and puts more value on a more sympathetic methodology based on close observation of the particular evidence and an analysis of the best possible way of dealing with the individual child. He stresses the need for sensitivity and a less rigid standard of controlling behavior problems in the schools.

The mental hygiene viewpoint on school discipline stays one jump ahead of chaos. To a large extent, practice is governed by outmoded concepts. Methodology tends to be polarized: some advocates cling to a simple-minded hope that affection and acceptance will conquer all; others are just as certain that the only way to manage recalcitrant youth is to get tough and kick them out when they do not respond. Such a primitive dichotomy, based as it is on vastly oversimplified notions of how to influence behavior, is no longer worthy of attention by serious students of personality dynamics.

The current effort of the mental hygienist is to work out a more appropriate and adequate basis for school discipline. As a matter of fact, mental health concepts have had less actual influence on the everyday workings of schools than we wish to admit. The reason is that proposals have lacked realism. School people are rightly concerned with concepts which will function in the educational milieu rather than esoteric ideas useful in other settings. But the mental hygiene movement in and out of schools is still dominated by concepts which, although valid in themselves, are remote from the Monday morning to Friday night routine of schools with thousands of children who must not only be "seen" in interviews but must also be controlled in the social world of the school. The new look in school mental hygiene has parallels in psychiatry where the art of helping is now moving from the interview room to social psychiatry in the community. The social psychiatry of Caplan[1] and the school assistance of the Newman group[2] are examples. These approaches consider the total milieu, the use of crisis situations and new methods of intervention to teach young people how to cope with difficulties.

One thing is certain. The new mental hygiene must provide more effective approaches than those of the past, for problems of discipline are of high priority in most schools. Perhaps it takes the form of helping a mildly deviate adolescent find a place in the school community rather than become a dropout. More likely it is how to handle such behavior as disrespect, defiance of teacher authority, peer aggression, calculated rejection of the school's goals, or destructiveness. While the

Reprinted from *The High School Journal*. Vol. 47, No. 6, March 1965, by permission of The University of North Carolina Press.
1. Caplan, Gerald. "Opportunities for School Psychologists in the Prevention of Mental Disorders in Children," *Mental Hygiene*, XLVII, No. 4, (Oct. 1963), 525-539.
2. Newman, R.G., Redl, F., and Kitchener, H.L. *Technical Assistance in a Public School System* (in press). School Research Program, 5410 Conn. Ave., N.W., Washington 15, D.C.

magnitude and chronicity is more evident in central urban complexes, similar behavior, though sometimes with a different format, is present in suburbia and the rural areas as well. Intensified pressures for academic accomplishment in schools produce more failure and frustration, and the many daily examples of raw aggression prevalent in society encourage impulse acting-out. At the same time there is the realignment of the socializing forces in the culture with the family influence diminishing while the school and other community agencies have yet to find the formula for replacement efforts. It has been termed a crisis in "character," which is the old-fashioned term being used again.[3]

There is no miracle drug to assuage the agony of cultural change. The school's portion of the responsibility remains uncertain, but this much is clear: we can help children through the use of appropriate disciplinary procedures. The following sections are a hurried look at three parts of this extensive problem. However, these excerpts are sketches of the new mental hygiene view.

1. Schools will broaden the techniques used in both diagnosis and intervention. A dual system of diagnosis and intervention is proposed. Both the traditional and the new approaches are necessary, but one offers more potential for the school milieu. This starts with theory regarding the cause of the behavior we wish to alter. Then it is necessary to know how to produce alterations in the desired direction. In traditional terms, this is all seen as a product of one's life history, oversimplification as follows:

CASE HISTORY APPROACH

A. The individual's life experience and its culmination is assessed by the psychologist with projective tests, by the social worker who unravels the family dynamics, and by the psychiatrist who searches for the underlying motivations in the pupil's inner life.

B. The individual life experience culminates in a diagnosis where the essence of the findings are summarized as a syndrome. This capsule description of the problem implies the major dynamics. For example, a youngster may be diagnosed as a "sociopath," "neurotic," etc. Even though there is less than complete agreement on nosology, these syndromes convey meaning to the specialists. But they frequently suggest very little to the educator of what should be done to help the child.

C. Behavior in question is seen as an inevitable outcome of the syndrome assigned, and a consequence of long-standing personality deviations. This tends to make the educator feel there is little the school can do.

D. Plans for intervention must then be based on altering the personality. The traditional method to alter behavior is through one to one (or sometimes group) therapy with the child and/or parents. This suggests that schools setting out to alter behavior will need to provide traditional therapy, since this is the key to alteration.

Many barriers become apparent when this methodology is seen as the single or major channel for change. The teachers and most other school personnel are left on the sidelines. The school must depend upon outside experts to produce change. Necessary communication between the teacher and the clinical personnel is often difficult to activate and sustain. It should be made clear that, in our experience, such traditional therapy may be the only method for really changing behavior in many cases and certainly it is a significant part in getting needed control in many others. But there is a growing awareness of a set of "causes" other than the historical. Contrasted with the case history approach is the life space approach. Here the search for causes of given behavior turns to the conditions in the contemporary scene, those here and now environmental forces

3. Peck, R.F., and Havighurst, R.J. *The Psychology of Character Development.* New York: John Wiley & Sons, Inc., 1960.

which impinge upon the pupil's self at any given time. Behavior is seen as a consequence of these forces. Situational analysis suggests a new schema.

LIFE SPACE APPROACH

A. The individual's life space is studied in terms of the major forces operating in his milieu. In the classroom, this means a study of the nature of the task in which the pupil is involved. For example, the task may contain the seeds of acute frustration, lead directly to misbehavior, and a discipline problem begins to grow. The group relationships are analyzed, for this second area may be the generator of forces producing unacceptable behavior. Groups may scapegoat or put strong pressure for certain behavior on members. Thus groups "cause" behavior. Finally, the authority relationship may contain the source of misbehavior, so the adult-child interaction must be scrutinized. A youngster who is rejected or feels he is rejected by the teacher may act out to get a response. There are methods of studying a classroom milieu to better know the play of forces. In addition, more remote forces are studied to fill out the contemporary pressures of family, siblings, neighborhood, etc.

B. These forces are seen as filtering through a particular "self." Forces alone do not produce behavior. They filter through a particular self. Knowledge of self-esteem, self-aspiration, and role helps educators appreciate the nature of the given pupil. School personnel can do much to understand the self-concept of students. From this point of view behavior and misbehavior are the consequence of contemporary forces interacting through the self.

C. Plans for intervention can then be directed both at the nature of the self and at the field of forces. If behavior has to be controlled, it may be possible to get alterations by modulating the tasks assigned, the group involvements, or the authority relationship. In fact, it may be that these stresses, objectively viewed are, in some instances, inducing the undesirable behavior. Through counseling with pupils, it may also be possible to change certain perceptions that need remedy.

It is clear that environmental manipulation may not in itself significantly alter the self, and case history methods as previously indicated, may be needed. But adjusting the forces to the level that the pupil can learn to cope with is in line with current theory of mental health work. The individual who is able to maintain himself within the range of acceptable behavior has already learned coping skills to manage situations. These can be taught to many other students by proper handling at crisis times. Now, schools often handle tense situations in a manner which encourages or consolidates unfortunate coping—we generate anger, we pile on rebuke, we belittle the pupil's intention and capacity to adjust—all in the guise of motivation and support.

Actually, building coping strength does not imply an easy intervention course. It is certainly no easier to accomplish than are changes by traditional therapy, but it does offer the opportunity to work within the scope of school responsibility—dealing in matters of curriculum, pupil-teacher relationship, group life, and so on. Flexible use of teaching personnel, new perceptions regarding evaluation and making the work relevant are all interventions to be considered along with many more. The most significant way to influence behavior and build coping capacity is to expose children to an environment reasonable for them, whatever this may be, and work through the steps until the pupil is able to accommodate to more stress. The preventive potential of this is well delineated in a recent paper by Bower[4] which includes some specific procedures. While the life space approach is not a panacea, it is a new direction proposed by school mental health.

4. Bower, Eli. "The Modification, Mediation and Utilization of Stress During the School Year," *Amer. J. Ortho.*, XXXIV, No. 4, (July 1964), 667–674.

2. School personnel are gradually understanding the new concept of acceptance. One of the most vexing concepts in dealing with discipline is the matter of acceptance. Is it "accepting" a pupil to exclude him from a room or school? To restrict his freedom? To put high demands on him for compliance? To give him a chance to try something we know he will fail? The answer to each statement is both yes and no because psychological acceptance is not a set pattern of adult behavior, but rather depends upon the nature of each child, and what will help him learn. To do this requires "differential diagnosis" looking behind the symptoms to basic patterns of behavior.[5] We accept the child psychologically only when we react in such a manner as best to teach him that which he must learn. All children do not learn to control their impulses in the same way. While there is no place for adult hostility to children, there is a place for differential handling in many other ways. This is an extensive topic. We can only touch on it here, but it is central to the new look in mental hygiene.

For example, an adolescent with a minimum of conscience will exploit permissiveness and thus learn little of how to cope with his impulses from this type of "permissive" acceptance. He needs to know that his environment will always be less rewarding if he misbehaves. He is restricted when he violates others' rights. When gratifications are denied him, however, it is never with hostility. With a youngster of this nature, words are largely wasted: clear action is necessary. He is "accepted" by being restrained. In fact, some children in a crisis may require physical holding, though never hurting.

An anxious child, on the other hand, needs to talk and work his problem through. His "acceptance" follows another pattern even though his behavior may have to be drastically curbed. Piling on pressure for control may encourage some pupils to seek self-punishment as a relief for inner guilt. The variety of patterns of "acceptance," in effect, match the variety of personality patterns found in pupils. To accept the child requires an appreciation of the nature of the pupil's personality as indicated in the case history approach, and then selecting responses which will help him learn necessary conformity. The many faces of acceptance leave no place for a split between counselors who listen (viz., accept) and principals who discipline (viz., punish). The pupil needs unitary handling based upon his true nature.

3. Schools are using new ways of talking with youngsters. Old-style moralizing gets nowhere with most young people today. The need is for an effective way to discuss behavior with pupils. As indicated, traditional therapeutic methods are not suited to teachers and other school personnel.

The life space diagnostic schema has also been the foundation of a new way for teachers to discuss problem situations, called Life Space Interviewing.[6]

Discussion is derived from the actual behavior which has taken place, usually in the presence or at least in the awareness of the adult. This "situation" then becomes the focus for talking through the nature of such behavior even in quite disturbed children. It is a most useful mode of confrontation for discipline situations. Again this is not easy to do, and it does not always bring success even after extensive use, but it is school relevant. Teachers have found it most useful, and, with supervised training, they have been able to develop real skill in such interviewing. Our thesis is simply this: Schools need to break new paths if they are to be effective in handling discipline without resorting to excessive repressive acts. A new mental-hygiene-oriented methodology has already been started. The techniques offer an infusion of control techniques with mental hygiene principles.

5. Lippman, H.S. *Treatment of the Child in Emotional Conflict.* New York: 1962.
6. Redl, Fritz. "The Strategy and Techniques of the Life Space Interview," *Amer. J. Ortho.*, XXIX, No. 1 (January 1959), 1–18.
Morse, W. C. "Training Teachers in Life Space Interviewing," *Amer. J. Ortho.*, XXXIII, No. 4 (July 1963), 727–730.

Father Francis Chiaramonte

THE OTHER SIDE OF THE COIN

Adolescence has always been known to be a time of questioning and inquiry, and today we are even more vitally concerned with the attitudes and behavior of this age group. Since there is a growing problem of violence and protest on the part of teen-agers, including a demand for sexual freedom and independence, psychologists are increasing their concern with this section of our population.

The complex role and responsibility of the parent by the time the child reaches adolescence cannot be overemphasized, and a reevaluation of the important function of the family is badly needed. Parents need suggestions and direction, as well as reinforcement from professionals. Certainly the psychologist is in a key position to aid the parents and the other professionals who deal with this age group. Their search for answers, and their attempt to correct the existing problems often come from the failure of parents to accept responsibility for the child. Teachers and parents are often unaware of the great psychological impact they have on youth by the things they say and do. For this reason, one must make certain that these impressionable youth are surrounded by healthy people who will exert positive influences on them. The adolescent needs group support and he often retreats to his peer environment, one which may have a stronger influence on his actions. But he also continues to be aware of the adult world much as he did as an infant and child.

To show the ultimate harm of early parental neglect in the training of children, Father Chiaramonte deals with the problem of teen-age drinking and mores in this article. He points out that the basic training of children must begin during infancy and continue throughout their development to adulthood. The most important years of influence on the growth of a child are those immediately following birth, during a time of complete dependency. At this time, the parent begins to mold the future behavior of the child. One hopes by the time of adolescence that most of the responsibility for the control of one's behavior has been internalized by the individual, who is, in fact, preparing himself for independent thinking and action.

Teen-agers are not solely to be blamed for their delinquency. Neither can we blame parents alone. Society must take the blame for much of the juvenile delinquency found in our communities. By society, we mean the collective notion of the people who compose it – you and I. We play a major role in the corruption of youth. As members of society, each one of us has the responsibility of creating a healthy atmosphere for the moral growth of our children.

The majority of parents, and all schools and youth organizations in the community, *are* committed to the moral education of our youth. They strive to provide a healthy atmosphere in which children can grow. Parents try to provide their children good examples of behavior. Teachers are conscious of their conduct before their pupils. Youth organizations try to give their members good principles of life.

Unfortunately, this is not enough. Society neglects its responsibility and without the cooperation of society whatever is taught in the home or school is of little consequence.

As members of society every parent, every teacher, every civic leader, every adult in the community must continue to influence teen-agers towards positive goals. This is where we fail.

Adults frequently are caught up in a double standard of life. We propose one standard, we follow another. We preach one thing to be wrong in the home, the school, or the community, and proceed to live according to another set of principles. This double standard, so prevalent today, is a cancer eating away at our youth and causing its moral breakdown. All of us must share this blame.

For example, we are harsh with the rapist, the bankrobber, the murderer, the kidnapper, etc. – and we should be! On the other hand, what attitude do we convey to teens about "lesser" types of crime? Do we condone, either by word or action, the existence of "White Collar Crime"? While we are hard on the bankrobber do we slide over the case of the embezzler? While we scream out for justice in the case of the hit-and-run driver, do we help the speeder get away with his crime? Whenever the question of enforcing the law comes up, are we more concerned with personal influence, "a friend downtown," the "fix," than with justice?

If we must answer yes to these questions, then we are the very people responsible for tearing down our community's moral and civil standards, thereby giving our teens the idea that a certain type of crime, a "White Collar Crime," is all right "if you can get away with it." Is it any wonder then that our teens try to do the same? For even though we never directly admit these crimes are all right, our adult attitude towards them makes our teens feel they are.

Our example wields a far greater influence over teen-agers than our words. As long as we adults allow "White Collar Crimes" to exist and feel that something is wrong and punishable only if we cannot get away with it, then we, the members of society, must assume the responsibility of breaking down the moral backbone of our youth.

Before any of us adults can do anything to rectify our unhealthy influence, which is widespread among teen-agers, we must first identify the problem. To identify a problem at its roots is to initiate a healthy change.

Integrally connected to the wider problem of an unhealthy adult influence on youth is society's concept of the teen-ager. Many adults feel that teen-agers are a plague to local communities and synonymous with trouble. In many different ways they tell teens the adult world is suspicious of them. They "let teens know" they cannot be trusted. They make them feel unwanted. At times they accept them into the adult culture – primarily when it is to the adult's advantage.

Even some parents with teen-age sons or daughters are not exempt from similar *attitudes*. Consequently, instead of adopting an attitude that their teen-ager needs guidance and understanding, they adopt one of distrust. This is why they constantly warn against "doing things." This is why they berate their teen-ager with what will happen if he gets into trouble. In such instances, I feel these parents are so filled with their own anxieties about raising children that their warnings and threats are at best empty and at worst a catalyst for a defensive and hostile attitude of "I'll show you."

These and similar *attitudes* contribute to the lowering of the teen-ager's self-image and can sentence him to a state of ambivalence for the duration of his teen years.

What is happening is that adults who, in the mind of a teen-ager, are mature and well balanced in their judgements, have chosen to judge them, not on the grounds of their individual merits and faults, but collectively on the grounds of the numerous crimes committed by a small number of teen-agers.

In spite of the statistics indicating an increase in crime among teen-agers we must realize that the juvenile delinquent is not the typical teen-ager. Yet, many adults condemn the majority because of the misconduct of the minority. Ask yourself what you really see (what your attitude is) when you meet a couple of teen-agers walking towards you on the street dressed in their latest fashions and perhaps even clowning around. Do you go beyond the clothes and haircuts? Do you see the individual teen-ager for what he is or do you condemn the group because of appearances? Do you automatically see a tough, rowdy, sex-crazy group of kids? Do you see your own or a neighbor's son or daughter who was seriously beaten? Do you see your own teen-age son or daughter with whom you are having serious trouble? Do you see the woman you read about having her purse stolen and being thrown to the sidewalk by a couple of rough teen-age boys? Do you see the únmarried mothers you either know or read about? Perhaps you see your car that was stolen by a couple of boys out for a thrill? What we *see* in these cases mentioned does not matter. It is what we do *not see* that is more important.

Adults often refuse to see each teen-ager as an individual with his own faults for which he is accountable and with his own merits for which he is to be respected. Only by seeing the teen-ager as an individual can we avoid blaming the innocent majority for the crimes of the guilty minority. Anyone who works with teens can tell you that this adult attitude is extremely discouraging to the teen-ager himself. A teen-ager's sense of fairness and honesty is much more acute than is an adult's. He can put up with almost anything much more easily than with unfairness. An adult attitude that insists on blaming every teen-ager for the crimes of the few, regardless of the individual's worth, is being unfair to the millions of teens who try their best and who have a right to resent being pegged unfairly.

To further accentuate the bad adult influence on teens, consider for a moment the teen-age drinking problem.

This is a serious problem in our society. The reasons for it are as varied as our teen-agers. Some admit doing it for "kicks," because they like the taste, to feel grown up, or to be accepted by their friends. Others admit to it because of adult example. This last reason, by far the most serious, is due to adult irresponsibility. Unless this adult influence is eliminated, the efforts put forth by schools and other responsible organizations to stop teen-age drinking will be ineffective.

At parties we find adults, even relatives, prodding teen-agers to take a drink. Adults boast about the great time they had getting "loaded." Many judge the success of a party by the amount of liquor consumed. They pass these standards on to our teens. We even find parents encouraging their teen-agers to take a few drinks, justifying it on the principle that they might as well get used to it now as later.

No wonder we have the problem of teen-age drinking! Adults, either directly – by encouraging it – or indirectly – by example – put psychologically immature youngsters in a position they cannot manage.

Teens cannot buy liquor without adult aid. In many instances, an irresponsible friend who is "of age" buys it for them. Or some "alky" buys it for the price of a cheap drink. In rarer cases, bartenders are irresponsible and do not check the identification of a customer who seems to be under age.

In all these instances immature and irresponsible adults are directly encouraging the continuation of juvenile delinquency. For proof, look at the automobile accidents, the unwed mothers, the attempted rapes, the car thefts, etc., attributed to the influence of alcohol. Many of the teen-agers concerned would never have been "brave" enough to commit these crimes if it had not been for the "confidence" alcohol gave them.

It is up to the mature adults of each local community to take charge of the situation and help our schools and our law-enforcing agencies. Reveal the names of the adults buying or selling alcohol to our teen-agers to the proper authorities, such as the juvenile officers. Take precautions that will prevent your own teen-ager from buying drinks. Some responsible liquor stores have gone so far as to hire their own police officer to stop any suspicious adults from buying liquor for teen-agers.

Before we can curb the drinking problem among our teen-agers, we must be aware that good cooperation is necessary among the four main branches of authority: the parents, the schools, the police, and the judiciary. But before this cooperation can be possible and effective, each adult in the community must see it as *his* responsibility to do something about the problem.

As I have said in the beginning of this article, I feel that much of the blame for teen-age crime and delinquency must be placed at the foot of adult society. I do not intend to change this position by what follows. However, I feel that since parents play such an important role in our adult society, something must be said directly to them.

Parents with delinquent teen-agers frequently try to escape the serious predicament they find themselves in by asking for help too late. Their plea generally takes one of the following forms: "What can I do?" "How can I get through to him?" "What am I doing wrong?" "Where have I failed?"

Parents failing to seek help expect a quick remedy—a prescription guaranteed to cure any teen-age ill. Candidly, there is no magic formula for teen-age ills. This applies especially when parents have been negligent of the child's training throughout his younger years.

These parents, while their children were developing physically, mentally, and emotionally during the formative years, should have adopted an attitude of preventive discipline.

Unfortunately, industry displays more wisdom in promoting production than some parents do in training their children. Actually, industry spends millions of dollars annually to keep machines running. On the other hand, little money or training has gone into educating these same machinists in the specialized "art" of rearing children. Neglected children break down as quickly as neglected machinery. Industry takes great pains to establish an intricate system of preventive maintenance. Even a less efficient business-man knows it is far more profitable to prevent a breakdown of machinery than to lose production time in repairing machines.

Parents deeply interested in their children conscientiously practice preventive discipline. Understanding and confidence have developed from the child's earliest years. Responsible parents always encourage their children to share their problems with them. They also insist upon their children being home at a reasonable hour. By supervising their children's study, reading, television programs, and recreational activities in general, alert parents are aware of the ways in which their children spend time. Interested parents foster wholesome friendships and try to prohibit their youngsters from patronizing questionable as well as undesirable "hangouts."

Parents must begin training the child during his infancy and continue unrelentingly through his childhood and adolescent years. Neglecting an early start in molding a child's character and in developing his attitudes is bound to produce an undisciplined, uncontrollable, maladjusted individual.

The parents who have followed a consistent training program for their children have by far a greater assurance of the successful realization of their aims and goals. On the contrary, parents who have neglected to train their children, either out of misguided love or through some faults of their own are strongly counseled to seek help through their schools or other professional services. It is never too late, but the chances for success are lessened in proportion to the extent of negligence during the formative years.

It is one thing merely to tear down, but it is something else to tear down with the intention of rebuilding. Since I have spent quite a bit of space tearing down attitudes and opinions I feel the responsibility of offering certain positive elements for your consideration which may, after sufficient reflection and discussion, contribute to the rebuilding of more positive attitudes towards our teen-agers. For it is my contention that a series of positive attitudes on the part of adults will evolve into a series of wholesome influences upon our teens.

The young people of our nation, represented for the most part by our teen-agers, have their own dignity which is anchored in their generosity. It is the responsibility of adults actually to honor and respect these youngsters of our country for their extreme generosity.

The respect of a noble human trait is not something foreign to Americans. Throughout our heritage we have honored and respected man because of what he contributed to the progress of our nation. We honor and respect the Fathers of the American Revolution because of what they gave us. We honor and respect our writers for what they added to our culture. We honor and respect our scientists; we even honestly envy them for the technological advances they have made possible. We cherish our astronauts because of their daring deeds in space.

Therefore, why cannot we cherish and respect our own teen-agers for what they are contributing to America and in particular, to our own community?

Perhaps the answer lies in the old adage: "Familiarity breeds contempt." In other words, we live in such close contact with the young people of our country that we begin to take them for granted, and once something is taken for granted it no longer holds its proper place in our hearts.

The generosity of our young people has never been more evident in any period of American history. The last thing in the mind of any young man or woman today is to waste his life. He is searching for a worthwhile cause to embrace or a leader to follow. For example, consider the tremendous response our youngsters gave to the late President Kennedy. When he appealed to the youth of America to cooperate with him in his Peace Corps project, Washington was flooded with requests for further information and application blanks a few days after the announcement.

The majority of teens today are very much concerned with dedicating themselves to some worthwhile profession—religion, medicine, nursing, law, business—and at the same time they are seriously pondering the major walks of life through which they will fulfill their aims: namely, a ministerial life, a married life, or a single life.

A youngster who thinks like this is not some empty-headed scatterbrain with no regard for the future. There is no justification for the cry: "What is the future generation going to be like if our teen-agers continue the way they are?" These youths today are serious. They want to give themselves completely to some noble cause in the interest of mankind. Consequently, if we honor and respect scientists, astronauts, writers, etc., for their deeds on behalf of a country or city, why cannot we honor and respect the average teen-ager for seeking to dedicate his whole life to some worthwhile cause?

Furthermore, teen-agers perform a great service to the country by just being around. They serve as a check on the morals of the country. They are in a very real sense the "Watchdogs of Adults." To understand this, all that teachers, parents, or those honest adults associated in any way with the youth of our community need to do is search their own experiences to find out how often they have changed a plan of action because of the young ones associated with them.

How often did you ever wish no "kids" were around you so you could begin or continue a disreputable conversation? How often have you decided not to drink at all or at least not too much because of the children? Have you ever decided not to divorce or separate because of the children? How often have the children brought Mom and Dad closer together?

If you must answer affirmatively to one or more of the above questions, you owe respect and honor to some of the youths of our country.

Teen-agers' contributions do not stop with merely curbing an adult's moral life. Their forthright honesty and sincerity compels them to speak out bravely, even though at times, recklessly, against the injustices perpetrated by adults. Adults find this hard to accept, but once they bring themselves to separate what was said from who said it they frequently must retrace their footsteps admitting they are wrong. In such instances we can thank teen-agers for being our conscience thereby checking our own moral direction.

We have so much to be proud of in our teens that we should spend more of the short time they are with us respecting them rather than rejecting them. When we criticize them for irresponsible and flighty behavior, keep in mind all those thousands of teen-agers who belong to the 4 H clubs, Junior Achievement, Scouts, etc., who are already accepting responsibility and training themselves to accept more. When we criticize their wild driving, be conscious of that large group of careful and highly skilled teen-age drivers who are aware of the tremendous responsibility of driving. When we are inconvenienced by the sounds coming from healthy teen-agers playing in a nearby lot, let us respect their needs and not call the police in order to quiet the neighborhood.

Remember that we can bring out whichever qualities in a teen-ager we want. If we constantly criticize him and tear him down unfairly, we will begin to make him feel mistrusted, and he will despair of growing up. Thus we will force him to join the very mob from which we wish to protect him. If we respect him for what he is — a generous individual in search of a goal — we will encourage him and successfully bring him to fulfillment.

Part V

APPLICATION OF LEARNING THEORY TO BEHAVIOR PROBLEMS

The search continues for ways to motivate children to want to learn, to grow, to adjust, to succeed. Because children are more alike than they are different, general statements can be made concerning which methods are most effective. Rewards were long ago found to be more effective than any variety or combination of disciplines or deprivations. However, questions arise as to how to determine meaningful rewards and how to adjust the rewards to the variations one finds within a group. What is meaningful and rewarding to one person may not necessarily be so to another.

Children with problems so severe that they are labeled as "behavior problems" or juvenile delinquents pose even more serious questions for the psychologist and educator. Methods that motivate and help control one group in a classroom of average, normal children often are not effective at all among the special groups of children with unique personality maladjustments. In some extreme cases, such children have to be removed from the regular class situation and placed in special rooms or groups within the school or sent to separate schools. This solution may not always be best for the child concerned, as he might profit from contact with normal children. Sometimes, however, his influence on them and the school situation may be so disruptive that in the best interest of the normal children it is wise to make the separation.

Taking a cue from the experiences of many parents, teachers have come to realize that the most rewarding and effective thing they can give a child is their attention, concern, and love.

A child reared by healthy and intelligent parents has learned in the home, even before starting school, the importance of love, and has developed the potential for accepting it and using it to meet his basic psychological needs. As he matured in the home, he learned that he first wanted and received recognition from his parents, and then gradually began to recognize that there were other sources of affection. At first, his immediate family and then relatives and friends could also give him the love essential to his happiness.

By the time a child reaches school, he has learned the subtle cues by which love, recognition, and acceptance are indicated by others; teachers can use these subtle indicators to reward the child and thus direct and guide his behavior. The difficult or problem-prone child either has never generalized his ability to recognize signs of love and approval, that is, he has been so psychologically damaged that he cannot perceive them and cannot accept them. Such children then need special care and attention. Their needs are found to vary in degree and type from the average child, and their potential for satisfying their unusual needs is often warped and damaged. Until the school is able to analyze children with special problems and adjust school programs not only to meet the needs of such children but also to help them learn to adjust to their unusual needs, there will be trouble in classrooms which annoy and upset the other children, distract the teacher from her plans, disrupt the learning progress, and in general cause confusion that will slow down the progress of all the children. Behavior problems cannot and should not be ignored for their own sake but must be resolved in a way that promotes the welfare of all children.

Carl A. Clark and Herbert J. Walberg

THE EFFECTS OF INCREASED REWARDS ON READING ACHIEVEMENT AND SCHOOL ATTITUDES OF POTENTIAL DROPOUTS[1]

Doctors Clark and Walberg's report on the effects of immediate rewards on achievement and attitudes has some very practical suggestions.

Learning results from fixation of responses which reduce one's needs, and is more apt to occur if a child is rewarded in a meaningful way, on a regular basis, and if the reward is clearly related to the behavior one is trying to encourage.

Teachers and parents for years have been told by psychologists what many of them had already found by experience with the children; rewards are more apt to bring about learning than anything else and are much more effective than punishment. But many teachers and parents continue to fail to heed this fact. Doctors Clark and Walberg have demonstrated in a classroom setting (rather than in the usual animal laboratory) that this principle of reward is the most effective motivation for learning. Perhaps this approach in a familiar classroom setting will be more effective in convincing teachers and parents of the wisdom of rewarding children for the learning behavior one wishes to encourage.

For a number of years we have been undertaking experiments on rewards and learning in the classroom, in which we have been assigning children and classrooms at random to experimental and control conditions. We have found the classroom to be a satisfactory laboratory for learning experiments, particularly in classes of slow-learning and so-called mentally retarded pupils, where there is more homogeneity of ability, and where there are interesting research questions concerning special methods of teaching.

The classroom can be made similar to a laboratory situation in several respects:

1. Temperature, light, and air are controlled.
2. All the subjects at all times are subject to observation while they are in the classroom.
3. The selection of subjects is controlled and randomly assigned to treatment.
4. The independent and dependent variables can be chosen and the independent variables can be administered in any amount.
5. Records of experimental procedures may be obtained.

For these reasons, it should not be necessary to say very often: "The laboratory results have not been tested under classroom conditions," or "It may work in the laboratory but not in the classroom." When there is greater recognition that the classroom can be an excellent laboratory for learning experiments, when rigorous experimental conditions are permitted and encouraged, hopefully the progress of psychological research and educational practice will be accelerated, and there will be less reliance on pedagogical philosophies and methods which are subjectively based upon authority or fad.

STUDY 1

Towards these ends, one of our first experiments was the controlled use of secondary reinforcement in the learning of spelling (3). The motivation was competition, one of the strongest learned drives in humans. The

1. Dr. Concetta V. Romanow participated in guiding studies 1, 2, and 3. Studies 4, 5, 6, and 7 were conducted within the Chicago Project of The Great Cities School Improvement Program, which was sponsored by the Ford Foundation and administered by the Chicago Public Schools.

children had been classified as mentally handicapped, for whom academic competition is usually unrewarded. Such motivation has not often been used with the so-called mentally handicapped in academic situations, since it is often assumed that these children have had their learned competitive drives for scholastic success extinguished, or that competition would be even more defeating.

Five classrooms of educable mentally handicapped (EMH) children in the Chicago Public Schools took part in this study. Ten children were selected at random within each classroom. Five were chosen at random from each class to receive the experimental treatment. The subjects were assigned to conditions entirely at random, and the ages and IQ's for experimental and control groups were very similar: the mean age for experimental group was 13 years 6 months: IQ, 70; and the average number of semesters in EMH class was 5.44. The mean for control group was 13 years 7 months: IQ, 69; and the number of semesters in EMH classes, 5.92. Twice each week the experimental subjects took part in a spelldown while the control subjects had regularly conducted spelling lessons, consisting of routine drill and copying. The reinforcement of winning in the spelldown was controlled so that every child in the experimental groups had successes.

To assure distribution of rewards to all students, easier words were occasionally given to poorer spellers and harder words to better spellers. The experimental group gained over twice as much as the control group in number of words correctly spelled on a post-test given at the end of the semester (significant at 5 per cent level).

This study illustrates the use of a particular reward (success in competition) based on aroused competitive motivation—a secondary drive. It indicates that competition should be considered as motivation for even so-called mentally retarded pupils provided all are to have some success.

STUDY 2

Another experiment, carried out by Dawson (2), was a study of praise given by a teacher to mentally handicapped pupils. The principal idea was to control the amount and distribution of praise given to the children in order to determine its effect on verbal learning. In this experiment both a primary and an advanced EMH classroom were used. In each group there were exactly 16 children. For four weeks the teacher gave increased praise to a random half of each class. There was no indication to any of the children that they were participants in an experiment and no changes apparent to the children were made in the regular classroom procedures. The teacher praised all of the children at least as much as usual and gave extra praise for the experimental subjects in ways that would make detection by any of the children—experimental or control—unlikely. As a usual practice children frequently left the room for special instruction, errands, or counseling. These occasions were used by the teacher to give additional praise to the experimental children. She also praised the children by writing comments on test papers and homework.

After four weeks, the post-test was given, and the gain in the number of words correctly spelled by the control groups, primary and advanced, was found to average between seven and eight. The highly praised children, however, gained an average of 16 words, a definitely significant greater gain (p=.05) statistically and educationally. There was no significant interaction of initial ability, primary and advanced, with conditions of praise.

STUDY 3

Rigorous secondary reinforcement of classroom verbal responses may not only result in direct learning but the concomitant learning of other responses that occur simultaneously with the response being reinforced. Some of these coincident responses are "attitude," "level of aspiration," a tendency to respond to the teacher and to the on-going classroom procedure, and, very generally, whatever responses that occur frequently and coincidentally with the specific dependent variable. The cues produced by some of these responses might also operate as secondary drives and thus provide further bases for secondary reinforcements in classroom learning situations.

In a study of several of these attitudinal variables (1), 64 children in two fourth-grade classrooms were randomly assigned to experimental and control groups within each class. They were aged from 8 to 11; average, 9.4 years: the average Kuhlmann-Anderson IQ was 95.5. All lived in a low-rent public housing community on Chicago's southwest side; the median family income of the residents was $2,920 per year. Forty-three per cent of the families in the community received public welfare assistance.

The experimental variable was praise administered by the teacher. All children got at least the normal amount of praise, and the experimental subjects received a much greater amount of praise per child. Half of each group (randomly assigned) were of the same sex.

There were five dependent variables. One was vocational level of aspiration as defined by a test constructed for a thesis. There were separate comparable forms for boys and girls. A second dependent variable was a word-making task, in which the subjects were to form as many words as possible from each of a given set of longer words. A level of aspiration score was also obtained for performance on this task. Third was dart throwing at a target; level of aspiration scores for these tasks was another dependent variable. All of these variables were measured before and after the experimental period.

During the experiment school work was conducted as usual, but increased praise was administered to children of the experimental group. The children were unaware that an experiment was taking place, and they did not have any reason to expect that the dependent variable tasks would be administered again.

Analysis of variance showed that the high praise group gained significantly more than the control groups in level of vocational aspiration. In fact, there was practically no change in the control group, while the high praise group raised their sights much higher in their future vocational expectations. There was no significant interaction with sex, i.e., the boys gained about the same as girls.

The same results were obtained for aspiration on both the word-making task and the dart throwing. The highly praised children significantly improved their scores on the word-making task as compared to the controls, and, again, there was practically no change for the control children. On actual scores for dart throwing, however, there was no significantly greater change for the experimental subjects though the mean change for the experimental group was slightly greater. The latter result is not surprising since there was no interpolated dart-throwing practice and since this skill is much less related to the interpolated classroom activities than the word-making.

The study, in summary, showed that the effects of reinforcement in a regular classroom situation will generalize to attitudes and also to skills not usually studied in class. Rewarded success in regular work in class may therefore make for greater success in future vocational work and even for success in physical activity. We hasten to point out, however, that since our subjects were tested in classrooms by teachers, more research is necessary to test the generality of the effects of teachers' praise on behavior outside the school.

STUDY 4

But will increased rewards outside the classroom, such as in the home, generalize attitudes toward the classroom or the teacher? To study this question, we administered a teacher attitude scale (developed by Dr. Benjamin D. Wright and colleagues at the University of Chicago) to 200 children, 11 to 13 years of age, in special classes for slow learners. The teachers were asked not to be present when the scale was administered, and the pupils were assured that none of the teachers or school administrators would be given the results for any pupil. The parents of the children were then contacted and asked if they would participate in a home quiz program with their children, for which we would furnish the materials.

Some 60 parents indicated initial interest in participating, but only 40 followed through to the point of commencing actual participation. These parents were assigned to two groups, using a table of random numbers, one group being the control. The control parents were told that since all who offered could not participate at once, they could take part in the study in the following semester.

The parents in the experimental group read the questions to their children and then immediately informed them when they got the right answer, which was given on the question sheet. The questions were designed by the writers to be of easy to moderate difficulty levels. Thus the children were frequently reinforced during the twice-weekly sessions with their parents. Each week the parents sent the two question sheets back, with checkmarks indicating the responses of their children.

Occasionally some of the parents would lapse in their sessions with their children. When this happened, and they did not respond to a follow-up letter, they were visited by a counselor. The final count of those in full participation to the end of the experiment was 14 for the experimental group. One pupil was not available for the final testing in the control group, leaving 19.

At the end of the fall term all 200 pupils were given the teacher attitude scale again. The over-all result was a significantly less fa-

vorable attitude toward their teachers. The control group loss in teacher attitude score was very close to that of the total group. The children of the experimental group, however, showed a large statistically significant gain. Reinforcement by parents in the home in connection with a school-like quiz session, therefore, apparently helps create a better attitude toward the teachers in school. This study also indicates that in the absence of a stepped-up reward program by the parents or teacher, there may be a gradual deterioration of the pupils' liking for the teaching during the school term.

STUDY 5

In a correlational study of six classrooms of about 20 students each, at the same school as used in Study 4, students in an educational psychology course observed the recorded rewards and reproofs given by the teacher throughout the semester. There was a low correlation, 16, between the child's initial rating of his parents at the beginning of the semester and total rewards received by the child during the semester. The correlation between total rewards and the child's rating of his parents at the end of the semester was .41 (a difference between ratings significant at the .05 per cent level). The more highly rewarded children tended to have favorable attitudes toward the parent. There is reason to believe, therefore, that for children like these, generally slow learners, praise from the teacher at school may improve the attitude toward the parent. This complements the finding of the previous experiment that working with parents on school-related quizzes improves attitudes of the children toward teachers.

STUDY 6

What effect will rewarding children have on the teachers who give the rewards? The one study we made that has some bearing on this question does not give a clear-cut answer. Five teachers each had two randomly assigned classes in a summer reading program. Each teacher was asked to present extra rewards in the way of praise and comments on papers to one of the two classes – which was again randomly determined by the experimenters – for each teacher. The teachers also kept a daily tabulation of types of behavior of each pupil. The behaviors were classified as positive, e.g., "asks questions about classwork" and "volunteers answer to question," and negative, e.g., "misbehaves" and "not working on assignment." The experiment continued for three weeks. The distribution in experimental and control groups of positive assessment as compared to negative deviated very far from chance expectations (beyond the 1 per cent level). The experimental pupils had more than five times as many positive marks as the control and only half as many negative.

This study indicates that teachers tend to rate those pupils more highly when they have rewarded them more. Possibly the rewarded pupils behave better, thus contributing to a more favorable attitude toward the pupil; but it is also possible that the fact of rewarding improves the attitude of the rewarder to the subject even apart from responses made by the subject. This point requires more investigation. In any case, the fact that rewarding increases a favorable attitude to the subject on the part of the rewarder seems definitely established.

STUDY 7

Perhaps the most important factor in the application of secondary reinforcement in classroom learning is the systematization of the distribution and measurement of the rewards. In the regular classroom rewards are given to pupils continuously throughout the day. But often they are a response on the part of the teacher to rewards the teacher receives from the pupils through their meeting teacher expectations of behavior. A vicious circle is thus set up between the teacher and a certain number of pupils who are meeting the teacher's desires for achievement and who are therefore being rewarded, and therefore achieving more. Other pupils are achieving less and therefore being rewarded less or not at all, and thus are achieving still less or not at all. The pupils who really need rewards the most are the misbehaving or non-behaving, non-achieving pupils. The rewards they seem to get the most come from the attention they get for misbehaving or from doing poor quality school work, and these, therefore, are the behaviors that are being reinforced. They are really being taught to misbehave and do poor school work.

It is necessary to break these vicious circles through carefully planned reward systems for continuous application throughout the school life of every child. One might think that such a planned reward system would make for a mechanical classroom situation lacking in spontaneity. In our experiments we have found the reverse to be the case. This was shown not only by the measurements of attitudes of pupils and teachers, but in the statements made by teachers participating in the experiments. They were, with very few exceptions, highly enthusiastic about the reward systems, and they often referred to the increased eagerness for participation in learning by the pupils. Such was the case even in one of our more mechanically contrived reward systems, used in an experiment now to be described.

In this study individual cards were given daily to each pupil, each card containing sequentially numbered squares which the pupil could circle when rewarded and told to do so by the teacher. The cards were collected at the end of each period and the number of rewards for each pupil tallied. In order to help control the possibility that a pupil could mark his card when he was not receiving rewards, the pupils were given special blue pencils with blue-colored "leads" which they were to pick up and use only when they were told to circle a number after being praised. Numbers circled with their ordinary pencils would not count, and it would be fairly obvious if a pupil picked up and used the special blue pencil— obvious to the teacher and to the other pupils.

A special problem with the use of the blue pencil and card reward recording system was the possible "gadget effect." But as this effect in itself contributed a reward, there was not much of a problem since we were more concerned with the fact of a reward than the type of reward. We did two things, however, to lessen and to control for a "gadget effect" and for the so-called "Hawthorne effect." One was to have both the experimental and control groups use the cards for tallying rewards, and the other was to have both groups go through a control period of several weeks during which time the novelty effect could wear off.

The dependent variable was reading achievement in this experiment. When pre- and post-test scores are used over a comparatively short time interval, several problems are introduced into the analysis: there are effects of regression toward the mean, item memory, and practice to confuse the results. It was decided, therefore, that the main analysis would be based on a single reading test given at the end of the experiment. Some control over initial individual differences would be attained by using 10's as a control variable in an analysis of covariance procedure.

The experiment took place in a Chicago school located on the southwest side of the inner city, an area consisting largely of slum dwellings and public housing apartments, populated by Negroes, many of them fairly recent migrants from Southern states. The neighborhood is characterized by low standards of living and high rates of unemployment, crime, delinquency, and of school dropouts.

The children in the experiment were from 10 to 14 years of age and were from one to three years behind the typical achievement grade levels. They were potential dropouts selected for special training in the Chicago Great Cities School Improvement Program.

The children were assigned on a random basis to nine classes in an after-school remedial reading program with 10 to 15 in each class and a total of 110 in the experiment.

At the beginning of the experiment all the teachers and children were asked to follow the same instructions. Each child received the specially prepared tally card which we have described, and the teachers were asked to distribute the praise rewards so that each child, even the very slow ones, would get at least several each day. After the teacher made a rewarding remark, she directed the rewarded child to make a tally mark on his card on a list of numbers, from 1 to 50. The child made the marks sequentially, beginning with number one. At the end of the class session he wrote down the total number of tally marks (therefore of rewards) he had received for the day. The teachers checked the card markings for accuracy, and sent the cards to the experimenters after each class.

After six sessions the reward rates per child and per teacher appeared to stabilize, and the five teachers (previously randomly determined) of the experimental groups (randomly constituted) were confidentially asked to double or triple the number of rewards while the four teachers of the control groups were asked to "keep up the good work." After these requests were made, large increments appeared in the number of tally marks on cards for the experimental group while the numbers for the control group remained at approximately the same levels.

At the end of the second three-week period, the 62 children in the experimental groups and the 48 in the control groups took the Science Research Associates Reading Test (Form A, grades 4 to 6). The first three sections of this test were administered and scored, using the standard directions. The mean total score for the experimental groups was 31.62, with a standard deviation of 7.43, and the mean for the control groups was 26.86, with a standard deviation of 3.60. The analysis of variance for the unadjusted raw scores produced an F-ratio of 9.52 (significant at the one per cent level).

In the covariance analysis with Kuhlmann-Anderson IQ's as the control variable, the F-ratio was 7.90 (still significant at the one per cent level). The smaller F-ratio for adjusted scores resulted, even though the error mean square was smaller, because of a slightly higher mean IQ for the experimental group. The mean IQ for the experimental group was 92.05, and for the control group, 90.73. This difference was not statistically significant.

A scale designed to measure the pupils' attitudes toward the teacher was also administered with the teachers not present. The pupils of the experimental groups showed more favorable attitudes toward their teachers than those of the control groups. This result is in line with other reward studies we have conducted, which also show that highly rewarded pupils have more favorable attitudes toward school and school materials, and that rewards tend to raise their levels of aspiration for future goals.

The teachers in the experiment were questioned about the reward system. All stated their pupils were enthusiastic about it, though one teacher said, "At first they thought the idea of circles funny; later they were competing for circles." In response to the question concerning generation of enthusiasm, most of the teachers went beyond mere affirmation to say "very much," "a great deal," "to the extent that we were late leaving at times."

The teachers did, though, have reservations about the use of circling as a continual classroom method. Indeed, we are well aware of the need for investigation of possible satiation effects of such a method. The main points here, however, are:

1) That the use of a systematic distribution of praise apparently will not lead to a dry classroom atmosphere devoid of enthusiasm, and
2) that increased, distributed praise leads to increased achievement.

CONCLUSIONS

We have long known that rewards enhance learning, but that is not the issue. What is necessary is that our knowledge be applied systematically, continually, and consistently. A great deal of research is necessary to find out how to do these things. We believe that we now have enough knowledge and evidence of its effects in application that we are able to make systematic use of this knowledge. For example, when we ask teachers to apply rewards systematically, their pupils show gains such as have been described; and as a rule the teachers and pupils are delighted. The teacher must increase the number of rewards and see that they are evenly distributed, as well as being alert to the optimum time to reward a particular child. The pupils, too, are more alert and work harder. But when an experiment ends under the pressure of time, curriculum, and tradition, application ends also and pupils and teachers revert to previous routines. The alternative is the dismal prospect of leaving the systematic application of rewards entirely to teaching machines.

The implication is clear. All teachers need to be trained in the systematic application of rewards, and their ability to use this approach should be considered a basic professional skill subject to assessment. There is too much left to chance when we rely on those things that we often assume just happen in teachers—such as insight, empathy, warmth, knack, and so on. Also, if we are going to speed up the educational process in our fast-changing, complex society, extend it effectively to more persons, so that it will include the so-called slow learners and the mentally retarded, and make the process more pleasant for all concerned, it is necessary that an explicit system of reward applications be expected of all teachers in all school systems. It is also of the greatest importance to us that research on reinforcement variables in classroom teaching not only be continued but be greatly expanded.

K. Daniel O'Leary and Wesley C. Becker

BEHAVIOR MODIFICATION OF AN ADJUSTMENT CLASS: A TO EN REINFORCEMENT PROGRAM

What meaningful and satisfactory reinforcement systems for children prove effective to motivate learning and to bring about desired behavioral changes? This question has been carefully studied by O'Leary and Becker. Their research may be a partial answer to the parent who questions whether he should give money as a reward for good marks or satisfactory behavior. Some "back-up" reinforcers such as candy to a small child may be even more effective than money, depending on the momentary deprivation of the child.

The ideal plan, as studies by these authors show, was to transfer control to the more conventional classroom rewards (teacher attention, praise, and grades) with less frequent use of the back-up reinforcers. In any case, the introduction of the token reinforcement program brought about an abrupt reduction in deviant behavior. The suggested use of token reinforcers as used in this experimental study might well be tried both in schools and at home.

Praise, teacher attention, stars, and grades provide adequate incentive for most pupils to behave in a socially approved way. However, for some students — notably school dropouts, aggressive children, and retarded children — these methods simply do not work. Nonetheless, where the usual methods of social approval have failed, the use of token reinforcement systems has proven effective (Birnbrauer, Bijou, Wolf, and Kidder, 1965; Birnbrauer and Lawler, 1965; Birnbrauer, Wolf, Kidder, and Tague, 1965; and Quay, Werry, McQueen, and Sprague, 1966). Token reinforcers are tangible objects or symbols which in and of themselves probably have little or no reinforcing power. However, they attain reinforcing power by being exchanged for a variety of other objects which are reinforcers, such as candy and trinkets. Such items which are used in exchange for tokens are called back-up reinforcers. Tokens acquire generalized reinforcing properties because they frequently have been paired with many different reinforcers. The generalized reinforcer is especially useful since it is effective regardless of the momentary condition of the organism. For example, the effectiveness of money as a reinforcer is less influenced by the momentary deprivation of the organism than is the effectiveness of candy.

The generalized reinforcers such as the verbal responses "That's right" or "Good" and token reinforcers such as grades usually are effective in establishing academic or appropriate classroom behavior. However, these generalized social reinforcers did not maintain appropriate behavior of the children in this study. In fact, their teacher noted that prior to the introduction of the token system, being called "bad" served to increase the children's inappropriate behavior. "They had the attitude that it was smart to be called bad. . . . When I tried to compliment them or tell them that they had done something well, they would look around the room and make faces at each other." It is a moot question whether the poor academic behavior of these children was caused by their disruptive social behavior or vice versa. It was obvious, however, that the disruptive behaviors had to be eliminated before the teacher could administer an academic program.

Although classroom token reinforcement programs have proven effective in modifying behavior, the pupil-teacher ratio has usually been small. For example Birnbrauer's (1965) classroom of 17 retarded pupils had four

From *Exceptional Children*, Vol.33, No. 9, May 1967, pages 637–642. Reprinted by permission of the authors and the publisher.

teachers who were in the classroom at all times. Quay (1966) had one teacher in a behavior modification classroom of five children. Therefore, one purpose of this study was to devise a token reinforcement program which could be utilized by one teacher in an average classroom. A second purpose of this study was to see if a token system could be gradually withdrawn without an increase in disruptive behavior. Our plan was to transfer control to teacher attention, praise, and grades with less frequent exchange of back-up reinforcers.

METHOD

The subjects for this study were 17 nine-year-old children described as "emotionally disturbed." Fifteen of the 17 children were Negro. They had IQ's (Kuhlmann-Anderson) ranging from 80–107. They were placed in the adjustment class primarily because they exhibited undesirable classroom behaviors such as temper tantrums, crying, uncontrolled laughter and fighting. The children were in the classroom throughout the day with the exception of some remedial speech and reading work.

Observation

Although the token reinforcement system was in effect for the whole class, observation focused on the eight most disruptive children. The observers were instructed never to talk to the children, nor were they to make any differential responses to the children. In short, the aim was to have the raters function in a manner such that they would become merely a part of the classroom environment and thus not have an effect on the children's behavior.

Observations of the children's deviant behaviors were made by two students who were in the classroom from 12:30 to 2:10 three days a week. A third student made reliability checks two days a week. Among the behaviors recorded as deviant were the fol-

lowing: pushing, answering without raising one's hand, chewing gum, eating, name-calling, making disruptive noise, and talking. Each student observed four children in random order for 22 minutes each session. Observations were made on a 20 second observe, 10 second record basis. Deviant behaviors were recorded on the observation sheets during the last ten seconds of each 30 second interval. While the observations were being made, the children had three structured activities: listening to records or stories, arithmetic, and group reading. During these activities instruction was directed to the whole classroom and the children were expected to be quiet and in their seats.

Base Period

The teacher was told to handle the children as she would normally. The aim of the base period was simply to obtain data which reflected the frequency of pupil behavior under usual classroom procedures. The observers were in the classroom for three weeks before any baseline data were obtained. At first the children would walk up to the observers and try to initiate conversation with them. However, the observers consistently ignored the children, and the children's approach behaviors diminished. Thus, it is likely that initial "show-off" behavior was reduced before baseline measures were obtained.

The average inter-observer reliability for individual children during the four-week base period, calculated on the basis of exact agreement with respect to time interval and category of behavior, ranged from 75% to 100% agreement (Table 1). A perfect agreement was scored if both observers recorded the same behavior in a 20 second interval. The reliabilities were calculated by dividing the number of perfect agreements by the number of different responses observed. The percent of deviant behavior for a child on any day was calculated by dividing the number of intervals in which one or more deviant

TABLE 1

AVERAGE RELIABILITIES

| | Base Period | | Token Reinforcement Period | |
Subject	% Perfect Agreement	# Reliability Checks	% Perfect Agreement	# Reliability Checks
1	85	3	88	9
2	82	2	94	9
3	92	3	96	9
4	100	1	93	5
5	77	3	87	9
6	75	4	87	9
7	80	4	80	8
8	75	3	88	8

behaviors occurred by the number of observed intervals for that day.

Token Reinforcement Period

On the first day of the token period the experimenter placed the following instructions on the blackboard: In Seat, Face Front, Raise Hand, Working, Pay Attention, and Desk Clear. The experimenter then explained the token procedure to the children. The tokens were ratings placed in small booklets on each child's desk. The children were told that they would receive ratings from 1–10 and that the ratings would reflect the extent to which they followed the instructions. The points or ratings could be exchanged for a variety of back-up reinforcers. The back-up reinforcers consisted of small prizes such as candy, pennants, comics, perfume, and kites. The prizes ranged in value from one cent to 29 cents, and the total cost of the back-up reinforcers used during the two-month token procedure was $80.76. Thus, all the pupils received reinforcers in the same manner during class while individual preferences were considered by providing a variety of

items for exchange. Having a large variety of back-up reinforcers available for exchange maximized the probability that at least one of them would be a reinforcer for a given child at a given time.

The experimenter repeated the instructions at the beginning of the token period each day for one week and made his own ratings of the children in order to give the teacher some norm upon which to base her ratings. It was the teacher, however, who placed the ratings in the children's booklets during the short pause at the end of a lesson period. The ratings reflected the extent to which the child engaged in the task appropriate behaviors listed on the blackboard. Where possible these ratings also reflected the accuracy of the child's arithmetic work.

The number of ratings made each day gradually decreased from five to three, and the number of points required to obtain a prize gradually increased. For the first three days the tokens were exchanged for back-up reinforcers at the end of the token period. For the next four days the points were accumulated for two days and were exchanged for back-up reinforcers at the end of the token period on the second day. Then followed a three-day delay between the receipt of token and back-up reinforcers which lasted for 15 days. Four-day delay was employed for the remaining 24 school days. During the three- and four-day-delay periods tokens were exchanged for back-up reinforcers at the end of the school day. By requiring more appropriate behavior to receive a prize and increasing the delay of reinforcement it was hoped that transfer of control from the token reinforcers to the more traditional methods of teacher praise and attention would be facilitated. The teacher was instructed with regard to changes in the number of ratings, the delay of back-up reinforcement, and the patterns of social reinforcement throughout the eight-week period, but the teacher was able to make the ratings and execute the token system without aid after the first week. Procedures were never discussed when the children were present.

The children also received group points which could be exchanged for popsicles at the end of each week. The group points ranged from 1 to 10, as did the individual points, but the group points were based on the behavior of the whole class. The group points reflected the extent to which the children were quiet during the time the ratings were placed in the booklets. The number of group ratings made each day gradually decreased from five to three as did the individual ratings. However, since the children were usually very quiet, the number of points required to obtain a popsicle did not increase. The points were accumulated on a thermometer chart on the blackboard, and the children received popsicles on seven of the eight possible occasions.

At first the teacher was reluctant to accept the token procedure for fear that the ratings would take too much time. However, the ratings took at most three minutes. As the teacher noted, "The class is very quiet and usually I give them a story to read from the board while I give the ratings. One model student acts as the teacher and he calls on the students who are well-behaved to read. . . . This is one of the better parts of the day. It gave me a chance to go around and say something to each child as I gave him his rating. . . ." The rating procedure seemed especially effective because the teacher could reinforce each child for approximations to the final response that was desired. Instead of demanding perfection from the start the teacher reinforced any evidence of progress.

In addition to the token procedure, the teacher was instructed to make comments such as the following when appropriate:

"Pat, I like the way you are working. That will help your rating." "I am glad to see everyone turned around in their seats. That will help all of you get the prize you want." "Good, Gerald. I like the way you raised your hand to ask a question."

Another technique utilized by the teacher consisted of extinguishing the deviant behavior of one child by ignoring what the child was doing while at the same time reinforcing the appropriate behavior of another child. For example, if one child were talking, she would say to the child next to him, "Fred, I certainly like the way you are doing your work without talking." As a consequence, the child who was talking would usually stop talking. This method enabled the teacher to refrain from using social censure, as she was instructed, and to rely almost solely on positive reinforcement techniques.

The investigators also were prepared to use a procedure called time out from positive reinforcement (Wolf, Risley, and Mees, 1964) to deal with those behaviors which were especially disruptive and which might not have come under control of the token procedure. The time out procedure involves isolating the child for deviant behavior for a specified period of time. In addition, the child must be quiet for a specified period of the isolation time before he is allowed to join the group. This procedure was not used, however, since the frequency of disruptive behavior was very low at the end of the year.

The average inter-observer reliability for individual children during the token period ranged from 80% to 96%. As indicated in Table 1, the reliabilities were recorded separately for the base and token periods because it was much easier to obtain high reliabilities during the token period when the frequency of deviant behavior was low.

RESULTS

The average percentage of deviant behavior at the end of the year was very small. The daily mean of deviant behavior during the token procedure ranged from 3% to 32% while the daily mean of deviant behavior during the base period ranged from 66% to 91%. The average percentage of deviant behavior for all children during the base period was 76% as contrasted with 10% during the token procedure. As can be seen from the F-ratio (Table 2), the change from the base period to the token period was highly significant ($p < .001$). Using an omega squared, it was estimated that the treatment accounted for 96% of the variance of the observed deviant behavior.

An examination of the individual records clearly shows the small degree of individual variation and differences in deviant behavior from the base to the token period. Although Subjects 2 and 7 exhibited more deviant behavior than others during the token period, the percentage of deviant behavior was obviously less than during the base period. It is noteworthy that the percentage of deviant behavior went down for all pupils from the base to the token period.

DISCUSSION

There are at least two variables in addition to the token procedure and social reinforcement which possibly contributed to the change in the children's behavior. First, during the baseline and token phases of this demonstration the teacher who administered this program was enrolled in a psychology class which emphasized operant and social learning principles. The influence of this class itself cannot here be assessed, although the dramatic and abrupt change from the base to the token phase of the demonstration makes it seem highly implausible that the psychology class was the major variable accounting for the change. However, a

TABLE 2

ANALYSIS OF VARIANCE ON DEVIANT BEHAVIOR SCORES

Source		df	MS	F
Between subjects		7	72.86	
Within subjects		8	2203.00	
	Treatment	1	17424.00	609.87*
	Residual	7	28.57	

*$p < .001$

replication of this study now being planned will use a teacher who will receive only a short introduction to the basic principles involved and subsequent instruction by the experimenter throughout the procedure.

Secondly, the reduction in deviant behavior enabled the teacher to spend more time giving children individual attention during the token phase of the experiment. She had time to correct the children's work and return it promptly, giving them immediate feedback. She was also able to use teaching materials that she could not use before because the children would not pay attention. Some children who had not completed a paper for two years repeatedly received perfect scores on fully completed work. The immediate feedback and new materials probably contributed in and of themselves to the maintenance of appropriate behavior.

A typical individual experiment within the Skinnerian paradigm involves the establishment of a stable base rate of behavior; next a set of environmental contingencies are applied and the maladaptive behavior is reduced. The contingencies are then withdrawn and there is a return to base conditions. Finally, the environmental contingencies are again instituted and the maladaptive behavior decreased. The results of this procedure of operant decrease, increase, and finally decrease of maladaptive behavior in association with specific environmental conditions demonstrate the degree of stimulus control obtained by the technique.

A return to base conditions early in the treatment period of this study was not carried out because of a concern that the tremendous enthusiasm and cooperation generated by the program throughout the school system might be severely reduced. There is little doubt that such a return to base conditions following three or four weeks of the token procedure would have resulted in an increase in disruptive behavior. For example, when a reversal was used by Birnbrauer, et al. (1966), a number of children showed a decline in the amount of studying and an increase in disruptive behavior. As an alternative procedure, it was planned to return gradually to baseline conditions during the following fall. Unfortunately radical changes in pupil population prevented this reversal.

It should be noted that without a reversal or a return to baseline conditions it cannot be stated that the token system itself and not other factors, such as the changes that ordinarily occur during the school year, accounted for the reduction of deviant behavior observed in this study. In order to clearly demonstrate the crucial significance of the token procedure itself, a systematic replication of this token reinforcement procedure using different children and a different teacher is planned. The replication will not be repeated for the purpose of finding out whether the observed phenomena are "real," for the treatment procedure is considered sound. However, as Sidman (1960) noted, "An investigator may, on the basis of experience, have great confidence in the adequacy of his methodology, but other experimenters cannot be expected to share his confidence without convincing evidence." The purpose of the replication and reversal is to determine whether uncontrolled or unknown variables might be powerful enough to prevent an equally successful repetition of the system.

Two results of this study which have interesting implications include the effects of delay of reinforcement and generalization. The use of tokens provides a procedure which is intermediate between immediate and delayed tangible reinforcement. In Birnbrauer's (1966) class of severely retarded children this delay was extended from a few seconds to over an hour. Some educable children would study for many days for only checkmarks and presumably the knowledge that they were approaching a goal. All the children in the present study would work for four days without receiving a backup reinforcer. In addition, more than one child made the comment toward the end of school that next year they would be old enough to behave and work well without the prizes.

Anecdotal evidence indicates that the children were better behaved than they had been prior to the token procedure during the morning session, music, and library periods when the token procedure was not in effect. These reports suggest that a transfer to normal classroom control using social reinforcement and grades would not be very difficult. Also, the gang-like behavior of frowning upon "doing well" disappeared. Some children even helped enforce the token system by going to the blackboard just before class began and reading the instructions to the class. In sum, the teacher's work was more pleasant, the children behaved in a much more appropriate manner and they seemed to be learning more.

Wesley C. Becker, Charles H. Madsen, Jr., Carole Revelle Arnold, and Don R. Thomas

THE CONTINGENT USE OF TEACHER ATTENTION AND PRAISE IN REDUCING CLASSROOM BEHAVIOR PROBLEMS

A detailed study reported in the following article shows that much can be done by the teacher who applies proven behavioral principles effectively to modify and change the actions of problem children in the classroom.

"Rules" for behavior in classrooms are not sufficient incentives for managing problem behavior. Teachers found that the technique of praising the child who has shown an appropriate response when another child was misbehaving was especially effective in controlling the deviant behavior by comparing it to a proper example. This action keeps the teacher from directing class attention and interest to the misconduct and at the same time provides reinforcement for the appropriate behavior. The article points out that praise and the directed teacher attention are successful techniques for reducing classroom behavior problems.

The influence of the teacher's attention, praise, nearness, and other social stimuli in maintaining deviant as well as positive social behavior in children has been repeatedly demonstrated with preschool children (e.g., Allen, Hart, Buell, Harris & Wolf, 1964; Harris, Johnston, Kelley & Wolf, 1964). The expectancy that attention in almost any form may maintain deviant behaviors lies in the high probability that attentional responses from adults will be repeatedly followed by relief from aversive stimulation or the presentation of positive reinforcers in the history of most children. With such a history, stimuli produced by attentional responses are likely to become positive conditioned reinforcers which function to strengthen responses that are followed by such attentional stimuli. An essentially similar process is involved in the establishment of the effectiveness of praise comments such as "good boy," "that's fine," "you're doing great," which acquire conditioned reinforcement value through their repeated pairing with positively reinforcing stimuli.

Various forms of attention by nursery-school teachers have been used to modify such behaviors as "regressive" crawling, isolate behavior, excessive orientation to adults, "aggressive" rather than cooperative peer interactions, and lethargy or passivity, among

From *The Journal of Special Education*, Vol. 1, No. 3, Spring 1967, pp. 287–307. Reprinted by permission.

others. In addition, a similar procedure has been used to train mothers to modify the demanding-aggressive behavior of their children (Hawkins, Peterson, Schweid & Bijou, 1966). There is little question in the face of the extensive research by Sidney Bijou, Donald Baer and their students that a powerful principle for influencing the development of social behaviors has been isolated.

The group of studies to be reported here demonstrates how the selective use of teacher attention and praise can be effectively applied in managing behavior problems in elementary classrooms; the studies also explore methods of training teachers to be more effective in this regard.

THE SETTING

The studies were carried out in Urbana, Illinois, in an elementary school whose population was 95% Negro. Our research group was invited into the school because it was believed that we could provide a service and they would provide us with a research laboratory. Seven teachers (half of those invited) agreed to participate in a workshop and seminar on the application of behavioral principles in the classroom. This report covers studies involving five of these teachers carried out between February and June 1966.

The conduct of our research was guided to some extent by the necessity of establishing good relationships within the school system. Even though we had been invited by the school administration to see what we could do, there was still a need to convince teachers to participate, to keep them participating, and to help them feel comfortable with observers in their classrooms. The comments of one of our teachers express better than we can the background into which the research had to be adapted.

At one time few teachers wanted to work at our school, and only those who could not find a better position would teach. Suddenly the school found itself qualified under

Title 1 of the Elementary and Secondary School Act to receive Federal aid. A large per cent of its population was termed "culturally deprived" or perhaps more aptly, "deprived of middle-class culture." The school was bombarded with specialists, aids, volunteers, and experimental groups from the University of Illinois, all wanting to borrow the children or to help the children. By planning carefully, class interruptions were held to a minimum, but even then planning was done around a music teacher, an art teacher, a language teacher, special small group speech classes and language classes. With all of this going on, plus many other items I shall leave unmentioned, it became increasingly more difficult to develop a continuous daily program. A self-contained classroom was a thing of the past. My attitude began to become very negative. I am not capable of judging the merits or demerits of this program; only time will measure this. I am merely attempting to describe briefly the setting, from my vantage point, into which a class in "behavior modification" was introduced. The enthusiasm held by some for the possibilities of behavior modification did not particularly excite me. The observing would interrupt my class and make it very difficult for me to function comfortably. The plan of the experiment was a bit nebulous, since too much knowledge of what was to be done would affect the results. To add to all this, these people were psychologists! My reinforcement history of working with psychologists need not be discussed here. I will simply state my relationship with them was inconsequential and negative; their reports were read carefully for some new information, but, finding none usually, the reports were filed as useless.

I vacillated for days on whether to take part in the class or not, finally deciding, despite my anxiety about the observation, that the only way to make educational psychology practical was to allow psychologists into the classroom to observe for themselves the classroom situation and problems.

Because of the need to sell ourselves to the teachers and maintain close contact with them, the seminar-workshop was initiated at the beginning of the second semester. At the same time we began to train observers, select target children, and make baseline recordings of the children's behavior. This sequence of events is not ideal, since the teachers were likely to try out the procedures they were learning in the workshop before we wished them to do so. The fact that they did this is suggested by an occasional decreasing baseline of problem behavior for a target child. Most changes, however, were dramatic enough that this potential loss in demonstrating an experimental effect did not grossly distort possible conclusions.

Most work in this area has used designs of the ABAB type. After baseline (A) an experimental effect is introduced (B), withdrawn (A), and reintroduced (B). We did not use this design (though we had an accidental counterpart to it in one room where the second (A) condition was provided by a student teacher) because: (a) we were afraid it might jeopardize the teacher's support; (b) the values of the experimental processes involved have been repeatedly confirmed; (c) "accidental" influences which might have produced changes in behavior would be unlikely to happen to ten children at the same time in five different classrooms; (d) we were unimpressed by arguments that Hawthorne effects, time alone or other "uncontrolled" variables such as the "weather" are causative in view of (b) and (c) above. By electing not to use an ABAB design we were also able to show the persistence of effects maintained by conditioned reinforcers over a longer period of time (nine weeks) than is usually the case. As a result of our caution and our success, we are now in a position where teachers and administrators in other schools are allowing us to establish controlled designs; we in turn help with their problem children.

PROCEDURES

Selection of Target Children

The authors began by observing in the classrooms of the teachers who had volunteered for the project, and then discussing possible problem children with them. After tentative selection of two children in each class, explicit behavior coding categories were evolved and tested. The final selection was contingent upon demonstration that problem behavior did occur frequently enough to constitute a problem and could be reliably rated.

Rating Categories

During the first four weeks the rating categories were repeatedly revised as reliability data demanded. Where it was not possible to get rater agreement for a category above 80%, a new definition was sought or a category abandoned. For example, in three classes (A, B, and C) inappropriate talking and vocal noise were rated as separate categories (see Table 1). In two classes (D and E) the behavior patterns made it difficult to discriminate between these behaviors, so they were combined. The general rules followed in establishing categories were as follows:

1. They should reflect behaviors which interfered with classroom learning (time on task) and/or,

2. They should involve behaviors which violated the rules for permissible behavior established by the teacher and/or,

3. They should reflect particular behaviors a teacher wanted to change (e.g., thumbsucking).

4. The classes should be constituted by behaviors which were topographically similar in some important way.

5. The classes should be mutually exclusive.

6. The definitions must refer to observables and not involve inferences.

7. The number of classes should not exceed ten.

Table 1

CODING CATEGORIES FOR CHILDREN WITH TEACHERS A, B AND C

Symbols	Class Label	Class Definitions

A. Behaviors incompatible with learning: General Categories

X	Gross motor behaviors	Getting out of seat; standing up; running; hopping; skipping; jumping; walking around; rocking in chair; disruptive movement without noise; moving chair to neighbor.
N	Disruptive noise with objects	Tapping pencil or other objects; clapping; tapping feet; rattling or tearing paper. Be conservative, only rate if could hear noise with eyes closed. Do not include accidental dropping of objects or noise made while performing X above.
A	Disturbing others directly and aggression	Grabbing objects or work; knocking neighbor's book off desk; destroying another's property; hitting; kicking; shoving; pinching; slapping; striking with object; throwing object at another person; poking with object; attempting to strike; biting; pulling hair.
O	Orienting responses	Turning head or head and body to look at another person, showing objects to another child, attending to another child. Must be of 4 seconds duration to be rated. Not rated unless seated.
!	Blurting out, commenting and vocal noise	Answering teacher without raising hand or without being called on; making comments or calling out remarks when no question has been asked; calling teacher's name to get her attention; crying; screaming; singing; whistling; laughing loudly; coughing loudly. Must be undirected to another particular child, but may be directed to teacher.
T	Talking	Carrying on conversations with other children when it is not permitted. Must be directed to a particular child or children.
//	Other	Ignoring teacher's question or command; doing something different from that directed to do (includes minor motor behavior such as playing with a pencil when supposed to be writing). To be rated only when other ratings not appropriate.

B. Special categories for children with teachers A, B and C (to be rated only for children indicated)

+	Improper position *Carole and Alice*	Not sitting with body and head oriented toward the front with feet on the floor, e.g., sitting on feet; standing at desk rather than sitting; sitting with body sideways but head and body both oriented toward the front with feet on the floor.
S	Sucking *Alice and Betty*	Sucking fingers or other objects.
B	Bossing *Carole*	Reading story out loud to self or other children (do not rate ! in this case); acting as teacher to other children, as showing flash cards.
//	Ignoring *Charley*	This category expanded to include playing with scissors, pencils or crayons instead of doing something more constructive during free time.

C. Relevant behavior

———	Relevant behavior	Time on task, e.g., answers question, listening, raises hand, writing assignment. Must include whole 20 seconds except for orienting responses of less than 4 seconds duration.

As Table 1 indicates, some codes were usable with all ten target children; others were devised especially for a particular child. For convenience we will speak of the Categories A and B in Table 1 as "deviant behaviors."

Observer Training and Reliabilities

Observers were obtained from undergraduate classes in psychology and education and were paid $1.50 an hour. Initially they worked in pairs, often in conjunction with one of the authors. After each rating session of 40 minutes, ratings were compared and discussed and reliability examined by category. Definitions were clarified and changes made when necessary. Reliabilities were above 80% before the baseline period was begun. Several reliability checks were made each week throughout baseline and periodically thereafter.

The observers were carefully trained not to respond to the children in the classes. They were to "fade into the walls." This procedure quickly extinguished the children's responses to the observers. Several incidents were reported where children were surprised to see the observers respond to a request from the teacher to move. After a while it was possible for other visitors to come into the class without distracting the children as they had in the past.

Rating Procedure

Except for a few occasional absences, target children were observed for 20 minutes a day, four days a week. In the experimental phase of the study frequency of reliability checks were reduced so that ratings of teacher behavior could also be obtained. Each observer had a clipboard with a stop watch taped to it. Observers would start their watches together

Table 2

TEACHER CODING CATEGORIES

Symbols	Class Label	Class Definitions
C	Positive contact	Positive physical contact must be included-such behaviors as embracing, kissing, patting (on head), holding arm, taking hand, sitting on lap, etc.
P	Verbal praise	This category includes paying attention to appropriate behavior with verbal comments indicating approval, commendation, or achievement such as: "That's good." "You're studying well." "Fine job." "I like you."
R	Recognition in academic sense	Calling on child when hand is raised. (Do not rate if child calls teacher's name or makes noises to get her attention.)
F	Facial attention	Looking at child when smiling. (Teacher might nod her head or give other indication of approval—while smiling.)
A	Attention to undesirable behavior	This category includes the teacher's verbally calling attention to undesirable behavior and may be of high intensity (yelling, screaming, scolding or raising the voice) or of low intensity ("Go to the office." "You know what you are supposed to be doing." Etc.) Calling the child to the desk to talk things over should also be included, as well as threats of consequences. Score the following responses to deviant behavior separately:
L	Lights	Turning off the lights to achieve control.
W	Withdrawal of positive reinforcement	Keeping in for recess, sending to office, depriving child in the classroom.
/	Physical restraint	Includes holding the child, pulling out into hall, grabbing, hitting, pushing, shaking.

and check for synchronization every five minutes (end of a row). They would observe for 20 seconds and then take ten seconds to record the classes of behavior which occurred during the 20-second period. All data are reported in terms of the percentages of the time intervals during which deviant behavior was observed to occur. The activities in which the children were involved varied considerably from day to day and contributed to daily fluctuation. For this reason only weekly averages are reported.

Ratings of Teacher Behavior

At the beginning of the experimental phase for four teachers, and for a week prior to the experimental phase for teacher E, a 20-minute sample of the teacher's behavior was also obtained. The rating categories are given in Table 2. The main purpose of the ratings was to insure that the experimental program was being followed.

Experimental Phase Instructions

Following a five-week baseline period (for most children) teachers were given instructions to follow for the nine-week experimental period. In all classes the teachers were given general rules for classroom management as follows (typed on a 5″ × 8″ card to be kept on their desks):

General Rules for Teachers
1. Make explicit rules as to what is expected of children for each period. (Remind of rules when needed.)
2. Ignore (do not attend to) behaviors which interfere with learning or teaching, unless a child is being hurt by another. Use punishment which seems appropriate, preferably withdrawal of some positive reinforcement.
3. Give praise and attention to behaviors which facilitate learning. Tell child what he is being praised for. Try to reinforce behaviors incompatible with those you wish to decrease.

4. Examples of how to praise: "I like the way you're working quietly." "That's the way I like to see you work." "Good job, you are doing fine."
Transition period. "I see Johnny is ready to work." "I'm calling on you because you raised your hand." "I wish everyone were working as nicely as X," etc. Use variety and expression.
In general, give praise for achievement, prosocial behavior, and following the group rules.

In addition to these general rules, teachers in classes A to D were given specific instructions with respect to their target children. An example follows:

Special Rules for Alice
Attempt to follow the general rules above, but try to give extra attention to Alice for the behavior noted below, but try not to overdo it to the extent that she is singled out by other children. Spread your attention around.
1. Praise sitting straight in chair with both feet and chair legs on floor and concentrating on own work.
2. Praise using hands for things other than sucking.
3. Praise attention to directions given by teacher or talks made by students.
4. Specify behavior you expect from her at beginning of day and new activity, such as sitting in chair facing front with feet on floor, attention to teacher and class members where appropriate, what she may do after assigned work is finished, raising hand to answer questions or get your attention.

The fifth teacher was given the general rules only and instructed not to give the target children any more special attention than was given the rest of the class. This procedure was decided upon because our observers felt that general classroom management was a problem for Mrs. E. She relied heavily on negative control procedures, and the general level of disruptive behaviors in the room was high. In view of this, we decided to see if the two target children in her class might not be used as barometers of a more general effect on the class of a change in control procedures.

When we first initiated the experimental phase of the study, we attempted to give the teachers hand signals to help them learn when to ignore and when to praise. This procedure was abandoned after the first week in favor of explicit instructions, as given above, and daily feedback on their progress. While hand signals and lights have been found to be effective in helping parents learn to discriminate when to respond or ignore (Hawkins, Peterson, Schweid & Bijou, 1966), the procedure is too disruptive when the teacher is in the middle of a lesson and is consequently placed in conflict about which response should come next.

At this point, the seminar was used to discuss and practice various ways of delivering positive comments. For some teachers, delivery of positive comments was difficult, and their initial attempts came out in stilted, stereotyped form. With time, even our most negative teacher was smiling and more spontaneous in her praise (and enjoying her class more). Shortly after the experimental phase began, one teacher commented, "I have at least 15 minutes more every morning and afternoon in which to do other things."

The experimental phase was initiated March 30th and ended May 27th. A breakdown in the heating plant in part of the building for the week of April 8th (Week 7) accounts for the loss of data for some children that week.

RESULTS

The average "deviant" behavior for ten children in five classes was 62.13% during baseline and 29.19% during the experimental period. The t-test for the differences between correlated means was significantly well be-

yond the .001 level. All children showed less deviant behavior during the experimental phase. However, differential teacher attention and praise were not very effective with Carole and did not produce much change in Dan until his reading skills were improved. Each child and class will be discussed in more detail and a breakdown of the behaviors which changed will be examined.

Teacher A

Mrs. A is an anxious, sensitive person who expressed many doubts about her ability to learn to use "the approach" and about whether it would work with her middle-primary adjustment class. Both of the children on whom data were collected changed remarkably, as did Mrs. A and other members of her class. The teachers' views of what happened to themselves and to members of their classes are very instructive and will be presented elsewhere.

Albert (age 7–8) tested average on the Stanford-Binet, but was still on first-grade materials during his second year in school. He was selected because he showed many behaviors which made learning difficult. He talked, made other noises, did not attend to teacher, and got in and out of his seat a lot. He loved to be "cute" and arouse laughter. In Mrs. A's words:

"He was a very noisy, disruptive child. He fought with others, blurted out, could not stay in his seat, and did very little required work. I had to check constantly to see that the minimum work was finished. He sulked and responded negatively to everything suggested to him. In addition, he was certain that he could not read. If I had planned it, I could not have reinforced this negative behavior more, for I caught him in every deviant act possible and often before it occurred. I lectured him and, as might be expected, was making only backward motion. In November Albert came to me to tell me something and I was shocked by the intensity of his stuttering. He simply could not express his thought because his stuttering was so bad. I declared an 'I like Albert week.' I gave him a great deal of attention, bragged about his efforts, and was beginning to make some progress. This turned out to be the basis upon which an 'ignore and praise' technique could be established. When the class began, I could see quickly what had happened to my relationship with Albert and had to fight to keep up my negative remarks until the baseline was established. Finally, I was free to use the technique. He quickly responded and his deviant behavior decreased to 10%, the lowest recorded. Along with the praising and ignoring, I attempted to establish a calmer atmosphere in which to work, and carefully reviewed class behavior rules. A good technique with Albert was to have him repeat the rule because 'he was following it.'"

During Weeks 8 and 9 Albert showed less than 12% deviant behavior on the average. His worst performance out of seven observation days was 18.77% and he was under 5% deviant four out of seven days. Then an unplanned experimental reversal occurred.

Mrs. A relates what happened:

"As my student teacher gradually assumed more and more of the teaching load, the deviant behavior increased again. She made the same mistakes that I had. I deliberately planned her work so that I would be working with Albert most of the time. She felt the efficiency of the direct command, but she also realized that this was not modifying Albert's behavior in a lasting way. Gradually, she accepted the positive approach and in the last week or two of her work the deviant behavior began again to decrease. She had learned that with so negative a child as Albert, only building rapport by using positive reinforcement would succeed.

"Albert has improved delightfully. He still blurts out, but makes an effort to stop this. He is often seen holding his hand in the air, biting his lips. He completes his work on time, and it is done well. Often, when he has to redo a paper, he takes it cheerfully and says, 'I can do this myself.' No sulking. He still finds it difficult to sit for a long period of time, but time on task has increased. He works very hard on his reading and has stated that he can read. His stuttering has decreased almost to zero. When the observers were questioned concerning this, they had detected little, if any stuttering. Most important to me, Albert has become a delightful child and an enthusiastic member of our class who feels his ideas are accepted and have merit."

Examination of the separate categories of behavior for Albert only serves to confirm the teacher's reports about which behaviors were most frequent and which changed the most.

The record of Mrs. A's behavior showed that she attended to and praised positive behaviors more than 90% of the time during the experimental period. Similar effective following of procedures was demonstrated for all five teachers.

Alice (age 7–8) scored 90 on the Stanford-Binet and was doing low first-grade work. The data on Alice are less clear than those for Albert since her average deviant behavior showed a decline prior to the experimental phase. Mrs. A considered Alice a "sulking child." She would withdraw at times and not talk. She would sit inappropriately in her chair, suck her thumb, and make frequent movements of her hands and legs. Mrs. A said that Alice would report headaches after being scolded.

Mrs. A also indicated that two weeks before the end of baseline she told Alice that she was "disgusted with your sulking and would you please stop it." Mrs. A felt that this instruction in part accounted for the drop in deviant behavior prior to the experimental phase. Analysis of Alice's separate classes of behavior indicates, however, that the motor category declined from 45% to 25% to 8% the first three weeks of baseline and remained under 12% the rest of the experiment. Following this decline in "getting out of seat," frequency of odd sitting positions went from 0% to 25% to 18% over the first three weeks of baseline and declined to zero over the next two weeks. There was also a decline in talking during the first two weeks of baseline. In other words Mrs. A got Alice to stay in her seat, sit properly and talk less prior to the experimental change. The behaviors which show a correlation with the experimental change are decreases in *orienting*, *sucking* and other (ignoring teacher) response categories.

It is probable that the maintenance of Alice's improvement, except for the short lapse when the student teacher took over the class, can be attributed to the experimental program. Mrs. A reported at the end of the year as follows:

"Alice is a responsible, hard-working student who now smiles, makes jokes, and plays with others. When a bad day comes, or when she doesn't get her way and chooses to sulk, I simply ignore her until she shows signs of pleasantness. Through Alice I have learned a far simpler method of working with sulking behavior, the one most disagreeable kind of behavior to me. Alice is a child who responds well to physical contact. Often a squeeze, a pat, or an arm around her would keep her working for a long while. This is not enough, however. Alice is very anxious about problems at home. She must have opportunity to discuss these problems. Again through the class suggestions, I found it more profitable to discuss what she could do to improve her problems than to dwell on what went wrong. Alice's behavior is a good example of the effects of a calm, secure environment. Her time on task has lengthened and her academic work has improved."

Teacher B

Mrs. B had a lower intermediate class of 26 children. Before the experimental phase of the study, she tended to control her class through sharp commands, physical punish-

ment, and withholding privileges. The two children on whom observations were made showed considerable change over the period of the experiment. Observers' comments indicate that Mrs. B was very effective in following the instructions of the experimental program. Only occasionally did she revert to a sharp command or a hand slap.

Betty (age 9–7) scored average on various assessments of intelligence and was doing middle third-grade work. Her initial problem behaviors included "pestering" other children, blurting out, sucking her thumb, making noises. She also occasionally hit other children. Often she said or did things that evoked laughter from others. Many of her problem behaviors showed a reduction during the baseline period (as happened with Alice), but thumbsucking did not. The experimental program brought thumbsucking under control for a while, but it increased markedly the last week of the experiment. Betty's other problem behaviors showed continued improvement over the experimental period and remained at a level far below baseline for the last five weeks of the experimental period.

Boyd (age 9–7) was of average IQ. His achievement test placements varied between second- and third-grade levels. During baseline he was high on getting out of his seat and making other gross movements, talking out of turn and making noises. Mrs. B also reported that Boyd had difficulty "saying words he knows," giggled a lot, and would not try to do things alone. He very much liked to be praised and tried not to do things which led to scolding. During this period Boyd was getting a great deal of teacher attention, but much of the attention was for the very behaviors Mrs. B wished to eliminate. Through a gradual shaping process Boyd learned to sit in his seat for longer periods of time working on task. He has learned to work longer by himself before asking for help. Mrs. B reports that he is less anxious and emotional, although we have no measure of this. Blurting out was not stopped entirely, but now he usually raises his hand and waits to be called on in full class activities and waits for his turn in reading.

Teacher C

Our biggest failure occurred in Mrs. C's middle primary class of about 20 children. Mrs C was one of our most positive teachers, and we underestimated the severity of the many problems she was facing. With our present knowledge, we would likely have gone directly to a more potent token economy system for the whole class (see O'Leary and Becker, 1967). The above misjudgment notwithstanding, the experiment reported below is still of considerable value in pointing to one of the limits of "the approach," as our teachers came to call it. Besides focusing on Carole and Charley, as described below, we assisted Mrs. C in extinguishing tantrums in Donna (beginning Week 8), and in reducing swearing and hitting by Hope. The work with Donna was very successful.

Carole (age 7–5) scored from 78 to 106 on various intelligence tests. She was working at the mid-first-grade level. Carole is an incessant beehive of activity. She scored high on response categories which indicate that she spent much time talking out of her seat, bossing other children and hitting others. Her most frequent behavior was talking when she should have been quiet. She was very responsive to peer attention. At times she would stand at the back of the room and read out loud to everyone. She liked to play teacher. She was also described as good at lying, cheating, stealing and smoking. Like most of the children in the study, Carole came from a deprived, unstable home. Descriptions of home backgrounds for most of the children in this study consist of sequences of tragic events (see Mrs. D).

The experimental phase of the program reduced Carole's average deviant behavior from about 75% during baseline to 55% for Weeks 7 to 9. A detailed analysis of Carole's responses shows that talking out of turn and blurting out still constituted over 30% of her deviant responses during Weeks 7 to 9. However Carole was in her seat more, sitting properly, responding more relevantly to teacher, and was on task 50% of the time. We were not satisfied with her improvement and felt that Charley (our other target child) while doing well, could also do better.

On April 25th (Week 9) we instituted a program in which ten cent notebooks were taped to Carole and Charley's desks. Mrs. C told the children that every 30 minutes she would put from one to ten points in their notebooks, depending on how hard they worked and how well they followed the class rules. At the end of the day if they had a certain number of points they could exchange the points for a treat. The initial reinforcer was candy. During this phase the rest of the class could earn a candy treat by helping Carole and Charley earn points. In this way they were not left out. The number of points required was based on a shifting criterion geared to Carole and Charley's progress. Charley responded well to this added incentive and was gradually shifted to saving points over two, then three, then five days to earn puzzles. Carole still resisted. She worked for points for several days, but on May 3rd (Week 10) she announced she was not going to work for points today, and she didn't. She was a hellion all day. Over the following two weeks Carole worked for a ring and then the components of a make-up kit. We were seeking stronger reinforcers and were stretching the delay of reinforcement.

On May 17th Mrs. C reported that Carole had earned points for three days in a row and was entitled to a component of the make-up kit. The 20% deviant behavior of that week showed that Carole could behave and work. The last week of May, Carole was back to talking and blurting out again. While some of our reinforcers were effective, Carole still needs a classroom where the structure would require her to depend on the teacher for praise and attention and where peer attention to her deviant behavior could be controlled.

Charley was presumed to be age 8 years and 2 months at the start of the study, but in fact was two years older. His IQ was given as 91, but with a proper CA was 73. He was doing mid-first-grade work in most subjects. Charley picked on the girls, hit other boys and bullied them (he was larger), got loud and angry if reprimanded, and at times he sulked and withdrew. No one was going to force him to do anything. Our ratings showed him highest in categories labeled *motor activities* (out of seat), *ignoring* teacher's requests, *turning* in seat, and *talking* to peers.

Initially Charley responded very effectively to rules and praise. He loved to receive praise from Mrs. C. However, praise was not enough to keep him on task. Also he was still fighting with Donna at recess. As noted above, a point system was initiated April 25th (Week 9) which worked well for the rest of the semester, while the delay of reinforcement was gradually extended to five days. On April 25th Charley was also informed that further fighting with Donna would lead to a loss of the following recess.

Comments on May 10th: "Charley is great. He ignores others who bother him as well as keeping busy all the time." May 26th: "Charley seems much more interested in school work and has been getting help with reading from his sister at home."

It is not possible to evaluate whether the point system was necessary for Charley. At best we know that social reinforcement helped considerably and that the point system did help to maintain good classroom behavior.

Teacher D

Mrs. D teaches a lower intermediate class of about 25 children. One group of her children had been in a slow class where the teacher allowed them "to do what they wanted." A brighter group had been taught by a strict teacher who enforced her rules. Since September the class has been divided and subdivided six times and has had seven different teachers.

Mrs. D describes the families of her two target children as follows:

"Don has average ability and achieves below the average of the class. The father works late afternoons and evenings. The mother, a possible alcoholic, has been known to do some petty shoplifting. She is frequently away from home in the evening. One older brother drowned at the age of seven. An older sister with above-average ability left home at the age of fifteen. She later married. Her husband was killed this spring in an automobile accident. Another older sister lost an arm at a very early age and is an unwed mother at the age of fourteen. Another sister attends Junior High School.

"Don's mother is of mixed parentage and has been in the hospital this year. The mother is divorced. The father remarried and it appears that there is a good relationship between the two families; however, the father has been in prison because of 'dope.'"

Mrs. D was initially quite bothered about being observed, but quickly learned to look more carefully at the way in which her behavior affected that of her class.

Don was 10 years and 4 months old at the start of the study. In April of 1961 he was recommended for EMH placement. Since kindergarten his performance on intelligence tests had risen from 75 to 102. He was obviously of at least average ability. His level of school achievement was between grades two and three, except for arithmetic reasoning (4.3). Observations revealed a high frequency of moving around the room and talking when he should have been working. He was called "hyperactive" and said to have poor "attention." His talking to other children was quite annoying to his teacher and interfered with classwork. Don appeared to respond to teacher attention, but obtained such attention most often when he was acting up.

The experimental procedures quickly brought Don's level of deviant behavior down from about 40% to under 20%. He was particularly good at working when the task was specifically assigned. When he was left to his own devices (no stimulus control) he would start to play around. These observations suggested that Don would greatly profit from more individualized programming of activities. He was reported to show improved behavior in his afternoon classes involving several different teachers.

Danny was age 10 years, 6 months at the start of the study. He measured near 85 on several IQ tests. His classroom behavior was described as being generally disruptive and aggressive. During baseline he scored high on *motor, talking, orienting, ignoring* and *noise*. By all standards Danny was a serious behavior problem. He seldom completed work assignments and was in the slowest reading group. Because of the severity of his difficulties, an educational diagnosis was requested during the early part of baseline. The staffing at Week 2 indicated a two-year reading deficit and a one-year arithmetic deficit. The following comments from the psychological report which followed the staffing are of interest:

"Danny's lack of conscience development and other intrinsic controls still presents a serious problem in controlling his behavior. His immediate impulsive aggressive reaction to threatening situations may hamper any educational remediation efforts. The evidence presented still suggests that Danny, in light of increasing accumulation of family difficulties, lack of consistent masculine identification, his irascible and changeable nature, and educational pressures will have a difficult time adjusting to the educational situation.

"It is our opinion that unless further action is implemented, i.e., school officials should attempt to refer this boy to an appropriate agency (Mental Health Institute for Juvenile Research) for additional help and correction, he is likely to become a potentially serious acting out youngster."

The data on Danny are most interesting. They show a small improvement in his behavior the first two weeks of the experimental phase. Generally the observers felt the whole class was quieter and better behaved. Danny especially stayed in his seat more of the time. However, a most dramatic change occurs when tutoring sessions in reading were begun (Week 8 to 9). It would appear that unless the child is capable of following the assigned activity, social reinforcement for "on task" behavior is not enough. In Danny's data this point is supported by an analysis of the kinds of activities where he showed the most improvement. Dan was averaging 80% deviant behavior when the activity was workbook assignments related to reading and language. In the reading group, where the teacher was there to help and direct activity, he averaged only 40% deviant behaviors. By early May (Week 11) the amount of deviant behavior during "seat work" activities had dropped to an average of 15%, with only an occasional bad day.

Well into April, Danny had not shown much improvement in his afternoon classes (with teachers not in our program). Several observations suggested that he would still show high rates of deviant behaviors on days when he was otherwise on task, if the activity shifted to something he could not do. For example, May 5th showed 25% deviant behavior during a period of seat work (reading), 30% during spelling, and 55% an hour later during grammar and composition. Danny was just beginning to move in reading, but was not ready for composition. The increase during Week 13 is due to one day where he was rated 40% off task. The rater comments indicate the basis for the "deviant" rating: "Danny should have been sitting quietly after doing his work, but instead of just waiting for the next assignment, he was playing with clay with another child. However, he was very quiet." Comments from May 9th and 10th give some flavor of the changes which occurred.

"May 9th: Mrs. D reported that Danny, after he finished reading, immediately started on spelling. This is a highly unusual occurrence. Until now Danny has avoided spelling activities until made to work on them."

"May 10th: Danny completely surprised the observer when he was on task the whole observation period, except for one minor talking to neighbor."

In view of the rather dramatic changes Danny has made in classroom behavior through a combination of remediation and social reinforcement, perhaps it is necessary to question the assumptions implicit in the quotation from Danny's psychological report given earlier. It should be noted that no attempt was made to work on family problems, his conscience, his masculine identification, or his "irascible nature" in changing his adjustment to school.

Teacher E

We have saved until last the most dramatic of all the changes produced in teachers and children. Mrs. E had a lower primary class of 23 children.

Observation of February 1, 1966:

"Six children were in a reading group and 15 were working on individual projects. The noise level for the entire classroom was extremely high and went higher just before recess. Some behaviors noted included whistling, running around the room (5 occasions), yelling at another child (many times), loud incessant talk, hitting other children (7 times), pushing, shoving, and getting in front of each other in recess line. Mrs. E would re-establish quiet by counting to 10, after giving a threat."

Observations suggested that control was obtained mainly by shouting, scolding, and the like in an attempt to suppress unwanted behaviors. This approach would work for a while, but there was a gradual buildup in noise until quiet was again demanded.

Mrs. E's responses on three days prior to a shift to positive reinforcement contained very few positive statements. Essentially, there was nothing to maintain appropriate classroom behaviors. The focus was on what not to do rather than what to do. There is a good possibility that the attention given deviant behavior in fact served to reinforce it.

Edward and *Elmer* were selected as barometers which might reflect changes for the whole class. Mrs. E was given the general instructions presented above but no special instructions for Edward and Elmer. They were not to receive more attention than other members of the class. She was to make her rules clear, repeat them as needed, ignore deviant behavior, and give praise and attention to behavior which facilitated learning. We wanted to see if a general approach to classroom management would be effective with children showing a high level of deviant behavior. The rating of Mrs. E's behavior before and after the change clearly shows an effect of the experimental instructions and training on her behavior.

Edward (age 6-8) tested 95 on the Stanford-Binet. Mrs. E considered him to be "distractible," to have poor work habits, show poor attention, and not to comprehend what he read. He never finished assignments. He could sight read and spell first-grade words. The baseline observations showed a high incidence of wandering about the room, turning around in his seat, talking at the wrong time, and making odd noises. He also showed little peer play.

A psychological examination in January of 1966 stressed Edward's poor social history (his parents had not talked to each other for three years), his lack of enthusiasm and emotional responsiveness, the apparent restriction on his peer interaction by his mother, and his need for better listening and language skills. Edward received speech therapy while in kindergarten. Throughout the baseline and experimental phase of this study, Edward was seen by a social worker and continued in speech therapy. In view of the fact that his (and Elmer's) behavioral changes were found to be directly associated with the change in classroom procedures, other treatments do not offer convincing alternative explanations for the data.

Edward greatly reduced the time he spent in aimless wandering, twisting in his seat and talking. He responded well to praise in both the reading group and class activities. Mrs. E reports that he began to complete assignments. He also showed better give and take with his peers, and would laugh, cry and make jokes. While still "distractible," he has learned to work independently for longer periods of time.

Elmer (6 years, 10 months) scored 97 on a group IQ test. He apparently started out the school year working well, but his work deteriorated. He seemed "nervous," hyperactive and would not work. He threw several tantrums and would cry if his work was criticized. His twin sister was also in the class and was doing well. By comparison Elmer often lost out. The parents expected as much of Elmer as of his sister. During baseline he was rated as showing inappropriate gross motor behaviors as much as 70% of the time. *Talking* was as high as 50% at times. *Noise* and *turning* in seat were at about 10% each. Initially our observers thought he was brain damaged.

Elmer's rapid response to positive reinforcement and a better structured classroom made it possible for him to stay on task longer. However, he did not improve greatly in his reading group. When the children were silently reading, he would at times clown and make noises. More work on reading will be necessary for academic progress.

Elmer's father came to work as a teacher's aid in one of our other classes just after the shift off baseline. His work with Mrs. C and changes in Elmer led slowly to his accepting the value of a positive rather than a punitive approach. Very likely father's attempt to be more rewarding with Elmer contributed to the maintenance of Elmer's improved classroom behavior. More to the point, however, is the fact that Elmer's improved classroom behavior (we showed father the graph dur-

ing Week 9) served to reinforce father's acceptance of a positive approach.

In her report at the end of the semester Mrs. E felt that 12 of 23 children in her class definitely profited from her change in behavior, that six children were unchanged, three somewhat improved, and two more deviant. The children who were reported unchanged tended to be the quiet and submissive ones who escaped Mrs. E's attention much of the time. From her own comments, it is likely that those reported to be more deviant seem so only because they stand out from the group more now that Elmer and Edward are not such big problems.

IMPLICATIONS

The results of these investigations demonstrate that quite different kinds of teachers can learn to apply behavioral principles effectively to modify the behavior of problem children. These results extend to the elementary classroom, with normal teacher-pupil ratios, the importance of *differential* social reinforcement in developing effective social behaviors in children. Work now in progress suggests that rules alone do nothing and that simply ignoring deviant behavior actually increases such behavior. The combination of ignoring deviant behavior and reinforcing an incompatible behavior seems critical. Nearly all of our teachers found that the technique of praising a child who was showing an incompatible appropriate behavior, when another child was misbehaving, was especially effective. This action keeps the teacher from attending to the deviant act and at the same time provides vicarious reinforcement for an incompatible behavior. In the future we hope to bring together a group of techniques which various teachers found effective in implementing the general strategy of this project.

These findings add support to the proposition that much can be done by the classroom teacher to eliminate behaviors which interfere with learning without extensive changes in the home, or intensive therapy.

Wesley C. Becker, Charles H. Madsen, Jr., Carole Revelle Arnold, and Don R. Thomas 173

Part VI

REACHING FOR ADULTHOOD

There is no one age group or period in the maturation process more interesting, more important, or more prone to problems than adolescence. Adolescents are literally "reaching for adulthood"; they are growing so fast physically and psychologically that they themselves, their parents, and society cannot easily adjust to the complex questions and difficulties that develop at this time. Physiologists point out that the onset of puberty has been advanced by two years during the past fifty years in the United States; this fact is primarily due to improved nutritional practices, particularly in the consumption of greater amounts of protein during childhood and youth. As a result of this change and of many other new developments in the family structure and function, in community organization, and in the role of the church, educators have had to focus more attention on the problems of adolescents.

Primarily it is a question of getting the necessary, pertinent, and accurate information to the right people at the right time. With increased knowledge about physical growth and development, particularly the physical changes that occur at puberty, there is a great need for the physician to keep up-to-date with as well as to furnish such information to other professionals, parents, and the developing adolescent himself. Not only matters concerning physical growth but changing standards and mores of society, alterations in the attitudes of various religious groups, and changing opinions among peers affect the behavior of the adolescent.

Teachers and parents are often at a loss in their attempts to communicate with the adolescent. If free and healthy habits of expression have not been established during infancy and childhood, it is likely that there may be a complete break at this time between parents and their children. This is often dramatically disruptive of family life and may remove the parent from his traditional sphere of influence just when the growing and maturing youth needs him most. The redefinition of roles is often confusing when a new relationship between parent and child is being defined. The maturing youth must now move into adulthood and begin to assume the responsibilities implied, be ready and willing to accept an independent position, to make decisions for himself, and to accept the results of his actions. The parent must release his offspring from strong control and supervision, must learn to rely on the child's judgment and allow him freedom to assume an adult role and personality.

With his growing sphere of freedom, the adolescent must make up his mind about many matters he encounters. Sexual mores and related topics have grown increasingly complex with the gradual acceptance of early marriages, divorce, illegitimate births, and the availability of the pill. Without thoughtful consideration of the so-called "revolution" in contemporary moral standards, the adolescent may find himself overwhelmed b the rapidly changing customs and attitudes toward sex. Of primary importance, then, are the choices he must make and the responsibility he must take to develop viable principles for his own actions which will lead to adulthood.

WHAT ADOLESCENTS SHOULD KNOW ABOUT ADOLESCENCE

The adolescent's biggest problem is learning to réason about his feelings and emotions at a time of heightened tension, both psychologically and physically. He needs to develop a positive attitude about this period in his life and toward himself, knowing that he is facing problems similar to others of his age group. He most likely will make a successful transition into adulthood.

These four short articles stress the more optimistic aspects of adolescence and stress the unique, humorous, and happier aspects of growing up.

A TIME FOR LAUGHTER

Richard Armour

In *Through Darkest Adolescence* I considered adolescence clinically, as a disease. "You wouldn't hit a sick person, would you?" I asked parents, hoping to discourage violence. (I have never struck my children myself, being a man of peace and two inches shorter and thirty pounds lighter than my son.)

If I have contributed to the stereotype of adolescence, I am sorry. Adolescents have enough to worry about with acne and homework and the opposite sex, without having adults writing books about them, especially books in which they recognize themselves — or their friends.

But honestly, I think there is nothing wrong with writing books about adolescence if you avoid such expressions as "compulsive rebellion," "imperious urges," and the ever-present "search for identity." I never use such language myself, partly because I want to be understood. I worry less about presenting adolescents with a stereotype of adolescence than I do about stereotyped writing on adolescence (or anything) — written, I presume, on a stereotypewriter.

Adolescents may or may not be "trying to find themselves" (after all, they have only to look in a mirror), but they are curious about themselves, as they are curious about life. They want to read about this thing they are going through and to know from others who have been through it that it is inevitable, it can be fun, and it won't last forever. One of their favorite books is *Catcher in the Rye*, which (being a novel instead of a psychological or sociological tract) never once refers to "compulsive rebellion" or "search for identity" but tells the adolescent plenty about what it is to be an adolescent just the same.

Novelists can tell adolescents all they need to know about being adolescents without *obviously* telling them — that is, without teaching or preaching. A good novel about adolescents can do what Aristotle said a good tragic drama can do: purge and cleanse the emotions. As for tragic drama itself, adolescents can learn something about the parent-child relationship from *King Lear*. As one student said, somewhat ambiguously, after reading Shakespeare's great tragedy, "I felt better when I had finished it."

But my own way of helping adolescents get from childhood to adulthood — a way that I recommend to others — is not through tragedy but through comedy. Not tears but laughter. And not all the time, just occasionally. Someone has said that life is a tragedy to those who feel and a comedy to those who think. If you can get adolescents to *think* about their moments of ridiculousness, and laugh at themselves, you will have done them an incalculable service — especially if they get the hang of it and go on to do it without any prompting.

This of course is a delicate business. Adolescents don't want to be laughed at; they

From the *PTA Magazine*, Vol. 62, September 1967. Reprinted by permission.

want to be laughed with. The last thing in the world they want, or anyone wants, is to be made fun of, whittled down to smaller size, in front of others. But happily the sense of humor is at its height (and breadth) during adolescence. The adolescent, when he is not taking himself and life too seriously, laughs with little provocation. Unlike the adult, who becomes a specialist in this area as in most others, the adolescent is a generalist when it comes to humor. He can enjoy both the subtleties of James Thurber and the wildness of *Mad* magazine.

One way to get the adolescent to laugh at himself (a sign of sanity and perhaps maturity) is to take the initial step by making light of some imperfection of your own. As an eighteenth-century physician wrote in a letter of advice to his son, "He is never laughed at who laughs at himself first."

I suggest an easy, relaxed approach to adolescents. Your own relaxation will relax them. Appeal to their minds (they *do* have them) rather than to their emotions.

Or else turn them over to the novelists and the humorists.

LISTEN, WORLD

Ralph G. Eckert

A young person today has something important to say to the world. The gist of it is, "I am myself. I'm me, not another edition of my father or mother or somebody my teacher or anybody else wants me to be." Your adolescent is unique, but his urge to express himself is not. All adolescents feel that way. That is why young people need a group in which they can be heard—and understood.

Many of us grew up in small towns, small schools, small church groups, and the like. In these groups we felt we had a part in decision-making. But nowadays fewer and fewer adolescents are having such experiences, so they have to create their own small peer groups. To make sure they are being heard, they feel impelled to disagree with the adult world (even more vehemently than other generations have done).

Television and the mass media find these rebellious teenagers interesting "news." Encouraged by the publicity, young people become more rebellious than ever. Thus the mass media capitalize on—you might even say they exploit—the normal rebelliousness of young people.

The spectators and the reporters who flock to photograph their activities are in a sense egging them on and encouraging them to break out in rashes of pointless rebellion. They need to learn that simply flouting what society upholds is not reforming it. Parents and teachers should try to help them find more mature ways of questioning established ideas and discover more constructive ways of patiently improving them.

All of us would find it helpful to become more conscious of our struggle to balance feeling and thinking. At birth, the mid-brain, the hypothalamus, is already pretty well developed. Within the first few months of life an infant can laugh as well as cry, get angry, experience frustration, and so on. His first communications to his parents are the expression of his feelings. His early motivations are all in terms of the satisfaction of these feelings. "I want what I want and I want it now."

Gradually the cortical area of the brain, the so-called gray matter, begins to develop. He can walk at one, but he can't talk until two or three; he will read and write at six or seven. He begins slowly to perceive cause-and-effect relationships, and as he approaches adolescence he begins to base his decisions more and more on what his "thinking brain" tells him, as opposed to his earlier decisions based largely upon what he felt.

At ten, if his mother said, "But Johnny, you've already had four helpings of pudding; if you eat any more you'll burst," he probably said, "Pass the pudding and get out of the way." But by the teen years, young people can respond understandingly to the statement, "Your emotions are like the motor in a car. They give you the drive to go, but how far can you go without a steering wheel?"

A thirteen-year-old boy was able, with some help, to reason his way to the conclusion that "I guess my thinking brain was telling me it was wrong and warning me that we might get caught, but when this kid said, 'Don't be chicken,' well, I guess I was more afraid of being chicken than getting caught. When we did get caught, all I could say to myself was, 'You stupid egg, why did you do it?'" But had his parents carped at him instead of trying to understand him (as I was), his self-condemnation would have been projected outward as hostility against them.

Finally, adolescents need to know that they are an in-between generation. Their parents grew up in a culture where desirable and undesirable behavior was clearly prescribed by authority—God, the Bible, the minister, priest, rabbi, parents, teachers, rules, law. And nearly all these were in agreement. Most of them agreed that smoking, drinking, and premarital sex were wrong for young people. Today you can get an argument on any of these in any group of teenagers.

What is desperately needed are parents and teachers who, by asking good questions, can help young people learn to reason about problems that are primarily "feeling problems" and thus increase their self-control. The teenage girl who gets into trouble has probably let her "love feelings" override her reasoning. The boy who gets her—and himself—into trouble has probably let his "sex feelings" silence his judgment. Despite a weakening of the old double standard, girls are still likely to suffer more from the emotional involvement of a premarital sex experience than does a boy.

Today's youth are being brought up on a science program that teaches them to think in terms of cause and effect. Many teenagers who are "fighting the system" have parents who do not know how to reason with them. These parents *dictate* as long as they can and then *abdicate*. The most successful parents are those who learn to ask good questions that make youngsters think, rather than continue to try to tell them what to do (or even make suggestions) except as questions: "Have you thought of . . . ?"

The schools too are teaching them how to think. We parents can learn what young people are thinking and feeling and help them make better decisions, if we can *learn to listen*, and *listen*, and *listen*. And this would do more than anything else to improve communication between generations.

TIME OF TENSION

Helen F. Southard

Adolescents need to know that puberty, with its physical changes, is bringing them nearer to adulthood. They need to know too that growing up includes learning to live with feelings. During adolescence, feelings are heightened as body chemistry is undergoing changes and the new phase—developing into a man or a woman—proceeds. Young people need especially to understand their sexual tensions and the broader kind of love feelings toward another person. Such feelings can grow into meaningful relationships but, when they are not returned, can give a sense of failure and rejection.

Hostile feelings, very common in adolescence, must also be understood, for these are often directed, through words and acts, toward the very persons young people love. As a result, guilt feelings may become overwhelming. Adolescents need to understand that these feelings are not intrinsically bad or indicative of emotional ill health but are simply a part of adolescence.

Boys and girls need to know how the other sex grows and develops and how each sex feels about the other. With this knowledge, perhaps they will be less prone to exploit each other, as they often do—perhaps unintentionally in trying to find immediate gratification of their needs. Examples of exploitation? When a young man, in an effort to justify sexual intercourse, tells a girl he may want to marry her some day; when a young woman leads a boy on but doesn't want to give what she seems to be offering. Such situations present an elementary lesson in responsibility that should be wisely prepared for.

Adolescents should understand that when the going is rough they may want to avoid some of the hard tasks with which they are faced, and the escape nature of some of their choices should be pointed out. Marriage is a common form of escape for girls, who may choose it rashly as a shortcut to adulthood and happiness. Boys may think that dropping out of school and taking some kind of job will make life easier or more interesting for them. Exciting possibilities do lie in store for those who are able to forge ahead toward a goal, but some realistic options have to be presented to young people.

Today many superficial guides to success are put before youth. They need to understand that maturity is tested over and over again during adolescence as various choices are offered them. Choosing not to do something, as well as doing it, is a positive part of being an adult. Adolescents should understand that many adult restrictions can disappear when young people learn to make wise choices. There is a popular image of adolescents as a big group of nonconforming persons given to antisocial behavior. This picture would have a less negative impact on young people if they understood that as one feels comfortable with oneself and knows more clearly what one hopes to be, it becomes easier to make choices that are different from those of one's group.

For young people to learn to choose wisely, rules, standards, and guidelines have to be offered by adults. Adolescents must understand that families may have differing ideas on these. Not all adults, like young people, have the right to consideration as persons. Grasping this fact is another lesson in responsibility.

Adolescents are often called dreamers, lazy and shiftless, and they may fall back on that role as a cushion. They must be helped to see that as a young person shapes up his individual self he acts out not one but many and varied roles. At one time a young boy may dream of becoming a great scientist or an actor or a gang leader; a girl may see herself as a TV star or the wife of a successful executive. Such dreams may temporarily supplant action toward a compassable goal, and friends may be chosen to fill in the gaps in the personality of the one being dreamed about. Adolescents must know that they will have low moments, periods of inactivity, and short-time goals and that they will outgrow many of their friends.

It is not easy to grow up to be a man or woman in our society. Adolescents need to be reminded of this and be given the assurance that their family and teachers will support them as they make their way.

CORRECTING THE IMAGE

Amelia John

Nobody ought to know more about adolescence than adolescents themselves. After all, they're living it, parked sometimes on Cloud 9, sometimes in the valley of despairing depreciation of themselves. But experience isn't knowledge. Not until it's transformed by reflection and perspective. Not until the emotion is recollected in tranquility.

Far too few adolescents, I think, have had what mental health people call *anticipatory guidance*. Rather, I should say *sound* anticipatory guidance. Anticipations of adolescence they certainly have. And the view they get from paperback novels about teen-agers, articles in popular magazines and newspapers, programs on TV, and songs on records and radio all lead them to expect the worst. They expect to be sad and lonely, terribly misunderstood by parents, unable to talk with adults. They expect to be fenced in by regulations set up by old fogies who don't know the world has changed, who are still living in the "olden days."

The popular rehashings of what scientific

information we have about the period called adolescence leads young people to believe they'll have uncontrollable sexual urges, black moods, fierce resentment—maybe even hatred—of their parents. They expect they'll have to put up a stiff, stout battle—fight a real revolution to gain their freedom and independence.

They expect that the only comfort and understanding they'll get will be from each other. They expect they won't be proper adolescents unless they're nonconformists, rebels, experimental researchers into the mysteries of sex, alcohol, drugs, and whatever else may be far-out and offbeat. What they hear and read about adolescence and teen-agers may lead them, with delicious fear, to anticipate the worst.

To my mind most of the material on adolescence that filters down to the youngsters themselves deals with the pathological aspects—the extremes of adolescent feelings and behavior, not the norms. The danger is, of course, that some teen-agers may try to live up to the stereotype—to feel what they believe they're supposed to feel, to behave the way adolescents are expected to behave. Others may suspect they're abnormal if they don't fit the stereotyped image.

The task for home and school is to supplant misinformation with information, lack of facts with real facts. Obviously the preteen should be supplied with real facts. Obviously the preteen should be supplied with physiological information. (In fact children should be learning about human growth and developing respect for their bodies and minds from the early grades on.) Probably a very important fact for adolescents to know is the fact of individual differences—that some persons develop and mature more rapidly or more slowly than others and that there is a range in emotional development and in the intensity of emotions. Above all, they ought to be charged with responsibility. They ought to know that adolescence isn't a bowling ball that will inevitably knock them over. They ought to know that in a large measure they can be masters of their feelings and their conduct. They ought to know that a good many young people strive successfully to make their teen years the best times instead of the worst.

Adolescence, they should know, offers the best opportunity they will ever have to reshape, remold, rebuild themselves into the kind of persons they want to be; and most really want to be very fine persons.

Laurence A. Flaherty

ADOLESCENCE: BETWEEN HOME AND SOCIETY

Adolescents as a group are misunderstood but they have a tremendous impact on society. Together with the physiological changes which occur at this time and the radical changes adults expect in their attitudes and behavior, adolescents must resolve tensions which hopefully lead to the mature role they will ultimately play in life. There invariably is a struggle to move from dependency to independent self-actualization in the conflict with all forms of authority. This struggle is the constant fluctuation in adolescent behavior that gives its impression of confusion and hopelessness. It is based on doubts and fears about the adult world into which he must move. Along with ideological and behavioral adjustments, the genital development and hormonal changes pose added problems.

In this article, Dr. Flaherty presents a comprehensive picture of the time between puberty and maturity. He discusses a new psychiatric theory—one where adolescents are often "acting out" the desires and ambitions of parents who may find vicarious satisfaction of their subconscious needs and impulses. Throughout, he stresses the complex problems of adolescent personality development.

Adolescence is a period of time which is not understood and easily forgotten by adults. In our society there is no clear-cut role for the adolescent nor any immediate prospect that such a role will be established. Adolescents, however, especially in recent years, have had a tremendous impact on society. Many have large personal sums of money, much leisure time, and an involvement in society which is neither vital nor necessary. There are vast economic markets whose advertisements are directly appealing to the billions of dollars in the hands of the adolescents. Adults have many fantasies and habitual reactions toward the adolescent which compound the complexity of understanding adolescent behavior. Perhaps this leads to the teen-ager's frequent defense "no one understands me." It is true that young people in this in-between-age are action oriented. They attempt to find causes for the vague sense of anxiety, uncertainty, and unanswered questions which are at the root of their attempt to seek identity, status, and a role in their immediate society and wider society. They challenge, attack, and question the basis of our needs and beliefs which contribute to our sense of security. This insures an adult response which may be critical, based on "adult wisdom," or the expectation that their questions can be postponed until they "grow out of them."

ADOLESCENCE: DEFINITION

This is a time which may be divided into three phases: preadolescence, early adolescence, and late adolescence. The preadolescent is content with his body proportions and is usually self-assured, energetic, enthusiastic, and content with himself. Early adolescence corresponds to puberty. This period is marked by the acquisition of secondary sexual char-

acteristics and ability to reproduce. The physical signs of sexual maturity begin in girls about thirteen, although puberty may start as early as age ten or as late as sixteen. In boys, some of the earliest to mature begin early adolescence around age eleven, the average about fourteen, and the latest around seventeen. These somatic and physiologic changes set in motion new thoughts, behavior, and bodily sensations. Growth and sexual hormones mediate this change. The physical changes initiate psychological unrest which promotes a seeking of a new "modus operandi" to manage the emerging sexual maturity.

Later, there is increased stress upon the older adolescent to develop a plan for a chosen vocation. He must learn what vocational opportunities exist for someone of his abilities, aptitudes, habits, and sentiments. The older adolescent must decide about his personal beliefs which are dependent upon his perception of the world and significant people in his private life. There is distinct change in the twelve- to fifteen-year-old as compared with the fifteen- to eighteen-year-old. Their views on the meaning of life, personal values, a moral code, and successful courtship skills are different. Early adolescents are preoccupied with their new physique, surprised with the effect on the opposite sex, and confused with new urges and physical sensations. Girls of this age are prone to outbursts of tittering and giggling for no apparent reason. Boys, especially under the influence of a barely audible remark, react with snickering laughter. The late adolescent has a more serious mien. He considers the ultimate goal of selecting a marital partner.

Basically, adolescence is a period of time between puberty and maturity; it is marked by the appearance of secondary sexual characteristics. The age range may vary from

Laurence A. Flaherty 181

twelve to twenty years, although the variation is peculiar to the individual. The change in adolescence encompasses gonadal maturity and a replacement of emotional security in the home for emotional security in wider society. No facet of maturation is of utmost importance, rather all aspects are equally important; so that, stunting in one area leads to conflict, compensation, or even impairment in other spheres. From evidence available, neither early adolescence nor late adolescence is a time of inordinate emotional stress for a boy or girl. The amount of inner conflict or disorganization experienced depends on the success of the individual in accomplishing earlier steps in development.

STRESSFUL AREAS IN ADOLESCENCE

1. The adolescent must bring every authority figure in his life into some type of harmonious working relationship with the other. Teenagers often meet adults whose attitude toward authority and responsibility are different than the standards which existed in the home during childhood. As a child the mother or father was available to limit and protect the child from his impulses, the impulses of others, and the demands of the environment. External controls are a temporary necessity until the child is able to postpone immediate impulses and effectively manipulate his environment. The parents provide the daily structure which gives external controls. This situation leads to a sense of security in the child and over-determined reliance on parental authority.

The child learned through his experience that his security was maintained by adhering to the guidelines formulated by the significant adult. The child is now dependent on the significant adult. These over-determined, emotionally charged, parental dictates become internally validated. When the child enters adolescence, the internalized parental dictates are challenged. They are exposed to wider society and pushed by the need of the adolescent to separate from the parents.

The internalized original situation no longer meets the new reality of the adolescent. New internal dictates are needed; however, they must be consensually validated for return to the earlier sense of security.

The adolescent is exposed to a spectrum of standards outside of the home. The standards at home may be higher than the standards he sees in the classroom or homes of his friends. They might be below standards maintained by other adults, legal agencies, or in his classroom. This impact challenges the internalized dictates and leads to a process of mentally comparing the past with the present. This creates a pervading sense of uncertainty and searching in the adolescent. Often, we find in the adolescent a "pan anxiety." There is no obvious reason for the apparent insecurity. We frequently note that suddenly they are fearful, anxious, and afraid although there is no specific fear. A host of rationalizations and verbalizations offer no appropriate explanation of their insecurity and pan anxiety. This seems to pervade the mental state of all adolescents. It is also shared by the neurotic and emotionally unstable adolescent who becomes a psychiatric casualty. This pan anxiety seems natural for the adolescent. The sense of uncertainty motivates adolescents to find personalized, internal dictates which aid in reestablishing their relationship to themselves, parents, and other authoritarian figures in the environment. Before adulthood is possible, they answer to themselves important questions – Who am I? Where am I going? What am I going to be? How will I get there? How will I be able to assume the responsibility of a job or family?

In dealing with adolescents, one is repeatedly impressed with their perpetual state of fluctuation. On one hand, they must separate from the security of the parents and, on the other, they must shape their own role in society. This process of separating from the parents often involves angry outbursts, accusations, mutual abandonments, reconciliation, and finally, if everything is successful, total separation. Usually, the stormier the adolescence, the harder the separation and persistent dependence on the parents. The continual devaluation or challenging of the parents' style of life often is the pivotal point upon which an adolescent finally is able to separate from a parent and form his own relationship with the never ending series of authority figures who play a large part in the success or failure of his life. The "love in" might represent a distorted intermediate in seeking security in a type of shared frustration instead of charting an individual solution to the problem of unresolved dependency.

2. Social relatedness is an over-determined inner need of the normal adolescent and explains the fads and customs adopted by adolescents to insure approval. The pressures are multiple. The family wants the child to be popular. The child, whether boy or girl, wants to be popular with the opposite sex. All adolescents are preoccupied and sensitive in maintaining their reputation and position in their peer group. Many adults and educators are unnecessarily anxious when the adolescent adheres to the mores prevalent in the group. Educators feel threatened when confronted by the genuine regard of the adolescent for the value system of the peer group. We must realize the deep needs of the adolescent to shape his own life yet conform to his social group.

The social group facilitates interaction and communication among the adolescents. In order to belong to the group, the member must temporarily suppress urgent individual desires in order to sustain the common concerns of the group. The group places obligations upon the member to promote unity and maintain loyalty. Membership satisfies an underlying feeling of rejection and loss which is a residual of the movement out of the original family. The prevalent sense of insecurity functions as a potent binding force which facilitates cohesion among the members. The presence of similar experiences and conflicts leads to identification and kinship feelings among the members. The purpose of group membership is to mod-ify the immature, unconscious, internalized dictates so that a reliable compromise is found to meet the adolescent's need of validation from wider society.

The adolescent, it is true, is vulnerable and can be exploited by certain groups, especially the dyssocial group. The dyssocial group still must deal with chaotic or destructive behavior which evokes reality-based fears in its members. Adolescents go to great lengths to identify with their group, acquiring skills, customs, activities, and codes required for participation in their peer group. This is usually accomplished in early adolescence and differs from earlier group attachments. This need to belong is extremely strong so that conformity to the group customs is an extremely compelling motive of itself.

Adolescents who concern me the most do not attempt to form group relatedness. They seem to be dominated by their earlier experiences with the parent. The group provides other models for the adolescent. In the group, a person who is a little bit older is usually available. He does not arouse the distancing techniques that adolescents may use in communicating with an adult. The presence of many individuals with different backgrounds and of different ages allows the adolescent a prolonged experience with conflicts "in vivo" he can identify in his recent past and models upon which he can learn to anticipate his immediate future. The process of continual separation from the home and parental values to the acquiring of the capacity to deal with, belong to, and become a part of the interaction with peers is clearly seen in his adjustment to the expectancies and demands of the peer group. One of the tantalizing elements in the adolescent's dilemma is the need for independence yet the frustration of having no role in adult society. He is also dependent in attaining the experience to achieve a progressively more mature pattern of adjustment.

3. As the impact of genital development forces itself on the early adolescent, he is faced with the task of learning to understand

his new bodily functions and containing the inner tension that occurs with responsible, reproductive maturity. The adolescent is placed in the position of fulfilling and identifying his sexual role which is biologically determined. Early in adolescence he learns the social behavior appropriate to his biological sexuality and important to maintain his emotional security in the face of sexual tensions and maintaining approval from parents, teachers, and peers. To accurately identify his sexual role is one thing, but the ability to win the admiration of the opposite sex is another.

There are many myths, misunderstandings, and outright ignorance which compound his task. There are many medieval fantasies which describe the devil as residing in females and tempting males. This leads to conflicting thoughts ranging from the sinfulness of sex to the depreciation of the female. Victorian mores view the female response as being desirable in passivity and intimating guilt, deviancy, or other obnoxious labels to any activity on the part of the female which would tend to enhance her enjoyment of sexuality or participate more fully in the sexual act.

Fears of pregnancy are often used as a weapon to discourage female sexual involvement or taught as being the only thing that needs to be feared. Many adolescent boys obtain mistaken notions about the results of masturbation. Masturbation comes to be associated with sin, disease, and insanity. On the other hand, many adolescent boys are under pressure to obtain sexual experience. Somewhere they have learned that the lack of sexual gratification is associated with weakness or homosexuality. In subtle ways intercourse becomes the way to hurt and humiliate the sexual partner. The excitement of sexual experience is felt to rest upon the elements of the bad, forbidden, or mischievous manner by which sexual gratification is obtained. Sexual intercourse is desirable because it is a "forbidden fruit."

The adolescent learns from his peer group about forbidden literature which perpetuates itself from generation to generation. There seems to be a continual process of replacing new myths with old myths or old myths with new myths. One pseudoscientific proclamation is the value of sexual experience under the influence of psychotropic drugs which has never been substantiated, although no doubt sexual behavior is more frequent in circumstances where inhibitions and prohibitions are removed.

Recently, the work of Masters and Johnson has shown marked similarity in the orgastic response between the sexes rather than any superiority of one sex. Masters and Johnson are in the process of investigating in future studies some of the psychological determinants that affect the sexual response. In psychiatry, especially in investigations on the nature of the psychotherapeutic relationship, it is evident that highly intricate and complex transactions are necessary to promote the full physiologic, psychologic, and emotional consequences of physical intimacy. The need for mutual regard, tenderness, and freedom of action seems to be possible inside the security of an enduring, stable, warm relationship. The exact nature of this relationship leaves many unanswered questions. In some way, so many other needs are met that the term "sexual relationship" may limit and not represent in reality the actual nature of the transaction.

As this information becomes available, it is difficult to understand why so many pressures are exerted upon adolescents. They seem to be forced to premature sexual relationships before they have adequately comprehended the nature of the relationship. Some of the recent statistics on this matter are disconcerting, and actually tragic. There is a rising rate of venereal disease. Roy W. Menninger estimates that one out of every six teen-agers becomes pregnant out of wedlock, one third to one half of all teen-age marriages are prefaced by illegitimate pregnancy. The number of unwed mothers under eighteen has doubled since 1940, and one teen-age marriage in every two ends in divorce within five years. In some ways it seems that the cultural events are not keeping pace with the utilization of new insights. One of the prevalent ideas is that the need to communicate fully involves a total physical relationship, even before a relationship, at least in my sense of the term, is secure. In many ways it appears that sexuality is being used as a substitute and opiate for a partial return to the state of infantile dependency, bliss, and closeness.

The roles relative to authority and dependency, group relatedness, and sexual role are three vulnerable facets of the adolescent's development. In late adolescence these roles are synthesized in choices which deeply affect the adolescent's future career. He must decide about educational and vocational goals. He must determine what is possible for him. What does he really value? What does he believe in? Implicit in the idea of emergence is the need to postpone and live with impulses for later satisfaction. The presence of models in his daily life is a tremendous acceleration for him in the attainment of future goals. These goals are extremely important and permanently fix his place in society, among peers, and reflect daily to him the fruits of his endeavors and achievement. If he does not prepare himself for these choices, and take necessary steps to achieve them, then we find the adult haunted by adolescent ambitions. Often he is in a perpetual state of cynicism, despair, and dissatisfaction.

PERSONALITY AND ADOLESCENCE

The adolescent is often confronted with anxieties, doubts, misunderstandings, and apprehensions which result from insecurity in the face of greater social demands, sexual responsibilities, or the whole force of economic uncertainty. In understanding the individual we attempt to understand the characteristic manner utilized to attain individual goals. In helping the adolescent we should have some understanding of this

"cognitive blueprint" which emerges from the interaction of the individual adolescent with his environment and the forces which influence his learning of roles involved in establishing interpersonal relationships. Personality is the term we use to describe the manner in which the adolescent maintains his anxieties, insecurities, and forms his identity, values, sexual roles, vocational choices, and personal responsibility. Personality is an enduring organization of emotions and sentiments, patterns of behavior, physical traits, personal goals, concept of self, environmental evaluation, and the characteristic manner of meeting obstacles for the immediate and remote attainment of his personal goals. Adolescence is another step in providing further experience in integrating and coordinating the inner life of the individual to meet in a harmonious fashion the demands of reality. The individual who has been prepared for adolescence uses this time to perfect his historically earlier methods of achieving his aims and acquiring new social and technical skills during this period. Harry Stack Sullivan has made valuable contributions to our knowledge of adolescence, the dynamic effect of interpersonal relationships and the need to maintain one's security with "significant others" during this process of "growing up." He stresses the importance of the mothering experience with its overriding importance in effecting future "object relationships." The infant's first interpersonal relationship is vis-à-vis the mother. The infant (later child) engages in activity which arouses anxiety in the mother by a process he refers to as "empathy." The infant and mother communicate via an affective process (empathic bond). This occurs at a primarily nonverbal level (meta-communicative). The empathic bond restricts the "trial and error" method of exploration in the child. It directly affects the so-called *defensive activities* (ego functions). The bond will hold attention in one area which expressed in terms of personality organization describes selective inattention. This prevents confusion and disorientation by restricting the entrance of other stimuli which might interfere with the object attended to. The development of thinking is another example of an ego function which is adaptive, integrated, and assists in reality testing. Thinking is a way of holding the musculo-skeletal apparatus in abeyance and using logical activity until there is a more appropriate opportunity to gain satisfaction. The personality development in adolescence is internally guided by the earlier anxiety that was felt at the displeasure of the "mothering one" and the continued acculturation which occurs by the reestablishment of empathic bonds with significant others in the individual's life. The amount of anxiety, inner conflict and emotional stress appears to depend upon the success of the particular individual in accomplishing the earlier developmental stages. Certain happenings in the earlier life of the adolescent will make it more difficult for the adolescent to experiment, participate, engage, or involve himself in the struggle of adolescence. The particular troubles brought to adolescence are invariably found in a troubled family. The parents who have problems in controlling their drinking patterns psychologically give permission for the use of similar intoxicating agents during the teen-age period. The unfaithful parent has already taught the adolescent the basics of sexual delinquency. The mistreated mother who thinks sex is dirty will influence the daughter to avoid contact with boys and limit the adult roles available for the girl. The parents who always provide plausible rationalizations for inappropriate or destructive behavior encourage psychopathic behavior in the offspring. The man who controls his family by temper tantrums gives example to the son in always demanding his own way and disregarding the rights of others. These children in their approach to adulthood from adolescence are fated to have handicaps in attaining social responsibility and making vocational choices which provide the inner security necessary in adulthood.

Dr. James F. Masterson, Jr., in a recent study and publication in the *Journal of the American Psychiatric Association* calls attention to the signs of the troubled youth. Many of us rather consistently pay no attention to the provocative behavior of the adolescent because of our own need to deny their behavior and ignore them completely. For some reason it seems that adult society thinks of adolescence as an extension of childhood, and if we wait long enough some magic will provide the change, when in reality only some drastic changes in the immediate environment, parental attitudes, adolescent reactions, and insightful therapeutic engagement is necessary. He has noted that in the past it was felt that so-called "adolescent turmoil" was normal. That is what under other circumstances would be called a neurosis, psychosis, character disorder, or the clinical picture of the symptomatic adolescent would subside with further growth of the adolescent. However, in his five-year follow-up study of adolescents diagnosed this way, results have not borne out the above conclusion. He studied a group of adolescents of the diagnostic category "adjustment reaction of adolescence." He found that "adolescence was but a way station in a long history of psychiatric illness that began in childhood and followed its own inexorable course." His conclusion was that adolescents will not grow out of their illness and that any treatment or intervention should be quite intensive.

USEFUL PSYCHIATRIC CONCEPTS

For those people, whether parents or educators, who deal with adolescents and their challenging behavior, it is easy to become angry, confused, or perplexed. Many adolescents have individual talents and are perceptive, energetic, idealistic, and enthusiastic. Most adolescents never work up to their intellectual capacity. There are no clear guidelines to deal with the adolescent. When they reach a certain age they become an adult, they are considered capable of assuming the responsibility that goes with adulthood. Adolescents are not children even though we may tend to view them as being overgrown children and react to them in this fashion. Many of us feel victimized by adolescents and try to bargain or bribe them. Often when their behavior becomes provocative we withdraw from them both physically and emotionally. This may have disastrous results upon the adolescent, especially if this was the technique used by the parents to force the child to conform to parental demands.

Adolescents are well known to act out, especially if given a task that is not relevant and absorbing of their energies. In understanding and dealing with children who are not able to report or express their symptoms or emotional feelings, we use play techniques. We know that children will displace their problems into play, and through this medium we can communicate directly back to children. However, with the adolescent who spends so much time thinking about his own place in the world, we learn more by listening to him and understanding what he communicates. As he verbalizes, he helps himself to internalize his anxiety. In listening and responding to adolescents, it is important to attend to both the overt and covert meanings of their communication as it regards their concerns and needs. This requires considerable skill and also appropriate consultation to avoid personal feelings which might entail capitulation, judgmental attacks, or angry critical comment which would adversely influence the quality of the adult-adolescent relationship.

Two concepts which might be of value in understanding and reacting to adolescents come from the psychiatric experience of dealing with the delinquent adolescent and the schizophrenic. The first concept that I would like to briefly explain is the result of work done by Adelaide Johnson and S. A. Szurek. They began publishing their findings in the early 1940's and had considerable experience dealing with the delinquent child

and adolescent. They have considered the character problems posed by the antisocial delinquent. The delinquency has been in the area of truancy, stealing, or sexual deviancy. They used the method of carefully detailed collaborative studies. Incidentally, further study might find socially constructive modifications like "acting out" of parental ambitions in socially useful achievements.

Their thesis states that parents may find vicarious gratification of their own poorly integrated, forbidden impulses in the acting out of the child through some type of unconscious permissiveness or inconsistency toward the child in the sphere of behavior under consideration. They feel that there is an unconscious defect in the conscience of the child which corresponds to the area of conflict in the parent. Earlier investigators had noted that antisocial children identified and acted out gross ethical distortions of the parent, like forgery in the parent and stealing in the child. In Johnson and Szurek's work, antisocial behavior in the child was traced to the unconscious encouragement of its expression by the parent. The behavior was the resultant of pathological binds which existed between the child and parent. This subtlety of communication has even been used by sensitive therapists for treatment purposes.

Adolescents are especially perceptive of conflicts in parental figures and lack the defensive activity to utilize logical activity or reality testing in evaluating much of the consequence of the direct expression of the conflicting thoughts they perceive. They are quite susceptible to the influence exerted on them from "omnipotent figures." In the communicational sequences they are sensitive to the type of communication that permits the thinking of unstated alternatives. Many parents "who want to make certain" adopt a detective-like attitude when it comes to doing homework. Often it is found that the homework is not done. Many fathers, who are preoccupied with the length of their young daughter's dress, are outraged when it is discovered that the daughter is illegitimately pregnant. There is also the mother's relationship with her Don Juan son in which he very punctually and promptly comes into her bedroom, sits on the bed, and entrances her with a vivid account of his date earlier in the evening. Therefore, what often appears to be the problem area in the adolescent's behavior, upon further investigation, may be found to be that of the parent who obtains gratification in a vicarious fashion through unconscious permissiveness, inconsistency, unwitting encouragement, or actually sanctioning of personal, parental, predatory behavior which has been acted out through the adolescent. Many of these parents do not understand the part they play in fostering this behavior and are oblivious to their instigating, perpetuating role in furthering the disordered behavior. For this reason, they often receive sympathy in reciting the outrageous behavior to their friends. In treatment, as these parents become aware and gain insight into their covert complicity, they experience genuine suffering. Additionally, when the psychiatric investigation reveals parental fostering of various aberrations, psychological advantages become apparent. When the adolescent is punished, the parent is also vicariously punished as the youth is caught and the parent identifies with his fate. In this way, the parent's conflict is externalized, takes place in another person so that the parent does not have to face his internal problems but can focus on the misdoing of the child and also, in many instances, allows the seemingly rational hostility which has always been present to have logical focus on the wrongdoer. These parents are especially sensitive to outside criticism and seem to delight in responding with righteous indignation and/or undeserved punishment of the child which further confuses the child and gives reason for a vicious cycle of reactive angry behavior at what is perceived to be a "betrayal" by the parent.

Professor Aichhorn in his book *Wayward Youth* describes the provocation of truant-

like behavior in a boy who was unable to relate in a trusting open fashion. Professor Aichhorn made subtle suggestions about the attractiveness of the outside world. This resulted in the boy's running away as expected. The child did return as Aichhorn thought when he found that the outside world was quite frightening. Professor Aichhorn may have had some second thoughts about this therapeutic device when the boy didn't return as soon as he thought. However, following this incident and the exploration of its meaning in their relationship, the relationship became quite positive. It was mentioned that other areas of psychiatry are developing new concepts in dealing with the disturbed individual. In the investigation of schizophrenia in 1956, Bateson, Jackson, Haley, and Weakland published a paper "Toward a Theory of Schizophrenia." The basis of their hypothesis lies in communications theory, and by using tape recordings, intensive psychotherapy, and clinical observation, they found certain particular sequences of events which they called the "double bind." Here they postulate that a "victim" is put in a bind with another person or persons and repeatedly exposed to communicational patterns which create a situation in which no matter what the victim does, he "can't win." They further suggest that the susceptible individual in this bind responds in a schizophrenic fashion. They point out the two levels of communication – the logical and the meta-communicative. The latter is often nonverbal and ordinarily is used to amplify the meaning of verbal comments. In the "double bind" the meta-communicative message (posture, gesture, meaningful action) contradicts the verbal symbolic message. The variations of the "double bind" are almost unbelievable. The two orders of the message communicated by the aggressor and victim may include such subtleties as "do not see this as a double message," "do not question what I am saying," "do not submit to my instructions," "do not obey me." When this is taken into consideration and communicational patterns evaluated fully, one would not be surprised at the statement "appearances can be deceiving."

ALCOHOL AND ADOLESCENTS

For many adolescents there are several serious pitfalls. The one I wish to comment on is germane, although it may not frequent newspaper headlines like the use of amphetamines, barbiturates, or LSD. Adolescence is often associated with adventure seeking, thrill seeking, and taking risks. Often they are expected to spend their time on the bench although they are full of energy, curiosity, and tempted by the seeming pleasures that are available to the adult. Many dire statistics are given of high-school and college kids using various psychotropic agents, especially marijuana and LSD. Although the use of these agents has increased in the past few years, the easiest psychopharmacologic agent to obtain remains alcohol.

Most state laws prohibit the teen-ager from using alcoholic beverages at least until the age of eighteen. Although this is the law in many states, a large percentage of teenagers have their first drink somewhere between the 9th and 12th grade. Urban communities have a higher percentage of teenagers initiated to alcoholic beverages than do rural communities with their stricter mores. The time of the first drink is largely determined by familial and socio-cultural factors. There is a relative lack of drinking among the offspring of parents who abstain. Today it is felt that both drinking and smoking among adolescents are serious health hazards. Drinking is not as serious a hazard in the sense that a teen-ager will become a hard-core alcoholic. The danger to the adolescent lies in his inexperience with the anesthetizing, intoxicating effects of the alcohol.

It is important that education conveys these health hazards in a univocal fashion. It is conservatively estimated that there are 5 million alcoholics in the United States.

Everyone who has contact with an alcoholic has a distorted view of drinking either from the view of being permissive or attempting to "stamp out" alcoholism. It is also estimated that every alcoholic has contact with 4 or 5 other people who, since they are directly involved in the alcoholic's social, psychologic, and economic problems, are incapable of having a healthy attitude toward alcohol. It is well known that drinking, especially to the point of intoxication, affects reflex time, judgment, and dulls perception. It lowers the awareness of the consequence of action and is frequently involved in behavior, especially among adolescents but also among adults, which is later regretted. Today with the ready access to automobiles, the adolescent who has been drinking becomes a definite menace when driving. Adolescents lack appreciation of their vulnerability, and this is often greatly exaggerated under the false optimism and group-induced euphoria where much adolescent drinking begins.

It bears repeating that there are many psychopharmacologic agents available, however, none as readily available as alcohol in its various forms, or so clearly related to destructive behavior in terms of reputation, aggressive behavior, or traffic accidents. The suggestibility of the teen-ager in the group works to his disadvantage where drinking is concerned. Alone he might experiment and try out something new. However, in a group other dynamics operate. There is the need to conform, outdo another, prove potency, or assure popularity. Every educator should have definite ideas on the use of agents which alter mental functioning so that such ideas can be imparted to the youngster in a relatively conflict-free fashion. At this point, the most important determinant in the use or abuse of alcoholic beverages resides in the example and early models that have been available in the family.

THE EDUCATOR

This term is used in its broad sense referring to the individual whether he be parent, teacher, or counselor, who functions in society to lead forth or draw out of the adolescent residing principles that are applicable to meeting the demands of reality. The most important principle that should shape the educator's techniques is his need to meet his own personal obligations and responsibilities. The educator will undoubtedly be influenced by his own successes and failures in accomplishing his own developmental task of adolescence. The manner in which the educator feels about himself and the world he knows will have great influence upon how his students successfully resolve their own pertinent development task. The educator should be prepared to take a hard look at himself, his techniques, and preparation that he is using in his daily activities with the adolescent. No matter what he has consciously communicated to the student, the meta-communicative attitude which conveys disdain, pedagoguery, autocracy, indifference, fear, or criticism, will surely be recognized. The methods must be continually reexamined in light of the aims and goals to be accomplished. One must not be satisfied with merely imparting "content," but have awareness of the multiple factors which influence the amount learned. Significant help is necessary to the adolescent in his quest for greater psychological, social, and physiological control of the new sensations and needs to manage new skills, customs, and self-doubt.

The educator will find that in meeting obligations to himself, he is also meeting obligations to the student and providing himself as a model and interpreter in the transition of adolescents. The educator who promotes and facilitates assimilation of values of a wider society communicates his own sense of worth. The challenge presented by the teenager should not be dealt with by withdrawal or the unanswerable argument of emphasizing "adult wisdom." The adolescent as opposed to the child is articulate and naturally turns his attention inward upon himself. He is attempting to find his place in society whether he expresses himself as curious, intrigued, provocative, or defiant.

It is important that we neither underestimate nor overestimate the adolescent. He may give the appearance of being mature; however, this is in appearance only. Under the guise of sophistication, the adolescent is often asking highly personal and anxiety-provoking questions. In listening to the adolescent we are always impressed, not always in agreement; however, the vigor of their commitment is undeniable.

SUMMARY

Adolescence is a period of time between puberty and maturity. During these years there are profound changes that occur in the psychological, social, and physiologic spheres. New experiences, loyalties, and relationships replace the emotional supports of the family as the phases of preadolescence, early adolescence, and late adolescence are mastered. The role of the child dependent upon the parent is replaced by a role in wider society where new civic, social, vocational, and sexual responsibilities are learned in preparation for the next phase of development. Out of the turmoil that confronts the adolescent, he ultimately has to determine his own course. It is hoped that this presentation is neither oversimplified nor complex beyond the point of comprehension. The meeting of obligations is the prime task of the educator and adolescent. Today, this is far more difficult than it was ten years ago.

Marvin G. Brook, M.D.

GETTING ON TALKING TERMS

Often problems which may lead to deep-seated psychological difficulties could be prevented entirely, or at least kept at a minimal threat, if only the individuals involved had learned to communicate. Many children grow up in homes where there is little or no talking; others grow up where there are words but little or no feeling expressed. These children usually have great difficulty relating to and associating with peers and with adults in particular. As Dr. Brook points out, they have not learned to talk—to communicate.

Talking gives a child the opportunity to understand the world around him and the people with whom he associates daily. It improves his interpersonal relationships. It helps in the development of his self-identity by allowing for the expression of feelings rather than an unhealthy suppression.

Psychologists, and particularly teachers and counselors, are constantly trying to help others develop a heightened sensitivity toward life and toward people. They can help individuals acquire this increased awareness by encouraging them to express themselves. Caution must be taken to prevent rigid rules or customs which inhibit spontaneity and feeling.

There's more in talk than meets the ear, as everybody knows who has taken note of the friendly smile, the eloquent wave of the hand, or the edgy voice that can add so much to the message of the spoken word—or so completely contradict it. This is especially true when a child is at one end of the communication line. He knows that our line of communication is made up of many threads, and he weaves them all together and gets our total message.

Yet talk remains the most important thread in our line of communication with a child. Through talk, parents and other educators can teach him, reason with him, encourage him, remind him, warn him. Through talk we can accomplish remarkable things for his healthy emotional development.

By talking with a child we help him learn about the countless things and creatures that make up his world, learn to make his needs known, and gain the vocabulary he must have to communicate with others. By *talking* with a child I mean *listening* to him as well—listening to what he says about facts and events, to his questions, his agreements and disagreements, and particularly

the feelings he expresses. And I also mean *answering* him, perhaps correcting his view of the facts, perhaps pointing out limits and rules to his behavior, and surely stressing courtesy and consideration toward others.

Being on talking terms with a child may give a parent a chance to explain how *he* feels about the things young Bruce is confiding in him—about "old" Mr. So-and-So across the street, who hates dogs, or about thunderstorms or the fascinating picture-book story they have been reading together. He may casually give Bruce a different slant by mentioning various people's differing views on Mr. So-and-So or storms or the story.

Of course, most parents *do* talk with their children, but are they doing it as well as their personalities, the situation, and the child permit? There are few of us who cannot improve our skill in this important kind of communication, given time, thought, critical self-examination, and assistance. Both parents should share this responsibility just as they share the job of teaching and discipline.

From the *PTA Magazine*, Vol. 62, September 1967. Reprinted by permission.

Although a mother has many more opportunities in the course of a day, there are advantages (and joys) for all concerned if Father and Mother alike are on good talking terms with their child.

Naturally, to certain problems talking does not provide the full answer or even the best answer. Moreover, sometimes the topic or the time of day suggests that the wisest action for the parent is to say nothing. There are occasions when children will not listen to, or talk with, their parents. There are times when parents are too rushed or disturbed or worried to answer children helpfully or even to listen well. In other words, we need to be selective in talking with our children. We need to be aware of obstacles and frustrations that may occur in even the most casual conversation, so that they will not blind us to the many pleasures both we and our children can gain from talking with one another. True, these are quiet pleasures, but they can be very satisfying.

WHEN THE TIME IS RIPE

It is never too early to begin. Long before he can understand the words we use, long before he can talk plainly or even try to talk, he gets comfort and a sense of closeness from the very fact that his parents are talking to him—from their voices, gestures, and the feelings they express. At older ages, too, these attitudes and relationships remain a crucial part of the communication between parent and child. Too often we ignore this silent, invisible backdrop as we concentrate on whatever we are discussing. And that's a pity, for the background of concern and respect continues to be important at every age.

It is best not to wait for a major crisis before we really take the child aside and talk with him. If we have given him plenty of talking time during tranquil periods and during minor crises, we have built up a sort of leverage for the major ones. This is true because parent and child respect one another and also because talking has become a natural path that is easy to follow even when a serious talk is needed to set things straight.

In a major crisis, and indeed in many minor ones, we cannot expect to resolve our child's difficulties or perplexities with a single talk. We should plan to return to the disturbing issue, perhaps repeatedly. If the child fails to bring up the matter directly, the parent can do so himself. This doesn't mean nagging; it means mastering the art of returning to a subject in a casual but reasonable way, or waiting patiently for clues from the child that show he is ready to talk about it again.

There is much, then, to be said for talking to a youngster in advance of an oncoming crisis. Talk can ease the experience of going to the doctor or the dentist, or prepare the young child for the absence of his father or mother. This gives him time to mobilize his forces to meet the problem in the best way he can—to master as far as possible the excitement, fear, and anxiety that he naturally feels when faced by the new experience. How he copes with his reactions to it is as important as the experience itself, for quite often those feelings are a greater burden for him than the actual event. So it's a good idea to talk about it with him several times, over a period of days or weeks.

Some young children just don't care to talk or be talked to, especially when they are beginning to feel independent and "on their own." They resist both listening and talking. Their parents, eager to "get a word in edgewise," may be tempted to save their discussions for a time when the child cannot easily get away—when he is in the bathtub or on the toilet or undressing for bed or in bed. But since a captive audience is not likely to be receptive or responsive, this approach may lead only to toilet difficulties or disturbed sleep. There are far better approaches, such as frankly acknowledging the strong barrier between them. ("You and I don't talk much with each other nowadays, do we? I wonder why.") If the child still keeps mum, advice from a specialist may be needed. A barrier that remains rigid and unchanged may reveal deep unconscious disturbances.

On the other hand, there are certain subjects that a youngster finds especially hard to talk about. And there are periods when a child may feel such a strong need to demonstrate his independence that he just doesn't want to accept someone else's views and judgments. At such times his privacy should be respected.

WINNING WAYS

So much for the "when" of talking with children. Let's go on to the "how." There are many ways, each reflecting the parent's own style of talking, listening, and getting himself in tune with another person. Also, how he talks depends on what he is talking about. In a highly exciting crisis—as when little Joan starts to ride her "trike" into a busy street—Mother's voice, tone, and gestures will be very different than when she and Joan are deciding what route to take to the nearby supermarket.

If either parent or child is overwhelmed by emotion, it is wiser to postpone lengthy discussion. There are other steps that may be taken at the disturbing moment. Support can be given to the terrified child, controls to the overly excited one, limits and acceptable outlets to the enraged one. Later, when emotions are no longer feverish, the parent can explore the child's ideas and feelings in a more relaxed and deliberate fashion.

Manner and tone are indeed almost as important as words in parent-child conversations. A child's smile or scowl, the wistfully pleading note in his voice, can give Mother or Dad helpful insight into his feelings. Then, too, many a youngster can be amazingly perceptive about grownups' expressions and tone of voice. He will quickly pick up and interpret a deprecating or ridiculing manner, and just as quickly register one that expresses concern and consideration. Sometimes, however, after the mercurial fashion of children, he will completely misinterpret his parents' manner because of his own strong feelings. The mildest, most loving reproach may seem like the harshest criticism—all because the voice of his own conscience is mingled with the voice of his parent.

Ways of talking with children depend also on the personal characteristics of the child. Even brothers and sisters vary greatly in their articulation, fluency, and manner of expression, and parents must be ready to change their style of talking and listening to fit each youngster. Furthermore, children change in personality, attitudes, and expression as they grow older. How we talk with a two-year-old differs greatly from how we talk with a six- or twelve- or seventeen-year-old, and so does what we talk about. Most parents make this continuing adjustment half unconsciously, but it may come about more easily if Mother and Father recognize it and perhaps discuss it together.

Parents who themselves enjoy a good "talking-over" relationship have a more substantial basis for getting on talking terms with their child. Having previously worked over—in thoughts, feelings, and words—their own views and responses to many problems, they can bring a unified and consistent perspective to their talks with their child. They are also likely to be more flexible and at ease in responding to their child's notions and expressions.

As we consider the "how" of talking, we remind ourselves of the fundamental importance of the relationship between child and parent, for this may be revealed as much in their manner of talking as in the words they use. If they share an abiding trust, confidence, and good will, obviously they will enjoy talking with each other. But if they are full of excitement, fear, and hate, communication is certainly blocked, and child or parent or both is likely to misuse whatever talk they may have together—to confuse rather than to clarify, or to discharge feelings rather than to accept and master them. The conversation may turn into a shouting session, the child aiming to provoke and hurt the parent and the parent retorting with harsh criticisms.

TALK TOPICS

What should parent and child discuss? The list is interminable. Minor crises, everyday rules, regulations, and courtesies are all suitable topics. So are the child's views about these things and his reactions to them. Nor can we overlook the importance of discussing with children certain serious events that may prove shocking – the death of a member of the family, an illness, an accident, or an emergency operation. A young child can be shocked by his mother's pregnancy or the birth of a baby, even by starting nursery school or kindergarten. Sometimes parents can use certain books and recordings produced to help children over crises. However excellent these aids may be, they cannot replace talks between child and parent. They cannot give the same support as a parent, nor do they give the child a chance to express his feelings, relate his fantasies, or ask questions.

Take, for instance, a four-year-old lad who is told that he is to go to the hospital for an operation. Since, as we know, young preschoolers may react in quite primitive ways, the little boy may feel, deep inside, that he would not be made to go through this experience if he had not done something wrong – or if his parents loved him more. Or he may imagine that, since he is being forced to suffer, he can rightfully expect to receive a magical reward or perhaps to make someone else suffer in return. The reward fantasy leads to increased disappointment and distrust, the revenge fantasy increases his primitive aggressiveness. Both fantasies lead to heightened anxiety.

WHAT'S IT ALL FOR?

Why do we talk with our children? One purpose is to improve the child's understanding, not only of events but of himself and his parents. Understanding brings greater mastery of himself and, later on, more realistic ways of dealing with other people. Also, talking may well improve relations between the child and his parents, helping each to perceive the other as an individual. Another aim of talking is to express feelings in a constructive way, rather than discharging them irresponsibly or, at the other extreme, suppressing them completely. The child who has a chance to vent his emotions in talk is in the long run a freer, less inhibited, less frightened child.

Though we have been concentrating on talk between parents and child, the child can also benefit by talking with others – teachers, for example. Now that schools are trying to increase children's participation, initiative, and activity, teachers rightly shy away from passivity and excessive memory work. But talking can be a still more meaningful classroom tool than it is today. Perhaps what is needed first is a better understanding by teachers of the real nature of the talking process. Consider the following example of a missed opportunity.

Certain schools have an unofficial tradition by which the children bring gifts to their teachers relatively early in the school year. Presumably, the relationship between teacher and child has little depth at this point. The gifts are seldom made by the children. They are more often purchased, and not from the children's allowances. In fact, parents usually shop for the presents.

This tradition is doing no good to the children or the teacher. Rigid custom has replaced talking and understanding, feeling and spontaneity. But the practice could be turned to good effect. Somewhere along the line the children could discuss how giving with love and thoughtfulness is distinguished from giving without feeling. They could be led to see that real giving is spontaneous, growing out of a positive feeling and a good relationship. Feelings about giving and not giving, and about classmates' giving, could come out in the talk.

Certainly headway has been made in recent years, at home and elsewhere, in the constructive use of talking. But there is room for further improvement. This improvement should rest upon an understanding of the ways in which talking is connected with thinking and feeling.

To establish clear and uninterrupted communication with our children, we don't need to send a satellite hurtling through space. But we do need built-in antennas that are sensitive to intellectual and emotional weather conditions. If we have set up such antennas, we can tune in at the right time on the *when, how, what,* and *why* of talking. That way we're safe in saying, "All systems GO."

Paul Friggens

SHAMEFUL NEGLECT OF SEX EDUCATION

For much too long we have been closing our eyes to the obligation to provide teen-agers with the necessary information concerning sex. Sex education includes not just the biological facts of reproduction and the sex act but also its relationship to the development of one's sexual role, of masculinity or femininity, as well as attitudes toward one's moral behavior.

Information needs to be introduced gradually. Interest in the various aspects of sex develops at different rates and the child must be ready and able to grasp the subject with understanding. Friggens is concerned with responsible sex education and distinguishes it from mere sex information.

This is not an area of education that can be assigned to the schools exclusively. The family must play its important role in this matter as well as the church or other agencies that mold attitudes and influence conduct and behavior. Parents, in particular, need help with the handling of a more complete method of sex education. In the role they do play, often the parents lack information and a feeling of security with regard to what kind of information they should make available to their children. They themselves may have unresolved problems and resulting anxieties concerning various aspects of sex. If the parents can't or aren't doing the job, schools will have to do it and work with the parents so that they can provide the proper guidance.

We are now reaping the fruits of our "sexual revolution" in America, and the statistics are infinitely shocking and sad.

At least one teen-age girl in every six, it is estimated, today becomes pregnant out of wedlock.

Illegitimacies are swelling our welfare rolls all across the nation, while dozens of American cities now provide special schools, tutoring, or night classes in which the entire enrollment is young, unwed mothers-to-be.

There's a startling rise again in venereal disease: an estimated 200,000 to 300,000 teen-age infections yearly.

What accounts for these tragic developments? One answer emerges from a recent public school health education study of some 18,000 children in 38 states: It revealed appalling ignorance and misinformation. While our so-called "sophisticated" teen-agers have been bombarded with sexually oriented films, books, articles, and advertising, probably no generation has been kept so ignorant of the true meaning of sex and sexuality.

Reprinted with permission from the May 1967 *PTA Magazine*. Copyright 1967 by The Reader's Digest Assn., Inc.

Complicating our teen sex problem still further is the "pill." Recently, on the West Coast, exploiters were reported selling single contraceptive pills to gullible high-school girls—a dollar for one night's "protection"—while across the country, I found that the contraceptive is further confusing our already muddled morality. One of the frequent questions that early-maturing teen-age girls now boldly ask in their high-school health classes is, "If I use the pill and don't get pregnant, then what's so wrong about having relations with a boy?"

The sex problems and concerns that we used to see in college and then in high school have now hit the junior-high level—the twelve- and thirteen-year-olds. A Denver, Colorado, teacher laments, "It would tear you apart if you could hear all the problems and questions that both children and parents confront us with."

"Shocking!" parents say. "But what can we do?"

They can recognize that as parents they have, by and large, failed in their job of providing effective sex education.

They can see that our schools step into the vacuum.

CAN PARENTS TEACH ABOUT SEX?

Ideally the home is the best place for sex education. But embarrassed, fear-ridden parents (often working mothers and absentee fathers) have been neglecting their responsibility. "We can't talk to our folks" is the children's universal lament. Says Dr. G. G. Wetherill, director of health service for the San Diego, California, schools: "Our lack of understanding and miserable attitudes toward sex are not helping young people in making choices as they grow up. And even if parents conscientiously try to prepare their children, there comes a time in the teen years when communication breaks down and parents have great difficulty discussing these highly sensitive and personal matters with their sons and daughters." "As parents we become too emotionally involved," says Dr. Vivian K. Harlin, director of health services in the Seattle schools and herself the mother of three.

Not only have we parents largely failed in the home, but by our abysmal ignorance and inhibitions we have obstructed and denied sex education in the schools.

"It seems almost incredible, but there are still many school systems in this country in which human beings are supposed to have nothing between the navel and the knees!" So Dr. Ruth A. Frary, Santa Cruz County, California, physician and marriage counselor, testified before a state senate committee.

In many communities parents are up in arms for fear that teaching of reproduction will show children "how-to" techniques and thus encourage sexual experimentation. Some parents seriously distrust the schools' training and ability to handle this sensitive subject, while still others are honestly opposed to such schooling on moral and religious grounds.

"Leave the teaching to the home and church," critics insist, despite evidence that most children get their sex education elsewhere.

"Actually we have no choice but to teach about sex in our schools," says Dr. Mary S. Calderone, physician, dynamic grandmother, and right now the nation's number-one crusader for sound sex education throughout our total society. Dr. Calderone is executive director of the Sex Information and Education Council of the U.S. (SIECUS), a voluntary health organization formed to meet the needs of members of the family-helping professions which is doing much to promote wholesome and realistic sex education. "It's nonsense to argue whether the schools should or shouldn't enter the field when our children have been getting sex information of one sort or another from the day of their birth: from their parents (whether or not they say a word!), their peers, the movies, TV, newsstands, advertising, phonograph records, society, and the street."

WHAT SHOULD SEX EDUCATION INCLUDE?

Many parents and communities are at long last trying to provide enlightened sex education for their children. School districts and governmental agencies in whole states are tackling the problem and drafting new curriculums in science and health. I have just visited a number of these areas from New York to California, and I found they are providing sound answers for the rest of the country.

"Enlightened sex education today is not just the facts of reproduction and certainly not education about the act of sex," Dr. Calderone emphatically declares. "It deals with one's total sexuality—maleness or femaleness, what makes you a man or a woman, the way you think, act, dress, marry. Sex is not something we do, but something we are, and the goal of SIECUS is simple: the use by every individual of his sexual faculties in mature, creative, and responsible ways in all his relationships, not just the sexual ones."

Helen Manley, executive director of the Social Health Association of Greater St. Louis, heartily agrees: "Sex education is not merely the physiological facts of reproduction or the health concerns in venereal disease," she points out, "and certainly it is not teaching the mechanics of the sex act." The nation's health educators, gathered recently at San Francisco to draft a suggested new curriculum, concluded simply: "Sex education should be distinguished from sex information. Perhaps it can best be described as character education."

Responsible sex education, says one authority, teaches that we achieve our greatest human happiness only in an enduring partnership, rooted in love, tenderness, and respect for the other person. The current trend is toward progressive sex-education or "family-life" programs that start as early as kindergarten or the first grade and continue through the twelfth grade. Usually the program is integrated with science, social studies, and home economics. Elementary school children are introduced to reproduction in nature, and teachers answer sex questions as freely as any others.

Under imaginative Edna Lehman, children of the Lincoln Elementary School in Evanston, Illinois, are introduced to the subject of reproduction in the second grade. Little tots tell about the new baby in their family, and they begin learning how flowers and plants are started. One year Mrs. Lehman soaked lima beans to illustrate the embryo stage; then children planted the beans and watched them grow and flower. Another year, the resourceful teacher hatched baby chicks in a small incubator in the classroom.

"At this age, before the children have been exposed to alley language, we can teach them the real beauty of birth," Mrs. Lehman explains. For example, they're fascinated by a film about the birth of baby kittens. "Look how the mother cares for them!" says one little girl. And the teacher interjects, "Wasn't it wonderful that God prepared a special opening for the birth of the mother's babies?"

"In this way, we seek to instill the wonder and reverence of it all," Mrs. Lehman declares, "and I believe we are laying the groundwork for responsible parenthood."

WHEN TO START THE TEACHING?

When should serious sex education begin? "Reach the children before it's too late!" most teachers urge, and that means about the fifth or sixth grade. Girls generally mature earlier than boys, and they're ripe for guidance at age eleven or twelve. It's important to reach both boys and girls at the age level when they are highly interested in their bodies, but in an uninhibited and natural way. Some schools find that in age and experience the sixth-grader is ready.

Evanston schools, however, have stepped up their sex education to the fifth grade, where children ask for the explanation of multiple births, just how fertilization takes place, and how to keep from having a baby.

"It's urgent not only to reach children with

physiology at this age," says Evanston fifth-grade teacher Robert Biddick, "but with the morality of sex. We must help them to realize early that sex is good, and not to be misused. We need to help them explore their feelings about themselves as sexual persons."

Some parents violently object to sex education at the fifth-grade level, claiming it exposes the innocent and unready. "True, it's over the heads of some, and they just aren't interested," Biddick explains. "We'll catch them again later, but meantime we see more and more children with real need."

I viewed a dramatic film, "Especially for Boys," which the Los Angeles schools had prepared for the sixth grade. With simple diagrams it discussed body changes and the glands, ovaries, and testes. It showed sperm and uterus and where and how a new life begins, and concluded on this lifting note:

"There is much to learn before young men and women can become good parents. Families are started after marriage because children need love and protection. Like your ancestors, you have within your body special cells which are the carriers of life. In this way life is carried on by every man—by doctor, teacher, mechanic, astronaut, or whatever you grow up to be."

At the junior-high level the program moves on from biological reproduction to the social aspects of sex: physical, emotional, and social transitions to maturity and adulthood; family health; and venereal-disease education. In senior high school special emphasis is put on marriage and the ideals of home and family, pointing out that the greatest human happiness is achieved only in enduring partnership, rooted in love, tenderness, and respect for the other person.

You should hear the questions that these anxious, confused youngsters raise in class, or read the more personal and pressing ones they leave in a question box. "Is it proper to have relations with a boy in a car if he uses contraceptives?" "Do people have sex only to make babies?" and "Can you get syphilis from a toilet seat?"

The skilled teacher never dwells on the sex act. "You don't have to go into intimate detail," as one told me, "but you can't and mustn't dodge the essential biology or the matter of individual responsibility."

At Tacoma, Washington, mini-skirted junior-high girls gather around their teacher to press personal questions after class. "What do you do with a boy with happy hands?" one asks. "Suddenly, I have warm, strange feelings and I'm boy crazy. Is it wrong?" another inquires. One day, after counseling with these youngsters, Patricia Fullerton, a poised, outgoing, young-married teacher, summed up her reassuring philosophy about sex education. "I wish that somehow teachers everywhere," she told me, "could put their arms around our youngsters and tell them 'Of course you have warm, intimate feelings. You want to love and be loved by the other sex. Well, it's life; it's normal. Never be ashamed of it! You must use self-discipline and control these drives, however; understand them, don't fear them.'"

WHAT KIND OF TEACHER?

It takes a specially gifted teacher indeed to stand up before a class of insecure, over-stimulated teen-agers today and impress on them that sex is precious, infinitely complex, and not just an act.

At San Diego, Kathleen Lochtefeld, an attractive, warm, and understanding woman, talks earnestly to a class of high-school girls about kissing, petting, and premarital sex.

"You have to answer their questions truthfully," Mrs. Lochtefeld stressed. "This generation is certainly questioning the 'code' of continence before marriage, and girls bitterly resent the double standard." She added: "It's difficult to teach morals today when we have downright worship of sex appeal and not one but several American sex codes. No wonder our children are anxious and confused. I don't preach, but I let my students know where I stand, what I firmly believe. Kids need this kind of support."

Thus, without fanfare or furor, sex education is meeting poignant, pressing needs in our schools today. "The big problem is our change of mores," says Ann Cotter, who teaches in the suburban Kenmore, New York, high schools. "Most of these young people are good kids. They want to be moral, but also they want to be accepted by their peers. They want to get along, and they desperately need somebody to give them some spine. Unfortunately, many can't talk to parents; others come from broken homes."

Unhappily sex education—and indeed the whole area of health education—lacks the academic prestige that it deserves, equal to that of English, Mathematics, or Social Studies. Says Nora Page Hall, director of Health Education for the Tacoma, Washington, public schools: "Most health majors get into the field through athletics and sports, and the schools treat health as a subordinate subject, something the gym teacher or school nurse can teach on a rainy day."

Says Miss Manley: "Our teachers have had little or no preparation for teaching sex education; they feel inadequate and resent crowding it into their already heavy schedule. Others feel they need much more information in physiology and anatomy. Lamentably the vast number of teachers graduating today lack a background in health. And an indiscreet teacher may do irreparable harm."

So first, we must look to our teaching qualifications and training if we are to expand successful sex education in the United States. There are capable, well-rounded, sensitive men and women in every school, who can fill the job if they are just motivated and given the chance, Nora Hall believes. Miss Hall is working with a small core of Tacoma teachers, who in turn are recruiting and inspiring others. At San Diego, Dr. Wetherill has developed a staff of five who cover both the ninth- and twelfth-graders in one session a week for six weeks. Lessons are also available to the sixth-grade classes. Courses are voluntary and the parents must consent. Ninety-nine per cent of the youngsters sign up.

Does sex education pay off? Critics contend that there is insufficient proof. Admittedly it's difficult to measure. "But neither can you measure the anguish of an unwed mother or the tragedy of a student suicide," an Evanston teacher comments. One danger is that a community is apt to clamor for a crash program, hoping for a prompt reduction in the incidence of VD and early pregnancy. A good program can reduce both, but sex education is neither a panacea nor disaster insurance, and communities shouldn't expect too much too soon.

IN YOUR COMMUNITY

What can your community do? First, develop a program that fits your local needs. Parents, doctors, clergymen, and teachers might well team up to draft the curriculum, as has been done in a few places. Next, see that your community understands the program. Over much of the country sex education is still an emotion-charged topic. Thus it is imperative to get the backing of key people in the community. Advises Dr. Wetherill, "Call them together and ask, 'Are you satisfied with the way your children are receiving their sex information now? If not, do you feel that we as teachers and parents are mature enough in our thinking about sex to do better? If you agree, we can begin planning a program.'"

The American Association of School Administrators has endorsed a comprehensive health education program for kindergarten through twelfth grade, in which sex education would be a normal part of a unit on human growth and development. After a study of successful programs, the National Association of Independent Schools, composed of some 790 of the oldest and most distinguished private schools in the United States, is strongly encouraging the incorporation of sex education in the curriculum. NAIS recognizes that children increasingly need guidance in coping with their confusion about sex.

Significantly, too, more and more church

and community leaders, plus the National PTA, are speaking up for enlightened sex education. "It is ironic that, in our so-called sexually liberated society, sex is still a dirty word," says the Reverend George Hagmaier, professor of religious education at the Catholic University of America. Father Hagmaier urges stepped-up sex education because "inadequate young people become inadequate parents."

It's a tragic shortcoming indeed that, while America spends increasing billions for education, we neglect a subject with such crucial importance for all of life.

Francis L. Filas, S.J.

PROBLEM IN TEEN-AGE SEX EDUCATION

Psychologists have long been aware of the ravages of venereal disease and of the fact that it has increased greatly, particularly among teen-agers in the past few years. Some of the seriousness of the problem, no doubt, is related to the promiscuity among school-age children and their relative lack of information. Father Filas has given careful consideration to justifying the need for a program for venereal disease education in our public and parochial schools.

Presentation of the information concerning these diseases can be considered part of the program in the department of biology, health, or guidance. If proper preparation is made for the introduction of the subject, none of the usual parent concern or objection need be aroused and it should contribute to a sound psychological attitude on the students' part toward health, sex, and social mores.

As these lines are being written, newspaper headlines and news commentators are stridently calling attention to an epidemic of spinal meningitis at Fort Ord, Calif. – some 85 cases within a year, and 14 deaths. The tragedy is that an epidemic unbelievably more extensive exists and is growing daily in our midst, and yet hardly a ripple of public attention has been stirred because of it. This is the hard fact of the social diseases: an estimated *minimum* 100,000 annual cases of syphilis, and a million cases of gonorrhea, 25 per cent of which are infections of teenagers (i.e., from the seventh grade or 12 years up to 19). This statistic does not carry its full impact until it is translated into day-to-day figures. Daily, 2,800 new gonorrheal and 280 syphilitic infections occur at a minimum, of which 750 affect teen-agers *per day*. Deaths from syphilis in the United States total 4,000 per year – more than ten

daily; and almost ten babies are born every day who have contracted syphilis – 3,000 per year.

As a final show of statistics, the 66 per cent of American youth who learn about the social diseases from their peers on the street usually get a batch of half-truths loaded with biological superstition and gross error on the methods of transmitting venereal disease and the chances for its cure. In this mass of shadowy half-truths, little or nothing is conveyed about proper means of prevention. The only genuinely effective method of preventing an increased spread of syphilis and gonorrhea is to avoid sexual promiscuity. The gang-in-the-gutter likewise knows little about the second elementary truth of venereal disease education: if infection has certainly occurred or is even suspected, a physician should be consulted so that the disease will not spread to possibly innocent victims.

A program of venereal disease education from the U.S. Department of Health, Education and Welfare has been worked out with consummate prudence for use in the schools. This program (embracing the two aspects of avoidance of sexual promiscuity and frank submission for treatment) is not truly a part of that sex education which ideally and theoretically should always be reserved in the first place for parents at home. Moreover, so many parents are themselves ignorant of the technical facts about venereal disease — as known in 1964 and not 1934 — that the schools must do this job of spreading the proper attitudes and information on venereal disease. A final problem occurs with regard to the inhibitions of parents who shrink from mentioning venereal disease, in the mistaken notion that "such things don't happen to nice people." The facts are that they happen in the nicest neighborhoods.

One of the reasons that have militated in the past against an approval of venereal disease education in the schools is the belief that such education necessarily implies something crude, shocking, vulgar and disgusting; or that the approach is on a strictly utilitarian basis, implying that "getting caught" with venereal disease is the sanction of a pseudo-moral order. More than this, the misunderstanding frequently persisted that venereal disease education meant a ridiculing of the God-given respect due to sex, so that it degrades sex as such. Even against venereal disease education in a thoroughly acceptable form, as outlined above, certain arguments recur that in many areas hinder a school program from going into effect. It will interest Catholics — and, let us hope, Catholic critics of parochial schools — to know that education programs have been introduced much more easily and with far greater cooperation in the Catholic parochial schools than in certain public schools. In these lat-

ter, the school boards or school administrators have feared to bring up the subject and have mistakenly thought that "religion" was against the idea.

There are a number of typical objections offered against this sort of program. One of them goes somewhat as follows: *"It is disgraceful to admit that our students need this. It implies that the character training in our schools has failed."* If this argument comes from an educator, it betrays a disgraceful selfishness and lack of interest in the welfare of the students. For the strongest way to combat venereal disease is to teach young people to avoid sexual promiscuity and hold up the moral ideal of a strict respect for sexual intercourse, so that the desire for it is satisfied exclusively within the bonds of marriage. The school must also realistically admit that its character training cannot be counted on to reach each individual student, just as the Church's moral training will to some extent inevitably fail. There is simply no argument against the fact of the widespread increase of venereal disease among teen-agers. And this certainly indicates that character training, first in the home and secondarily in the school, has failed. Why should a first and possibly relatively inculpable failure be compounded into culpability by a refusal to take necessary and irreproachable action?

A second objection is based on a complete caricature of the proper education: *"The inclusion of venereal disease education units in a general science or social science curriculum implies that there is no immorality in the use of sex outside marriage, and that the only norm is: 'Don't get caught; and if you get caught, treatment is so easy and certain that you can keep doing this again and again with impunity.'"* Here again, the opponent forgets that the best prevention of venereal disease consists in teaching the moral standards of the proper use of sex in marriage. The use of this education in other departments of the curriculum does not mean an invasion of the sphere of theology and moral religious training. Venereal disease education properly prescinds, abstracts from, any explicit moral and religious judgment; it does not, however, contradict these. And as for the treatment being certain, though penicillin treatment can cure, this is hardly an infallible remedy. Moreover, the temporary disappearance of primary lesions of syphilis can lull the ignorant teen-ager into thinking that all is well. He or she does not know that a killing, crippling or mentally debilitating germ is latent until a later flare-up indicates that irreversible organic damage has occurred.

A further objection: *"This will call the attention of innocent students to what they should not know and what they do not need to know."* The only answer to such a statement is a flat denial. Any health problem involving so many thousands of teen-agers is something the American student should know about.

"Our parents and grandparents got along without this; why can't our children?" Yes, our parents and grandparents got along without this—but how? With what shame and heartaches and further unnecessary spread of disease in their own day, under the hush-hush atmosphere of an era when reliable cures did not exist. Moreover, the times have changed. If the incidence of venereal disease had been as critical in our parents' and grandparents' times, they, too, should have been given education about it in their schools with the same critical imperativeness with which it is justified today.

"There is too much talk about sex already in the air. The less of it the better. Besides, our children in seventh and eighth grade and early high school are too young to hear it." It is thoroughly correct that too much undigested and improperly presented raw information about sex is being circulated. Much of this comes from 1) an openly prurient press, which seems to be almost beyond control because of court decisions on the legal meaning of obscenity; 2) from the respectable press and radio and TV, which

none the less at times inject their "respectable" snide comments and sexy emphasis for the sake of circulation rises and ratings—and this often in the name of what must be called, for want of a better name, pharisaical concern for public morality. A double standard on sex openly exists: on one page, an editorial decrying juvenile delinquency, and for the next ten magazine pages, the latest pictures about the hottest sex kitten. But it should be remembered that venereal disease statistics begin in the seventh and eighth grades and early high school. Hence the need to start the education early.

"The Church is against such mention of venereal disease and the means of stopping it." This objection is a puzzling one, since no reasonable basis exists for it either in biblical theology or in official Church teaching—to speak at least for Catholicism. Papal documents on Catholic attitudes toward sex condemn "pansexualism" as a philosophy of attributing all human ills to a uniformly sexual cause. The Church might also be listed against any coeducation of the sexes where male and female are treated as completely identical human beings. They have, indeed, identical human dignity; but they do not have the same talents, needs, potentials and approaches. The Church is truly opposed to any implication that the body of any man or woman is a purely animal entity that must have its sense desires satisfied whether or not they conflict with one of the laws of the Creator. The Church is opposed to any implication that sexual intercourse or sexual pleasure is an absolute necessity for mental and physical well-being. But proper venereal disease education offends against none of these approaches, and either does not touch on them or implicitly supports them.

"Venereal disease is the punishment of God. Let the culprits suffer." In the present context, this objection is the most raw and uncharitable expression one can imagine. Jesus admitted no excuse when He said: "He who is without sin, let him cast the first stone." The love that God expects us to show

toward our neighbor means at the minimum that we should not callously wish evil even on those who seem to have brought such evil on themselves. The biblical dictum "Mine is vengeance, says the Lord" does not mean that God is vengeful, but that only the Creator knows the innermost sanctum of human free will; only He knows, satisfactorily and adequately, how blameworthy or how innocent any man or woman or teen-ager is. Even if we were to admit as true so bigoted an interpretation as that venereal disease was the divine punishment for sin and that those who received it must stay with it, we would then be forgetting that venereal disease can also strike those who are completely innocent. How about the child of a syphilitic mother, infected from her? How about the subjectively innocent, namely, the teen-agers who have not been given adequate character education at home, and who have been led astray by bad companions or temporarily blinded by strong passions, which confuse them and which they do not fully know how to control?

The main objections against such a program of education in schools can thus be met. It becomes obvious, then, that the real educative process must begin with school administrators and, through them, teachers.

For unless they are persuaded, the program will not succeed. It cannot be too strongly stressed, in this connection, that a reverential attitude toward sex must always be maintained. In this way it can be made clear that the lawful use of sex – according to conscience and religious teaching – is not wrong; what is being decried is the abuse of sex and the disastrous effects that follow from it.

Of all the objections to venereal disease education, the one that needs refuting more than any other concerns what it tells students about treatment. It is a popular misconception that the program describes the treatment as so certain, so infallible, that anyone can indulge in sexual promiscuity again and again with no risk through reinfection. Education about venereal disease may indeed seem to imply that prompt application for medical treatment makes reinfection harmless. But no such implication is contained in current literature from reputable agencies interested in this field, for as we have noted, cure is by no means certain. Public misunderstanding on the point, however, may be an obstacle to wider introduction of a program badly needed in our schools.

Part VII

DROPOUTS AND DELINQUENTS

In the past decade, no group has been given more professional attention by psychologists than the dropouts. Today the dropouts hold the attention of psychologists and all related professionals because they pose a great threat to the stability and continuity of our way of life. There is no question that the growing urbanization of America and the resultant changes in family structure have altered the traditional respect for staying in school and avoiding conflict with the law. Of course, several generations ago the schools were making little or no attempt to keep children in school beyond the eighth grade — certainly not to the age of seventeen for all individuals. The percentage of dropouts, therefore, is much greater today. Then too, fewer and fewer young people can find employment before the age of eighteen; this leaves a great number who leave school or are asked to leave school without a chance to find a job. Such young people are potential problems to society.

Generally, psychologists agree with educators who feel that the best place for most unemployed youth is in some type of organized and supervised setting. The dropout cannot fit into the school of the past with its rigid curriculum and unrealistic goals and methods. Either the schools have to adjust to the fact that different types of individuals will be coming to them and remaining until age seventeen, or society will have to create other agencies to cope with persons whose needs cannot be met in the traditional school but who are not yet employable. Psychologists can see the need for involvement and activity, particularly on the part of the adolescent who has little or no opportunity to express frustration, aggression, anger, or violence in socially acceptable ways. Often, parents fail to reinforce the school's attempts to sustain a child's interest in school and to cultivate the feeling that education is necessary for real and lasting happiness and for the "full" life.

Professionals today are interested in the problems of "hard-to-reach" children and delinquents as well as those of the dropouts. Gangs and rumbles have become the symbol of a large per cent of unhappy and disenchanted youth, particularly in the large cities of America. There have been real gun-shooting episodes involving gangs in most of our major cities. This development has not been limited to the socially-economically disadvantaged but has also been found in all segments of society. At first, the gang phenomenon was studied primarily by the sociologist, and then by the social psychologist; now it has become the subject of intense psychological study and experimentation as well. It is felt that behind the group behavior are varied and serious psychological problems and disturbances within the individuals involved, and between them and their peer and family groups.

By studying the individuals who make up these antisocial and destructive groups, one is better able to understand their meaning and behavior, and to help various agencies and schools alter their plans so that they can develop preventative programs and corrective schemes. The application of sound psychological principles, such as the recognition of the basic need for acceptance and status, love and attention, has proven a basis for the more successful attempts to work with gangs and hard-core delinquents.

Gilbert Derr

PROMISING PRACTICES FOR THE CULTURALLY DEPRIVED

Throughout the country there is increasing interest in the potential dropout and preventive programs. Mr. Derr's article explains various programs instituted with adolescents who had not progressed beyond elementary school level. He has applied unusual techniques and devices by taking into account the latest thinking in group techniques and has utilized such teaching instruments as the newspaper, the mail order catalog, the voting machine, club activities, part-time work, and special clinics. Recognizing the uniqueness and importance of the father role, he has also experimented with a "father's club" among a group of fatherless families.

This special research also reports an interesting counseling technique, with proven psychological bases, that assists those individuals most needing counseling: the physically handicapped, the mentally retarded, the indigent and the unemployable. These various programs point up the wide range of needs and the variety of possible approaches to the problem of the lesser-motivated student in the school system.

In the interest of keeping potential dropouts in school, many promising practices have been developed by the Special Project at the Douglas School in District Eleven.

PROMISING PRACTICE I

Separating the Elementary School 15 Year Olds and Up

This was the basic step in the organization of the program for potential dropouts. Generally speaking, it is the overage grammar school pupil who is most likely to drop out. Further, because of his age, and his still being in grammar school, it almost always follows that his problems are compounded: under-achievement; borderline I.Q. and below; large family; no father; disciplinary difficulties; peer wrangles; and poor self-motivation. But this does *not* imply that he is not creative. He is doubtless a more basic individual with greater possibilities than the advantaged.

This meant that all students in that particular school, who were 15 years old and older, were placed in ten classrooms. These pupils were separated for purposes of instruction, guidance, and testing. They participated in

normal school activities with the school at large; that is, lunch, assembly programs, etc.

This is the basic promising practice in the potential dropout phase out of which has emanated many useful approaches for working with the culturally deprived.

Dynamic teachers were selected, followed by well-organized and executed orientation and workshops. The instructional effort was concentrated in the communication and arithmetic areas. There was a "soft-pedaling" of science and social studies since it was felt that the more basic skills were of greater use to these students. Working with the overage pupils, who were also often underachievers, discipline cases, from large and often fatherless families, were nobly-spirited and hard-working teachers and a group of specialists, including an assistant principal, the administrative head; an adjustment teacher, educational counselor, school social worker, home economist, youth activities coordinator, parent and community counselor, and job placement counselor.

Because of team effort, the pupils were more highly motivated, achievement levels were raised, many social problems were solved, and many were placed on jobs. Follow-up has shown that of the first Special

Project class which is now in high school, 97 per cent are still in school.

A new concept has been developed from this experiment. From the separation of overage pupils in *one elementary school* has come the separation of overage pupils in *all of the elementary schools in one school district*. This means that all overage grammar school pupils have been placed in one building. This recent concept in the public schools in Chicago is known as the Educational and Vocational Guidance Center. Thus, there has been a city-wide implementation of an effort that came to fruition because the problem was identified and isolated.

Summarizing Promising Practice I. Separating elementary school 15-year-olds and over with a concentration of instructional efforts toward developing communication and arithmetic skills gave rise to a new concept in education.

PROMISING PRACTICE II

Forming Homogeneous Achievement Groupings

The action research program was faced with an extreme poverty in reading achievement. The execution of reading in the conventional manner would mean one of two things: either the utilization of *one* textbook for all of the reading levels in a class or the setting up of as many reading groups as there are reading levels. Both of these approaches are unsound and the advancement of reading levels would be questionable. The majority in a reading program could not benefit in a situation in which *one* book is used for all levels; and it is almost a physical impossibility for a teacher to work with as many groups as there are reading levels.

It is a known fact that educational philosophers frown on homogeneous groupings. However, this very necessary departure proved quite successful in raising the reading and arithmetic levels.

The Special Project reading classes were set up in half-year achievement levels, that is, 3.0 to 3.4 and 3.5 to 3.9, etc. This meant further that there was a complete reorganization for such a 90 minute reading period. The same procedure was used in arithmetic for 60 minutes. In this way, a teacher can unify his materials and supplementary texts are more beneficial because the pupils can be reached. For those pupils who need phonics, and 75 per cent of them do, a teacher is given a workable and surely sensible situation that he can handle.

Regardless of the fact that there is a "cross-cutting" of ages, the pupils are so highly motivated toward raising achievement levels basic to academic success and school completion that the older ones do not seem embarrassed to be with the younger.

Evaluation has shown that within the first year of the Special Project classes, both reading and arithmetic levels have been raised as much as 4 years. Further, there was improvement in the achievement level of each pupil in the program. Because of the success of the Special Project achievement classes, several schools have organized reading and arithmetic programs in such a fashion.

Summarizing Promising Practice II. Homogeneous achievement groupings raised the reading and arithmetic levels of each pupil in the program.

PROMISING PRACTICE III

Organizing After-School Vocational Classes

The expressed goal of the action research program, otherwise known as the Special Project, was to stimulate potential dropouts toward school completion. It was felt that guidance in the form of a definite concrete program was necessary to transform the idle hours after school into something meaningful. Without a constructive after-school program, the many negative forces at work during idle hours could pull the potential dropout away from his goals, despite strong motivation. Let us not forget the "power of the peer group."

As the philosophy of the After-School Program was being formulated, the following consideration was eminent: vocational training, or a form of vocational training such as a skill involving the use of the hands, was highly relevant in the lives of these pupils. The psychology of the effort was simply this: to initiate thinking in the direction of a vocational occupation and to be given the opportunity to make a choice plus the time and instruction to develop the practice. This, in itself, would be a strong motivation to want to stay in school so that these vocational goals could be realized.

The Special Project pupils were given the opportunity to voluntarily participate in the After-School program. The response was 100 per cent following the announcement, and rightfully so—after all, this was to be an experience that grammar school pupils had never had before. Few had ever heard of grammar school pupils going into the woodworking, auto, metalsmith, and electric shops in a vocational high school and also taking typing, office practice and dressmaking.

The shop classes were from 4:00 to 6:00 P.M. five days a week. Since the vocational high school was easily accessible—two blocks to walk, attendance was almost perfect. The pupils were given the opportunity to display their creations, and some were quite talented. Often, this was the first time that they had succeeded in anything and these pupils displayed their work with pride. Somehow, as they looked with the viewer at their creations, they were trying to say—"See what I can do when I am given the opportunity to decide?"

Summarizing Promising Practice III. The After-School Program did provide a vocational experience leading to self-motivation which is essential to the interest necessary for school completion.

PROMISING PRACTICE IV

Using the Newspaper as a
Teaching Device

Several techniques have been developed in the Special Project classes along with much new subject matter and "unusual" textbooks, all devoted to keeping the would-be dropout in school.

A most unusual textbook is the newspaper. It has been called the "poor man's university." Because it is an up-to-the-minute record of current events, it is a university in print. The daily newspaper has become a tool by which the youngsters expand their vocabularies. They may learn history through current events, discover science, and learn practical arithmetic by "shopping" the ads.

It has been observed that the newspaper is a number one "attention holder." The daily newspaper has a direct appeal because it is immediate—a part of the twenty-four hours at hand. Repeated tests have proven that vocabularies have been enlarged markedly and are traceable to the use of the daily newspaper.

Summarizing Promising Practice IV. The newspaper, because of its current appeal, has been successful in developing vocabularies, discovering science, and teaching history and arithmetic.

PROMISING PRACTICE V

Using the Mail Order Catalog
as a Teaching Device

Another unusual textbook which provided a great deal of interest as supplementary material was the mail order catalog. Besides opening up an entirely new dimension to the Special Project pupils, the catalog was extremely interesting in that they could see so many goods and services presented in such a manner as to stimulate interest in reading, science, social studies, spelling, art, music, vocational skills, and arithmetic. Immediately, the mail order catalog put them in the atmosphere of "a business world," and youngsters are attracted to the dynamic sense of commercialism. (Many times, teachers "lose" their pupils because of a lack of imagination and do not provide dynamic learning experiences. Boredom is a reason given by many students as to why they left school.)

Mail order houses – Sears Roebuck, Spiegel's, Alden's, Montgomery Ward's and others – provided each pupil with a textbook. With the catalog, they could learn about so many articles and products, their uses, how they are designed, the sales price, a discount consideration if ordered by the lot, fractional dimensions, and the variety of features connected with each article.

With such a teaching device, there is no end to the motivations just by examining the myriad examples shown. Since, according to Sigmund Freud, owning a home is a childhood wish and money is not, one can visualize the repeated satisfactions in fulfilling that "wish." As he turns the pages, he is saying, "I want this awning, this stereo, this power lawnmower, this set of golf clubs, this Ping-Pong table, this door knocker, or these draperies, this apron, this cookbook, this rug, this kitchen, this sofa, or this color in my living room.

Some pupils were motivated toward work with the design of products; some to clerical work in the mail order house itself; some to the manufacture of products. Moreover, filling out the order blank provides a learning situation with a definite carry-over. This is surely a good orientation for filling out applications for employment.

Studies have revealed that the mail order catalog, a most unusual textbook, proved to be the most popular.

Summarizing Promising Practice V. The mail order catalog, as a teaching device, opened up a dynamic commercial world to the student, with concrete examples of prod-

uct variety and design, with built-in motivation and clear-cut academic and vocational implications.

PROMISING PRACTICE VI

Using the Voting Machine as a Lesson in Democratic Responsibility

This was the brainchild of one of the Special Project teachers who was a practicing attorney as well as a teacher. He felt keenly the necessity of our youths' learning the value of exercising their political responsibility in a democratic government. He brought a voting machine to school and enlisted the services of experts to instruct the pupils in the operation of the machine. The pupils were so highly interested that the voting machine was brought back to the school several times.

The actual operation of the voting machine did more to encourage participatory interest in government than any amount of written material. This was evidenced by a greater interest in the activities of the student council, suggestion box, class elections, and opinion polls following the experience with the machine.

Summarizing Promising Practice VI. The voting machine stimulated an interest in preparing for the responsibilities of the democratic process.

PROMISING PRACTICE VII

Using the Bulletin Board to Raise Aspirational Levels

The Special Project pupils are mostly Negroes. There is a constant need for these pupils to identify with persons and situations which will help them aspire to higher goals.

These, and like pupils, need to identify with people in their ethnic group who *have* achieved reasonable success against the odds with similar problems and similar challenges. The son of the tycoon cannot correlate his experiences with the child of the asphalt jungle any more than the black city-dweller can relate his experiences to the white suburban child. To add to this problem, there is still a lack of valid information about Negro achievement in the textbooks.

It would be good for the Negro child to know that the founder, first settler, and builder of the first trading post in Chicago, as well as the first citizen, was a Negro – Jean Point Baptiste DuSable. There is no statue of the man – no founder's day – no city-wide commemoration.

Frederick Douglass, 1817-1895, was one of many outstanding figures in American Negro history. A self-educated man, he impressed the rulers of Europe with his eloquence as he toured and lectured there. The first twenty years of his life were spent in slavery. In 1838 he escaped to Massachusetts where he settled and lectured on behalf of the Massachusetts Anti-Slavery Society. Later he began the first Abolitionist newspaper in Rochester, N.Y., in 1847. How many black children know of him? And even fewer know about Benjamin Banneker, inventor of the striking clock, publisher of the first almanac, and one of the initial participants in the planning of the capital city of Washington, D.C.

They surely should know about the greatest soul and force in developing the scholarship of Negro history – Dr. Carter Godwin Woodson. Since textbooks don't mention him, how can the pupils know? The bulletin board must take on the proportions of a full-fledged teaching device and not just a "window dressing showpiece." The fact remains that if the dedicated teacher does not devise special means to inspire the little Negro boy and girl, they will never get it from the conventional tools and books because it is *not* there.

The bulletin board in the Special Project became a major learning situation – pictures, articles, library assignments, discussions, etc., were arranged by the pupils. Because of the interest generated by this, outstanding Negroes in Chicago were invited to meet the pupils who made up these displays.

Summarizing Promising Practice VII. The bulletin board, as a major teaching device, has been used to raise the aspirational level of Negro pupils by providing supplementary knowledge and information not available to students in textbooks.

PROMISING PRACTICE VIII

Participating in Urban 4-H

The Special Project pupils were given the opportunity to engage in club work after school and on Saturday. This activity was under the guidance of the Home Economist.

Often, there is a tendency to equate the 4-H activity with rural areas, but gradually, cities have been drawn into the movement.

The goal is to teach cooperation as well as competition, and to develop a savings account with their prize money. Activities of the 4-H clubs include sewing, cooking, photography, woodworking, leathercraft, and art. Emphasis is placed on creativity. The culmination of these skills is an event called a "Club-O-Rama." During this show, the creations are displayed and judged by 4-H officials from the State of Illinois. The winners are designated by blue, red, and white ribbons. These ribbons are redeemable for cash. The Club-O-Ramas are well attended by parents and guests. The element of competition keeps the pupils interested, and sometimes a few interesting things happened at the judging – prizes went to boys for cakes, pies, and biscuits, and to girls for photography.

Success is important to these pupils, but they were also made to understand that success is *achieved* and not given.

Summary of Promising Practice VIII. The Urban 4-H activity provided an opportunity to experience recognition through merit.

PROMISING PRACTICE IX

Placing Elementary School Pupils on Jobs

The action research program took a step that was almost unheard of in an official way. Only a few employers would consider hiring grammar school children, the main reason being that they are not covered by liability insurance until age 18.

The Special Project pupils were greatly in need of some "responsibility in action" because they were from relief recipient families—mainly without fathers. Added to this was the fact that they comprised the third, and sometimes fourth, generation on public aid and had never known anyone in the immediate family with an occupation. With a well-planned and executed program, the foundations of economic stability could be laid.

The job placement counselor made original contacts with the local Chamber of Commerce which had access to a block of employers, and with a bit of persuasiveness and tact here and there, the hard-boiled "wheels" who boasted that they would never hire a "grammar school kid" suddenly found themselves on the Project's advisory committee, making plans for a bigger operation. Altogether, there were 82 jobs secured from these businessmen.

Typical places of employment included grocery stores, laundries, dry cleaning establishments, hardware stores, medical offices, department stores, gasoline service stations, drug stores, mail order houses, and beauty shops.

Follow-up has shown that a number of students who have reached high-school age have the same employer they had during their Special Project days.

Early employment developed a wholesome attitude toward work and the value of a dollar was effectively "driven home" to them. In the orientation, it was stressed repeatedly in one form or another, that more money can be earned with an education than without it.

Summarizing Promising Practice IX. Placing elementary school pupils on jobs provided an early realization of the importance of economic stability.

PROMISING PRACTICE X

Developing Cultural Experiences

The Special Project pupils reside in the heart of the so-called "black belt"—where, with the expansion of city housing projects, a concentration of the deprived portion of our country's population is found. Many of the residents seldom venture beyond the general area, which means that the cultural outlets are limited. It was with this backdrop that the Special Project set about to broaden the pupils' background.

It seemed that Saturday was the only day left during the week to do this. Students were asked, on a voluntary basis, to come for the first trip, an eighty-mile tour of the greater Chicago area. Parents were asked to come, making a total of approximately four hundred and fifty who took the trip. The people saw landmarks that were new to them.

Besides sight-seeing, cultural trips were also organized. One outing provided for the play "Sleeping Beauty" on the campus of Northwestern University. Another trip went to the Young People's Symphony at Orchestra Hall, and once, pupils went to Ravinia Park to listen to a rehearsal of the Chicago Symphony Orchestra.

The experience at the Chicago Art Institute was most unique. The Institute was about to discard scores of prints from the old Masters, but decided to put them to better use. The curator received the pupils and their parents in small groups, gave a talk on the painting and the artist, and presented each family with a print for the home.

Another trip was taken to O'Hare International Airport and from the observation deck the students watched the jets "take off." Most of the pupils had never seen a plane on the ground.

The impact of these experiences can never be measured by objective means because they are so highly personal. However, the best evidence that the experiences were meaningful to the students was their enthusiastic response and questioning – "Where do we go next?"

Summarizing Promising Practice X. Developing cultural exposure provided an opportunity to appreciate new areas of experience and to instill curiosity in the students to take this initiative themselves.

PROMISING PRACTICE XI

Forming Interest Groups

For an activity during the summer, the pupils are asked to choose an interest group. Each interest group has two parent sponsors and an instructor. Activities were chosen such as dressmaking, developing pictures, making crystal radios, repairing small appliances, making model airplanes, cooking, and exploring the world through books.

A newsletter was developed and contributed to by each group as a source of information about the progress and activities of the interest groups.

Summarizing Promising Practice XI. Forming interest groups helped keep up an interest in a type of educational activity during the summer through the principle of group reinforcement.

PROMISING PRACTICE XII

Developing the Reading Clinic

Aside from emphasis on the communications skills and the formation of homogeneous reading groups, it was felt that special attention was needed to help the poorest readers. Therefore, during the summer, the services of two reading experts were utilized.

The reading clinic was a highly concentrated program. Pupils were required to attend two-hour sessions, four days a week. They were literally bombarded with the most up-to-date techniques, equipment, and materials. Live telephones were utilized, voices were recorded, and for the first time, many pupils listened to their own voices. New ways were used to build vocabularies and drills were given in such a way as not to become monotonous. The pupils seemed to enjoy the reading clinic thoroughly, and immediate testing showed a marked improvement in reading achievement levels.

Because of the success of the clinic, parents in other grammar schools wanted their children to have an extra session in remedial reading and now there are after-school reading classes in several grammar schools.

Summarizing Promising Practice XII. The summer reading clinic affected achievement levels markedly upward – so much so that reading clinics operate in many grammar schools after school hours.

PROMISING PRACTICE XIII

Forming a Father's Club

The majority of the pupils in the Special Project classes are from broken homes. When the father is the missing member, there is no male example for boys, especially, to understand responsibility and positive discipline. Ironically, the "Father's Club" had no fathers as members.

The school social worker and this author began making contact with large families (those with seven children and over). We contacted thirty-eight families with at least seven children. The first contact was made in person. The mothers seemed quite enthused that a Father's Club would be organized, but always asked who the fathers would be? Some mothers referred us to a brother, an uncle, her father, her boyfriend, or an older son to participate in the Father's Club. One mother could not find anyone, so she, herself, came. Another mother said, "You know, you came one day too late. If I had known about this yesterday, maybe I could have persuaded my boyfriend to stay on at least for the club meetings." Of the 38 large families involved, there were only five natural fathers participating.

The purpose of the Father's Club was to aid these fathers or "stand-ins" in becoming better paternal figures. As it was felt that the "cue" should come from the members, sponsors asked the participants about what they felt they would need to know. Among the problems, "fathers" expressed concern for recreational facilities for the boys; urban renewal plans and the effect on their homes; installment buying and pitfalls; property and inheritance; education and completion; employment opportunities; social security; public health; civil service exams; and armed forces opportunities. Experts in the areas in which the "fathers" were interested were invited to club meetings to discuss the problems. The sessions were "down-to-earth," and much of the time was consumed with practical questions and answers. Though the club was organized during summer vacation months, attendance was phenomenally high. Interest and enthusiasm were strong during each session. At a meeting between the Father's Club and the staff of the Special Project, the fathers became better acquainted with the Special Project through pictures, slides, and the opportunity to meet and talk with the administration and teachers.

Summarizing Promising Practice XIII. The Father's Club sought to develop leadership in the *male* members or friends of families without fathers.

PROMISING PRACTICE XIV

Involving the Parents

Involving the parents has resulted in the development of several activities:

1) Home sewing groups meeting under the guidance of a home economist, where moth-

ers learn to make and alter clothing and make draperies and slipcovers.

2) Cooking and nutrition programs under a home economist, using a housing authority apartment kitchen as a laboratory.

3) Field trips with the home economist to supermarkets and department stores for practical lessons in consumer buying.

4) School-oriented parent education meetings to help parents understand the school program and learn how to work with their children.

5) A large-family program involving 25 families with 6 or more children, directed toward developing family unity, mutual respect, family goals, and family recreation. Activities included trips to museums, art fairs, the zoo, cultural events, plays, and concerts.

6) A parent education organization relating to a particular group of youths known to the police.

Summarizing Promising Practice XIV. Involving parents in educational programs helped to make the home a better place in which to live.

PROMISING PRACTICE XV

Organizing Educational and Vocational Guidance Centers

The educational program in these centers is designed for students in the elementary school who are one or more years overage for their grade level, or who are beyond the normal graduation age for the elementary school though still enrolled in the elementary school. Under ordinary conditions, many would never reach high school, and many of those reaching high school would soon become dropouts. The majority of the students entering the program are either in the sixth or seventh grade. The class size is twenty pupils. Overage pupils in each contributing area are given the opportunity to transfer to the center. Priority is given to those who are oldest and most retarded for their grade level.

The educational program emphasizes basic subjects with special emphasis on developing the communication skills in which the pupils show the greatest need. Those unable to develop their basic vocational skills to a degree necessary for success in high school, are helped to develop simple occupational skills which will enable them to become employable on leaving school.

The small class size, together with good guidance and counseling, special counselors, individual help from teachers, many instructional aids, special help in reading, and an atmosphere of interest in learning, motivation in terms of a goal within reach, and a new chance, all combined to produce substantial gains in achievement on the part of large numbers of pupils.

In the new and changed atmosphere, pupils with previously low achievement have manifested an eagerness and readiness to learn. The median gain in reading for all pupils during one-half year was one-half grade. This was a remarkable accomplishment when it is considered that improvement was made by a group of previously low-achievers or nonachievers. More than 10 per cent of the pupils enrolled during the year advanced sufficiently to be transferred to a high school with a reasonable prognosis of success. Pupils remaining in the centers have indicated a desire to learn employable skills rather than drop out of school when they reach the legal age.

Summarizing Promising Practice XV. The Educational and Vocational Guidance Centers have provided for the academic and vocational needs of overage elementary-school pupils who would find it difficult to succeed in a regular elementary school.

PROMISING PRACTICE XVI

Taking the Teen-Age Census

An effort was made to find out who the dropouts were in School District Eleven. Some leads were discovered in the schools, but since this is a highly transient area, the schools often had no records on dropouts living in the area. Other leads were provided by relatives, but generally, people in large cities are highly skeptical about those seeking information and very "tight-mouthed" about providing it. The files of the local Housing Authority were examined to locate dropouts.

In District Eleven there were found to be 1,687 teen-agers out of school and out of work.

Summarizing Promising Practice XVI. The teen-age census provided information on the school dropout and pointed up the numerical seriousness of the problem.

PROMISING PRACTICE XVII

Establishing Census and Counseling (CC) Centers

The purpose of the Double C phase is to ascertain who the dropouts are and to extend counseling assistance to them through "reaching out" letters and follow-up services.

The census is acquired by requesting high-school counselors to forward a carbon copy of a standard dropout clearance form to the central office of the Urban Youth Program. This copy furnishes the personnel data for each young person included in the census. A record is made of the name, address, and telephone number for each dropout as well as the name of the school left and the date of leaving. Every two weeks forms are compiled for forwarding to a reception center which has been established in one of the high schools in each of five locations in the city. The reception centers are open during the evening sessions of the schools, Monday through Thursday.

After the referral forms are mailed to the reception centers, individual letters are sent to the young people inviting them to come to a reception center named in the letter to talk with a counselor, whose name and room location also appear in the letter.

Those dropouts who accept the invitation to counseling may be provided with the following services:

1) Referral to the evening school programs at the reception center or to counseling and assistance about returning to full-time school.

2) Referral to social agencies for help in solving personal problems if needed.

3) Referral to a pre-employment counseling workshop, part of the Double C program, preparatory to entering either the Double E or Double T phase.

Summarizing Promising Practice XVII. The Census and Counseling (CC) Centers provide counseling and job orientation in preparation for placement in either Double E or Double T phases of the Urban Youth Program.

PROMISING PRACTICE XVIII

Providing Education and Employment

The Double E phase is a cooperative work-study program in which a dropout returnee spends twelve hours per week in school classes and twenty-four to thirty-two hours per week on the job in a merchandising or clerical occupation. School classes are conducted in the subject areas of English, social studies, business, and essential mathematics. Content in these areas is job-oriented, but is so designed that academic knowledge may also be furthered. Special workshops provide opportunity for independent study for those individual students who can be assisted toward a high-school diploma by completing required subjects or electives not regularly offered. The school-work program terminates at the end of a 40-week period; high-school credit is given for both school subjects and supervised work.

The Double E program began on an experimental basis during the summer of 1961 as a cooperative venture in which the Chicago public schools furnished the educational experience for the participating students and Carson, Pirie, Scott and Company provided the work experience. During its first year, the program was financed partially by the Ford Foundation. The first class completed training in May, 1962. Many more classes were financed by the Board of Education and have since completed training. New classes begin approximately every ten weeks.

Students employed in merchandising establishments work in such jobs as stock, shipping, clerical, sales, merchandise checking, gift wrapping, and display lettering. Those employed by other types of organizations are working or have worked in such jobs as telephone operator, biller, order filler, general clerical worker, messenger, display man, studio assistant on closed-circuit television, lens grinder-polisher, winding machine operator, IBM burster operator, addressograph operator, printer, alteration tailor, laundry loader, busboy, sandwich maker, and lay-up man.

Summarizing Promising Practice XVIII. Education and Employment provide the dropout with the opportunities to realize his goals in a responsible way.

PROMISING PRACTICE XIX

Providing Training and Transition (TT)

The Double T phase gives direct vocational training to develop skills in the following occupations: hospital aides, small-appliance and radio repairmen, garage and service station helpers, typists, office machine operators, personnel for clothing alterations and pressing, beauticians, and welders.

PROMISING PRACTICE XX

Providing Training for the Terminal Educable Mentally Handicapped

The educable mentally handicapped who are in high school and who have passed the second year, or who are approaching age seventeen, are forced automatically to leave school, and in a sense, become dropouts.

The purpose of this orientation is to provide a ray of hope to parents who might feel that it is "all over" for their children or to assure them that their children can learn a skill – can become productive – and can be of value to themselves and others. The Training and Transition Program is explained, and students are instructed to make appointments. These EMH pupils are especially grateful and seem to work so hard that many times they approach perfection. According to reports, one of the best shoe repairmen was a terminal EMH pupil. Many EMH students are also encouraged to participate in remedial reading and to attend evening school.

Summarizing Promising Practice XX. Providing training for EMH pupils stimulates them to become useful members of society.

PROMISING PRACTICE XXI

Providing Training for Continuation School Pupils

Continuation school provides one day per week in school and four days on a job. There are no academic credits given. Many pupils are not transferred to continuation school until they are almost seventeen. The services of the Double T and Double E are extended to continuation school pupils. Once they become involved, they can obtain a release from continuation school and if they are at least sixteen years old, they can enroll in evening school and obtain academic credit.

Summarizing Promising Practice XXI. Providing training for continuation school pupils has enabled them to gain both academic training and a skill.

PROMISING PRACTICE XXII

Cooperating with Industry, Labor and the State Employment Service

Perhaps for the first time in the history of education, there was a four-way "tie-in" in the development of a training program. The Chicago Board of Education, Illinois State Employment Service, Amalgamated Clothing Workers of America Labor Union, and the Clothing Industry – specifically Hart, Schaffner and Marx and Kuppenheimer and Weinberg Corporation (Oxford Clothes). The ultimate was that MDTA would be the recipient of a Needle Trades Program, but in the interim, the Special Project would aid the pilot project.

The cooperative tasks were divided so that the Board of Education would do the recruiting, provide the place for instruction, the counseling, job orientation, and the instruction. Industry would provide most of the basic power machines, all of the specialty machines (blind stitcher, basting machine, cuff machine), employees in the industry for job orientation, and scrap material for practice work. The labor union would provide an expert to give orientation relative to the union. Illinois State Employment Service served as the catalyst, did the screening, and provided experts for job placement.

Because of this close-knit cooperation, a very well-coordinated Needle Trades Program was put into operation, providing training and employment for dropouts. To date, approximately 115 young people have received employment.

Summarizing Promising Practice XXII. Because of the cooperation of the Board of Education, industry, labor services and employment services, over 115 persons have been gainfully employed in the clothing and garment industry.

PROMISING PRACTICE XXIII

Cooperating with Hospitals

The Hospital Occupational Training Program is a cooperative work-study program for school dropouts. The training leads to occupations such as assistant lab technicians, dietary workers, and nurses' aides. The training period provides for one month of theory and one month of practical work in the hospital. An advisory council has been formed with a representative from each cooperating hospital. Some of the graduates have earned promotions to significant jobs. One young lady is now chief technician in the hematology lab; another is chief aide in the operating room; the only male from the class has been granted a scholarship to a school of pharmacy; another young lady is in pre-medical school.

Summarizing Promising Practice XXIII. Cooperating with hospitals has provided careers in the general field of medicine and hospital care.

PROMISING PRACTICE XXIV

Cooperating with Cook County Department of Public Aid

Many trainees in the Double T phase of the Urban Youth Program are public aid recipients, and one of their ultimate goals is to master a skill in order to get off relief. A cross-referral system has been developed between the project program and the Public Aid Department. Among the first graduates of the needle trade, hospital occupational training, and cosmetology programs were public aid recipients who are now working regularly and are off relief.

Summarizing Promising Practice XXIV. Cooperating with the Public Aid Department has stimulated aid recipients towards self-sustenance.

PROMISING PRACTICE XXV

Accelerating Cosmetology

To qualify to take the state examination to become a licensed beautician requires 1000 hours of training. In order to make the program more beneficial to the trainees, they met 5 hours a day, and reached their mark in 10 months. Eighteen students have qualified and are now licensed beauticians. One student has opened her own shop.

Summarizing Promising Practice XXV. Accelerating cosmetology has meant a shorter path to gainful occupation for our trainees.

PROMISING PRACTICE XXVI

Cooperating with YMCA and a Large Appliance Store

The project's small-appliance repair shop has an arrangement with one of the largest appliance stores in the city of Chicago. The store donates small appliances to the project on the condition that none will be sold. The trainees repair these small appliances and they are distributed among needy families. A local YMCA also donates new but broken electrical toys. Our trainees repair these toys and the YMCA distributes the toys on Christmas to needy children.

Summarizing Promising Practice XXVI. Cooperating with the YMCA developed a sense of pride in good workmanship because the students approved of the purpose to which their efforts were directed.

PROMISING PRACTICE XXVII

Cooperating with the State Employment Service

Illinois State Employment Service is cooperating with the Double T program in a most remarkable way. ISES has committed itself to honoring those certificates granted upon the completion of a training course by doing one of four things: placing the graduates on a job; providing on-the-job training; placing the graduate in an apprenticeship training program; or placing the graduate in MDTA.

Because of this excellent relationship with the top employment agency, the trainees have a goal while they learn skills.

Summarizing Promising Practice XXVII. Cooperating with the State Employment Service has given a purpose to the training.

PROMISING PRACTICE XXVIII

Developing Civil Service Examination Preparation

One of the most popular classes in the Double T program is that which prepares students for Civil Service exams. This class offers a review of math, reading, and English, and goes into the techniques of taking the exam. Experts from the Civil Service Commission are invited to meet with the class. Samples of old tests are used to prepare students for the actual testing.

In the follow-up, it has been learned that the Civil Service course has enabled trainees to write other exams successfully. Within fifteen months, seventy Civil Service exam preparation trainees were placed on jobs. Such jobs included work in U.S. postoffices, mail order houses, chain drugstores, Illinois Bell Telephone Company, Social Security Administration, and U.S. Armed Forces.

Summarizing Promising Practices XXVIII. Civil Service exam preparation has aided in teaching techniques of exam writing and has improved test results.

PROMISING PRACTICE XXIX

Developing In-Service Training for Automobile Services Trainees

Aside from having excellent shop facilities for teaching trainees to become service station attendants, the program also aims to give students practical experience with cars at an operating service station.

For this reason, a given portion of time is allotted for in-service training. For one month, each trainee spends four days a week at a station, and one day in class. Each trainee is also required to qualify for and obtain his driver's license before he can earn his certificate for graduation.

Summarizing Promising Practice XXIX. In-service training has enabled the auto service trainee to have direct experience with service station work.

PROMISING PRACTICE XXX

Combining the Vocational Program with the Academic Program

Each Double T trainee is encouraged to attend evening school and earn academic credits as he learns a skill in the Double T program. In the same building Double T classes are offered from 4:00 P.M. to 6:00 P.M. and evening school begins at 6:30 P.M. So it is convenient to prepare for a job and to work toward a diploma at the same time. Approximately 95 per cent of the Double T trainees attend evening school.

Summarizing Promising Practice XXX. Combining a vocational and academic program has given the dropout the opportunity to achieve job training and a high-school diploma.

There are more promising practices in operating a credit union with an account in a local bank; the material and instruction center for teachers; a weekly in-service training for teachers; group meetings with parents; individual counseling by experienced graduate students at Chicago State College; cooperative programs with the Cook County Department of Public Aid providing counseling; training and further educational programs for dropouts in foster homes; and a food service training program for school lunchroom attendants.

In Chicago, practical approaches have been developed to build experiences leading to positive thinking, self-assurance, and self-guidance; to counteract the negativity that characterizes the culturally disadvantaged; and to guide them towards the understanding that they possess the qualities and potential to become useful members of society.

Significant steps have been taken to stimulate the potential dropout toward staying in school and to encourage the actual dropout toward school completion and vocational training. For the potential dropout, promising practices have taken the form of basic and novel teaching techniques, vocational training, interest groups, job placement, and parent and community emphases which have resulted in the development of a revolutionary concept in the field of education for the overage grammar-school pupils: The Educational and Vocational Guidance Center. For the actual dropout, promising practices have taken the form of well-organized and correlated programs, cooperative efforts of employment agencies, industry, labor with Board of Education, and work-study programs which have resulted in the development of revolutionary techniques in working with school dropouts: the Double C Center; the Double E Program and the Double T Program.

Ultimately, these programs seek to develop a positive sign in the lives of the disadvantaged leading to a restoration of faith in themselves and an awakening of society to the realization that, if the needs of the disadvantaged are not discovered and cared for, serious consequences of disunity and dissension can become permanent aspects of our society. It should be remembered that a democracy characterized by negatively experienced members can never realize positive goals.

John E. Roberts

THE DROPOUT

For years the dropout has been of concern to educators and psychologists, but of late, because of the increasing percent of students involved, the dropout has become a major problem. A number of approaches have been attempted, and from the very start of this new attempt to deal with dropouts, John Roberts has been working with special programs designed to encourage them to consider returning to school, or to take part in specially designed curricula and programs for such unique students. It has been felt that the school itself is in the best position to cope with the problems surrounding the dropout, despite his intensified reaction. The approaches made by outside agencies, such as government or community sponsored groups, often are better received by students.

The idea that one should research the current causes of dropouts and then face these causes realistically is a sound basis for designing new concepts and new programs to meet the existing needs. Whether the conventional school program and its administrators can be flexible and imaginative enough to create and operate programs which are psychologically sound and academically respectable is questionable. At least, it is an attempt which should be carefully investigated and, if successful, be continued and extended accordingly.

Dropping out of school is generally the culmination of a long and tedious period of frustration and defeat, not only for the student, but for the parent and teacher as well. It comes as no surprise to anyone, least of all to the dropout himself, for his has been a history of failures and defeats. His parents have been aware of his lack of progress and have been forewarned of this eventual outcome on numerous occasions. His teachers, in many cases, look forward to this day when the struggle is terminated. When this occurs, all parties concerned tend to blame one another for failing to meet their responsibilities.

A realistic and unbiased appraisal of the dropout will indicate that he is confronted with a constellation of long-standing problems and has reacted in the most characteristic way—avoidance. He may be culturally deprived, socially maladjusted, overprotected, or emotionally disturbed. Or, he may be one of that vast group of our population who are classified as slow learners. In any and all cases, however, special attention must be paid to the most basic causes of the failure.

For all except the slow learners, these problems block his learning ability and his capacity for interest. With regard to the slow learner, a normal distribution of the school population will include about twenty per cent who suffer from varying degrees of mental retardation, and it would be unrealistic to pretend that everyone is capable of absorbing the general high-school curriculum. Unless provisions are made to adjust subject matter to varying levels of attainment, many students of lesser ability will continue to become discouraged and leave school.

Another important factor in the dropout's situation is the area of attitude. A student's attitudes are important in determining the type of adjustment he will make toward the school environment. Unless a student has a favorable attitude toward education and desirable goals for himself, his school experience will be relatively ineffective. Attitudes are persistent and difficult to change. Those that are deep-seated will require long periods of time to alter or modify.

In addition, parental mismanagement often contributes to dropping out of school. Some children are given so many privileges and possessions that they never learn the relationship between effort and reward. Overprotection stifles initiative and does not prepare the student to face problems in a realistic manner. Instead, he would prefer to sidestep the difficulty or give up rather than meet the problem head on. The parent who excuses the child's behavior by condemning the teacher merely reinforces the child's unwholesome attitude toward legitimate authority. Some parents refuse to realistically accept the child's ability and potential and insist that he earn grades which are beyond his capabilities. This can only add to his frustrations and sense of failure. On the other hand, parents who exhibit an interest and place a high value on education will generally impart this attitude to their children.

American education as it is now organized and conducted is failing with approximately a third of our children who eventually wind up in the dropout pool. For these people, a more meaningful and realistic program of education and training is necessary if they are expected to become contributing members of our economic society.

It is not enough to catch failing and underachieving students in their final year of high school. They should be detected early, and corrective measures should be taken as soon as the problem becomes apparent. It is far more simple to shape the sapling than remold the tree. As unwholesome attitudes become more deeply entrenched, campaigns to encourage youths to stay in school will generally fall on deaf ears. This is especially true if they are expected to remain in the same type of learning situation which they have grown to abhor. Appeals which are directed toward the long-range financial rewards of education mean little to uninspired youths who live in a world of today.

A number of innovative educational programs have demonstrated that many of these youths can be motivated to learn and adjust their behavioral patterns when they are provided with skillful teachers and the proper climate for learning. It is unrealistic to assume that these special programs provide all the answers or ready-made solutions to all of the problems which teachers face in their classrooms. However, the fact that vast numbers of problem youths who are enrolled in such programs do cooperate and succeed indicates that they are provided some inducement or incentive which motivates them to learn.

A description of the structure and philosophy of one such program which has successfully provided training and education for thousands of school dropouts may provide an insight into some techniques to which these reluctant learners have responded. Due to the diversity of handicaps which these dropouts possess, a variety of training programs is necessary to more adequately meet the needs of a segment or group of dropouts with similar problems.

Before a youth is enrolled in one of the units of the Urban Youth Program he receives intensive counseling. In these conferences the dropout is assisted in a process of self-evaluation. It is important that he be aware of his limitations or handicaps and voluntarily decide on a proper course of action. His interests, abilities, and needs are evaluated, and he is offered a spectrum of self-help options that might include referral to special schools, social agencies, special training programs, or jobs. If he is interested in furthering his education or learning a

skill, he is informed of the specific programs for which he may qualify.

One training unit of the Urban Youth Program is designed for the youth with a pressing financial need who requires short-term training preparatory to employment. Another offers long-term training in clerical office skills for the more capable student. A third unit offers long-term training in industrial-service skills, coupled with basic education. Finally, another unit is available which is a combination of education and employment, and which provides high-school credit as well as a wage.

This variety of plans is broad enough to meet the needs of a vast segment of the dropout population. Yet, regardless of the type of training the individual dropout chooses, a common denominator at these installations occurs in terms of staff, supportive services, and curriculum.

The quality of teachers and supportive personnel is the most important and irreplaceable factor in the readjustment and eventual success of each student. Ironically, the best teacher in these situations is not necessarily the one who has achieved advanced degrees or years of seniority in the educational profession. Instead, the most successful teacher is the one who, first and foremost, is a warm and understanding individual. He has a feeling of empathy and is willing to accept the student as he finds him. Through this relationship, he can contribute toward the development of positive feelings toward self and others which makes learning possible. When this relationship is established it provides a source of motivation and a focal point for positive identifications. The problems of discipline diminish and a base for learning is established. The dynamic teacher who possesses these qualities in addition to advanced training and experience is, of course, ideally qualified to provide learning experiences that result in pupil satisfaction and success.

The effective teacher, though, is aware of his own limitations and readily accepts the help and resources of other personnel. The counselor, social worker, and psychologist can provide valuable assistance as well as insights into student behavior. Likewise, the reading teacher can provide the individual attention which is beyond the capabilities of the classroom teacher. Also, these staff members operate as a team and participate in a program of weekly in-service training as a means of pooling their ideas and planning curriculum innovations.

In the area of curriculum, learning activities are provided in basic subject areas and are designed to contribute to the economic and social, as well as the academic, growth of the student. Throughout the program emphasis is directed toward the development of confidence and self-assurance in the student and the establishment of teacher-student rapport. Subject matter is relevant to pupils' circumstances and is timely in terms of their own concerns. Whenever possible, learning experiences are provided which are real and tangible, and in many instances cut across subject matter areas. An application of these principles was demonstrated in a unit on "Rights and Responsibilities Under the Law."

Early in the unit, a tour of City Hall was arranged to arouse an interest in local government. The students attended a City Council meeting and were stimulated to learn how laws are enacted and the city is governed. This was followed by a visit to the Municipal Courts to learn how these laws are enforced.

Much was done to stimulate the thinking of the group in everyday legal matters. A judge and a lawyer talked to the group and answered questions. As a culminating activity, the students acted as a jury in practice trials at the John Marshall Law School. Particular attention was devoted to the study of fraud, misrepresentation, legal contracts, and other cases in which these students could easily become involved.

An excellent opportunity was provided for the development of arithmetic and commu-nicative skills as well as providing needed information. Credit buying was analyzed with special emphasis on the variety of plans available. Automobile financing plans were evaluated and students learned about the savings which could be achieved through proper financing. Interest charges on borrowed money were studied. Throughout, the legal implications of fraud and misrepresentation were emphasized. With the cooperation of the Better Business Bureau periodic releases of fraudulent practices were studied, and students were encouraged to contact this organization for information on specific companies.

In short, the students' classroom experience was made relevant to situations which were real and tangible and in which they were deeply interested. They were learning, learning in an environment that made knowledge a useful tool for continued success. All of their studies—civics, mathematics, and English—took on new meaning. No longer were they dry, boring subjects; they were part and parcel of a productive life.

Another highly motivational curricular device which involved the entire student body while cutting across broad subject matter areas was concerned with the study of the newspaper. It involved the use of textbooks and supplementary projects to clarify concepts introduced via the newspaper articles. By using the daily paper to impart values as well as information, the faculty did an excellent job of lifting spirits, sights, and goals. The mathematics teacher prepared a list of ideas which provided a method of reviewing all of basic mathematics, using the newspaper as a primary text. The social studies instructors did much the same thing and taught everything from social identification to United States History and Government, again using the newspaper as the primary text. Other subject areas included taxes, budgets, banking, insurance, job training opportunities, geography, and law.

Because of the overwhelming acceptance

of the newspaper as a primary text by the students, their annual dinner featured a newspaper format, including excerpts read and dramatized from their newly-formed student newspaper. The kick-off attraction in the fashion show which was a part of the program following the dinner was, of course, a newspaper mini-dress.

A program which offers a degree of help and encouragement in school, and which demonstrates some achievement or reward in return for the expenditure of energy, will generally find acceptance among most youths. The teacher, however, is the prime motivating force, and the manner in which he contributes toward the development of positive attitudes within the youth will determine the degree of learning which takes place.

The following guiding principles for teachers have been most effective:

1. Accepts and treats students with respect and dignity.
2. Fosters situations which permit students to experience responsibility and cooperative effort.
3. Gives each student a degree of individual attention and makes him feel important.
4. Maximizes success and minimizes failure.
5. Devises flexible classroom procedures and extracurricular activities to meet the needs of students.
6. Accepts guidance and counseling as a concomitant responsibility.
7. Respects the views and opinions of students.
8. Provides continuous opportunities for written and oral expression at a level commensurate with each student's abilities.

In addition, the resourceful teacher enhances the learning process through the use of the following devices and techniques:

1. Audio-visual aids such as the tape recorder, overhead projector, teletrainer, radio, television, and film projector.
2. Trips to institutions and firms related to the areas of instruction.
3. Use of outside speakers.
4. Activities which involve active student participation, such as role playing, dramatization, pantomime, and plays.
5. Use of concrete materials.
6. Experience-approach, centered around life problems.
7. Short units and immediate goals.
8. Continual evaluation.

Many of these young people, whether they be potential or actual dropouts, can be reached when provided with a realistic learning situation. When they begin to develop a positive attitude toward education most of their behavioral and antisocial attitudes will improve.

However, it must be emphasized that positive results are only achieved through patience and understanding. Immediate or spectacular improvement is unrealistic, and failures and setbacks en route will be experienced. Lapses in behavior are normal and progress should be measured by what the student was at the outset rather than what we would like him to be.

Working with disadvantaged youths is a difficult and challenging task and requires all the ingenuity and resources the teacher can devise. But it must be remembered that dropouts are people who have the same hopes and desires, and, in many cases, the same abilities as stay-ins; and, if given the opportunity and proper direction, they will prove themselves. Educators, then, must have a commitment to the responsibility of converting these potential public liabilities of tomorrow into the productive assets of today. To do otherwise is to write off one third of the future.

Robert Jemilo

YOUTH ACTION

One of the most exciting and promising programs dealing with the problems of the dropout and the gang-oriented youth has been developed under the direction of Robert Jemilo. The following article describes the history, philosophy, and operation of the program. It should be noted that it has been in progress for several years and many refinements and revisions are being made as the need develops. This report covers the current philosophy and reorganization of the program.

Many of the principles derived from behavioral problems in the streets are psychologically relevant to the classroom situation, and teachers may well profit from this research. For instance, the principle of identification with leadership is recognized and implemented, and the development of leaders drawn from the ranks of the gangs themselves has proved to be the most unique and functional aspect of the program.

The problems of passing into adulthood are accentuated for adolescents of this sort by problems involving their introduction to alchohol, drug addiction, sexual behavior, and cultural and group pressures in general. To meet these problems, stress is placed on developing good communication, using all language and nonlanguage practices known to the psychologist, sociologist, and educator. *Recognition* and *status* are the key issues in the success of the program because they are values held in high regard among the youths themselves.

Much can be learned from this project because of its explicit goals and its wide range of suggestions for implementing a comprehensive and effective program.

HISTORICAL BACKGROUND

In 1956, the Youth Gangs Program of the YMCA of Metropolitan Chicago was launched. During the ensuing years, street-club-work programs of other private agencies such as the Chicago Boys Clubs, Chicago Youth Centers, and Hull House Association were either intensified or initiated. While there had always been communication and a "loose league of cooperation" between the agencies, each, nevertheless, ran its own separate street-club-work program. In May 1965, these same agencies entered into a cooperative street-work program known as STREETS. The notable differences between STREETS and its predecessor programs were that (1) STREETS, in part, was funded by the Chicago Committee on Urban Opportunity, (2) it represented a first cooperative street-work program by the private agencies, and (3) a Coordinator, whose responsibility was to establish and/or intensify channels of communication among all four agencies and attempt to integrate services of the STREETS program across the board, was built into the organizational structure.

In January 1967, for a host of fiscal and operational reasons, the STREETS program initiated the metamorphosis of that program into Youth Action. The decision to alter the structure carrying out street work in the city of Chicago was not arrived at lightly. The Youth Action program is a complete amalgamation of all street-work programs previously carried out under the auspices of the four separate agencies, into a single structure, with a single Director. The amalgamation was deemed necessary in order to: (1) eliminate duplication of administration, thus making a maximum of funds available for program services; (2) increase communication and enhance cooperation between existing units of street workers and provide for a more effective distribution of skills and talents across the city; (3) provide all four agencies with more effective knowledge of community and gang problems identified by staff, thus creating a better mechanism for bringing the growing cooperation of the four agencies in combining resources to attack specific and significant community problems.

The administrative staff has been drawn from men who have worked in the project and in the street. In addition to the professional staff, there is a part-time staff made up primarily of indigenous youths and local adults. The practice that has had considerable publicity and has been of great concern to the administration as well as the community consists of making use of members of the gangs who have demonstrated their leadership potential and who are willing to cooperate with the professional staff. These youths are paid a stipend each month with a degree of flexibility which allows for mobility and acts as a motivating force. After some experience, "consultants" may be promoted to "senior consultants" at a higher rate of pay.

It takes a worker with what is called "street smarts" to do the job: to first gain the confidence of the gang leaders—often bitterly disillusioned young people—and begin the slow job of transforming negative behavior into positive actions, to replace the gang's activities with the kind of program that can lead to better lives.

The gangs don't come into program offices but must be reached on the street. It takes a worker who can really "get out where they are," someone with heart, who knows his way around, who knows how to communicate, and who has the ability to maintain perspective and adhere to long-term values which may contradict the ones considered immediately functional by those being served.

In addition to that street know-how, the worker must be wise in understanding the young people's need for status (that problem of self-respect) and an expert in offering real

alternatives to the gangs, such as athletics, jobs, or education.

Athletic programs are an important key, even to the gang leader who may sullenly respond, "We don't dig athletics." The workers have balls and bats in their station wagons, and a basketball, and maybe some tickets to a ball game. Most of these boys have never identified with an adult male who wasn't a hustler or a pusher. When a man begins to work with them, plan with them, show them he's interested, they become interested. The boys—maybe they're 18 or 19—begin to see that hanging around corners, getting chased by "the man" (the police), getting called "punks" by other elements of the community, is just not "where it's at." The hardest part of the job starts after that initial reaching out.

Besides the gyms and basketball courts, there is the Jobs Now Agency, set up to match a boy with a job even if he was a dropout in the seventh grade. The workers there often were gang leaders themselves. They give each boy two weeks of intensive training in things like how to fill out a job application, how to dress for an interview. And they find him a job. If it doesn't work out, they'll find him another job where he can stay.

The Central YMCA High School and College are other valuable "tools" for the street workers. They serve many of the older boys, too old to go back to the public schools they dropped out of.

The workers have another aim, too: to get the youths to give up the guns that are so much a part of gang life. But guns mean status, and "getting a boy to give up his status isn't easy." It's part of the process to find other alternatives to provide status, and once a worker builds rapport and offers realistic alternatives, implementation of the firearms policy has not posed any major problems.

It's often harder to build rapport with tough white kids in a middle class area. They have more, so the program is less exciting to them.

Aside from an inferior educational system

in the ghetto, housing problems, etc., the Negro youth, even if he overcomes the aforesaid obstacles, has the problem of race, which has unjustly negated many legitimate and significant opportunities.

The consultants have a variety of duties determined by the detached worker, and by the very nature of the group to which they are assigned and the community in which they reside. They attempt to control delinquency and particularly to control behavior of the group, and can make a most significant contribution in changing negative group norms and behavioral patterns. They help the worker operate programs which may be designed for the total neighborhood or an area that the worker serves. Success or failure of the program depends for a great part on the individual detached worker, as it is his responsibility to select, train, and manage the consultants. The stipend referred to above tends to explain and justify the role of the consultant among his peers, legitimizing his role, and is a positive alternative in providing and maintaining status and recognition in the group and, in some cases, in the larger community.

The consultants as part of their work operate athletic tournaments and publish a newspaper for the various groups in the entire city. The consultants regularly attend planning meetings with their workers and other consultants in the administrative staff. They have an opportunity to take trips as an incentive for those doing something outstanding or a particularly good job. As an example, a trip to New York was arranged as a token of appreciation from the administrators of the project. Also an elaborate Christmas party was arranged at which they brought dates and wore their best suits. The consultants are aware that, if arrested, they are automatically suspended until they are found innocent or fired if they are found guilty. So that they do not make a profession of being a consultant they are required to be either working or going to school full time. They can remain consultants only for two years in order to keep moving in terms of rank and responsibility; many have moved into full-time professional roles.

The program is designed to work with individuals from sixteen to twenty-one years of age, although the ages range from twelve to thirty-four. This group needs the most attention since youths of this age tend to serve as models for younger boys in the area.

The administration encourages each detached worker to operate in his own way; there are general policies which have been developed and are explained in Part Two of this article. There are two basic roles: (1) The worker must take action. That is, if there is a disturbance the worker must do something about it or he must withdraw from the situation for the moment so as not to legitimize it by his presence. (2) The worker must not allow himself to be put in a compromising position. He is warned against becoming a pawn between various segments of his group or allowing misinformation to jeopardize his effectiveness as the worker.

The workers are often involved in handling problems concerning smoking, drinking, sexual behavior, narcotics, and spontaneous attacks on personal property. In addition, they often have to deal with problems resulting from group attitudes and racial problems as well as fights resulting from subcultural activities and inter-group conflict.

The program and its success are highly dependent upon the individual worker. Management is responsible for training these workers and for obtaining financial support and equipment, and for initially directing workers.

To be successful, it is felt that each worker must be able to operate effectively within whatever subculture his group is a part of. Each worker must exert a direct influence, not only on the group, but particularly on the key members and the leaders of the group. He must develop an understanding of and basis for dealing with the total community, that is, the police, social agencies, institutional facilities, the courts, the schools, and the families. The primary effort of the program is group oriented. Each worker must provide opportunities for activities with status which are seen as desirable by the youths. But also, workers must develop interest in activities of a type that are generally considered important and acceptable by society, particularly in the area of education and job placement.

GOALS AND OBJECTIVES

The long-range objective of this program is to create a lasting and permanent effect on the communities we have served; to reduce delinquency; to erect positive and legitimate opportunity structures and implement successful methods or techniques to deal with the continuing problems which affect the lives of hard-to-reach youths.

Phase I

A. To build *communication*, and when applicable, to utilize community agencies, police, local power structure, etc., in the communities where we are working.
B. To *contact*, *neutralize*, and *build rapport* with the delinquent subcultures through effective use of our own tools which lead in the direction of socialization, recreation, education, and employment.
C. The development and training of the negative power structure in order to facilitate the change of negative group norms.

Phase II

A. To develop and train other indigenous, unaffiliated (regarding "gang element") youths and adults in a subprofessional role in order to meet the needs of the Senior, Junior, Midget, and Pee-Wee elements of the gang structure.
B. To lean heavily on the training aspect, through proper utilization of program tools and the development of individual self-respect and motivation of the total gang element.
C. To develop cooperative and collaborative attitudes and practice in the community among professional and indigenous persons.

Phase III

A. To develop community pride and responsibility through exposure and training.
B. To develop a realistic approach to personal, group, and community problems.

SELECTION AND INVOLVEMENT OF AN INDIGENOUS STAFF

I. *Commitment*. In selecting people as paid staff members, the worker should be sure of the person's sincerity and commitment to the Program. He should:
  A. Take into account the person's past record as a volunteer.
  B. Make him responsible for certain tasks, such as collecting rosters, chaperoning and managing groups, making out time and report sheets, being responsible for equipment, helping set-up and carry out programs, etc.
  C. Observe such things as dependability, responsibility, punctuality, and performance.

II. *Trial Period*. New program aides should be asked to function on a trial basis for the first few weeks.
  A. This will allow the worker the chance to see the aide in a variety of situations and give him the basis for his final commitment.
  B. The aide will have an opportunity to see what is expected of him and decide if he wants to accept the responsibility.

III. *Potential Ability: Time and Energy.* Paid staff members should have the potential of performing the tasks assigned to them with a reasonable amount of instruction. They should also have adequate time and energy to devote to the Program.

A. Consideration should be given to the kind of activities in which the new aides will be expected to engage. Training should figure in the worker's plan for the aide.

B. School or employment should be considered, along with other factors affecting the time an aide has to devote to the Program.

IV. *Ability to Relate.* Probably the most important characteristic a program aide must have is the ability to relate to and work with people.

A. Start working with people at their own level.

B. Program aides should not tell local people what to do, but instead should assist, encourage, give direction and motivation.

C. Don't attempt to move faster than groups or individuals are willing to move, and yet not too slow. Watch for cues; *listen* to the people.

V. *Aides Should Be "Indigenous."* Every effort should be made to select aides who live in the communities they will serve. Because they live in the area, these aides are more likely to:

A. Be involved in the life and activity in the neighborhood.

B. Know the area, the institutions, and the people.

C. Be in the neighborhood when they are not "working," and when the worker is absent. They can, therefore, serve as a positive influence on a constant basis.

1. These aides may be able to curtail negative activity by accidentally observing a conflict on the street.

2. They may elect to make a visit to a youth, adult, or an agency simply because they live nearby.

3. Their commitment is likely to be greater because this is "their" community.

4. Because they are "insiders," their rapport with the community will be enhanced.

VI. *Key Factors: Commitment—Potential —Desire.* No person should be added to the staff simply because he is "heavy" with the group or in the neighborhood. A commitment to the Program, potential, and a desire to carry out the objectives of the Program should be some of the important factors which influence staff selection.

A. A staff member should have broader responsibility than just being a "control" factor.

B. The worker should be wary of the guy who is just "interested in the buck" and who does no more than is necessary to get by.

C. In selecting staff, consideration should be given to what effect— positive or negative—the experience will have on the individual.

1. Will he react to this as a "handout" with no feeling of accountability?

2. Will it be taken as an opportunity to learn and develop one's ability?

3. Are adequate guidelines being set up to assure that the aides can handle the situation rather than being overwhelmed?

VII. *Developing Leaders.* Staff positions should be used to encourage and assist the development of dedicated community leaders.

A. Making a person a program aide can be a means of providing the recognition which may be the difference between a passive, non-involved citizen, and an active community supporter.

B. It is a means of providing the tools and experience that a person needs to make his life more successful.

C. The program aide's position can serve as motivation for neighborhood youth and adults to be more active in the community and move them to think in terms of community service.

COMMUNITY SERVICE AGENCIES: CONTACT, NEUTRALIZATION, UTILIZATION

One of the most important assets that a street work program can possess is good, harmonious relations with other community-serving agencies. A program such as ours relies heavily on the mutual respect and cooperation which we encourage among all community-minded groups. In order that these relations may continue to flourish and develop, it may be of value to discuss the techniques of community cooperation.

I. *Initial Contact.* It is of extreme importance that initial contact be made early upon the worker's entry into an area. Adequate preparation should be made in advance to assure a successful meeting—first impressions are often lasting impressions.

A. Learn what you can about the role and function of the agency before making contact. Seek knowledge of the leadership and staff; i.e., their attitudes and outlook on the community, how the community views them and their agency, etc.

B. When the first visit is made to an agency, be it a youth center, CHA office, church, Urban Progress Center, school, police station, PTA, or block club meeting, the new worker should be accompanied by the previous worker or the present worker, if there is one.

C. All significant personnel should be met and cordial relations established. Emphasis should be on the agency director and his "action" staff.

D. When contact is made with an agency which has had no previous experience with our Program, arrangements should be made to introduce the agency director to the unit supervisor. This will have an effect of establishing an "agency-to-agency" relationship.

II. *Follow-up.* Of even greater significance than the original contact is the need for constant follow-up. To visit an agency "once in a blue moon" is of little value since no rapport can be established. You must get to know the staff and they should know you.

A. Seek to meet regularly on a weekly or biweekly basis with pertinent staff members where matters of mutual interest and concern can be reviewed and discussed.

B. Attempt to involve agency staff members in your area and unit staff meeting. When possible, visit agency staff sessions.

C. Explore the feasibility of joint training sessions where a clearer view of differing goals or methods may be obtained.

III. *Neutralization.* There are many important reasons for fostering and maintaining relations with other agencies—chief among them is communication. We must constantly strive to keep the community aware of what our Program seeks to achieve. At the same time, we should be aware of what programs and activities are being offered by other youth and community organizations.

Another reason is to bridge the gap between these groups and the youth and adults we service. In this way, old disputes and animosities may be reduced and overcome. Of equal importance is the need to prevent new misunderstandings based on misinformation or no information. In this area we seek to neutralize those individuals, groups or agencies where such problems might occur.

A. In meetings with agency staff members, discuss our Program frankly. Explain the goals, methods and techniques of the detached worker. Make the worker's role clear.

    1. We work on the street and in "borrowed" facilities with delinquency-prone youth.

    2. We seek to involve all interested segments of the community in providing wholesome recreational, educational, and job opportunities for these and other youths.

    3. Wherever and whenever possible, we seek to set up jointly sponsored programs with other youth-serving agencies.

B. Don't overstate the case. Make realistic appraisals of the Program. Avoid suggesting that we have all the answers or that we solve every problem.

C. Use tact. When problems or misunderstandings arise, don't become defensive or self-righteous. Don't try to "Bogart." This is especially true where law-enforcement agencies are concerned. If someone gets busted, try to get the facts. Make no assumptions of guilt or innocence. In a word, *cooperate*.

D. Utilize the tools and opportunities provided by the Program to cement and strengthen relations with agencies.

    1. Share tickets to various events with staff and youth members.

    2. Offer to provide trophies or share expense for equipment needed by the agency for cooperative use.

    3. Encourage agencies to share the newspaper by contributing articles or announcements.

    4. Invite staff to luncheons, dinners, trophy presentations or banquets held by the Program.

E. Written communication can be of great value when properly used, but a letter which is confusing, untactful or provocative can do more damage than good. *All* letters should be tactful, to the point, and courteous.

WORKER RELATIONS WITH POLICE AND THE COURTS

The work of the Detached Worker often brings him into close contact with the law-enforcement agencies of our city. This is particularly true where the police and the courts are concerned. Since the inception of the Program, we have worked to maintain a mutually beneficial and supportive relationship with the Chicago Police and court systems. This has included close personal contact between the workers and the personnel of the police department, from the district commanders to the officers on the beat. With respect to the courts—especially Boys' Court and Family Court—a similar relationship has been fostered.

It is absolutely essential to the continued success of the Program that these relationships be maintained, broadened and improved. In this outline we shall discuss some of the techniques which make for good police and court relations.

I. *The Police.* The effectiveness of a worker can be greatly increased if he is known to the police officers assigned to his area. The worker, in turn, must be acquainted with the officers.

A. When you begin work in an area which is new to you, pay a visit to the district headquarters, meet and get to know the commander.

B. Suggest that you be introduced to the officers of the district at one of the police roll calls.

1. At such an introductory roll call, be discreet. State briefly your reason for being in the area and for being at the roll call.

2. Offer your cooperation, soliciting theirs in return, in matters concerning youth.

3. Answer all questions honestly and briefly.

C. On the street, know the patrolmen and the patrol cars. Be especially familiar with the youth officers and the gang cars.

D. In dealing with the police, whether in a conflict or a non-conflict situation, don't challenge them. Try not to threaten their position or their authority.

1. We want the cooperation and support of the police whenever we need it and they expect the same thing from us. If you make the "man" look bad in front of a group, he is not going to do much cooperating!!

2. If the group you are with is approached by the police, immediately identify yourself as a worker and let the police take the initiative. Once they have committed themselves as to their intentions, you can then re-enter the situation in behalf of your group. This will, of course, depend on what the "man" has in mind. Don't allow yourself to be put in the middle.

3. If you think the policeman is wrong, say so briefly and calmly and state your position. If his response is negative, wait until a later time to pursue the issue, i.e., aside from the group, at the police station or with the commander.

E. Contacts within the department should be utilized whenever a positive result can be gained for a group or an individual.

1. Occasionally, and as a last resort, it may be necessary to have a group "busted" or an individual taken into custody. Any such action must be for their own protection or for the protection of the general public.

2. The police should always be notified in case of serious group conflicts or any unlawful acts against persons or property.

3. On his own, the worker must strenuously enforce the Program's policies on firearms, autos, alcohol and narcotics.

II. *The Police Station.* The right to intercede for our groups in the city police stations was not won easily. This privilege was gained only after bitter struggle and controversy demonstrated the value and effectiveness of the Program and its work. This right must be protected at all costs.

No one has the right to walk into a police station and *demand* anything—not even a bona fide attorney-at-law—and nothing can jeopardize our relationship with the police quicker than practices of this kind. When you visit a police station to see about your boys—be cool.

A. Your main reason for going to a police station is to get information.
 1. Seek out the arresting officer or talk to the sergeant on duty. Ask what happened and why the group was arrested.
 2. Unless you were present when the action took place, be careful of your opinions as to what happened. Do not contradict statements made by the police unless you *know* the facts.
B. Depending on the charges and the circumstances, you may be able to get the group released. This will not always be possible or desirable—don't push it.
C. In any discussion with the police in the station, keep the group out of it. Take the officer to the side and talk to him privately. Confer with the group later, and avoid being "middled" by either side.
D. Be aware of the need for good human relations when dealing with the police. When an officer shows a cooperative attitude or helps a group in some way, give him credit.
 1. If the statements or actions of an officer get a group released from custody, make sure the group knows the officer was responsible. Impress them with the fact that he is trying to help them make it.
 2. If the guy seems negative, don't square him in front of the group. Nothing will be gained by this.
 3. Remember that you are an intermediary, not a law officer or a judge. Don't let your desire to help the group square you in these situations.
E. From every encounter with the police there is some lesson to be learned. See that the youths in-volved learn these lessons and that the *proper* conclusions are drawn.
 1. When a group or individual is released from custody, discuss the reasons for the arrest. Examine the facts and consider ways to prevent the same thing from happening again.
 2. If one member or segment "bagged" the whole group, point this out and attempt to bring group pressure to bear on the negative element.
 3. If the whole group was wrong, tell them how and why and let them know that you cannot help them when they "goof."

The maintenance of good police and court relations is one of the most delicate challenges faced by the Program. This is so because every single worker bears a large responsibility for the total relationship. A rash act or an ill-advised statement by any worker can seriously compromise the rapport that years of struggle and hard work have brought into being. This is a heavy responsibility that cannot be taken lightly by anyone.

III. *The Courts.* If our work with the police requires great tact and foresight, this is doubly true when it comes to the courts. In our appearances in court, in our dealings with judges and the States Attorney's office, we must always be clear about our roles, our motives and our objectives. We must know when to go to court, why we are going and what to do when we get there. We must at the same time know how best to serve the youth we support and the Program we represent. Only after these and other important factors have been firmly fixed in our minds can we be confident that our relations with the courts will rest on a firm and secure foundation.
A. Reasons for going to court.
 Contrary to the belief held by some professionals, both inside and out-

side the Program, our main reason for attending court sessions is not to get youths released from custody. While we realize that all youths are not guilty as charged, we also know that all are not innocent. We are not judges and must not assume the prerogatives which belong to a duly constituted court of law.

1. Moral support for youth. Have the group understand that you are there to give every assistance you can legitimately provide based on your *personal* knowledge of the facts.

2. Use court appearances to strengthen your rapport with groups.
   a. Let them know that you are interested and concerned about their welfare.
   b. Bear in mind that when these youths are finally released they will be back to your area of work.

3. Use these occasions to strengthen your work with members of the group who were not arrested.
   a. Discuss the issues of the trial, examine the facts and help the group see and understand what happened.
   b. Don't be timid in showing where the guilt lies. If those arrested were wrong, say so. See that the youths realize the consequences of their acts.
   c. Don't allow them to "pass the buck" on the courts or the police.

B. You cannot make every court session.
   1. During your entry period, you should take advantage of every opportunity to appear in court with a group. This will not only improve your relations with the groups, but will provide some insight into the individual and group problems which exist.
   2. As rapport is established with groups, it will become more and more difficult to attend all court sessions. You must then decide which groups, individuals or issues demand your presence when hearings are held.
   3. Key factors which should affect such decisions are guilt or innocence of the youth involved and opportunities for learning where the group as a whole is concerned.

C. When a case involving your group is scheduled to be heard, attempt to meet with the judge in his chambers beforehand. Under these private circumstances you can express your personal feelings about the case, be they pro or con.

D. In Family Court hearings rely on the probation officer as your friend in the court. Seek his counsel and express your views to him.

E. In Open Court:
   1. If you are unable to meet the judge in chambers, identify yourself as the hearing begins. Indicate to the States Attorney who you are and what your position is.
   2. Avoid giving direct testimony or recalling facts of the case.
   3. Your main role is to provide background to help the court understand the youth.
      a. Tell the court of the positive aspects of the youth's background. If he has assisted you in the past, mention this fact. Mention any positive characteris-

tics the youth may possess without committing yourself as to his guilt or innocence.

b. Be conscious of the effect such testimony has on the youth. Take care not to let him think that you would distort the facts to get him off the hook. Have him understand that he must be responsible for the issues involved in the case.

c. If you feel that detention should be the outcome of a given case, make this known to the judge or States Attorney in private, but never in open court.

F. Pitfalls to avoid

1. While you should stress alternatives to jail, don't fall into the role of the weeping social worker who "cops a plea" for every kid.

2. Don't play the role of a defense attorney, and avoid letting the court saddle you with the decision as to how a case will be settled. That is the work of a judge and we are not equipped for it.

3. Always remember that your conduct in court will be remembered when you return again. Play your part with the long view in mind.

The relationship which we now enjoy with the police and the courts is a process, not an accomplished fact. Like any process, this relationship requires constant care and attention. If we adhere to the simple principles mentioned in this outline, together with a fair amount of common sense, the coming years will show a constant improvement in our relations with these all-important public agencies.

TRAINING: METHODS AND OPPORTUNITIES

Training and instruction are essential if the indigenous staff is to effectively promote and implement the objectives of the Program. Some methods and opportunities for staff development will be discussed here.

I. *Staff Meetings.* The staff meeting should be more than just a weekly get-together where cold facts are run down and reports exchanged. This meeting can form the basis of the staff training program.

A. Discuss program policy and theory.

B. Use the problems and accomplishments of the individual staff member as your group discussion points.

C. Prepare in advance certain topics for examination, such as:

1. How to involve more youths or adults in meaningful program activity.

2. How and why to plan programs.

3. How to deal with group problems on the street.

4. Relating to agencies, utilizing community space and resources, and cooperating with other groups.

5. Reports, time sheets, forms, etc. – why they are necessary and getting them done correctly and on time.

II. *Individual Conferences with Staff Members.* This is the time to make sure things are clear to the staff member.

A. Deal with specific questions in depth.

B. Assess worker's progress and give assistance.

C. Discuss the work in the field, relationship with groups, individuals, agencies, etc.

D. Review certain reports, give direction and seek out problem areas.

E. Offer constructive criticism from which the worker can learn.

III. *Challenge – Opportunity – Responsibility – Motivation.* In assigning responsibilities, think of how the worker can learn from the experience. Make sure that there is constant challenge and the opportunity to grow and develop.

A. Try to assign tasks which will help the worker learn.

B. Don't keep a worker in one position so long that it becomes routine and boring.

1. If all a worker has been doing is "keeping the lid on" a group, try having him plan activities and let him select someone else to chaperone and keep the group tight.

2. Shift staff responsibilities so each member has a chance to function at all levels.

3. Assign tasks on the basis of increasing difficulty and responsibility.

4. Don't be content to get your staff "set." The job is to *train and develop people.*

IV. *Free Exchange of Ideas.* The relationship between the worker and his staff should be such that all members feel free and are encouraged to express ideas and opinions openly. A free exchange of ideas and information is essential to good communication.

A. Strive to control negative reactions to comments and opinions of staff.

B. Encourage *all* staff members to contribute to the pool of ideas and information. This will make them more involved and committed, and they will learn better.

C. Be aware of clique development that could result in some staff members being "left out."

D. Be accessible to staff. Make them feel that they can always come to you for help and support.

E. Group pressure and opinion can be useful methods to emphasize the need for improvement around certain problem areas such as missed assignments, tardiness, "goof-ups" in the area.

V. *Developing Potential Ability.* Training and instruction should be regarded as a necessity in developing the abilities of staff and non-staff personnel at all levels. This is especially true of non-staff members whose interest and potential are evident, but whose opportunity for development has been limited.

John P. O'Brien

YOUNG PEOPLE IN TROUBLE: THE CASE FOR PROBATION

Probationary techniques for dealing with delinquents have met with different opinions. The issues center on what psychological factors are considered in these cases of misconduct. The more sympathetic interpretations of probationary measures call for lenient means in dealing with behavioral problems and place a greater emphasis on the personal aspects of each case.

Mr. John O'Brien's report on the probation work of the Juvenile Court of Cook County, Illinois, describes liberal policies in handling probation cases. The court has found that the last resort is to take a boy out of his home and place him in an institution in order to correct his behavior. Instead, after careful study of each case, the court prefers to develop a plan for rehabilitation. The emphasis is not placed on *what* the child did, but rather on *why* he did it, and on working out a reasonable program for him. It has been found that mere punishment is not the most effective means and does not serve as a deterrent to others, not even to the child involved. Immediate rewards as well as long-range goals play an important part in probation work.

Success in a program of probation depends upon the qualifications and effectiveness of the probation officer himself, and on the resources and support which he receives from the community. In a program which calls for close human contact and concern, an officer must have knowledge of psychological principles. In his work he sees the obvious expression of the needs of adolescents and their determined attempts to meet these needs, not always by means which are considered socially legitimate. The child must be made to understand the aspects of his behavior which are undesirable and to understand the influences in his environment which must be changed in order to make a successful adjustment.

Next year, some 15,000 Cook County boys and girls, sick with anxiety, will stand before a high bench in a crowded and austere courtroom at 2240 W. Roosevelt. They will be charged with offenses ranging from truancy to armed robbery.

About half of these youngsters will sigh with relief when the judge places them "on probation." This means they will not be shipped off immediately to serve time in a state institution. They can return instead to their families and friends, to their homes and their schools.

Why are half the youngsters brought into the Juvenile Court placed on probation? If guilty of breaking the law, do they not deserve some more severe form of punishment?

The answer is that the Juvenile Court was not established to provide punishment. It was established to provide help. When the Cook County Juvenile Court was organized in 1899 it was the first court in the United States with the sole purpose of helping children — delinquent, dependent or neglected. It deals daily with children in need of protection because of parental neglect or abuse as well as with children who have done things which would be a crime if committed by an adult.

The Juvenile Court, or Family Court as it has been called, is based on the concept of

"parens patria" — the state as a parent. Whenever parents do not or cannot fulfill their responsibility to guide, control and care for their children, the Juvenile Court steps in temporarily. The primary concern of the court is the welfare of children in trouble.

The creation of a Juvenile Court in Cook County was a great humanitarian step which set a pattern for the nation. In 1905, the Pennsylvania Supreme Court described the function of juvenile courts in a moving decision which pointed out that when a child comes into court, he is not to be tried for a crime but rather to be saved from an ordeal with the prison in its wake " . . . whether the child deserved to be saved by the state is no more a question for a jury than whether the father, if able to save it, ought to save it," the court ruled.

Mrs. Joseph T. Bowen, a noted Chicago civic leader, wrote almost 40 years ago about the founding of the Juvenile Court in Cook County. She recalled a cartoon which she had seen.

"The first part represented a steep precipice over which little children were constantly falling," Mrs. Bowen wrote. "At the bottom stood a long row of ambulances to take the injured to the hospital, but no at-

From *Viewpoint*, the *Chicago Sun-Times*, December 26, 1965. Reprinted with the permission of the author and publisher.

tempt was made to keep the children from the edge of the precipice. The second part showed how the Juvenile Court formed a fence at the top of the precipice and the children were prevented from falling over.

"At any rate," she stated, "that cartoon, ahead of its time, described very well the effort of the Juvenile Court to save children and since then the court has made a continuous effort to educate parents to raise the standards of the home, and to keep children from committing the various crimes and misdemeanors which take them into police stations."

How can a child who has broken some law be helped? If there is anything good at all in the child's home and family background, the child will have a better chance to grow up to lead a happy and useful life if he stays at home, supervised and assisted by officials of the court. The only alternative—placing a child in a state institution—is viewed as a last resort, because it indicates that all other efforts at rehabilitation have failed.

The whole philosophy of the Juvenile Court system in America is based on the idea of probation—an idea even older than the concept of a special court to deal with children.

The American probation system began around 1824 in Boston. A shoemaker named John Augustus, who was visiting a courtroom, felt strongly that some of the prisoners whose cases he heard deserved another chance. He spoke to the judge, offering to give one of the prisoners a job in his shop if the judge would not send the convict to prison.

The experiment worked. Other prisoners who showed promise of rehabilitation were given an opportunity to work in John Augustus' shop. The practice spread slowly across the nation, and a new career was born . . . the probation officer. However, probation as an accepted way of rehabilitating law offenders didn't really come into vogue until after the passage of the Illinois Juvenile Court Act in 1899.

In Juvenile Court, the probation officer is a man or woman with many duties. First, he must seek to learn the reason each child is there. About 75 per cent of the youngsters—boys 16 and under and girls 17 and under—will have violated the law, while the rest will be those without parents or whose parents have abandoned or neglected them. Many will have run away from home. Some will be involved with the police for the first time, perhaps because they were with the wrong friends at the wrong time and didn't understand what was going on. Others will have long records of more or less serious delinquent behavior and brushes with the law.

All of the youngsters whom the probation officer sees will be unhappy, miserable, and frightened. To the probation officer, what each child did is less important than why he did it.

The probation officer, after it is determined that the court has jurisdiction over the child, will conduct an investigation into his background. The probation officer will go about this task in many ways.

He will ask the parents how the youngster behaved as a child, and how he acts at home, and whether they know where he goes after school, and who his friends are, and how they feel about the trouble he is in and what plans they have for more effective supervision.

He will ask the youngster's teachers how he does in school, whether he is a troublemaker, whether he is a leader or a follower.

He will seek out the clergyman who knows the child best and ask for information and guidance about the child's spiritual life.

Finally, after talking to friends, relatives, and anyone else who might help in putting together the complicated story of an unhappy child, the probation officer will make a report to a judge in Juvenile Court. If there is enough "good" in the child's background, probation may be granted.

If probation is granted, the job of the probation officer starts in earnest.

To be effective, the probation officer should

have intensive contact with the children under his supervision. For some youngsters this requires a weekly contact. The officer must gain the confidence of these young people, who usually are fearful and suspicious of this new authority in their lives. He also must make sure they live up to the terms under which they were granted freedom.

The probation officer should be so skilled, well trained, and experienced that he can anticipate trouble and take steps to prevent it. He must serve as a counselor and friend to the youngsters he works with, and to their families as well. He may be a vocational adviser, helping a youth to find a job and keep it. He may be asked for advice about school work, about girl friends and boy friends, and about all the problems which a child must face while growing up in our complex and often savage society.

Are we too lenient with juvenile offenders? This question is asked by people who are legitimately disturbed by the rising rate of delinquency in our society and the apparent breakdown of community controls. The cure which they propose usually is a simple get-tough policy which would do nothing to solve the problems faced by our society or the problems faced by the individual child.

Getting tough with delinquents usually means locking them up for a short time, and it never has been demonstrated that this improves them in any way, or serves as a deterrent to others.

If getting tough were any kind of solution, the problems of both juvenile delinquency and adult crime would have been settled long ago. Getting tough is the easiest thing to do, once an offender has been caught.

Committing a youngster to a "training school" is at best a temporary measure. All must be released, at the latest, when they reach the age of 21.

Putting a youngster in an institution is expensive too. It costs about 10 times as much to lock up a child as it does to keep him on probation.

Some children who wind up in Juvenile Court have been involved in repeated violations of the law. We have no choice but to send them to a state institution for the protection of society, and hope that the passage of time may bring about some personality change. Even the most dedicated member of a juvenile gang does not regard the gang as a way of life forever; it's only a temporary way of overcoming the problems of adolescence.

How well does probation work? Exact figures are hard to come by, because there is no way to measure the value of a human life against what it might have become. Nevertheless most children placed on probation in Juvenile Court will make good if the probation staff is good. Many youngsters left in high school will graduate. Some will go on to college. Others will find jobs and become self-reliant and self-respecting citizens.

The key to the success of any probation system is the probation officer. Naturally, the more skilled the probation officer, and the more time he has for each case, the more successful he will be in selecting youngsters for probation and in helping them afterwards.

The Juvenile Court probation system in Cook County works better than we have any right to expect, because it is severely handicapped by a shortage of staff, time, and community resources.

At present a total of 134 probation officers are authorized to handle the 15,000 young boys and girls who come before the court every year. Furthermore, the probation department does not even have the 134 officers to which it is presumably entitled. The turnover rate is high, as skilled personnel leave to go to higher-paying courts and to social service agencies. There is constant difficulty in recruiting college-trained men and women for a comparatively low-paying, overburdened, difficult, and dangerous job.

The present caseload in Cook County Juvenile Court is so great that even the most dedicated and efficient probation officer has difficulty doing his job properly.

One probation officer may have 80 or 90 children in his care at one time, and be expected to investigate 10 to 15 new cases each month.

The probation service is doing a good job— but given more time and resources, it could do a far better job. More youngsters could be rescued from their misery and helped to live useful adult lives.

We need more treatment alternatives available to the court. Right now, the alternatives are probation or commitment to an institution. Experiments have been tried in other cities with "half-way houses," day camps, weekend camps, and other systems of control which leave a child with his family or in school while in the course of rehabilitation.

The situation is growing more critical daily. Families are being uprooted, neighborhoods are changing, the population is increasing, and the job of learning to be an adult is harder than ever.

In 1961 in California, state law-enforcement officials were shocked to learn that even if the rate of delinquency did not increase, the growth of the teen-age population would require them to double the capacity of their state institutions for delinquents within a few years. In an effort to meet the problems, they tried cutting down the caseload for a selected group of probation officers. The results were remarkable. By making it possible for some members of the probation staff to do their job properly, the state actually saved money. First, children were locked up awaiting court action for a shorter time, and second, fewer children were committed to state institutions.

One of the most significant studies of the effects of the probation system was started in 1959. The National Council on Crime and Delinquency undertook a three-year project in the Circuit Court of Saginaw, Mich., to test the effectiveness of probation when a service is adequately staffed with well-trained officers. At the end of the three years, it was found that the number committed to state institutions decreased by 14 per cent. At the same time, the number who violated probation was reduced by 50 percent. This is an impressive record of success.

A well-staffed and wisely administered probation system seems to be the best method ever found for dealing with many juvenile delinquents. We know that probation can work. It must be made to work. Otherwise, we must vastly increase our police force, at least double our present institutional facilities, and probably face an increased crime rate in spite of our efforts.

Even if we could afford to pay many times what we do now to protect society against delinquency, we would have to add the incalculable cost of ruined lives that a good probation system could save.

The Cook County Juvenile Court has had its ups and downs. At times, it has been outstanding as a result of the work of sincere, understanding and compassionate civic leaders, and legal and political authorities. At other times, as a result of civic indifference, it has stumbled over rocky ground. Nowhere more than in the record of our treatment of children is it apparent that good government is a never-ending job for the citizen, who must keep informed about the work of the court and support those policies and budgets that will strengthen it.

Judge Orman W. Ketcham of Washington, D.C., one of the leading Juvenile Court authorities in the nation, has pointed out that when the state acts as a substitute parent, the interests of the state and the welfare of the child are not in conflict, but in fact coincide.

"Those interested in justice for children, as well as those concerned with their social welfare now and in the future, cannot afford to be complacent. . . . They must insist that the state take prompt steps to perform on its promises.

"Roscoe Pound regarded the establishment of the Juvenile Court in America as one of the most significant advances in the administration of justice since the Magna Charta. But the bright hope of this new form of jurisprudence could be snuffed out by the failure of legislatures to support the juvenile courts and carry through on their promises. Unless this is done, the Juvenile Court's 'noble experiment' will never really have been fairly tried," Judge Ketcham wrote.

The Juvenile Court in a real sense is the court of last resort for children, for when they appear before a judge, they are in serious trouble. If society fails them at this time, their future becomes very dark.

With the support of public officials and interested citizens, much has been done to improve our treatment of the boys and girls who appear in Juvenile Court. The daily tragedy witnessed by those of us who work in the court is that so often, much more could be done.

Part VIII

TEACHERS AND COUNSELORS

Teachers and counselors play such a vital role in the education and development of children that it is important that the attention of the psychologist and psychiatrist be directed toward making certain that the "right" people are guided into the college programs leading to the teaching and counseling fields. Every possible psychological test and method should be used in the selection of candidates for degrees and certificates in these two areas. College and university admissions offices and the departments involved are relying more on the professional evaluation of students at the time of admission and often midway through their training program. Frequently the performance of students is not predictable; it is subject to changes which make it questionable or undesirable for them to continue in their chosen work without, at least, professional treatment. The mental health of such a worker is of concern to all: administrators, parents, children, and the person himself. He should strive to reach and maintain the best possible adjustment of his personal life, particularly when in a position to influence others professionally.

Attracting promising students into the professions of teaching and counseling has become so vital and pressing that much attention, research, time, and money are being devoted to the total problem by colleges, by the government, and by the people already in the field. A superior individual—intellectually, personally, morally, and ethically—is needed, if the educational system is to survive and the institutions are to turn out the type of professional needed to meet the continually higher demands of society and the increasingly complex problems that they are expected to handle.

Those working as teachers and counselors are constantly being encouraged to re-evaluate their role and personality, and the adjustment and compatibility of both. Continuing academic and in-service training are needed as there are rapid changes in the field, not only in the core of knowledge available, but also in the techniques, practices and therapy being successfully used.

The idea of interrelating the various professionals in a school setting—the principal, teachers, counselors, psychologists, and social worker—is becoming more and more an accepted practice. For too long, each operated in an intellectual and practical vacuum. Since all of the fields demand more psychological background, it is natural that the psychological principles affecting human behavior, particularly that of children, should become the basis of this interdisciplinary move. The practical method, using case-conference or intrastaffing techniques, promises a brighter future. These formerly separate professionals can now interrelate, find respect for each other's training and work, and apply all of their knowledge and experience toward the resolution of a common problem. In the past, jealousy between professions has been kept a secret and not openly discussed. Now it is time to face this fact and to apply all the newly developed techniques of group interaction and sensitivity in training individuals in varying professional programs to work together for the welfare of the very individuals they are committed to serve. Parents have been the last in the case-conference team to be recognized as of importance in understanding and treating various problems that arise. Finally, they, too, are being included in the diagnostic and treatment process.

John Naisbitt

THE NATIONAL TEACHER CORPS

The National Teacher Corps has as one of its major goals the attraction of promising, intelligent, imaginative, and healthy people into the profession of teaching. It seeks those who are truly interested in the problems of the poor and want to help them better their conditions of life. It particularly strives to find those who would not otherwise have considered teaching; and it makes it possible for such persons to enroll as prospective teachers in special programs at co-operating universities.

However, the work of the Corps represents more than this. It indicates the concern of many for the types of individuals who are being recruited into teacher training programs, and for the quality and emphasis of the training they are receiving. The mental health and attitude of the teacher are progressively becoming recognized as basic to good teaching. In addition to having the academic potential, the prospective teacher needs special, sincere, and healthy interest in what his future job will entail.

The experience of the National Teacher Corps is already giving educators and psychologists evidence of the need to re-examine their courses and techniques. The emphasis on a laboratory approach with paid interns may greatly change universities' concepts of how best to train future teachers. Selection of prospective teachers needs improvement and refinement. Professional course work needs updating and upgrading; teaching of such courses should be altered and team-teaching approaches used. Development of more and better teachers could be expected, if teacher-training institutions exhibited a willingness to learn from the experience of the Corpsmen.

Q. What's "national" about the National Teacher Corps? Is there a national pool of teachers specially trained to work with disadvantaged pupils, and can a local school system request to have such teachers work in schools?

A. The National Teacher Corps is a program for careers in teaching the disadvantaged. The program is "national" because it is funded by the U. S. Congress and because it recruits prospective teachers from all over the country and relocates them where they are needed.

But the way in which the program is handled varies from project to project. Each project is the result of cooperative planning by the state department of education, a local university, and the teachers and administrators of the school district, who jointly submit proposals to the Teacher Corps for a work-study internship in the education of the disadvantaged. The university outlines a master's degree course stressing the nature and needs of impoverished communities and of educationally deprived students – sociology and psychology, special methods of instruction, appropriate curriculums, and special work in disadvantaged schools and communities.

Local schools can obtain the services of Teacher Corps interns if these schools are in areas having concentrations of children from low-income families. The interns work part time in the school in teams of three to ten, under the guidance of an experienced teacher. A portion of the school day is also devoted to work in the community related to the problems of the students. The rest of the interns' time is spent at the university and with their studies.

From *The PTA Magazine*, May 1967. Reprinted by permission.

Although general recruitment is national and preliminary screening is done in the Washington office, all corpsmen must have been accepted by the local university, the local school system, and the state department of education.

The appeal of a "national" program has helped to attract bright, imaginative people who had not previously planned to teach. The Teacher Corps presents teaching as one of the great challenges in education today. It looks for excellence. It asks for warm, responsive people who are willing to engage themselves in the struggle to improve the opportunities of the poor. Thus the Teacher Corps is upgrading the image of the disadvantaged.

Q. Just how does the program operate? Whom does it benefit?

A. A university begins training Teacher Corpsmen during the summer in an eight- to ten-week pre-service program. This program usually emphasizes understanding of the poverty community in the locale where the corpsmen will be teaching. Corpsmen also begin their graduate course of study during this time.

In the fall the corpsmen continue to study at the university, but they also start to work in schools in poverty areas, supplementing the regular teaching staff. Their work is planned by the principal and the team leader to increase their professional competence gradually as well as to meet the needs of the schools. In the first semester the main activities are tutoring and small-group instruction. Later, corpsmen may teach regular classes for several hours a day, thus freeing the regular teachers for other professional activities. Sometimes a Teacher Corpsman is given responsibility for a group of difficult or failing students who have been selected by regular teachers for intensive work. Then the experienced teacher who is the team leader supervises the work of the corpsmen as they operate to develop a special program and team-teach.

Principals and regular teachers agree that a Teacher Corps team, by supplementing the professional staff, benefits those students who need more individual attention. The presence of young people who bring to their teaching an unusual understanding of the poverty community, a deep commitment to a difficult task, and fresh ideas that they can test in practical teaching situations tends to produce a healthy relationship between parents and the school.

The greatest benefit, however, can be expected in the years to come, when the Teacher Corpsmen will bring a more thorough preparation to their teaching careers. Seasoned by work in a poverty area, corpsmen will not undergo the culture-shock that causes so many beginning teachers to drop out of the profession. And again, they will teach in the slum schools because they want to teach in slum schools.

Q. Aren't departments and schools of education in universities and colleges already training teachers to work with disadvantaged pupils?

A. Yes. But the need is still great. Most teacher education programs are educating people who already intended to teach, and for the most part the curriculum is for prospective teachers in the more privileged schools.

The Teacher Corps is seeking the college graduate who has not previously expected to teach and presents him with the challenge of a new career.

The Teacher Corps stresses involvement in the local poverty community as the best orientation for teaching people who are disadvantaged.

Add this to the two-year internship of graduate study and service in a local school, and you get a pattern unique in teacher education.

Project directors at several of the best universities in the program frankly admit that the Teacher Corps program has opened their eyes to a whole new range of possibilities in teacher education. The close relationship with the daily life of the school from the very beginning of a teacher education program gives the teacher-intern a healthy, "show-me" attitude toward his academic studies. Usually he is eager to experiment with the new ideas he encounters through study, but he approaches them with an eye to their effectiveness in teaching.

Leon Ovsiew, assistant dean of Temple University's College of Education, said recently: "What we are doing at the College is learning from NTC. Oh, we are teaching. We have some very good teachers working with the corpsmen. No doubt! But more than that, we are learning. The National Teacher Corps has already had a visible effect on our programing. We are now planning to revise our total undergraduate and graduate teacher education program.

"We are learning through NTC how to involve potential teachers with people in the community, with other teachers in the school, and with administrators and students in these schools. We are learning how to give these people an opportunity to use their own creative abilities and intelligence instead of constantly telling them precisely what they ought to do so that they can be molded in our image. We are even learning more about what we need to do in teacher education in general. I think it's very safe to predict that a fringe benefit of the NTC money will be to revitalize teacher education throughout the United States."

Q. Federal funds, we understand, pay the corpsmen's tuition at the universities. Who pays their salaries? Are federal funds available to the participating universities and school systems for any other expenses of the program?

A. The interns' tuition, the administrative costs of the pre-service program, corpsmen's stipends during this period, and certain administrative costs are paid from federal funds. The federal government also pays 90 per cent of the corpsman's salary during the school year. The local school district pays the remaining 10 per cent. The salary for the experienced team leader is the same as he would earn in the local system, on the basis of his education and years of service.

The federal government also makes necessary payments to the experienced teacher's home system in order to protect all of his pension benefits. Bill H.R.7819 contains a provision that interns shall receive compensation equivalent to the lowest rate paid a full-time teacher in the local system to which they are assigned, or $75 a week plus $15 a week for each dependent, whichever is less.

Q. How are corpsmen selected? What are the criteria for selection?

A. Corpsmen are selected by experienced evaluators on the basis of the corpsmen's applications, their work and/or school records, reference information, and other such data as may be necessary to reach a decision. The main criteria are evidence of understanding of, and dedication to, the Teacher Corps mission; excellence of academic background; teaching or work experience; experience in other poverty programs; and high-quality references from those in the best positions to rate objectively. The final criterion is the general quality of the application itself.

Q. Does a corpsman have any choice as to the geographic area in which he will serve, or is he assigned to a school system?

A. The corpsman does not have any choice as to location. However, Teacher Corps-Washington, in recommending a person to a local program, weighs factors of both personality and experience that would make him better suited to work in a given region or a given situation.

The local university then admits the corpsman into graduate school. During the pre-service training period at the university the corpsman is interviewed by local school officials, who can either accept or reject him. If a corpsman is not acceptable to a local school, the national office of the Teacher Corps and the university reevaluate him. If they feel that the corpsman still meets Teacher Corps standards and should be given another chance, he is transferred to another program. If he does not measure up, his service is terminated.

The local school officials may terminate the service of a teacher corpsman in their system at any time during the period in which he is under contract to them.

Q. Do corpsmen commit themselves to careers in teaching the disadvantaged, or is their training applicable to work with other pupils?

A. Good preparation for teaching the disadvantaged is good preparation for any teaching. But the corpsmen are selected because of their social concern and their commitment to improving the education of the poor.

Their training will tend to deepen this commitment because it gives them an opportunity to broaden their understanding of the underlying problems of the poverty community, and it gives them a chance to succeed in a difficult assignment. Having found their Teacher Corps experiences satisfying and rewarding, they will probably continue in this area.

Q. Why wouldn't in-service training for teachers already serving in disadvantaged schools be more effective than the Teacher Corps program?

A. In-service training for teachers already in the disadvantaged schools would be a great thing. It is sorely needed, and it can be done under other federally funded legislation.

But the pupil population is rising, and we have an additional problem—a need not simply for better teachers but for more good teachers. This latter need is the one that the Teacher Corps was created to serve. Not that the Teacher Corps is the answer to the teacher shortage. But it can start a chain re-

action. It can attract more bright young people to teaching; put them into a program that has one foot in the local school and one foot in the university; create a demand in the university for a teacher education program more responsive to local school needs; cultivate an atmosphere in the local school that is more open to the kinds of changes needed to upgrade poverty education; and raise the image of the teacher of the disadvantaged to that of a competent specialist dedicated to serving the needs of the deprived child in school and in community.

Q. Is the cooperation of a university necessary, or could a school system have a Teacher Corps program without university participation?

A. The partnership between the university and the local school is the backbone of the Teacher Corps program. Only through increased cooperation between these two institutions will we really upgrade the education of our teachers and as a consequence the education of deprived children.

Q. What effect will the National Teacher Corps program have on teacher education programs at nonparticipating colleges and universities? On in-service programs for teachers?

A. We cannot say. It is difficult to predict what effect even successful programs at one institution will have on the programs of other institutions. As the Teacher Corps matures and has time to demonstrate that certain new approaches do produce a measurably better teacher education program, it is believed that other institutions will consider incorporating some of the features of the Teacher Corps program.

Q. What is the current appropriation for the Corps? Is it enough?

A. The 1966 appropriation for the Teacher Corps was $9.5 million, which enabled the Corps to become a reality. Today 1,213 Teacher Corps members, experienced teachers and teacher-interns, are engaged in service in 275 schools in 111 school systems across the nation. The 945 teacher-interns are grouped into 277 Teacher Corps teams.

Only $7.5 million was appropriated by Congress for 1967, out of the $64 million authorization. This barely covers the salaries of the 1,200 corpsmen who remained with the program through the fall, during the interim between summer pre-service and congressional action. The President has now requested an additional $12.5 million for fiscal 1967 and $36 million for 1968.

The first of these amounts would enable the Teacher Corps to recruit 2,500 additional people for summer programs and would fund the universities for their participation next fall. The 1968 appropriation would cover the salaries for the new corpsmen and the second-year teams.

In view of the spectacular success which the Teacher Corps has enjoyed so far, it is startling to reflect that it has been on trial for its life. Last March the House Committee on Education and Labor invited several educational organizations to testify before it to help the committee decide the fate of the National Teacher Corps. The National Congress of Parents and Teachers was among those testifying, as were the National Education Association and the National School Boards Association.

The National Congress on this occasion pointed out that the National Teacher Corps is a unique instrument for developing the kind of opportunities that disadvantaged children need. It reminded the committee that educational leaders find the Corps is developing methods for teaching disadvantaged children that are beyond any previously known or tried. The National Congress, therefore, urged the committee to extend and expand this unique and immensely valuable program.

Ray H. Simpson

SELF-EVALUATION AND PERSONALITY

We have become progressively aware of the impact of the personality of the teacher on the student. Not only does the teacher's personality affect and often determine what will be learned and how effectively and efficiently learning will occur but it also will have dynamic effects on the growth and development of the child's personality as well. Identification with the teacher is constantly operating in the classroom and the teacher projects many important aspects of life and adjustment to it; hence the need for individuals as teachers who are "healthy" in all aspects, and who make an ideal object for identification. Since the teacher needs to implement general principles of psychology, it is assumed he will have a sound, basic training in psychology, will keep up on current developments in the field, and will make frequent evaluations of his own personal adjustment to his classes. If personal troubles develop for the student (and well they may for even the best educated and functioning individual), the teacher, related professional personnel, or parent should sense the difficulty, evaluate the degree of seriousness, and know what to do about the problem by seeking professional counsel and developing a plan of action to resolve the difficulty.

No adult today can afford to "stand still." The teacher needs constantly to strive to keep abreast of the changing times, to adjust as he himself matures and grows as an individual. In addition, the teacher needs to be able to perceive and understand the ideas of his students. This makes the kind of relationship that exists between teacher and student most important.

Adequate teacher knowledge of subject matter and of appropriate goals, procedures, and resources is of great importance. Also of paramount importance is the teacher's understanding of himself. It has been suggested by Myers[1] that "understanding of the self is the most crucial of all understandings." If the teacher is accurately to interpret the behaviors of others, he should have a comprehensive picture of himself.

The importance of self-evaluation and self-improvement in the area of teacher personality is paralleled by the size of the difficulties involved. However, Burt[2], for example, concluded that self-rating is second only to life-record methods for accuracy in personality measurement. With cooperative individuals, self-rating ties for first place in accuracy.

Two interacting types of perception are closely related to teacher personality: self-perception and perceptions related to pupils. In an attempt to help the teacher evaluate himself, various facets of these types of perception will next be discussed.

SELF-EVALUATION OF SELF-PERCEPTIONS

As has already been noted, the understanding of self is possibly the most crucial of all understandings. Combs[3] has pointed out, "Perceptual psychology indicates that the behavior of the individual at any moment is a function of how he sees the situation and himself. . . . The behavior of a teacher like that of everyone else is a function of his concepts of self." Success in this area can be improved by examining and re-examining certain important issues the teacher may appropriately raise with himself:

1. Do I perceive my success as being closely tied up with the success of others? More specifically do I see my professional success as being largely determined by the success of the pupils with whom I work? In art, authorship, or research the lone wolf may be very successful. However, it is very difficult to see how a teacher's success can be divorced from that of his students. The teacher who is smug and self-satisfied with "his high standards" when over 25 per cent of his students fail would not seem to meet the criterion suggested here.

2. Do I visualize myself as a crystallized, complete person or as an intellectually and behaviorally learning person? The former type of individual is likely to be so "mature" that his ideas are outdated and his intellectual outlook is backward. The active, professionally growing person, regardless of chronological age, not only will be critically examining new events but will also be an active learner who is challenged by the quantity and diversity of what he does not know, such as the infinite complexities of young people and their relationships with their peers and with adults. The teacher who perceives himself as one who has completed his learning and who sees his job as one of "dishing it out" is bound to slip backward. One cannot stand still. He who is not learning professionally is going to be deteriorating professionally.

Carl Rogers[4] suggests that the continuous becoming of an individual must include his willingness to be a process that is ever changing. This becoming continues throughout the life-span. Some mistakes will be perceived as an inevitable part of the learning process. The learning person is one who can take a disappointing situation and learn something useful from it.

3. Do I cultivate a flexible self-assurance in myself? After an extensive study of teachers with contrasting success records, Olander and Klagle[5] listed emotional maturity

Adapted with permission of The Macmillan Company from *Teacher Self-Evaluation* by Ray H. Simpson. Copyright © Ray H. Simpson, 1966.
1. K.E. Myers, "Becoming: For Child and Teacher an Ever Changing Self-Image," *Childhood Education*, 41 (September 1964): 35–38. Reprinted by permission of the Association for Childhood Education International, 3615 Wisconsin Avenue, N.W., Washington, D.C.
2. C.L. Burt, "The Assessment of Personality," *British Journal of Educational Psychology*, 15 (1947): 107–121.
3. A.W. Combs, "The Personal Approach to Good Teaching," *Educational Leadership*, 21 (March 1964): 369–377, 399.
4. Carl Rogers, "What It Means to Become a Person," in C. E. Moustakes, ed., *The Self* (New York: Harper, 1956).
5. H.T. Olander and H.M. Klagle, "Differences in Personal and Professional Characteristics of a Selected Group of Elementary Teachers with Contrasting Success Records," *Educational Administration and Supervision*, 45 (July 1959): 191–195.

first among the four best predictive measures of success. It has been shown that teachers with an "integrative" pattern of conduct show significantly more spontaneity, initiative, voluntary social contributions, acts of problem solving, and fewer negative attributes such as conflict with others and boredom[6]. The need for developing flexible self-assurance is very understandable, since the typical working day for teachers is more than nine hours, and more than half of this time the teacher is responsible for leading a dynamic working situation in a group of 20 to 40 active young people[7]. Myers[8] has described flexible self-assurance in the following fashion:

"The replacement of fears and anxieties by self-assurance which can accept good times and bad and yet remain intact gives one knowledge that the self-image can shift if the occasion demands and incorporate the shift into the changing perception of what it means to become. Teachers who have this flexible self-assurance which allows them to change to meet the new and ever changing classroom challenges can help children achieve self-assurance."

4. Do I perceive myself as a person who not only tolerates diversity of point of view and procedure but even welcomes it? Am I comfortable when two students disagree on a subject appropriate for class discussion, or, even more crucial, when a student takes issue with me? Lack of appropriate perception toward diversity may be shown by irritation when controversial issues are discussed. Lack of tolerance for diversity of opinion may also be reflected in a desire to quickly give "the answer" in a discussion rather than encourage the clash of differing perspectives and the probable accompanying sharpening of intellectual abilities.

With desirable perspective the teacher will encourage an atmosphere where each student will not be afraid of being labeled foolish if he proposes a creative or offbeat idea even if it is extreme.

The teacher with a favorable perspective toward himself and diversity will avoid such expressions as: "The only way to teach ____ is ____." "The only good text in my field is ____." "The only way to solve the crisis in southeast Asia is ____." The traditions of democracy and the healthy search for the truth are not promoted by dogmatic assertions which reveal an intolerance for stimulating speculation and an honest search for the truth.

Not only in educational issues, but also in such fields as politics, economics, and art a realistically tempered intellectual vitality is hard to maintain without the constant challenge of divergent ideas.

5. Do I see myself as a person able to discuss my own personal and emotional problems? Do I accept and even seek criticism as a part of my personal and professional development?

As a teacher looks inward upon himself he inevitably sees areas of doubt and uncertainty in his search for meanings and values. The comprehensive study by Jersild to which reference has already been made suggests that excessive personal tension may appear "in disproportionate resentment, competitiveness, discouragement, efforts to impress or placate, to play the game and play it safe[9]." The study further showed that most teachers when given the opportunity found discussion of their anxieties and doubts a very useful venture. Jersild's interpretation is this:[10]

"Facing the issue of anxiety meant, to them, a way of sharing a human situation with intimate personal meaning. The discussion of anxiety was a discussion of something that to them was real, even if painful.

6. C.C. Anderson and S.M. Hunka, "Teachers Evaluation, Some Problems and a Proposal," *Harvard Educational Review*, 33 (Winter 1963): 73.
7. NEA Research Bulletin, "Teacher Time Devoted to School Duties," in the *Education Digest*, 28 (February 1963): 43–45.
8. K.E. Myers, *op. cit.*
9. Arthur T. Jersild, *Psychology of Adolescence*, 2 vols., 2nd ed. (New York: Macmillan, 1963), p. 9.
10. *Ibid.*, p. 64.

It was something that involved them personally, instead of telling them, as so many discussions in education do, how to do something to somebody else. It penetrated to some degree the wall of isolation that keeps people emotionally separate from one another."

SELF-EVALUATION AND
TEACHER PERCEPTIONS OF PUPILS

The preceding section has emphasized that the teacher's self-perception is strongly influential in determining his behavior. The teacher's needs, attitudes, tensions, and anxieties not only strongly condition his self-perceptions but also influence his perceptions of his pupils. Clarification and better understanding on the part of the teacher of his assumptions and perspectives with respect to his pupils are likely to decrease undesirable biases and distortions which would have adverse effects upon the teacher's leadership of learners. In this section we are concerned with issues that the teacher may appropriately raise with himself in better understanding his perceptions of his pupils.[11]

1. Am I sensitive to the private worlds of my students, particularly as these relate to me? In my interactions with them do I accept their perceptions, feelings, attitudes, beliefs, and understandings as extremely important? These issues are particularly significant to the teacher when a pupil's perceptions are at variance with his. Myers[12] suggests, "Teachers must be open to complete self-evaluation, for they must see themselves through children's eyes to evaluate the 'self' the children see. Children's evaluation is often an eye-opener for teachers who perceive themselves only through their own senses. . . . The critical examination of self is a difficult task, as self-acceptance must be achieved."

The teacher should be aware that his complex perception of pupils and the related ongoing interaction of him with them will be conditioned by a number of processes which have been revealed by careful experimentation in social psychology. According to Secord and Bachman[13] these include (a) "the tendency to see persons as unchanging entities," (b) "the tendency to see the cause of a person's actions as lying in him rather than in the situation," (c) "the coloring of perceptions by favorable or unfavorable evaluations of the stimulus person," and (d) "the placing of persons in ready-made categories associated with sets of personal attributes." Knowing that these things happen can alert the teacher as to prospective difficulties in relations with pupils, such as the danger of stereotyping as indicated by (d) above.

2. Am I primarily person-oriented rather than thing- or event-oriented? A teacher's training all too frequently is almost exclusively tied in with things (that is, in history, mathematics, etc.). The current emphasis on things and events is usually accompanied by a relatively small number of contacts with pupils of the age with which the teacher will later be working. Thus, it is very easy for the prospective teacher and the teacher to get into the habit of giving excessive weight to things and events and insufficient weight to pupils and their perceptions.

Not only is the good teacher person-oriented but he likes persons. Keliher[14] states it this way: "He is interested in them (children), is intrigued by their way of doing things, likes to watch them grow in mind and body, enjoys their emerging accomplishments. This teacher knows about the rough edges of growth—that boys and girls need help and guidance—that this is the reason for teachers."

In Ryans' six-year study[15], which involved 100 separate research projects and over

11. For a number of these issues the author is indebted to Arthur W. Combs, "The Personal Approach to Good Teaching," *Educational Leadership*, 21 (March 1964): 369–377, 399.
12. Combs, *op. cit.*, p. 3.
13. P. Secord and C. Bachman, *Social Psychology* (New York: McGraw-Hill Book Co., 1964), p. 90.
14. A.V. Keliher, "Environment for Learning," *Education Digest*, 28 (February 1963): 12–15.
15. D.G. Ryans, "Some Relationships Between Pupil Behavior and Certain Teacher Characteristics," *Journal of Educational Psychology*, 52 (1961): 82–91.

6000 teachers, he concluded that three of the key characteristics that differentiated between good and not-so-good teachers were: (a) the good teachers had attitudes favorable to pupils; (b) they enjoyed pupil relationships; and (c) they were generous in their appraisal of the behavior and motives of other persons.

3. Am I meanings- and significance-oriented rather than exclusively facts-oriented? This question implies the need to learn more about the interpretations and meanings that pupils do or should attach to some of the factual learnings. It suggests a need for the teacher to learn more about the perceptual experiences of his students, about why their perceptions may lead them to reject an assignment, about why the youngsters may believe that most of what they find in their texts is "phony." The growing teacher is concerned with how things seem to the pupils, for their ideas may turn out to be radically different from the teacher's. This difference, if unperceived by the instructor, may seriously interfere with learning.

4. In my contacts with a pupil do I characteristically look for causes of his difficulties on which I can possibly help him rather than shrugging off his behavior with statements such as: "Look at his mixed-up family, what can you expect?" or "His parents are divorced; he has no father; his mother works; you can't hope for much," or "He doesn't even know when to come in out of the rain"?

Much more constructive questions which give promise of eventual improvement in the pupil are ones like these: Why is the text I am using possibly inappropriate for this pupil? Which reading material would probably be better for him? How might I modify the nature of my assignments, possibly by giving optional ones so that the pupil will perceive the study to be of potential value to him? I have perceived the pupil as "failing." In what respects am I as the classroom leader "failing"?

It is always easy to find a variety of alibis for our failures, but it is more challenging, and much more effective, to search for constructive changes we can make in our own behaviors so that the pupil is more likely to succeed. The great potential in the wealth of professional reading materials should not be neglected when behavior changes are considered.

5. Do I regard each pupil as being capable? The traditional concept that each pupil in a particular class should be able to do "the work" of that class is an unfortunate legacy. It is a social vestige that prevents many teachers from dealing effectively with individual differences in varied goals, assignments, use of resources, and class procedures. When we really accept individual differences, we will recognize that the below-average pupil can do as well in terms of his abilities as the above-average student if we are capable of helping create a learning situation where each is expected to do according to his abilities.

Secord and Bachman[16] have concluded that "persons exhibit a general tendency to assume that others are similar to themselves." If a teacher denigrates his pupils or colleagues, there is a rather strong suggestion that he is unsure of his own abilities.

6. Does the personality I have developed encourage a love for learning? Possibly the greatest weakness in our schools today resides in our current inability to do an effective job in instilling a love of learning in our pupils. This suggests that each teacher has the responsibility to study each aspect of his approaches to teaching and attempt to determine which of his behaviors probably are promoting a longtime interest in teaching and which, even though they are getting immediate results, are probably killing the desire to learn after the teacher is no longer around.

Two incidents reported by Hughes[17] illus-

16. Ryans, *op. cit.*, p. 91.
17. Marie M. Hughes, "Teacher Behavior and Concept of Self," *Childhood Education*, Vol. 41, No. 1 (September 1964). Reprinted by permission of the Association for Childhood Education International, 3615 Wisconsin Avenue, N.W., Washington, D. C.

trate contrary approaches: "A third-grade child read to his class about dinosaurs, pronouncing the words 'tyrannosaurus' and 'brontosaurus' without hesitation." After this feat the only response the teacher gave was, "You left out an 'and.'" This would possibly be expected to have a negative effect.

Contrast that incident with the second one: "One morning Charles clomped into Sister Teresa's second grade, leaving a trail of large daubs of mud. He brought a bird with a broken wing held tenderly in his hand. After the bird's wing was attended to and the bird placed safely in the cage, Sister Teresa said, 'Charles, I know you are worried about the bird today but tomorrow you will take the mud off your shoes before you come into the classroom.'" The situational and perceptive understanding illustrated here can contribute much to the fostering of a love for learning more about the great unknown.

Philip M. Katz

THE CASE CONFERENCE THAT WORKS

This detailed material on the case conference technique is presented by Principal Katz in order to clarify the varying role and functions of the teacher, school counselor, psychologist, nurse, administrator, and their relationships with students and parents.

The case conference procedure can be utilized in any school regardless of its size or the age of the students. It is advisable for parents to become acquainted with various school personnel before their children become involved in behavior which interferes with acceptable school conduct and requires special attention.

So often parents and school functionaries meet for the first time when a child is about to be suspended or dismissed from school. How much better it would be if they could work together as the child grows and matures, handling each situation as it arises, developing a program to prevent serious problems from developing, and sharing professional knowledge about the child in a joint effort to understand his behavior and plan his future with and for him.

Mr. Katz has experience covering several years with a case conference technique that really works. It helps each participant see his role better, sharpen his professional techniques, and gain insight into the child's problem.

The teacher is in the forefront as far as identifying significant behavior that needs correction if learning in a group situation is to be possible. She should confer with the counselor when the situation appears to indicate a more serious problem than she is trained to cope with, or if handling it in a classroom setting would unreasonably interfere with learning on the part of the other children in the room. The counselor in turn relies on the professional testing, evaluation, and recommendations of the psychologist and/or other professional personnel. The administrator coordinates the information, works out arrangements to implement steps for helping the child through the school facilities, by community agencies, and by the parents.

Dr. Katz has developed procedures for applying known psychological principles in a productive, meaningful way.

The "case conference" or staffing is simply a method whereby individuals with specialized (or fragmented) knowledge pool or focus this knowledge on a single child to the end that the child may be helped. Although well established in the medical and social work professions, the case conference method has been underutilized in the public schools, despite the special values of this method —simplicity, productivity, and applicability —that commend it to the school situation. A caution is in order to the effect that the case conference method is a tool, not a panacea, and it must be used intelligently and properly to be effective.

The simplest way to start a conference team is for as few as three people to sit down together and seek to answer one question: How can we help this child? From that point on local conditions will determine the direction and scope of operations but no matter how many people become involved, how elaborate the recommendations, the procedure remains basically simple: The question, the tentative answers, the assignment of tasks, and provision for review. As a matter of fact, not only is the operation simple, it should be kept simple.

The productivity of the case conference method could probably be established empirically but for our purposes we can prove it logically by analyzing two arguments most often offered as disadvantages of the case conference method.

One supposed disadvantage is that the case conference method is time consuming. The services of many people are tied up for the consideration of one child when that time could be spent helping many other children. The answer to that contention is that a child with a problem will, in any event, take a disproportionate time from school personnel. The proper question is: Shall this time be spent productively in pooled efforts or dissipated in individual efforts? The validity of pooled efforts is illustrated by the following experience.

One of the first children brought to my attention in a new assignment as principal of a large elementary school was Fred W. (not his real name of course). Through sixth grade Fred was an excellent student, well-behaved and productive. In seventh grade he became so disruptive in his behavior and so poor in his school work that he was retained in the seventh grade. This child became the first case to be handled by the newly instituted conference team and this is what happened.

At the first meeting, in addition to the formal recitation of the record, the intangibles and subtleties that color and affect human relationships but never find their way into official reports were made evident. Before the session was over a strong sense of direction had emerged along with plans to augment that direction. Time would tell whether we were right or wrong but at least we had a starting point as the following example will show.

Our starting point had to be the relationships between the school and the family because of what emerged from the first session of the conference team. There was general agreement and evidence that the parents were uncooperative and somewhat hostile to the school, that the mother was more than a little overprotective of the boy and the stepfather tended to be defensive. Quite apparently something had to be done about these conditions. Regardless of the reasons for the hostility it was agreed that the school should make the first overtures to break down the barriers and establish or reestablish better feeling between the parents and the school. This task fell to the principal primarily because he was new to the situation and was in a position to offer all a fresh start. We were further advised that the mother was a very heavy woman who found walking stairs very difficult and that she would probably be reluctant to come to school on this account, if for no other reason.

Accordingly a meeting was scheduled for

From *The Illinois Schools Journal* (successor to *Chicago Schools Journal*), Vol. 40, No. 7 (April 1959): 331–339. Reprinted with the permission of the author and publisher.

the principal's office on the first floor. It was the principal's task, in addition to establishing a friendly tone, to tell the parents that the child was being promoted to the eighth grade under certain conditions, explain the conditions, inform the parents of any other steps the school had in mind for the youngster and then ask the help of the parents in making the promotion and the other plans work. At the start of the meeting the mother was obviously hostile and defensive so the principal simply chatted with purpose of establishing cordial relations. In a few minutes a visible relaxation became evident. The mother sat back in her chair, her hands resting in her lap, not clenched in front of her, so that when the teacher joined the meeting the parents were ready to listen.

The teacher pursued the theme of school-parent cooperation but when the mother protested that she always cooperated and did what the school asked, the teacher was able to cite specific dates, times, and requests that had been ignored. This was done, I might add, in such a masterful way that if the parent had taken umbrage at this information it would have told us that we were dealing with an impossible situation. As it turned out we were not.

The parents were appreciative of the changes in store for the boy and then the discussion turned to what she and the father could do. Among the recommendations were that the mother demonstrate to the boy her interest in his school work. "For example," said the teacher, "Fred has done considerable work on the bulletin board outside of the room. If you could see the board and praise Fred for it, it would show him that you really do care."

The mother didn't pause more than a second. "Come on," she said, "I'll do it." And up she went. Three laborious flights, one step at a time.

Are we home free with this case? Not completely, but the aggressive behavior has stopped and the school work is improved. The prognosis is excellent because we now have the machinery—the conference team—to convert significant deviations into corrective procedures.

A second argument frequently offered as an objection to the case conference method is that it creates problems where none existed before. The answer—that the case conference *acknowledges* problems, does not create them—is even more obvious than in the first argument yet the point in contention must be taken seriously because it is raised by teachers of good will and serious intent and has considerable merit from the perspective of the classroom teacher.

"Acknowledge, exist," says the classroom teacher, "all I know is that I have things under control and I want to keep it that way."

What is coming into focus in this argument is not the merit of the case conference method but the dilemma peculiar to the school situation of attempting to reconcile the welfare of the many against the welfare of the one. Sometimes we opt for one, sometimes for the other. The teacher, understandably, leans toward the group; the conference team, equally understandably, leans toward the one. These differences can never be finally reconciled but they must be dealt with by anyone attempting to develop a case conference team. There is no point in the conference team trying to win this argument but if they recognize why it is raised they will consciously be supportive of the teacher, offer concrete suggestions, and at all times be aware of the dilemma posed by attempting individual problem solving in what is essentially a group oriented institution.

The third value of the case conference method lies in its applicability to any kind of school situation regardless of the student's socio-economic level, ethnic origin, or other variables for which we often develop specialized methods. The case conference seeks to help people and their humanity is the common denominator. Every child who comes before the conference team is a human being in the process of becoming a person.

Some obstacle to his becoming a person has been raised and the task of the conference team is to do their share toward removing or reducing this obstacle so the child can continue on toward becoming a person.

Needless to say, the specific recommendations made concerning the child will take into account all the variables that go into making a person, will take into account all the variables that constitute his environment, and will seek to assess the effect of these variables on the child. But with all this, the dominant assumption remains that this is an unhyphenated human being and no other descriptive adjunctive is necessary.

At this point, a more detailed description of the actual workings of the case conference method might be in order. Some years ago a conference team was started at a small elementary school in Chicago and after two years of operation the results were summarized in the following article:[1]

"The group or clinical approach to problem solving has long been effectively used in the medical and social work professions. Whether this technique is applicable to solving academic and behavior problems at the local level is just now being explored. After two years of group or Clinic Team operation the evidence seems to indicate that the group approach can be greatly effective.

"One of the first cases handled by the Clinic Team serves to illustrate how the combining of talents leads to the development of a unified plan and makes it possible to put the plan into operation. It should be noted in evaluating this approach that all the relevant information about the boy in question, including health data and even substantially the same recommendations that the Clinic Team arrived at, were included in medical reports and a Child Study report made two years before the case was considered by the Clinic Team.

"The school personnel involved with this youngster prior to utilizing the group approach were not insensitive to his problem.

To the contrary, there is ample evidence that the problem had been properly identified and that diligent *individual* efforts had been made to help this youngster. At the time the Clinic Team took up the case, however, the child, far from having shown evidence of improvement, was rapidly becoming a more serious problem in the classroom.

"The child in question entered the school in April, 19–, as a 4A student of poor academic achievement and with a record of serious behavior problems at all previous schools. He had attended four other schools (two public, and two parochial).

"Joe (as he shall be known from here on) was a dark-thatched, heavy set (almost obese), eleven-year-old with a lumbering, bear-like gait and a seemingly uncontrollable temper. A Stanford-Binet test showed normal intelligence but the tester questioned the results as there were indications of above-average ability.

"The reasons for the study, which began in May, 19–, simply state: 'Poor classroom behavior, poor peer relationships, immature, excitable, nervous.'

"Some typical teacher's comments add substance to those simple observations: 'Joe has been shouting and hitting Bill.' 'Joe . . . took one and one-half hours to write one sentence of a letter of apology.' ' . . . has not started to work this morning. He is shouting across the room, tossing wax, and kicking the seat across from him.'

"A Child Study made in 3rd grade showed negative deviations from MA of 1 to 2 years. The examiner commented that ' . . . since MA may be higher, the negative deviations may be more serious than shown here.'

"The case was first considered at a meeting of the Clinic Team in June, 19–, at which Joe's mother was present. The Clinic Team made the following decisions as a result of the discussion: 1. We would obtain a medical report on Joe's condition from the hospital at

1. Philip M. Katz, *et al.*, "Solving Pupil Problems at the Local Level," *Chicago Schools Journal*, Vol. 40, No. 7 (April 1959): 331–338.

which he had been receiving treatment. 2. Joe's teacher was to give the parents his homework assignment so that they would know what work he was assigned. 3. Joe's mother was encouraged to concentrate on following certain recommendations which had been made to her by a Guidance Clinic that had seen the child during the time he was not in the public school system. (The Clinic Team had been shown the recommendations sheet by the mother in a previous interview.) 4. We would later consider the possibility of recommending counseling treatment for both parents.

"Information from the mother and a previous medical report in the folder revealed that at age 2 the child had spinal meningitis and had been hospitalized for some weeks. Recovery was difficult, involving relearning walking and speech patterns. An earlier teacher-nurse report recalled that Joe had several outbursts during an interview. The mother stated that this happened several times a day unless he was in a calm, secure environment.

"The mother was very tense at the initial interview but indicated a sincere wish to help. In the course of the meeting, it became clear that the need for keeping the child in a calm, secure environment had been translated by her to mean 'give Joe what he wants lest he get upset and have a seizure.'

"The first problem the Team had was to determine whether results of earlier examinations were still valid. Exploratory questions by the teacher-nurse member of the Clinic Team plus review of the records and observations of teacher and principal seemed to indicate that medication was controlling somewhat Joe's fits of rage: hence the possibility of seizure upon frustration was reduced.

"Evaluation of the child's behavior at school for the past two months seemed to indicate that 'acting out' and aggression had now become a part of Joe's behavior pattern and that instability resulting from disease was a secondary factor.

"At the conclusion of the first meeting the following course was indicated: 1. Review medication, possibly seek re-examination. 2. Interpret to parents the changed physical condition and stress the need for firm handling and setting of boundaries. Allay fears of seizures due to saying 'no.' 3. Construct new behavior patterns in school. With the coming of the fall semester the school set about constructing new behavior patterns. It was felt that when the aggressive behavior did not produce the desired results, another pattern would be substituted. What this new pattern would be we did not know but would have to watch and wait developments.

"It was agreed that when signs of aggressiveness were displayed, and long before a peak was reached, Joe would be sent to the office with his books and wraps and a brief note explaining what had happened. If the principal were in he would discuss quietly the incident, point out that other children had rights, etc. Joe would usually be given a choice of going home or working quietly in the adjustment room. At other times, depending on the circumstances, the principal would make the decision. The choice of returning was left to Joe. He was to return when he felt in control of himself. Quite obviously, Joe would not be allowed to return three or four, times to create fresh disturbances. If the principal were not available the clerk had instructions to send Joe home immediately. The mother was a party to this arrangement and in those cases would help the boy to decide when to return to school. Other situations were planned for, too.

"Progress was uneven. As the months went by there was ample evidence that the aggression was controllable, as it invariably followed situations in which Joe was frustrated in a course of action. By November it was felt that the permissiveness of the earlier months had built an awareness of the need for rules in an organized society and that a dramatic illustration was needed to impress upon Joe that he was now governed by the same regulations as others.

"After an incident involving spitting and fighting, the lines of tolerance were clearly drawn and the punishment to follow such behavior was clearly indicated to the boy. The following day a teacher requested Joe to return to his room. Instead of complying he began shouting, 'Shut up. I hate you,' and clapped his hands over his ears. It was in this position the principal found him. Joe was suspended from school for three days.

"During this suspension, in December, the Clinic Team again considered the case. The school was to continue with the procedures previously agreed upon and the bulk of the meeting dealt with means of assisting the parents in the home environment. The recommendations for December were that: 1. The teacher-nurse would make a home visit to discuss tantrums and physical disability with the parents. 2. On the basis of a report on this visit we would determine whether both parents should be invited to a January Clinic Team meeting. 3. At that meeting we would discuss the earlier-mentioned 'recommendations sheet' point by point with both parents.

"The parents could not attend the January meeting so they were invited to the February one. At the January meeting we noted: 1. The teacher-nurse had arranged to have the hospital re-evaluate Joe's medication. 2. The teacher-nurse in a home conference with the mother had stressed firm, consistent, unemotional handling of the boy. 3. Both parents were invited to the February meeting.

"By February Joe had a new teacher who had to be involved in the situation. This month, as it turned out, marked the turning point in the case. Notations for February started out prosaically enough: 1. Appointment has been made for re-examination at the hospital. 2. Materials are to be sent home for use when child is excused from school for misbehavior. 3. Arrangements have been made for child to play accordion for his classmates. 4. Arrangements made for a retest in reading ability.

"Both parents attended this meeting. The group suggested the father do more things with the child. Specific trips and activities were mentioned. The teacher had discovered that Joe, in addition to accordion playing ability, had a facility in chess. Arrangements were made for the youngster to teach the game to some classmates.

"Again the need for consistent, unemotional management was urged. Since the dosage of medication was increased, the school was requested to advise the nurse of any significant changes in adjustment.

"The school had occasion to do just that. A week after the meeting Joe walked up to a girl classmate and hit her in the eye while she was seated at her desk. Joe was suspended from school for one week. During this week the mother enrolled the child in a private school for retarded children. The principal counseled against this move on the grounds that Joe was not a retarded youngster. He requested, however, that if the mother insisted, she continue to keep in touch with the school. Before a week was up, Joe was withdrawn from the private school and returned to school.

"From this point there was steady improvement in his classroom behavior. March, April, and May saw fewer and fewer incidents, less severe and all more easily handled. With June and the end of the school year Joe again went to camp. He returned with a loss of many pounds and a gain of many friends. No further meetings were necessary. The success of the group approach in this case shows that it does and can work to solve serious problems for individual pupils. But how does it operate?

"When we first began Clinic Team operation we did so on the hypothesis that combined efforts would be more effective than individual efforts in dealing with problem cases. We further felt that face-to-face discussions with all those involved in an individual case would be more effective than formal written communications with each other. Problems raised by any source (teacher, parent, etc.) are screened informally by the principal and adjustment teacher to determine whether the problem would be handled by the principal (through other channels) or the Clinic Team.

"The adjustment teacher, after conferring with the principal, prepares the agenda of cases to be considered at the monthly meeting, assembles data, and later acts as secretary. At the meeting a definition of the problem is wrung from the free exchange of ideas that follows review of the case.

"As a result of this interchange, the group comes up with something more than a tentative hypothesis, something closer to an 'educated hunch' as to the nature of the problem and probable courses of action. The handling of each case at each session then concludes with three steps: 1. Produce concrete, practical recommendations based on the 'educated hunches.' 2. Assign responsibility for implementation of recommendations. 3. Schedule time for evaluation and review.

"Record keeping is kept to a minimum. The major form surviving this trial and error period is the Recommendation Sheet at the top of which are lines for name and birthdate. The left two thirds of the page is used for recommendations, the right third for comments. A line separates the two columns. Group recommendations are listed and when the case is reviewed notations are made as to status of recommendations.

"Rarely are dramatic or even novel suggestions needed. The strength of the Clinic Team lies in coordination of efforts, regularity of evaluation to check progress, and flexibility so a change of direction is quickly effected if necessary.

"The psychologist who served as a member of the Clinic Team felt that the approach has a number of real values. It makes the psychologist a participant in the treatment of problems as well as in their diagnosis. The group approach guarantees follow-up of cases once located so that there are fewer instances of children presenting the same problem (only in more severe form) five years or more after initial testing by the Bu-

reau of Child Study. Finally, the Clinic Team helps the school view the child as a 'child-in-his-world,' not simply as a problem student.

"The teacher-nurse member of the Team felt that the fully rounded picture of the child developed in the group meetings helped her to work more efficiently with both parents and medical authorities. Further, participation in Clinic Team sessions increased her sense of acceptance by and identification with the school. The regular clinic sessions afford real opportunity for personal growth and development to those participating.

"Most classroom teachers who participated in Clinic Team activities as a result of having one or more problem cases in their own classes are inclined to praise the program enthusiastically. They feel it helps them to gain insight into classroom problems and aids and supports them in conferring with parents. Another value, it is felt, is that the Team can give detailed long-range attention to individual cases which the classroom teacher, because of his major preoccupation with whole group activities, frequently cannot give, even when he sees the need for it.

"The adjustment teacher who functioned as a part of the Clinic Team began the program with some misgivings as to its value relative to techniques already in use. Her experience, however, served to satisfy her that the time involved was more than well spent. A particularly valuable quality of this approach is that it makes clear to teachers that they have the aid and interest of others in dealing with classroom problems, and to parents that the school is vitally, meaningfully, and continuously interested in their children's problems.

"Ultimately the principal must make the decisions involving these children. He needs facts upon which to base his decisions. At each Clinic Team session he gets all the dimensions of the problem in addition to available facts. The people with whom he must subsequently work in each case are at the same session getting the same facts, so a common background has been established.

Action can follow quickly when all people involved are simultaneously apprised of the problem and the agreed-upon approaches.

"As the responsible head of the school, the principal's main focus is usually and properly school-centered; with the Clinic Team he can share his concerns about an individual and for this session be completely child-centered. Back in his office he changes hats and tries to reconcile the two points of view if they are in conflict.

"The Clinic Team lends supportive status to the principal and faculty. In one instance a pupil had done absolutely no work for three semesters. The opinion of the Clinic Team, Board of Education psychiatrist, and agency psychiatrist giving therapy indicated that retention of the youngster in grade would be detrimental to him. Because each succeeding teacher was involved in the case and knew the background, each teacher had the courage (and that's the right word) to continue to work in what looked like a hopeless situation. At the same time, the principal felt secure in his decision to keep promoting the youngster. This story, by the way, has a happy ending, for in the fourth semester something or everything took hold and the pupil made a dramatic recovery and is proceeding satisfactorily.

"The problem of involvement of parents in Clinic Team participation must be carefully considered. The roles of the other participants are well established; that of the parent is not. Many approach such a conference with trepidation and anxiety. It is easy to forget that school, to many parents, is an unknown and hence strange and fearful place. A parent going to conference with four or five professional people can easily find it a traumatic experience.

"What allays parents' fears? What is it parents value in conferences of this nature? What are they looking for when they turn to the school for assistance? Here are the reactions of some of the parents who have been involved with the Clinic Team: 'It is a good feeling to know that we can have outside help when we need it. More parents (with problems about their children) should go to them because their advice is helpful.'

"A second parent says: 'The Team was composed of people who could discuss my son's behavior with an intelligent approach because they were not emotionally involved with my child. I felt they were making every effort to help my son by trying to understand him.'

"Still another parent who had received help wrote: 'I had the cooperation of a group of people trained in their field to assist me in the adjustment of my child both at home and at school. I think their personal interest has helped him greatly.'

"Tone and climate, it appears, are all-important in involving the parent as a working member of the Clinic Team. Broadly speaking, the proper climate grows as the Clinic Team develops a sensitivity to the feeling of the parents in this situation. But being just cheery and pleasant is not enough—conviviality alone can become a dead end. In which direction shall this pleasantness be channeled?

"These three points, repeatedly stressed in parents' reactions seem to suggest the answer. They valued the close personal attention, appreciated the objective viewpoints, and respected the specialized training of the team members.

"Experience has provided some generalizations concerning the Clinic Team approach which may be of use to others who might wish to adopt this system:

"1. The strength of Clinic Team lies in coordination of efforts, regularity of evaluation to check progress, and flexibility so a change of direction is quickly effected if necessary.

"2. A properly functioning Clinic Team leads to community acceptance of the school as a place where help is offered. It is a positive expression of good community-school relations.

"3. Genuine acceptance and respect for one another as equals is necessary. The physical environment should match the emotional climate. This usually rules out the principal's office.

"4. The thorny problem of communication with the classroom teacher needs more attention.

"5. Adjustment service should be geared more closely to the operation of the Clinic Team. Utilization of the adjustment teacher in this fashion will go far toward improving communications with the classroom teacher."

In the years since that article was published, the case conference method has been proved to be an effective tool for solving selected academic and behavior problems at the local level. But what else has been learned in ten years of operation? For example, what qualities are needed by the personnel involved?

Basic, of course, is acceptance of the child and a desire to help the child. All of us claim these virtues but these claims should be subject to rigorous (albeit private) scrutiny because acceptance—genuine acceptance—of children with different backgrounds and mores than our own is not easily come by.

Compassion is needed to appreciate the human condition but it should be coupled with objectivity that respects the human integrity. Compassion without objectivity may dissolve into the kind of maudlin sympathy that suffocates the child and leaves him more helpless than we found him. The objectivity that is desired proceeds from a respect for human integrity which reduces the temptation to take a moral stance or to pass judgement. This is not to say that teachers do not attempt to transmit moral values or make judgements about them; it simply means that during the time the conference is in operation moral judgements and value judgements only get in the way of the immediate goal of resolving the problem under consideration. A doctor setting a broken limb is only concerned with the fracture, not the conditions that led up to the fracture. After-

wards he may well concern himself with the conditions that led up to the fracture, but at the moment, no.

One question that inevitably arises in a discussion of the case conference method is "how do you choose from among the many cases that offer themselves?" A practically useless bit of advice is to try to pick the cases that can be helped by the case conference method. A not much better suggestion is to look first for some academic problem on the sound assumption that behind the academic problems are a whole host of other problems. I suppose the answer is that we just do without wondering too much how we do it.

In practice, the people charged with selecting cases soon develop a "seat-of-the-pants" expertise that seems to work fairly well for our purposes so no serious attempt has been made to set up better screening procedures. And if we did, the results probably would not justify the time and effort needed to establish and carry out screening procedures. There is also some feeling that the staffing itself should be part of the screening process. All these arguments notwithstanding it is in the area of selection that improvements could be made. If a more scientific or more structured method of selection could be developed that would be true to the principles of the case conference method and take into cognizance the school situation, it would probably make for a more efficient and effective operation.

Over the years some conditions necessary to the successful operation of the case conference have been reaffirmed. None of these observations are startling and in fact most are rather prosaic, but then directions for keeping a paintbrush are also prosaic while they tell nothing of the uses that can be made of a paintbrush. So too the suggestions offered here are suggestions for the maintenance of a tool:

1. Keep to a simple operation with a minimum of record keeping, reports, etc. You will find that nearly always the data you want about a child has already been recorded

some place. The function of the staffing is to pull together information, not to create new records.

2. Regularity of meeting seems more important than frequency of meeting because the strength of staffing is cumulative. Benefits tend to accrue; they do not spring full blown from one sensational meeting.

3. A certain amount of staff continuity is necessary. The nucleus must work together long enough to develop a tone and to learn to work together. If the nucleus remains fairly constant then peripheral members can change and still be absorbed quite rapidly into the team.

4. Avoid working under pressure. There is no such thing as an emergency staffing. The time and place for the sessions should be carefully chosen so the participants can be as relaxed and unhurried as possible.

5. Avoid the tendency to take on too many cases. If the initial cases were carefully selected to yield successes (and they should be) a false feeling of confidence is engendered and the team thinks they are ready to take on the world. Guard against this. Staffing is only a tool and to be used effectively it must be used selectively.

6. Probably the most important condition is to know your limitations.

Other than its general value, does the case conference method have any special relevance to contemporary educational problems? The answer is a hopeful "maybe."

In this century we are seriously coming to grips with the problems encountered in educating "all the children of all the people." The ferment in education engendered by the responses to this problem is having a healthy effect on education in toto. New methods and materials appear daily to compete for favor, and old methods and materials are being examined for new applications. The case conference method falls in the latter category.

Staffing is a neutral technique that can be used to advantage whenever you have a person and a problem but the particular way in which it will be used will vary with the personnel of the team, factors in the school situation, the problem under consideration and other pertinent variables. Aside from these considerations is there a particular way in which the case conference can be used in schools that are situated in culturally disadvantaged neighborhoods, in neighborhoods where the family unit has deteriorated or never existed in a viable form? One way that we are exploring is to staff the entire family instead of just an individual child.

If we assume that to alter environment is to alter behavior, and if we accept the fact that many children cannot, literally, learn in a disintegrated family unit, then the school ought to do something about patching up the family unit. Remedial or compensatory education given to a frightened, anxious, or hungry youngster is largely wasted because of negative environmental conditions. This is true even when the instruction is given by highly trained personnel who have at their disposal unlimited time for diagnosis and the most modern equipment for treatment. These ideal conditions, it should be noted, are seldom met. But if we could shore up the family unit, then conceivably we would reap more benefits from remedial or compensatory instruction. There is no suggestion here that the schools can do the entire job, or even a major portion, but they ought to do what they can in this area, if only to protect their investment.

It is with all this in mind that we are exploring family staffing. What would happen if, instead of convening conventional remedial or coaching groups, a coaching group would consist of all the children in the family enrolled in that school who would be allowed to work on their regular school assignments under the guidance of a teacher or other qualified person. In this situation would arise ample, natural opportunities for the older to help the younger, for the younger to see the older ones as helpers and protectors. In other words, each child could learn what constitutes proper sibling relationships.

Within this kind of a framework the teacher or other personnel available to work with these families would need only the skills possessed by teachers and the proper compassionate attitude. In effect, the teacher becomes a surrogate mother, father, big brother, big sister, or friend as circumstances and his personality permit. In family staffing the school conference team is in a sense the quarterback for this operation. They call in experts in other fields and other agencies to contribute their special talents or resources to the reconstruction of the family unit.

Would this work? The odds are all with it because those of us who work in areas of the type described know all too well the many concerned parents who are simply overwhelmed by circumstances. If these parents and their children could be given the sustained attention possible through some form of staffing administered by or through an institution as close and as familiar as the school, they could become truly effective parents.

Bryant Feather and Walter S. Olson

LET'S GET THE SCHOOL COUNSELORS "OUT OF THE OFFICE"

The role and concept of the school counselor today is rapidly changing. Much of the counseling and guidance formerly done by the family, clergy, and/or family physician is now being done by the school counselor. With this shift in responsibility, it is now extremely important that the counselor look on his job as much broader, more demanding, and more vital to the well-being, adjustment, and growth of each child. To produce this kind of highly trained and skilled counselor, it is necessary that much of the training and behavior be changed as the following study suggests: it is most important to get the counselor out of his office.

One area where more practical application of psychology occurs than perhaps even in the classroom is in the school counselor's office. The school counselor is to be differentiated from the school psychologist and from the clinical psychologist by title, training, and nature of the job. The counselor is trained to deal with problems related to schools and school-age children. He works closely with teachers, administrators, parents, other related professional personnel and with individual students and groups of students. Since his emphasis has changed from purely educational counseling to now include vocational, personal, and growth problems, his need for training and experience has likewise grown. Previous programs and training have been inadequate in many instances, and current attitudes and demands by school administrators indicate that a great change is desirable and, as this study shows, is being encouraged and implemented.

Gradually, it is being recognized that counselors need to know the community agencies and facilities and to learn to work with them on a professional level as part of an integrated team.

THE CHANGING ROLE OF THE URBAN COUNSELOR

It is time the traditional principles of guidance and counseling and the training of counselors were updated to meet the changed times and altered demands found in this age of urban living. By accepting the "arm-chair" concepts of the past, counselors are failing to understand or to meet the needs felt and expressed by children with problems which are obvious to their parents and teachers.

Increased urbanization and overcrowding

in certain areas of the city have created an atmosphere of confinement and deprivation. In certain parts of every city, space available for "living" and constructive social interaction is limited or nonexistent. Today, in many instances, both parents work (both by necessity and, often, by choice) thus leaving children alone too much of the time. Counselors need to become aware of existing community agencies and facilities and to be encouraged to take advantage of them by stimulating active participation.

Our changing social order in the urban setting tends to eliminate the basic family structure or greatly alter it. In many instances, children feel a lack of closeness, of belongingness, of love, of even being a part of a family unit. Often there is limited or nonexistent communication between parents, adults, and children. Participating in agency or recreational programs offers a child an opportunity to belong to a group, to be part of a team, to participate with his family in an activity, or at least to have his family watch him as an appreciative audience.

With children having less, if any, duties or work around the home, and having less opportunity for part-time work, more time is available for other activities. For reasons of physical and mental health, some of this time should be channeled into worthwhile community activities, with proper supervision and direction.

Culturally deprived children have a greater need for guidance and counseling than the average child. Especially is their need greater for consistency in programming and for a well organized, definitely planned, and professionally supervised program. They exhibit a greater need for structuring than the more advantaged child. Their background and previous experience have tended to create an indifference to organizational activities, and often, an intolerance and prejudice; educational and recreational programs must broaden their appreciation for people and new experiences.

It has long been proven that recreation is instrumental in the physical, social, and mental growth and maturation of youth. Recreation not only gives the opportunity to belong, and to participate in group activities, but also to develop a habit of self-discipline. In such programs, the professional personnel often become parent substitutes or ideal models with whom the child may identify. Frequently, the child may have more respect for them than for his inadequate parents, especially when there is an absence of warmth or love in the home.

From such community program involvement, one expects to develop the leaders of the future. It affords opportunity for the shy youngster to overcome handicaps, for the under-developed to grow, for the potential leader to experiment in leadership, and for every child to learn to get along with his peers and with other adults.

In view of the changes noted in family structure, and the necessary involvement in community activities on the part of the children, it is important for the school counselor to become well acquainted with all the facilities available, and to establish good working relations with all of the participating agencies, their programs, philosophy and personnel.

MEASURING THESE CHANGES

To test and explore these changes and needs, and to determine the type of counseling and counselors needed today, the following types of individuals were surveyed and a portion of each group interviewed in depth:

1. Approximately one hundred and fifty students in the graduate program of counseling at Chicago State College:

These students were mostly experienced classroom teachers and counselors in the metropolitan Chicago schools and they represented many years of experience in the field of education and counseling as well as being advanced graduate students, many of whom were working for their second master's degree, and some with the equivalent of Ph.D. credit for college work.

2. A group of approximately fifty teachers and twenty school counselors employed in Chicago or one of the adjacent suburbs, representative of public, private, and parochial schools.

3. Thirty-three adults teaching psychology or related subjects in an adult-education program of the Chicago YMCA "Learning for Living Division."

4. Ten special counselors in the Urban Youth Development Program (a training program for dropouts [17–21] needing vocational training).

5. Twenty adolescents actively participating in private psychotherapy, sixteen of whom were attending school and four of whom were dropouts. All had serious psychological difficulties, and all had above a 90 IQ.

6. Fifty children ranging in age from 8–19 in supervised recreational programs of the Chicago Park District, and parents of the participating children.

7. Ten supervisors in the Park District Program.

The participants in this study were asked to state briefly what one expected of counselors and to make one sentence statements of principles and/or attitudes that would be most important to indoctrinate in them. The group was asked to keep in mind the many changes of the past five years resulting from urbanization, overcrowding, civil rights movements, and our changing economic order. They were encouraged to express unique needs to be met by ideal counselors. Their most frequently expressed principles are to be found below.

"OUT OF THE OFFICE"

The general conclusion was that in urban communities, emergency counseling services should be made available at the local community level, such as in schools or community centers, much as are found in medical clinics to meet emergency medical problems

when they arise. Also a *preventative program* should be established before problems become acute, preferably in their incipient stages. These services should not only be available, but also offerings and types of services should be known, understood, and acceptable to those needing them most. The fee for the service should be adjusted to one's ability to pay and should never preclude service when needed.

School *counselors should be mobile*, should "come out" of their offices, stop feeling glued to their chairs and limited to a four-walled office. They should be moving about their work-community, locating and identifying problems, potential difficulties, or problem-causing situations. It is important that they establish rapport with individuals in the community who may need their services or who are active in related community agencies. A counselor should be a leader in the community and a figure with whom members of the community may positively identify with good effect.

Counselors should know well all existing agencies, personnel, and services and should establish good functioning relationships with them; this might be done by regular visits to such agencies and participating in their programs as consultants, coordinators, or as participants in their work.

A true zest for life, and for living a rich and rewarding one, should be evident in the image projected by the counselor. They need to be open-minded and broadly experienced in all phases of life and living. It is important that they keep abreast of the life being lived by today's youth in cities; they must be aware that tradition and former behavior, attitudes, and mores may not apply at all to the contemporary world. One cannot know what is going on today among young people by recollecting an adult's younger years and assuming it to be the same today.

The traditional school counseling service, in its best and most complete form, should be extended to the dropout (no interruption in counseling service should occur when a youth withdraws from school or is thrown out) and to the graduates of the school for a reasonable period of time until referral to other community agencies can be made. One is used to going to the school counselor and should feel free to return even after graduation if one does not know where else to seek help. Such service might be terminated a few weeks after graduation, or when an individual has reached eighteen years of age.

In summary, counselors must live in the present, be aware of life and all its facets and ramifications; they need to be a vital force in the community, to utilize all the facilities it affords, and to interact with all its professional personnel and related agencies.

William Clark Trow

THE FUTURE OF SCHOOL PSYCHOLOGY BY EXTRAPOLATION

As the field of psychology has changed from that of test constructors and interpreters to the variety of specialties that are now called for in the field, so has the role and definition of the school psychologist changed and developed.

Dr. Trow has made an astute analysis of the history and status of the job of the school psychologist as it applies to our present system, and he has made some predictions for the future of the school psychologist. He feels that the present system of dividing work equally among a great variety of personnel with different titles ends in a form of chaos.

To bring meaning and order to this chaos, Dr. Trow suggests the further development and utilization of a job and a person to be called an "educational psychologist." This makes sense and should be implemented as specialists are trained and readied for this new coordinating and consulting role. He still feels that the team approach is sound and, when limitations of the size of the school and community warrant it, one individual may have to serve overlapping functions.

What should be the responsibilities of the school psychologist? This question has been discussed for some time, a number of valuable studies of different kinds have been made, and others are underway, which will undoubtedly serve to clarify the problems involved and point the way to various solutions. A somewhat different approach, and one not without interest, is to note the origins of present theory and practice and the changes that have taken place, and seek to project their course of development into the future. Thus by a kind of non-numerical extrapolation, some of the coming developments may perhaps be foreseen and evaluated in the light of current thinking. Since a school psychologist is a psychologist working in an educational setting, it is not inappropriate to note what has gone into the making of psychologists in the United States of America, and what bearing work in the educational milieu may have on their activities.

19TH CENTURY ORIGINS

The beginnings of American psychological theory are to be found primarily in British associationism, German experimentalism, and French psychiatry. A long line of eminent British philosophers employing the armchair methods of their discipline wrote

Adapted from *Psychology in the Schools*, Vol. III, No. 2, April 1966, pages 131–139, by permission of the publisher, Psychology Press, Inc., Brandon, Vermont.

on psychology as a part of their province. Taking their cue from Aristotle, and from their environmentalist *tabula rasa* assumption, Hobbes, Locke, Berkeley, Hume, the Mills, and others, developed the so-called "laws" of association which seemed to explain the mental processes, particularly those involved in learning: similarity and contrast, contiguity in space and time, recency, frequency, and intensity.

Experimentalism was primarily German in origin. The psychophysics of Weber and Fechner, the work on memory of Ebbinghaus, the experiments of the Würzburg school and others bear witness to this amazing development. But Wilhelm Wundt, the "father of experimental psychology" who founded the first psychological laboratory (1879), serves as an appropriate symbol. At about the same time, however, William James opened up a room for psychological experiments at Harvard, and in 1898 Thorndike presented his doctoral dissertation at Columbia containing his famous experiments on chicks and kittens. This was a different kind of experimentation from the brass-instrument, introspection in Germany, and made him the founder of comparative psychology.

In France, Charcot and others studied the personality deviations later catalogued under the head of abnormal psychology. There he was visited by Freud, who was familiar with British associationism, and who gradually worked out his psychoanalytic theory and free-association technique for the treatment of the neuroses. Adler, his Viennese contemporary, preferred the power goal to sex as the key to neuroses, and his concept of inferiority and compensation found its way to America alongside of Freud's more complicated unconscious. The influence of the third of the three leading psychoanalysts, Carl Jung, was not great in America, while in Europe, particularly in Freud's native Vienna, the environmentalist hypothesis upon which all three built has been largely rejected in favor of a genetic etiology.

These, then, are the three chief theoretical sources on which the early psychologists had to draw. They dealt mainly with the simpler cognitive processes and employed introspection in some cases supplemented by simple laboratory apparatus, to which should be added Thorndike's maze and puzzle box. There was no such thing as "practice" at the turn of the century; psychologists either experimented or taught or both. Associative principles had been laid down and inferences were drawn for school learning, but they were rather tenuous. The psychoanalytical base for clinical psychology had also been established, and scientific method had been adapted to psychological research. Meanwhile, five other centers of original thought were forming which were also to influence the practice of psychology in America—evolution, Geisteswissenschaft psychology, education, statistics, and mental testing. This motley array was perhaps more responsible for the development of psychology as a profession than the three theoretical sources already mentioned.

The fall-out from Darwin's *Origin of Species* has not yet been absorbed, since the theory of *evolution* it propounded attacked the universally held belief in the creation. The psychological ramifications of the doctrine, as developed chiefly by Herbert Spencer, formed the theoretical basis for comparative anatomy and for comparative and genetic psychology, the anecdotal method of Romanes and others, the child-study movement of Preyer, and the adolescence questionnaires of G. Stanley Hall.

Dilthey's *Geisteswissenschaft* (cultural science) psychology is known to American psychologists only through his descendants as exemplified by Eduard Spranger, and through the empirical branch, Gestalt psychology, by Köhler, Koffka, and Lewin. This group of Berliners opposed the elementarism of the associationist and experimentalist tradition, and in the United States brought their holistic philosophy to bear on psychological and educational problems.

Meanwhile, interesting psychological developments had been taking place within the field of *education* relative to the concept of child nature, rewards and punishments, and the learning process. Rousseau, in the preceding century in his *Émile* had derogated the societal influence on mankind in general and on youth in particular, which had started a back-to-nature fad. The Swiss school master, Pestalozzi, had rediscovered the power of love over hate and aggression in school discipline, and had also worked out a simple-to-complex system of content instruction which had no little influence on the early American normal schools. Froebel emphasized the educational value of the activity involved in play. In fact the original name he had given his little school was *Kleinkinderbeschäftigungsanstalt*, a German language mouth-filler, which means "small child's activity institution." The later name, *Kindergarten*, was much easier to handle and pointed to Rousseau's idea of the importance of the natural growth of the child, given the proper care and attention. The German philosopher, Herbart, objecting to the associationists' passive quality of mind as a *tabula rasa* on which experience writes, developed the more dynamic concept of apperception and contributed to teaching method the five formal steps of the inductive lesson.

In the fourth center, stimulated by the uncertainties of the race track, chance and probability were studied, and with the Gaussian curve and Galton's coefficient of correlation, followed by the work of Pearson and others, the principles of *statistics* came into being, a tool for handling the numerical characteristics of psychological and other variables.

And lastly, there was the center that triggered off the whole enterprise, the Parisian schools, where Binet was asked to find a quick and easy way to discover the feebleminded children in the school population. After years of empirical searching, he and his colleague, Simon, developed the series of *mental tests* which bear their names, and

also the concept of mental age. Their contribution constituted a genuine breakthrough. The tests were widely used, and in America the successive revisions were translated and revised and became the trade tools of the first school psychologists (see the chart on page 269).

20TH CENTURY DEVELOPMENTS

From these eight, largely separate beginnings, it is possible to follow the lines of development which led to present-day psychology as it is employed not only in the schools but also in other institutions and in private practice. At the turn of the century Thorndike, clearly a student of British *associationism*, subjected the "laws" to experimental verification, modified them accordingly, and pointed out applications to educational processes and learning situations. He was no doubt familiar with German experimentalism, and from William James he adopted the so-called functionalist approach, which led to the investigation of the mental processes employed in learning school subjects, in which he was followed by Judd, Freeman, and others, and a rapidly increasing number of studies, among which those of reading are probably the most numerous.

Wundt's structuralism, the study of mental states, was brought to America by his famous student, James McKeen Cattell of Columbia and by Edward Bradford Titchener of Cornell. Cattell was the first to use the term "test" in its present psychological sense and he devised a number of psychophysical tests which he administered to Columbia freshmen. Titchener preached the doctrine of structuralism pure and undefiled, and with his several textbooks taught generations of young people the precision of introspective experimentalism, particularly as related to the sensory processes.

Meanwhile, the Russian physiologist, Ivan Petrovitch Pavlov, had been studying the digestive processes of dogs, and ran onto what he called the conditioned reflex, which

TABLE 1

THE FUTURE OF SCHOOL PSYCHOLOGY BY EXTRAPOLATION

19th Century Beginnings	20th Century Developments	Extrapolation
Associationism Locke, et al.	Functionalism: (introspection) mental processes, applied to learning school subjects. James, Thorndike, Judd, et al.	Applied research, school learning. *Educational Psychologist*
Experimentalism Wundt, et al.	Structuralism: (introspection) mental states. Cattell, Titchener./Behaviorism: objectivism. Pavlov (CR), Watson	Pure research, learning theory. *Psychologist*
Psychiatry Charcot, et al.	Psychoanalysis: Freud, Adler, neo-Freudians. Clinical psychology; mental hygiene, counseling, therapy	Clinical psychology data, counseling. *Mental Hygienist*
Evolution Darwin, Spencer	Genetic psychology: child study, heredity, growth stages, child development. Harvard, Michigan, California, et al.	Physiological data, nervous system, glands; genetics, growth. *Medical Psychologist*
Geisteswissenschaft Dilthey	Gestalt psychology: Wertheimer et al. Combines with Sociology: social worker, visiting teacher, etc.	Sociological data, family culture. *Educational Sociologist*
Education Rousseau, et al.	Educational method: Pestalozzi, Froebel, Herbart, Dewey, et al. Activity, projects; progressive education vs. disciplines	Educational data, social learning. *Educational Psychologist*
Statistics Gauss, Galton	Measurement: Thorndike, Rugg, et al. Newer concepts: reliability, validity, significance, etc., research design, retrieval	Research techniques, computer services. *Statistician*
Mental Tests Binet-Simon	Testing: individual, group; aptitude, achievement, personality. Diagnose, recommend. Terman, Wechsler; Iowa, California, et al.	Test data. Measurement, evaluation. *Psychometrist*

seemed to indicate a physiological base for associationist principles. Thorndike considered it a special case of learning, and it is now referred to as classical conditioning in contrast with instrumental conditioning, the name given to the type of experiments Thorndike, and later Köhler and others, developed. Pavlov's work gradually became known to American psychologists, but none took it more seriously than John B. Watson whose concept of behaviorism was to dominate the field for the next twenty or thirty years. Thus introspective psychology as it had been known was no more, though other than overt behavior later became a respectable object of psychological study. The sharp boundary between associationism and experimentalism gradually disappeared, and research on any psychological problem, by whatever technique might prove to be effective, became the direction of future development. This included a growing interest in what came to be known as learning theory, in which the names of Skinner, Melton, Guilford, Bruner, Ausubel, and others are currently to the fore.

These learning and experimental developments, however, have had less effect on school psychology than the *psychiatric-psychoanalytic* influences which have enlarged amazingly. Neo-Freudians have accepted or rejected, emphasized or deemphasized one or another part of the master's teachings. Partly as a result of the influence of Clifford Beers' *A Mind That Found Itself*, mental hygiene or mental health has gained national recognition as a point of view emphasizing the importance of prevention and a way to treat minor mental or behavior disorders chiefly through environmental change, acceptance, and counseling, the latter largely "non-directive" (Rogers). And school psychologists have often found themselves cast in the role of clinical psychologists whether they were actually prepared for it or not. Though supplemented by group therapy, the counseling method is costly in time and money, and as in the mental hospitals there

is rarely time for it. So the harried school psychologists give the tests they are paid to give, talk to the teachers about mental hygiene, and in the case of pupils frequently diagnose and refer, leaving the teachers in class and homerooms to handle the treatment. But teachers claim the diagnosis is often incomprehensible to them, and if they do understand it, impossible to follow. And the referral may be to a Center which itself is overcrowded, necessitating delays and often not equipped to provide extended treatment. It is this kind of situation, though not necessarily typical, which perhaps raises the most questions about the role of the school psychologist.

Although *evolution* is apparently not producing any higher forms than *genus homo*, man's genetic origins and growth stages as influenced by his environment became subjects of study. Infancy, childhood, adolescence, and adulthood, their physiological and psychological manifestations and adjustments were characterized, and cross-sectional studies were followed by longitudinal records of developing structure and behavior. Some, like the Harvard, California, and Michigan growth studies involve careful measurements; others like those of Gesell and Piaget employed especially contrived situations and shrewd observations. Rousseau's trust in nature has tended to be favored over societal intrusion and intervention. Thus growth theorists tend to question the environmentalist doctrine. Given adequate environmental support, it is not the environment that determines the nature of the organism, but the organism that by the selection processes determines its environment. School psychologists are still in the process of discovering what the school can and what it cannot do for its population.

Gestalt psychology in general was more concerned with the larger, macrocosmic patterns of behavior than the finer microcosmic phenomena. Percepts and concepts differ if total situations are considered, and the behavior of the individual is to be explained as a part of a larger whole, i.e., the group. As a consequence of the influence of Kurt Lewin, the individual's total "life space" was considered, and group climate, leadership, and inter- and intra-group communication became of interest and concern. Students came to be viewed *sociologically*. Visiting teachers trained in social work investigated home and community influences in order to deal with problems of mental and emotional maladjustment, and Moreno's sociometry and sociodrama were invoked to better understand interpersonal relationships.

Educational theory and practice continued to develop. New experimental schools appeared including Maria Montessori's kindergarten and John Dewey's school at the University of Chicago. Kilpatrick and Bode interpreted the Dewey educational philosophy which built on that of his predecessors, and progressive education seemed to frown on all discipline and exalt freedom, play, self-selection of activities, and self-expression in the arts and elsewhere. Discipline, that much abused word meaning teachings, had come to mean punishment instead and was therefore banished along with the usual sanctions until psychologists and others, sensing something needful had been lost sight of, began to explore the nature and operation of reinforcement and of aversive stimuli, and to seek ways to set limits to undesirable behavior.

In the early years of the century Thorndike's *Introduction to the Theory of Mental and Social Measurements* was soon followed by Rugg's *Statistical Methods Applied to Education* and later by many other volumes on the subject. As a consequence, such concepts as reliability, validity, and significance became known and their meanings sharpened, and a new precision was brought into psychological and educational investigations. Partial and multiple correlation, factor analysis, and other techniques, card punch machines, and new computers have made *statistics* an indispensable tool for the research worker. Thus sociological,

educational, and statistical techniques were added to the school psychologist's kit of tools. But the most extensive developments came with the progress made in testing.

Revisions of the Binet individual *mental test* quickly appeared first by Goddard and soon after by Terman and his collaborators, and were paralleled by the development of group aptitude tests led by the pioneer Army Alpha for literates and Beta for illiterates. Aptitude tests adapted to school use followed as did achievement and personality tests and clinically inspired projection tests, of which the Rorschach is perhaps the most well known. The first role of the school psychologist was to administer Terman's Stanford Revision, and since these early days, a whole arsenal of tests has been placed at his disposal. Many consider the effective use of this arsenal still his proper role, but other roles have been thrust upon him so that there is at present no little uncertainty as to his proper function.

PROJECTING THE LINES OF DEVELOPMENT

One approach to an answer to the question of the proper role of the school psychologist is to consider what tasks other than teaching need to be done in the schools. Clearly janitorial and secretarial are now outside the bailiwick of teachers as well as psychologists. The remainder are performed by what are often referred to as student personnel workers and derive from various sources —from the ranks of attendance officers, social workers, health and physical education teachers and coaches, academic advisors, vocational guidance people, and homeroom teachers, while regular teachers are expected to enforce discipline and administrative officials are generally held responsible. It is not a system; it is a form of chaos—the natural product of successive attempts to satisfy needs, but guided largely by penuriousness and expediency.

If, instead of trying to decide what should be done, we ask what is likely to happen, if we assume the continuity of professional interests and project the lines of development of the past into the future (not the immediate future but say the next turn of the century), what will such an extrapolation show? What will be the division of labor among the psychological personnel of the schools?

It seems clear that the *associationist-functionalist* approach would continue in applied research on school learning, that is, the learning of school subjects and on social behavior. The people who do this research will probably continue to be connected with universities or research centers in colleges and the larger school systems. The developing educational technology, involving the new media and various projected reorganizations, is likely to result in an even increased interest of the armed services and industry, thus providing strong competition from the outside which may or may not be advantageous. But the outcome may well be a rather drastic modification of school practices including teaching procedures. School psychologists to date have had relatively little to do with possible major or minor changes in teaching practice that might result in more effective learning and a better adaptation to individual differences. Such matters have largely been left to teachers and supervisors with the result that the unsatisfactory *status quo* has been maintained with its fixed subjects, methods, time periods, and marking and promotion policies. Already, however, certain innovations from the outside, notably new science and mathematics programs and language methods have forced the organization of special workshops for instruction in newer content and skills. If improvements are to be made, it will be necessary for school psychologists to help bridge the gap between research and practice with the possibility of important changes in the latter. School personnel concerned with these problems might properly be called *educational psychologists.*

No sharp line is expected to be drawn separating applied research on learning in school from pure research on learning theory in the psychological laboratory. One additional step removed from school practice, *experimental* psychology is nevertheless of prime importance and a likely source of future breakthroughs.

The *psychiatric-psychoanalytic* tradition will necessarily continue, employing principles of clinical psychology as a basis for handling disturbed cases. The medical analogy—diagnosis, and treatment or referral, the advantages of which have recently been questioned, will nevertheless be appropriated for many cases, using the method of the interview—therapy as directive or nondirective as the occasion demands or as the practitioner subscribes to. But it is not necessarily a desirable model for all cases, many of which might profit more from some other kind of model of the problem-solving approach.

It may be surmised that specialists in this and in the other areas except research and statistics, might be expected to operate on one of two levels. On the first they would serve as data collectors to get the facts bearing on the case; on the second, they would provide treatment or indicate or bring about the environmental modifications that may be needed to solve the adjustment problem. The personnel worker in this field may well be called a *mental hygienist* unless he qualifies as a clinical psychologist.

The task of the *genetic* and growth specialist is not so clear chiefly, perhaps, because it has been so generally neglected. The environmentalist hypothesis which has dominated American psychiatry and psychology is beginning to break down with the discovery of new drugs and with longitudinal growth studies, which leaves the way open for more adequate attention to be given to genetic and physiological factors, particularly neurological, glandular, and others affecting growth and development. As a rule, neither physicians nor physiologists are adequately trained in all these areas so that a new kind of specialist may be called for, perhaps a *medical psychologist.*

Sociological and ecological specialization are beginning to be given the attention they deserve, although the importance of environmental influences of home and community have long been recognized. The school social worker, whether called a visiting teacher or something else, is a symbol of the recognition of the need for such data in dealing with behavior problems, as well as for providing an adequate education for all children whether or not they have been disadvantaged. The current names for the specialization are not particularly satisfactory. School psychosociologist or socio-psychologist says it, but it might be better to settle for something simpler, like *educational* (or school) *sociologist*.

The psychological tradition in *education* will no doubt continue not only with new experimental schools based on philosophical ideas, but also with experimental classrooms operated with precise laboratory control. Quite as important, the school population will be viewed as a supporting social environment in which children's social behavior may be improved, instead of one in which children acquire undesirable responses for the school to deal with. Hospitals for disturbed children have recognized the therapeutic value of education and have set up special classes adapted to the needs of the young patients. Similar efforts will undoubtedly continue to be made in the regular schools. The gap will have to be reduced between the psychologist's recommendations and the capacity of the school to provide an environment conducive to effective social learning. The person concerned with this aspect of student personnel work might well be the same *educational psychologist* who aims to adapt research findings to school learning. Curriculum and method will be his specialty, not for the disturbed only, but also for all the pupils in the school.

The *statistician* will provide what assistance is needed by those doing research, and might well be one of them. He might continue to help beginners and others in research design and in retrieval, confer with more mature investigators about their difficulties, and instruct in the use of statistical procedures, and data processing, including the use of computers. His function would be to expedite dependable research.

School *testing*, both individual and group, will probably continue as an important function much as at present, except that the person in charge, who will probably be called a *psychometrist*, in addition to administering the routine measurement program, will be an authority on tests for special purposes, and competent in interpreting them to students, teachers, and parents.

Thus for the complete student personnel set-up of school psychological services there would be the following officials: researchers (pure and applied), statistician, educational psychologist, mental hygienist, medical psychologist, educational sociologist, and psychometrician. For each, except the researchers and statistician, there would be two possible levels of training and responsibility. The first level would be that of the competent data collector, analogous to something a little above the laboratory technician in the hospital or the law clerks who look up the facts about cases and prepare briefs in a law firm. The doctoral level specialists would be data collectors, too, but they would also be expected to assume responsibility for correcting the conditions. Referrals would be made by the *school psychologist*, who would be a specialist in one or more of these areas but well versed in all, so that like the medical doctor he could make proper referrals to specialists and interpretations of data collected. He would be the staff officer who, in collaboration with the school officials, and also the community services, would be responsible for seeing to it that so far as possible the treatment including the environmental adjustments needed are carried out. He would be in charge of the whole program.

Of course, in many school systems, an individual would wear more than one hat, while in the larger systems each function would be performed by a large staff. But the tasks as listed seem to be the ones which need to be done, though some now receive relatively less attention than others. And furthermore, these tasks seem to be the continuation of the lines of psychological development beginning more than a hundred years ago. It may be that all that is necessary is to allow evolution to take its course. But it is a slow process. Perhaps the thing to do is to make plans along the extrapolated lines.

Ben N. Schuman, M.D.

SOCIAL PSYCHIATRY AND EDUCATION

Through the years, psychiatry and education have gradually moved closer together; each recognizes the contribution of the other and they are at last joined together in their research and exploration of problems and solutions. Dr. Schuman discusses the history of psychiatric therapy as a background for the current interest in group dynamics and various modalities of psychotherapy. In turn, he relates these to the milieu of the school and to the problems of learning. His findings agree with past research that indicated that those early experiences which predetermine the capacities to learn, also determine neurotic character traits. These first occur in the family and then in the school.

He raises an interesting possibility of combining teacher training with practical experience in therapeutic settings in the community. This may be the breakthrough that we all have been searching for for many years.

In this paper I shall attempt to discuss those modalities of therapy which fall under the rubric of social psychiatry and point out those aspects which are relevant to the concerns of educators at this time. In order to do so, I will discuss first, group therapy, family therapy, and then dwell at some length on the concept of the therapeutic community. Finally, I will try to bridge the gap, or point out common denominators between the therapeutic community and the classroom.

Perhaps the most direct route to these various viewpoints is the analogy of the microscope. Within this analogy, the psychoanalyst uses the oil immersion lens of his microscope to study the individual and attempts to discern his internal structures with the hope of eventually bringing about change which results in more acceptable behavior. The sociologist uses the magnifying glass or the low power lens of his microscope. He seeks to describe and understand the behavioral patterns of large numbers or aggregates of individuals with the ultimate hope of accurately describing, predicting, and planning for methods of influencing behavior of such aggregates. Aggregate behavior here is roughly synonymous with culture. The social psychiatrist uses an intermediate lens, or rather a zoom lens and studies small functional clusters. He seeks to understand the relationships between the apparently discrete members and thus comes to understand the forces which may be impelling one of a given cluster to aberrant behavior.

The family is one such cluster. One family member may be symptomatic and the others non-symptomatic. At first, it appears that the one member is "sick" and the rest of the family is "non-sick" or healthy. However, closer examination invariably reveals that the symptoms of the "sick" member, or identified patient, are a logical and inevitable outgrowth of the role assigned to him by virtue of the family constellation. The pathologic moods of behavior of the identified patient have, in a sense, been selected for him and have the unique importance to the family of supporting the steady state of the family.

For example, a sociopathic offspring may shield a weak and passive father. As long as the child remains sociopathic and inadequate, the father appears adequate and imposed upon. The modus vivendi reached by the parents comes to depend upon a sharing of their concern for their symptomatic offspring. The offspring or "victim" also depends upon this concern or steady state and does his utmost to cooperate in protecting the family myth so that others may fulfill their idealized roles. It is only when the entire system begins to decompensate that a family may be moved to attempt a different synthesis by expulsion of the scapegoat, or undergo therapeutic change. Clinically, this is evidenced by the rapidity with which certain symptoms tend to disappear as the therapist focuses on the covert interactional pattern peculiar to the family. This is not to say that intervention is marvelously effective and simple, but that the symptoms are directly and inseparably related to the pathology of the family as a unit, and that if the family changes, the symptoms may lose their utility and hence may be readily abandoned.

Beside the family, as a natural group, there is the therapy group. Retaining the same aperture, we may next examine the related phenomena of groups in a discussion of group therapy. Here, a collection of people, usually between five and ten in number, meets together with the therapist at regular intervals and becomes a group. A group is something more than a mere collection of people. There exists a pattern of relationships between the various members which establishes a common sense of identity or belonging. The group becomes an entity. It has an identity of its own just as the family does. Each member of the group shares in this identity, as well as contributes to it. It becomes a group because of the forces inherent in each individual which drive him to seek a genuinely human encounter. It is the task of the therapist to foster and abet this process.

The process of becoming a group in itself exerts a beneficial influence upon each group member. He contributes to the group identity, and in return, is able to redefine his own identity or lean upon the group to bolster or strengthen his own sense of self or ego boundaries.

It is the further task of the therapist to encourage and lead the group to examine its modes of interaction. This leads again to a more intense or more human type of encounter in which each member becomes more explicitly aware of his own habitual modes of relating to others. He may gain insight into the unconscious processes within himself which determine those modes and may elect to change such modes.

Thus, if one views identity as a continuing process, psychotherapy may be seen as a means of identity change. Anthropologists Fogleson and Wallace have described this as a "ritualized method of identity change."

Extending the analogy of the microscope with its various lens systems somewhat further to examine the psychiatric hospital with its central concept of the therapeutic community, we must adjust or alter the focus so as to find greater depth of field.

In the psychiatric hospital, the psychiatrist must keep the individual in clear view, and, at the same time, be acutely aware of the structure of the community in which he works. In order to discuss the concept of the therapeutic community with clarity we must digress for a time.

Mental illness was explained during the Middle Ages by the theory of demoniac possession. Zillburg suggests that this was a counteraction by Western society to the processes of change which were to herald the Reformation, the Renaissance, and the Industrial Revolution. The Inquisition in Spain and the hanging of witches in Salem may be seen as part of the same process, an attempt by societal forces to halt or turn back processes of change.

The emergence of the insane asylum represented an attempt to sequester the mentally ill as social undesirables since the theory of demoniac possession suggested possible contagion from the inmates of these asylums, who were, at the same time, objects of derision and purveyors of fear. Pinel, during the French Revolution, removed the chains from the inmates, valiantly recognizing them as human beings who were merely sick.

An ameliorative process was set in motion with occasional great names like the Tukes in England or Dorothea Dix in the United States, which resulted in the concept of the insane asylum as a place of benevolent custodial care.

Shortly after the Second World War, a British psychiatrist, Dr. Maxwell Jones, founded an industrial neurosis hospital, experimented with patient self-government, and expanded the concept of benevolent custodial care, cure through rest and the spa, to active intervention by the staff (largely non-psychiatrist) with the goal of helping the patient to rehabilitate or re-adapt to outside society. From his work came the expression "therapeutic community," an explicit recognition of the therapeutic potential in all staff/patient interaction. In the same period, sociologists were turning their interests to the state hospital systems. Weinberg and Dunham, Caudill Goff, Kaplan, Stanton, and Schwartzs, as well as others, described the psychiatric hospital, its values and structure, its explicit and implicit impact upon the patient.

Thus, within the past two decades, the concept of utilizing the entire surroundings, or milieu, in a therapeutic manner came into being. Initially, the environment of a mental institution was conceived as a means of correcting the evils of custodial care to the extent that it impeded psychotherapy. It soon came to be hailed as an important therapeutic moiety in its own right.

The quantum of therapy in analytic psychotherapy is the fifty minute hour. The quantum of therapy in milieu therapy is the ward meeting, which may last an hour or considerably longer. In the former, a one-to-one relationship exists; in the latter, each participant relates to many persons simultaneously, participants including patients and staff.

In this didactic setting the psychiatrist is relatively passive and offers "interpretations" only when he feels the patient is ready to accept them. In the milieu, interest may center on any observed part of the patient's behavior. Value judgments are made freely. In this setting the psychiatrist functions primarily to set values. He may exhort, condemn, coerce, cajole, threaten, display anger, contempt, or ridicule in an effort to promulgate these values. He does not, however, carry out this program from a seat of splendid isolation. Rather, he seeks to induce the formation of a group, that is, a cluster of persons interacting and *engaged* with each other, possessing beliefs, attitudes, and feelings which confer a sense of collective identity. In effect, then, a sub-culture which espouses his values gives the therapist the mandate to carry on his work.

By "engagement" is meant significant affective interaction. The isolated patient is not permitted to maintain his isolation. He may be carried bodily into a ward meeting —preferably by his fellow patients—and told over and over again that his presence is desired, and that his getting well depends on his participating in the meeting. The therapist also demands commitment on the part of the staff to the concept of milieu therapy and the significance of the group. Commitment on the part of the patient is to the affective nature of the group experience. Since the ward is his present world, these are the people he must care about. If a nurse should leave the hospital, she must be mourned. To fail to do so is to deny one's feelings, to be uninvolved.

Value systems and symptoms are to be legislated out of existence by group pressure. A patient who "acts crazy" disgraces the group. Staff and patients alike must confront him unremittingly until he abandons his symptoms. The goal is social recovery, that is, the patient must get well enough to stop being a patient. Thus, therapy for each patient falls into two phases: the initial phase of engagement and subscription to group values; and the secondary phase of separation and preparing to terminate his hospital stay and return to the larger community.

Prior to discussing the relevance of these three modalities of psychotherapy to the milieu of the school and problems of learning, it is necessary to consider learning as a process of socialization, akin to acculturation in one sense, and to the continuous development of a series of identity changes. The taking-in of knowledge and the acquisition of skills imply structural changes in the ego which accompany the act of absorption.

Professional training in law, medicine, or ministry for example, consists largely of the establishment of a professional identity which gives the individual sanction to do this particular type of work. Thus, the education of a professional consists of the acquisition by him of sets of values, modes of thinking, and points of view. In short, it may be viewed as a process of socialization to a given sub-culture. This process of socialization in turn depends to a large extent on the capacity of the individual to acquire or absorb the specific or general cognitive and/or affective patterns which are offered, made available, or thrust upon him by the teacher. With "capacity," I include a volitional component which may be truly as limiting psychologically, as the absence of a large bulk of cortical tissue would be biologically.

The capacity to acquire knowledge and skills from others involves the taking-in of kinds of supplies. Readiness to take in or incorporate is related to one's earliest experiences. Consider that the human infant requires a specialized environment to exist. He is dependent on his supply of food. For this the infant requires a *more* specialized environment, another human to meet his needs. When the process of taking-in is satisfactorily transacted, with neither excessive frustration nor gratification, this ability becomes

mostly conflict-free. When this developmental phase is not satisfactorily traversed, conflicts are set up which predetermine the ability to accept or take in, and this includes not only food, but protection, love, limitation, and instruction as well.

The relevance of the three modes of therapy discussed has now become more apparent. Early experiences which predetermine the capacity to learn also determine neurotic character traits. These experiences first occur in the family context.

Finally, we may now turn to consider the task of the school, with the understanding that the student comes from home with a role already assigned to him which is more or less fixed as to what expectations are placed on him, with injunctions which may be covert or explicit, but in either case are effective in channeling his energies and encouraging or prohibiting achievements.

This role assignment is effective and enduring by virtue of his internal psychic structure, which, during his pre-school years, has become elaborated out of basic needs and drives. In his personality and development he has traveled an arborized route with critical phases and turns largely predetermining what uses he shall be able to make of future experiences. However, this "arborized" path is replete with collateral and alternate routes. He retains always a measure of plasticity and capacity for growth.

The school, as the first instrument of society, transects the path of personal development outside the family. It does so with the aim of acculturating the student to values which have been sanctioned by ongoing generations. The content of the cultural message may be a mélange of reading, writing, arithmetic, etc., but the larger, implicit mission is to help shape the personality development into an instructable, achievement-oriented, "civilized" man, according to its definition of culture.

Thus, the classroom always becomes an arena of conflict, where compromises and solutions must be reached if the student is to be educated, to be led out of the primordial state. The student comes with predilections and limitations imposed by past ego development and family dynamics.

The teacher is charged with the task of imposing and maintaining societal standards of behavior appropriate to the task at hand. His training, however, has been largely in pedagogy, and his professional identity focuses primarily on content and not the process of education, in the larger sense of socialization.

Further, the teacher focuses explicitly on content with implicit and covert mission to set and uphold values and standards. He has the mandate to do so from society at large. If the community in which the school functions is at variance with this mandate, as in the ghetto schools, his effectiveness in this role is proportionately diminished. He then has the option of pressing for these values through whatever means exist or withdrawing from effective maintenance of standards and salvaging status by concentration on content at whatever residual level the milieu permits.

This same set of circumstances exists insofar as the maladapting student is concerned, but here the withdrawal is on the part of the student. He withdraws from the prevailing classroom culture, from any meaningful dialogue with the teacher, and attempts to set up a sub-culture with his peers, thus creating a mutual paranoid system between himself and the school system.

The similarities between the educational and psychiatric institutions become apparent. The active treatment center and a vital educational institution have a common task of attempting to acculturate a population which resists these efforts due to intrapsychic structure and concurrent family dynamics. Custodial institutions, psychiatric or educational, reflect the despair of surrender by the assignment of stereotypic roles to the population along hierarchal lines, with great social distance between staff, faculty, and patient or student groups.

An interesting attempt to intervene has been made by Drs. Kellum and Schiff in the Woodlawn Mental Health Center on Chicago's south side. Working with first graders in a "culturally deprived" area in an effort to reduce the prevalence of social maladaptation, they developed a set of criteria for maladaptive behavior by polling a group of fifty-seven teachers. A long list of items was eventually grouped into five basic categories:

1 – Hyperaggressive
2 – Shy/aloof
3 – Restless/fidgety
4 – Underachieving
5 – Immature

In addition to these, the term "global" was utilized to record a non-specific impression.

In an effort to reach the children as well as the school staff two basic techniques were used. The first involved weekly meetings with the school staff to deal with intra-staff anxieties and the problems presented by the pupils.

A second meeting included the principal, assistant principal, adjustment teacher, and first-grade teachers.

The second technique is the classroom group meeting, including the entire first-grade class, the psychiatrist, the teacher, and a focal group of the ten most maladapted children in the classroom (as defined by the five criteria above). The format of the group meeting is similar to that of the mental hospital ward meetings. It is essentially a program of intervention by the psychiatrist into the classroom sub-culture, applying the concepts of milieu therapy. Here, the therapist functions as a person who sets values and attempts to modify the student sub-culture so as to foster adaptation. His aim is to induce the formation of a group with a collective identity. The therapeutic aim is not the cure of psychiatric symptoms, but a reduction of maladaptive behavior in the context of the classroom. Outcome studies are in progress and indicate a reduction in maladaptation.

The Woodlawn experiment is admittedly an attempt at intervention addressed to the maladapted or symptomatic population. Thus, it ultimately derives from the medical model of restorative or curative attempts. What is required is a quite different attempt tantamount to a reformation of large segments of the entire primary educational institution.

In the Woodlawn experiment an attempt is being made to introduce milieu concepts and techniques into the school system. Moreover, this is done to reach a limited segment of the school population as a target population, and, in the process, to promulgate the values of milieu therapy among the first grade teachers and instruct them in the techniques as well. There is the idea that, ultimately, the teachers will be able to carry on and thus permit the psychiatrist-therapist to withdraw.

There have been prior experiments in indoctrinating numbers of teachers in psychiatric concepts. Psychoanalytic institutes have offered extensive training in the theory of child and personality development. Here, however, the focus has been on the intrapsychic development of each child. The question "What is the most effective method of intervention?" or indeed, "Is there any effective method of intervention?" has been left unanswered. The social psychiatrist in the therapeutic community has a somewhat more pragmatic, or, if you will, existential response. Whatever is appropriate to either conceptualizing the process of acculturation or making an effective intervention involves committing oneself to becoming an integral part of the system. Therapist or teacher must respond on a human level and not as a detached professional who retreats behind barriers of expertise.

Since it is not possible to communicate this point of view by a lecture or monograph or classroom work, since it must be experienced, why not begin by permitting teachers, or those who are about to become teachers, to experience the impact and methodology of this approach?

I propose the establishment of training centers in psychiatric hospitals or mental health centers where the concept of the therapeutic community is understood and embraced. Let groups of beginning teachers enter such institutions in a new category of student apprentice. They will be neither nursing assistants nor junior psychiatrists, but part students and part professionals. They will serve an apprenticeship that will last for some time between three months and a year, a length of time sufficient to permit them to enter into the life of the therapeutic community and to become integral members thereof, giving them an awareness of the processes of the community and the role of the professional in setting values.

Perhaps such apprenticeships could be carried out in connection with academic courses in the theory of personality development (although this would seem less essential in the actual experience of functioning as a community member). At the end of this time these teachers would be ready to return to the classroom and, hopefully, be able to make a synthesis of what they had learned of the techniques of teaching content, together with their experience of involvement in the community which focuses more entirely on processes.

To summarize: a parallel has been drawn between the concept of the therapeutic community in a psychiatric hospital and the process of "cure" has been related to the process of acculturation. Similarly, in education on either a primary or professional level, there has been a consideration of the process of acculturation, similarly and hopefully leading to identity change. A suggestion has been made that teachers be trained in and allowed to experience the techniques of the therapeutic community with the hope that they may be able to apply these techniques to the problems of the classroom, and thus address themselves more directly to the fundamental shortcomings of mass education in a disorganized community.

Ben N. Schuman, M.D. 279

Part IX

TESTING

The history of psychology is closely tied to tests and testing, and much has been written and said about this area of inquiry. The layman expects that psychological tests will answer any and all questions about intelligence. Parents and schools want to know a child's intellectual potential and just what can be expected reasonably of him; they want to be able to identify the talented and the gifted child as well as the retarded, brain-damaged, or handicapped child. There is a constant concern for the level of achievement a child has reached at different points in his development, since it is felt that the use of his abilities and the quality of his performance measure the effectiveness of the school he has been attending and its teaching techniques.

Achievement tests are related to intelligence tests, and the discrepancies and variations between them often are indicators of personality problems and potential difficulties. A general measure of intelligence is not enough now; society demands a greater breakdown of capabilities than just verbal and nonverbal aptitudes. Even though the perfect testing instruments have not yet been developed, great strides have been made toward improving the psychological tests we currently have, and toward developing and refining new ones to meet today's demands.

In addition to varying forms of intelligence and achievement testing, the psychologist has developed tests in the area of vocational preference and interests as well as in a variety of special personality aspects. Many school counselors and psychologists are using these instruments — hopefully only as indicators which are far from exact or definitive. Test information can be used meaningfully only by experienced and knowledgeable personnel in connection with other related materials and techniques.

Special attention during the past few years has been given to measuring the effects of cultural disadvantage with respect to the interpretation of test results. Many instruments used by psychologists were found to be inaccurate, if not inadequate, in evaluating the culturally disadvantaged. Much of the criticism leveled at the use of tests by psychologists stems from the use of instruments by nonprofessional aides and from the interpretation of tests by inexperienced people. The criticism — much of it justifiable — will continue to plague the psychologist and psychometrician until the use of these tests is limited to the area for which they are designed.

Psychologists often look with envy and respect at the related field of medicine and the progress it has made in diagnostic procedures. This advancement is explained by the history of the field, the long hours and great amount of money and energy that has been devoted to the research and development of superior instruments. Perhaps if such attention and resources were applied in the field of psychology, it might also achieve a comparable level of advancement.

Concetta V. Romanow

THE TEACHER, THE CHILD, AND THE INTELLIGENCE TEST

Students, teachers, and parents have long been perplexed by all the writing and talk about intelligence tests, I.Q., aptitude, potential, and ability. The confusion is both one of semantics and of fact and value. It is clear from Dr. Romanow's article that these matters must be treated separately by professionals and parents. Many of the professional tools and techniques should be limited to professional use and not be made available to the untrained person. Much damage is done by the misuse of information that is not really understood by persons outside of the field of testing.

In the following report, an explanation of the effect of both heredity and environment is discussed in terms of the many forces influencing human growth and development. The relationship between the more abstract measures of testing data and the specific experiences of each individual is discussed with emphasis on the need to understand the more concrete experiences to which a child is exposed, and to realize that there is no fixed and rigid knowledge to be gained from testing measures alone.

STRENGTHS AND LIMITATIONS OF I.Q. TESTS

The so-called intelligence test is frequently looked upon as a test of "native ability." The concept of native ability unfortunately conveys the idea that we are testing behavior based on some mysterious kind of innate potential without the influence of environment. This is simply not true.

One has only to look over items in an intelligence test to realize that knowledge of these items depends upon the learning situations encountered in experience. For example, intelligence tests include questions similar to the following: showing the child a picture with a number of objects and asking him to point out the one which is a "refrigerator"; asking him to define words such as "apple," "vanquish," and "bucolic"; having him count the number of beads on a string; asking questions such as: "How many quarts make a gallon?" "In what way are a cow and a sheep alike?"

Clearly, such questioning can be answered only if the individual has had the opportunity to learn about the materials they involve. The child cannot correctly identify the refrigerator unless he has either seen the object itself or a picture of it and has heard the word "refrigerator" associated with this object or picture. In other words, a child who has learned a language other than English would not be able to answer the questions, nor would a child who comes from the kind of environment which would preclude any contact with refrigerators.

It is also obvious that vocabulary items must be learned, number concepts (counting) must be learned, and items of information such as the number of quarts in a gallon must be learned before the child can deal with them in any "intelligence" test. But in order for such learning to occur, the child must be exposed to such materials or at least have the opportunity to come across them. Hence the child's performance on an intelligence test must be affected by his background and training.

Since environmental factors influence scores on intelligence tests, we must use caution in interpreting the scores or I.Q.'s of children whose backgrounds differ markedly from those of children on whom the test was

From the *Illinois Schools Journal*, February 1961, pages 209–215. Reprinted with the permission of the author and publisher.

standardized. The immigrant as well as the child of foreign language background may be penalized on intelligence tests, since their opportunities for verbal learning (as far as the language of the test is concerned) have not been equal to the opportunities of the child who hears English spoken in the home and who has learned this language from the beginning.

If the child has been raised in an environment in which little stress is placed on tests and achievement, he may have little motivation for doing well. Lack of motivation can lead to careless answers and can certainly lower the score on an intelligence test. Chance factors such as those we have been discussing and numerous others will affect the test score. As a result, our inferences as to the child's overall knowledge or "intelligence" may be in error.

We sometimes hear references to what the intelligence test does not measure. It may be said that the test does not measure personality traits such as persistence, cooperativeness, or emotional stability. It is true that the intelligence test does not yield a specific score for these characteristics; however, it is also true that such personality characteristics affect the test score. Since the intelligence test is actually a test of general knowledge, it is clear that the individual's persistence in seeking knowledge, his cooperativeness in various learning situations, his emotional stability will affect the extent to which knowledge is obtained and so will affect the test score. Lack of motivation, negativism, and emotional problems are personality factors which serve to depress or lower the child's intelligence test score.

Should a parent be told the child's intelligence test score: In the opinion of this writer, never. One reason is that some parents are liable to misinterpret its significance. They may think of the score as something immutable, unchangeable, innate, and eternal—a kind of brand fixed upon the child. As we have mentioned, this concept is completely erroneous.

There is also danger that if the child has a low intelligence test score, the behavior of the parents toward the child may be affected. If they treat him as an incompetent from whom very little can be expected, such an attitude is hardly likely to motivate the child for future achievement. He may become emotionally isolated and simply "give up."

On the other hand, it is possible for parents of a "high I.Q." child to treat him as if the high intelligence test score were an end in itself. It is not. Merely because a child has a high I.Q. score does not mean that he will automatically learn calculus or chemistry or Shakespeare. All such learning requires further effort. Unfortunately, the "high I.Q." has become a status symbol in our society and the parents of such a child may allow him to rest on his laurels (so to speak) rather than encourage him toward further learning efforts. Such distortions of the significance of the intelligence test score are not uncommon.

Finally, we may consider a question which is often asked: what is the difference between intelligence, aptitude, and achievement tests? Actually, all three types of tests are similar in that the scores obtained are influenced by the individual's environment and learning experiences within that environment. There is no such thing as an intelligence or aptitude test which is not affected by one's experience. As has been stated when discussing the word "potential," the concept of "aptitude" is misleading in that some people may think aptitude tests are completely uninfluenced by environmental factors.

Further, it is highly probable that the home background of these children involves a different cultural environment in terms of the habits learned and the objects and values to which the children are exposed.

Numerous studies also show that children from "deprived" environments tend to have relatively low scores on intelligence tests. Such children include those raised on canal boats, in isolated rural areas, and in orphanages. These children would tend to have limited contacts and in some cases little or no schooling. It has been shown that when the environment is changed, there is frequently an increase in the intelligence test score. For example, the children raised in orphanages showed no gain but rather a general decline in score. All this evidence indicates the effect of environmental factors on the intelligence test score.

As has been pointed out, there is no such thing as a test of "native ability" which is not influenced by environmental factors. Such a test would be impossible to construct. What kinds of questions could be asked which would have no relationship to the environment in which we live and learn? It is true that there have been attempts to construct "culture-fair" tests of intelligence. As the name implies, such tests are constructed so that they are "fair" to individuals from various backgrounds, for example, urban and rural children, children from wealthy homes and those from slum environments, and children of various nationalities. However, such "culture-fair" tests must of necessity have limited content.

A test which is to be used with children of widely different cultural backgrounds could not contain items requiring identification of such objects as umbrellas, automobiles, or papaya trees, because these objects occur with different frequency in different cultures. In some areas individuals may never use umbrellas but may know a good deal about papayas, while in other areas the opposite occurs. Further, if the test is to be used with Zuñi Indian children, Parisian children, and children living in Chicago, it is evident that language must be excluded from the test. Such exclusion is practically impossible to accomplish.

In any case, there is no such thing as a test completely "fair" to all groups regardless of background. Some cultural groups, for example, stress speed much more than others. A test with time limits therefore would not be fair to children raised in a culture where slow activity and careful deliberation are valued.

As all tests are influenced by environmental factors, just what conclusions about native ability can we derive from the intelligence test score? The answer is, nothing definite. The questions on intelligence tests are based on objects, situations, and symbols acquired in our environment.

If two children differ widely in the scores they achieve on an intelligence test, we would be justified in attributing the differences primarily to "native ability" only if the children had been exposed to precisely the same environmental factors for every moment of their lives.

This "if" is a very large one, for of course such a situation can never exist. No two people in the world—not even identical twins—are exposed to exactly the same environment from the moment of conception. Consequently, the role of hereditary factors (that is, of the individual's inherited biological structure) can never be clearly determined. All we can do is to assume that hereditary and environmental factors interact.

Since intelligence tests do not give an index of native ability as such, of what use are they? So-called intelligence tests *are* useful because they enable us to predict with some measure of accuracy the future scholastic performance of the child. In other words, we can predict that children with relatively high intelligence scores will generally do well in school, while children with relatively low intelligence test scores will generally do poorly in school.

The fact that this positive correlation between intelligence test score and scholastic achievement exists means that we can to some extent predict the child's future performance on the basis of his standing on the so-called intelligence test. This aid to prediction is a great boon to teachers and administrators, for we are enabled to set up, in advance, appropriate scholastic programs.

Thus, if we can predict that children with intelligence test scores considerably above average will generally show quick comprehension and high achievement, we can then go about setting up enriched curricula in order to expand the scope of their interest and knowledge. Similarly, if we can predict that children with intelligence test scores considerably below the average will generally have difficulty in the school situation, we can then go about setting up learning situations which are best suited to them.

In passing, we may note that the selection of children for the Educable Mentally Handicapped classes in the Chicago Schools depends in part upon their scores on an "intelligence" test. The establishment of the program and the selection of the children are thus based on the assumption that so-called intelligence tests generally have predictive value, that is, make possible the prediction of performance in the school situation. In this way, such children can be selected and given special training before they have undergone years of frustration in regular classes.

Intelligence tests are sometimes referred to as tests of "mental ability" or "potential." Since "potential" refers to the ability to perform some behavior which has not yet developed or appeared, it is obvious that we can never measure potential as such. The test does not measure potential directly.

Nor does any intelligence test measure "intelligence" directly, for intelligence is not a concrete object. The weight of an apple or the length of a hand may be measured directly, but all an intelligence test can measure is performance on a limited number of questions and at a particular moment in the individual's life.

Intelligence and potential are abstract concepts inferred from present behavior. A so-called intelligence test is one measurement of present behavior. "Ability" is inferred from test performance. An analogy can be expressed in this example: a three-year-old child is observed extemporizing melodies on the piano. The onlookers may say, "Aha! this child has great potential." What these onlookers really mean by the word "potential" is that they are predicting for this child, very superior future performance in the field of music.

Thus "potential" simply refers to the prediction of future behavior based on observations of present behavior. When we hear a statement such as "his potential never materialized," this actually means that the individual never achieved the level of performance which was predicted for him. In other words, our original prediction has not been borne out; there is a discrepancy between the prediction and later performance.

When we attempt to correlate intelligence test scores with measures of scholastic achievement, it is clear that we cannot predict perfectly from the intelligence test score. The teacher has also observed this discrepancy in everyday observations. Occasionally a child with an extremely high score on an intelligence test will be only about average or even below average in his scholastic achievement. Or, a fifth-grade child with an intelligence test score not very much above the average of his group may be reading at the eighth-grade level and generally show superior school work.

At first glance it may seem strange that some discrepancies between intelligence test scores and scholastic achievement should exist. But if we really think about this imperfect relationship between intelligence test scores and school performance, we can see that it is not at all surprising and in fact is to be expected.

One reason that scores on an intelligence test do not always coincide with school performance is simply that the test represents only a small portion of what the child may know or be able to do. After all, there are millions of possible questions which a test-writer might include on a test of "intelligence." But the test cannot go on forever, and so the writer must choose a very limited number of items—a few dozen or so. This means that out of the great pool of possible questions only a few can be chosen. Any test merely samples a limited portion of the individual's total knowledge. Consequently, we cannot expect that intelligence test scores will enable us to predict school performance in a variety of areas accurately for each child.

Another reason for the discrepancy lies in

the various factors contributing to error of measurement in any test situation. For example, on the day that the child takes the intelligence test he may be coming down with a cold; or he may not feel well because he has not had breakfast; or he may be distracted by the strange new situation; or he may be emotionally upset because his parents have had a violent argument that same morning; or the examiner may remind him of someone whom he dislikes, with the result that the child feels rebellious and does not give his full cooperation; or he may make some "lucky" guesses.

If the child has been raised in an environment in which little stress is placed on tests and achievement, he may have little motivation for doing well. Lack of motivation can lead to careless answers and can certainly lower the score on an intelligence test. Chance factors such as those we have been discussing and numerous others will affect the test score. As a result, our inference as to the child's overall knowledge or "intelligence" may be in error.

But since performance on all three types of tests is affected by the individual's experience, just what is the difference between them? We may say that an intelligence test calls upon knowledge of a more generalized kind, such as might be derived from everyday experiences, while an achievement test is based on knowledge of subject matter specifically taught in the school situation.

Thus there might be an achievement test on the content of intermediate algebra, while an intelligence test is not likely to contain such items. This does not mean that an intelligence test excludes all school-taught material. For example, an intelligence test might contain a question such as, "If two pounds of apples can be purchased for twenty-five cents, how many pounds can I buy for a dollar?" This item requires numerical skill which may be learned outside the school but which is also taught in the school situation itself. Further, we have reading achievement tests, but practically all so-called intelligence tests call upon reading and verbal skills. It is apparent that there is much overlapping in the content of intelligence and achievement tests. In general, however, intelligence tests require less specialized, more general knowledge.

An aptitude test (mechanical aptitude, musical aptitude, clerical aptitude, etc.) also differs from an achievement test only in that the knowledge required is less specialized. An aptitude test is simply a measuring device used before the individual has had *specialized* training in the subject. However, performance on an aptitude test is affected by the individual's previous experiences. An item on a mechanical aptitude test, for example, involves a sketch depicting various gears in a certain relationship to each other. It is clear the performance on such items is affected by the individual's prior experience in observing machinery, taking apart alarm clocks, exploring museums, or reading books.

Why have so-called aptitude tests? The only justification for their existence is the degree to which they allow prediction of future performance. Thus, a mechanical aptitude test is a valid test if the scores are correlated with performance in a mechanical job or with grades in a mechanical training course.

To summarize, it can be seen that the difference between intelligence, aptitude, and achievement tests is much less than is generally supposed; performance on all is influenced by environmental factors.

All of the above is not meant to imply that intelligence tests are of little value to teachers. As has been previously indicated, intelligence test scores, properly utilized, are an effective basis for grouping children, for determining the appropriate level of instruction and as general indicator of what pupils will do in school. Nevertheless, teachers and administrators must not "brand" a child with an I.Q. score and must not overlook the many important factors affecting a child's school record which are unmeasured or poorly measured by such tests.

James H. Ricks, Jr.

ON TELLING PARENTS ABOUT TEST RESULTS

Psychologists, school counselors, and teachers are constantly faced with the question as to what and how does one tell parents about the results of school tests. There is, of late, an increased interest on the part of many parents who are demanding information about the results of psychological examinations, or who are refusing to allow their children to be tested, claiming an invasion of privacy. Even law suits have been filed concerning this very point. It is a principle and policy that will no doubt be explored in depth during the next few years and precedents may be established which will change our present practice of testing and reporting of results.

Problems arise with group testing in school settings where there is no opinion on the part of the student as to whether he wishes to be examined, or in individual testing which is required and administered by school personnel, even with information on tests and results voluntarily submitted to or requested. In any case, the professional must evaluate and establish an operational policy concerning the entire field of testing and what is to be done with the results.

The consensus of the following article is that parents *do* have the right to know about the abilities and performances of their children, but the difficulty lies in the way in which the school personnel conveys this knowledge in terms parents can truly understand.

Like any other organization dealing with people, a school has many confidences to keep. School administrators, teachers, and especially guidance workers inevitably come to know items of private information. A gossip who carelessly passes such information around abuses his position and his relationship with his students. It is both right and important that some kinds of information be kept in confidence.

What about test results? Do they belong in the category of secrets, to be seen only by professional eyes and mentioned only in whispers? Or is their proper function best served when they become common knowledge in the school and its community? (In some towns, names and scores have been listed in the local newspaper, much like the results of an athletic contest.)

We think neither extreme is a good rule. Sometimes there is reason to make group data—figures such as the average and the range from high to low—generally public. Seldom should individual results be published except for the happy announcement of a prize won, a scholarship awarded, and the like. But short of general publication, school guidance workers face a particularly important question: Should parents be told their children's test results?

Hard questions, often, are hard because they deal with genuinely complicated problems. Simple "solutions" to such questions are likely to be a trap rather than an aid if their effect is to divert our attention from the difficulties we truly face. Simple rules or principles, on the other hand, can be of real help as one tackles complex problems and situations. This article will present some rules that we have found useful in facing questions such as—

"What should I say when a mother wants to know her son's IQ?" "Should we send aptitude test profiles home with the children?" "We feel that parents in our school ought to know the results of the achievement tests we give, but then it's hard to explain the discrepancies between these and the teachers' grades."

From the *Test Service Bulletin* of The Psychological Corporation, No. 54, December 1959.

No single procedure, obviously, can be appropriate for every kind of test. Nor for every kind of parent. To Mr. Jones, a well-adjusted and well-educated father, a report of his daughter's test scores may enhance his understanding of her capacities and of what the school has been giving her. To Mr. Green, a somewhat insecure and less knowledgeable man, the identical information may spark an explosion damaging to both child and school. And the counselor or teacher often has no sure way of knowing which kind of person he will be reporting to.

Two principles and one verbal technique seem to us to provide a sound basis for communicating the information obtained from testing. The two "commandments" are absolutely interdependent — without the second the first is empty, and without the first the second is pointless.

The First. Parents have the right to know whatever the school knows about the abilities, the performance, and the problems of their children.

The Second. The school has the obligation to see that it communicates understandable and usable knowledge. Whether by written report or by individual conference, the school must make sure it is giving real information — not just the illusion of information that bare numbers or canned interpretations often afford. And the information must be in terms that parents can absorb and use.

Few educators will dispute the first principle. It is in parents that the final responsibility for the upbringing and education of the children must lie. This responsibility requires access to all available information bearing on educational and vocational decisions to be made for and by the child. The school is the agent to which parents have delegated part of the educational process — but the responsibility has been delegated, not abdicated. Thoughtful parents do not take these responsibilities and rights lightly.

The parents' right to know, then, we regard as indisputable. But, to know what?

Suppose that, as a result of judicious testings, the school knows that Sally has mastered the social studies and general science better than many in her ninth grade class, but that few do as poorly as she in math. In English usage she stands about in the middle, but her reading level is barely up to the lower border of the students who successfully complete college preparatory work in her high school. The best prediction that can be made of her probable scores on the College Boards three years hence is that they will fall in the range which makes her eligible for the two-year community college, but not for the university. She grasps mechanical concepts better than most boys, far better than most girls. Looking over the test results and her records, her experienced teacher recognizes that good habits and neatness of work have earned Sally grades somewhat better than would be expected from her test scores.

All of these are things Sally's parents should know. Will they know them if they are given the numbers — Sally's IQ score, percentiles for two reading scores, percentiles on another set of norms for several aptitude tests, and grade-placement figures on an achievement battery?[1]

Telling someone something he does not understand does not increase his knowledge (at least not his correct and usable knowledge — we are reminded of the guide's observation about the tenderfoot, "It ain't so much what he don't know, it's what he knows that ain't so that gits him in trouble"). Transmitting genuine knowledge requires attention to content, language, and audience. We have already referred to some of the characteristics of parents as an audience. Let's look at the other two elements.

Content means that to begin with we must ourselves know what we are trying to get across.

We need to know just what evidence there is to show that the test results deserve any

---

1. The implied "No" answer to this question does not, of course, refer to those few parents trained in psychometrics — perhaps even to a point beyond the training of the school staff. Parents include all kinds of people.

consideration at all. We need equally to know the margins and probabilities of error in predictions based on tests. If we don't know both what the scores mean and how much confidence may properly be placed in them, we are in trouble at the start—neither our own use of the information nor our transmission of it to others will be very good.

Content—what we are going to say—and language—how we are going to put it—are inseparable when we undertake to tell somebody something. In giving information about test results, we need to think about the general content and language we shall use and also about the specific terms we shall use.

To illustrate the general content-and-language planning: a guidance director may decide that he wants first to get across a sense of both the values and the weaknesses of test scores. One excellent device for his purpose would be an expectancy table or chart. Such a chart can make it clear to persons without training in statistics that test results are useful predictors and that the predictions will not always be precise. Local studies in one's own school or community are of greatest interest. But the guidance director who lacks local data may still find

illustrative tables from other places helpful in preparing parents and students to use test results in a sensible way. (An example is given in Figure 1, following.)

Specific terms used in expressing test results vary considerably in the problems they pose. Consider, for example, the different kinds of numbers in which test results may be reported.

IQ's are regarded as numbers that should rarely if ever be reported as such to students or to their parents. The reason is that an IQ is likely to be seen as a fixed characteristic of the person tested, as somehow something more than the test score it really represents. The effect, too often, is that of a final conclusion about the individual rather than that of a piece of information useful in further thinking and planning. Few things interfere more effectively with real understanding than indiscriminate reporting of IQ scores to parents.

Grade placement scores or standard scores of various kinds are less likely to cause trouble than IQ scores are. Still, they may substitute an illusion of communication for real communication. Standard scores have no more meaning to most parents than raw

Figure 1. The guidance director found, in the classes of 1953 and 1954, 101 boys and 85 girls who had taken the *Differential Aptitude Tests* (including Verbal Reasoning and Numerical Ability) in their tenth grade years and the *Scholastic Aptitude Test* of the College Entrance Examination Board as seniors. Since the CEEB reports two scores—Verbal and Math—there were four sets of data: Boys-Verbal, Boys-Math, Girls-Verbal, and Girls-Math. The chart for the boys' CEEB Verbal results looked like this:

Of each ten boys in the tenth grade whose VR + NA scores are in the	on the CEEB SAT-V when they are seniors, how many will score				and how many will score 500 or above
	399 & lower	400-499	500-599	600 & over	500 or above
Top Quarter of the Class		2 figures	4 figures	4 figures	**4 out of 5**
Second Quarter	1 figure	5 figures	4 figures	1 figure	**3 out of 5**
Third Quarter	2 figures	4 figures	3 figures	1 figure	**2 out of 5**
Lowest Quarter of the Class	6 figures	4 figures			**Very few**

scores unless there is opportunity for extensive explanations. Grade placements seem so simple and straightforward that serious misunderstandings may result from their use. As noted in a very helpful pamphlet[2] a sixth-grade pupil with grade-placement scores of 10.0 for reading and 8.5 for arithmetic does not necessarily rank higher in reading than he does in arithmetic when compared to the other sixth-graders. (Both scores may be at the 95th percentile for his class—arithmetic progress much more than reading progress tends to be dependent on what has been taught, and thus to spread over a narrower range at any one grade.)

Percentiles probably are the safest and most informative numbers to use provided their two essential characteristics are made clear: (1) that they refer not to per cent of questions answered correctly but to per cent of people whose performance the student has equalled or surpassed, and (2) who, specifically, are the people with whom the student is being compared. The second point—a definite description of the comparison or "norm" group—is especially important in making the meaning of test results clear.

Much more can be said about the kinds of numbers used to convey test score information. Good discussions can be found in a number of textbooks.[3] But a more fundamental question remains—are any numbers necessary?

We intend nothing so foolish as suggesting a ban on the use of numbers in reporting test results. But we have been struck repeatedly by the fact that some of the very best counselors and many of the best written reports present numerical data only incidentally or not at all.

Along with the two "commandments" at the beginning of this article, we mentioned a verbal technique. Generally, we dislike formulas for writing or speaking. This one, however, seems to have advantages that outweigh the risks attending its suggestion. It's just a few words:

"You score like people who . . ."
Or, to a parent,
"Your son (or daughter) scores like students who . . ."

The sentence, of course, requires completion. The completion depends on the test or other instrument, the reason for testing, and the person to whom the report is being given. Some sample completions:

". . . people who are pretty good at office work, fast and accurate enough to hold a job and do it well."

". . . people who don't find selling insurance a very satisfactory choice. Three out of four who score as you do and become insurance salesmen leave the job for something else in less than a year."

". . . students who find getting into liberal arts college and getting a B.A. degree something they can attain only with extra hard work. On the other hand, they find a year or two of technical school interesting and they probably do well in the jobs to which that leads."

". . . students who are disappointed later if they don't begin a language in the ninth grade and plan to take some more math and science. It's easier to head toward business later if you still want to than to go from the commercial course into a good college."

". . . students who don't often—only about one out of four—manage to earn a C average their freshman year at State."

". . . students who have more than average difficulty passing in arithmetic—you (or to a parent, he) may need some extra help on this in the next few years."

Many more samples will come readily to mind. The most important thing to note is that a satisfactory report combines two kinds of information:

2. Katz, M. R. *Selecting an Achievement Test*. E. & A. Series No. 3, 1958 (Page 26). Available free from Educational Testing Service, Princeton, New Jersey.

3. See, for example, Chapters 17 and 18 in *Measurement and Evaluation in Psychology and Education*, by Thorndike and Hagen (New York: Wiley, 1955), or pages 556–563 and 584–588 in *Appraising Vocational Fitness*, by Super (New York: Harper, 1949).

1) the test results of the individual person, and
2) something known about the test or battery and its relationship to the subsequent performance of others who have taken it.

Also, a satisfactory completion puts the school or the counselor out on a limb, at least a little. Some variant of "That's not so!" or, more politely, "How do you know?" will be the reaction in some cases, probably less frequently voiced than it is felt.

Well, let's face it. The decision to use a test at all is a step out on a limb. Some limbs are broad and solid and the climber need feel little or no anxiety. Some are so frail that they offer only hazard, with the bait of an improbable reward. We climb out on some limbs of medium safety because there is evidence of a real chance that they will help us, and those whom we test, toward a worthwhile goal.

The words of the formula need not actually be used in each case. Sometimes percentiles, grade placement scores, or a profile may be what the parents should receive. But it is well to try first mentally stating the meaning of the results in the language suggested above. If this proves difficult or discomforting, a warning signal is on—reporting the numbers is likely not to be constructive in the case at hand!

The audience of parents to which our test-based information is to be transmitted includes an enormous range and variety of minds and emotions. Some are ready and able to absorb what we have to say. Reaching others may be as hopeless as reaching TV watchers with an AM radio broadcast. Still others may hear what we say, but clothe the message with their own special needs, ideas, and predilections.

The habit of using the formula, and of thinking a bit about what answer to give if the response is a challenging or doubting one, puts the interpreter of test scores in the strongest position he can occupy. In the case of achievement tests, it requires him to understand why and how the particular test or battery was chosen as appropriate for his school and his purpose. In the case of aptitude (including scholastic aptitude or intelligence) tests, it requires him to examine the evidence offered in the test manual and research studies to back up the test's claim to usefulness. And it reminds him always that it is in the end his thinking, his weighing of the evidence, his soundness and helpfulness as an educator or counselor that is exposed for judgment—not the sometimes wistful ideas of the test author or publisher.

The school—or the counselor—is exposed for judgment when telling parents about the abilities and performances of their children. The parents have the right to know. And knowledge in terms they can understand and absorb is what the school must give.

Bryant Feather

AN EXPLORATORY STUDY IN THE USE OF FIGURE DRAWINGS IN A GROUP SITUATION

During the past several years much has been said and written about the effectiveness and use of various psychological tests. In some states, the use of certain test results is being barred by law, which is a dangerously limiting trend. However, the issue does focus attention on the need for the development of more effective test instruments and for controlling the use of results of the various tests that we have.

Attempts are constantly under way to develop new and more effective test instruments; projective techniques seem to be one of the answers to the challenge. For many years, drawings have been known to be a significant tool for the trained psychologist to use in his diagnosis, treatment, and on-going evaluation of disturbed individuals. The following article reports on work being done to adapt this technique from the clinician's work with individuals to a group approach. There is clear indication that this approach might be used by a professionally trained psychologist to do rough group screening of large groups of supposedly normal individuals.

Research on the use of this group projective test is being continued by the author; current findings indicate that it is effective only if administered and interpreted by an individual carefully trained and experienced in the use of figure drawing as a diagnostic tool. This points up the importance of limiting the use of such tests to the professional, and to the importance of his interpreting and using the results only to the degree that such results can be understood and accepted by the client and others involved in a case. It is appropriate that people know of the techniques and tools much as they know of the X ray and its use. But they must also realize that they are not qualified to use the X ray or to make interpretations of the results. The results and application of these procedures should be presented in meaningful terms but the results can be used and checked only by the professionals.

During clinical interviews with maladjusted students, the writer has often employed the technique of having the student draw a person and then draw a person of the opposite sex of that of the first drawing. These sets of figures were found to be rich in psychoanalytical content; they were valuable tools in aiding diagnosis, and in advancing therapy. During the time this was being done, repeated reference was made to Goodenough (4) and Machover (6) and to the current studies in the professional literature as a point of departure in interpreting the figures.

It was believed that if such drawings could be revealing in a clinical situation, they might be adapted for group use, and they might also be an interesting method for studying students who had expressed no difficulties, and who were to all appearances functioning adequately in their current academic setting.

Following this hunch, the following study was undertaken to determine if there was a significant pattern to be found among the figure drawings of college students when Machover's Personality Projection in the Drawing of the Human Figure technique was modified for a group situation.

For the basis of the method employed in this study, one needs to turn to the underlying theories of all projective techniques. Rapaport best expressed this when he (11, p. 213) wrote:

"The projective hypothesis may be formulated as follows: All behavior manifestations of the human being, including the least and the most significant, are revealing and expressive of his personality, by which we mean that individual principle of which he is the carrier."

Schmidl has stressed the value of interpreting drawings as a help in preliminary diagnosis, as a method of noting changes and progress during prolonged treatment. He says (12, p. 96):

"No one will expect that a diagnosis should be based on form analysis of children's drawings alone, but it could be a valuable supplement especially in cases of children who do not express themselves verbally."

From the *Journal of Social Psychology*, Vol. 37, 1953, pages 163–170. Adapted with permission of the publisher.

Following along with a similar type of reasoning, one finds the following statements by Harms (5, p. 192):

"The appreciation of this new means for psychotherapy, that of child-art diagnosis, should be considered as an art of diagnosis without which no medical man and no psychologist can be a perfect master in 'the art' of understanding and helping broken and disturbed human souls."

Although these men have referred primarily to the drawings of children, the writer feels that the technique is equally applicable to post-adolescents.

Among the first individuals to publish findings related to the drawings of the human figure was Karen Machover (6), and she has so well stated the specific theory and principles that the following excerpts are reproduced at length to clarify the operational limits and techniques:

"Projective methods of exploring motivations have repeatedly uncovered deep and perhaps unconscious determinants of self-expression which could not be made manifest in direct communication. . . .The activity elicited in response to 'draw a person' is indeed a creative experience, as will be testified by the individual who is drawing. Wide and intimate tie-ups exist between the figure drawn and the personality of the individual who is doing the drawing (6, p. 4).

"When an individual attempts to solve the problem of the directive to 'draw a person,' he is compelled to draw from some sources. External figures are too varied in their body attributes to lend themselves to a spontaneous, composite, objective representation of a person. Some process of selection involving identification through projection and introjection enters at some point. The individual must draw consciously, and no doubt unconsciously, upon his whole system of psychic values. The body, or the self, is the most intimate point of reference in any activity. We have, in the course of growth, come to associate various sensations, perceptions, and emotions with certain body organs. This investment in body organs, or the perception of the body image as it has developed out of personal experience, must somehow guide the individual who is drawing in the specific structure and content which constitutes his offering of a 'person.' Consequently, the drawing of a person, in involving a projection of the body image, provides a natural vehicle for the expression of one's body needs and conflicts. Successful drawing interpretation has proceeded on the hypothesis that the figure drawn is related to the individual who is drawing with the same intimacy characterizing that individual's gait, his handwriting, or any other of his expressive movements (6, p. 5)."

For this study some 175 college students at Michigan State College in Effective Living classes were used. Effective Living was a formal general education course which draws concepts and material from the specialized fields in the areas of the humanities and social sciences that are useful in helping one to deal realistically and successfully with life's problems. In general, these are the problems of clarifying one's life goals and increasing understanding and skill in human relationships.

A random sample was obtained by choosing four sections of some 58 sections among which students were divided indiscriminately at registration time. In general about 60 per cent of Effective Living students were freshmen, 30 per cent sophomores, and 10 per cent juniors and seniors.

All of the students had made a study of "personality" for 10 weeks immediately preceding this investigation. During this survey of personality (which was defined as "the totality of one's characteristics"), its development, formation, and changeability; lectures, text readings, and discussions concentrated on symptomatology, diagnosis, therapy, and prognosis. During one of the lectures the sections were told that there were many interesting and apparently successfully projective techniques of studying personality. It was pointed out that the use of such procedures was limited to clinical settings and to trained personnel. However, for purposes of demonstration (and secondly for data for this study) the students were asked if they would care to see and take part in a limited demonstration

TABLE 1

An Analysis of 175 Drawings Made by Michigan State College Students in a Class in Effective Living

	Per cent No. of 175			Per cent No. of 175	
Location of drawing on page			Clothing used on figure		
1. Upper left	47	26.8	1. Overdressed	27	15.4
2. Upper right	5	2.8	2. Casual	117	66.9
3. Center	110	62.8	3. Scanty	18	10.3
4. Lower left	3	1.7	4. Naked	10	5.7
5. All over	9	5.1	5. Bust or head only	3	1.7
6. Turned page	6	3.4			
				175	
	175		Angle of figure		
Proportionate size of drawing			1. Frontal view	128	73.1
1. Very large	8	4.5	2. Side view	43	24.6
2. Large	50	28.5	3. Bust or head	3	1.7
3. Medium	81	46.3	4. Several	1	.6
4. Small	29	16.6			
5. Very small	7	4.0		175	
			Angle of head		
	175		1. Frontal	115	65.7
Sex of the figure drawn			2. Profile	57	32.6
1. Male drawing male	145	82.8	3. Both	2	1.1
2. Male drawing female	11	6.3			
3. Female drawing female	11	6.3		175	
4. Female drawing male	8	4.6	Treatment of hair		
			1. Normal	122	69.7
	175		2. Excessive	36	20.6
			3. Absence	17	9.7
Use of hat					
1. Absence	144	82.3		175	
2. Present with hair	20	11.4	Stance		
3. Present without hair	11	6.3	1. Secure	85	48.6
			2. Insecure	90	51.4
	175				
Treatment of feet				175	
1. Shoes shown	138	78.9	Treatment of hands		
2. Bare with toes	14	8.0	1. Details shown	126	72.0
3. Bare (Clublike)	8	4.6	2. Mitt type	20	11.4
4. None shown	15	8.6	3. None	29	16.6
	175			175	

of one of these methods. All of the limitations were pointed out that were resultant from using such a technique in a group setting. Once interest was aroused in the project, the following directions and explanations were given:

1. Because the method of studying certain aspects of personality that we are about to investigate is usually employed in an office, with only the therapist and subject present, it will be necessary for you to pretend that you are alone and that no other than the psychologist will ever see your drawing. Try not to look at nor pay any attention to the person sitting near you, and assume that he will completely disregard you.

2. For purposes of uniformity I shall furnish each person with paper and pencil.

3. In a moment I shall give you a specific instruction . . . the only instruction that I shall give you. Please do not ask any questions at all, as the question you ask might influence some other person in the room. When you have finished, merely turn in the paper and leave quietly. There is no time limit.

4. Remember that this is in no way a test of your ability nor of your talents, but rather a type of personality test.

5. Now I shall give you the only instruction necessary and the only one that I can give you. . . . Please do not ask any questions and do not consider any aspects of the method. Just let yourself go.

6. "Draw a person."

Once all of the drawings were obtained and a detailed consideration of them was made, the tabulations were compiled in Table 1.

From these tabulations one can hypothesize that the drawings of post-adolescents might conform to the following expectancies:

1. Centered on the page.
2. Of medium size.
3. The same sex as the person doing the drawing.
4. Casually dressed.
5. Frontal view.
6. Without hat.
7. With normal looking hair.
8. With hands shown in detail.
9. With shoes indicated.
10. Done with a medium type of line.

Of course it must be pointed out that all the judgments in classifying the drawings on these 10 points were made by agreement between two people only: the author and the assistant (a registered nurse, who had had extensive psychiatric nursing experience and college training in addition to her nurse's work).

After the drawings were tabulated as shown above, a series of interviews were scheduled with each of the individuals. During these conferences careful note was made of the physical appearance of the individual, and a record was made of such factors as: Sex, age, marital status, academic record, physical appearance, nervous mannerisms, introversion and extroversion, ambitions, means of support, vocational choice, history of previous psychological counseling, and present need for various types of counseling.

Although the 175 people were apparently functioning adequately (enrolled as college students, attending classes, living in approved housing, and participating in average social activities) it was found during the personal interviews that some of these subjects were, in reality, experiencing difficulties which were in turn reflected in their drawings. The 175 records were divided into five arbitrary classifications according to their degree of personal adjustment. The criteria used in making this judgment were:

1. All-college academic point average. An average of "C" was decided upon as a minimum level of satisfaction.

2. Subjective evaluation on the part of the interviewee. Each one was encouraged by a non-directive technique to judge his own adjustment.

3. Observations and judgment by the psychologist. During the interviews and classroom observations the following factors were given special attention.

a. Personal appearance of subject

TABLE 2
Classification Of 175 Students According To Their Degree of Personal Adjustment

Good	39
Fair	45
Average	40
Poor	43
Very Poor	8
Total	175

b. Nervous mannerisms

c. Physical health

d. Avocations and use of leisure time

e. Attitudes toward and/or relationships with:

  1. Self

  2. People of opposite sex

  3. People of same sex

  4. Sex

  5. College life:

    (a) Academic aspect

    (b) Social life

    (c) Recreational activities

  6. Religion

  7. Future

    (a) Vocational

    (b) Avocational

(c) Familial

(d) Personal

When the 175 students were classified according to their degree of maladjustment the results shown in Table 2 were obtained.

The extremely subjective method of making this evaluation is obvious. When these results were analyzed in view of this admitted limitation, it was found that not one of the drawings done by the eight individuals classified as "very poor" would fall within the group of drawings that could be considered as "average drawings." As a matter of fact they varied so radically from the other drawings that they could easily be picked out as symptomatic of some problem being experienced by the drawer. Table 3 shows in how

TABLE 3
Deviations From the Average Drawings Found Upon Analysis of the Drawings of the Eight Individuals Having a Rating as "Very Poor" on the Adjustment Classifications

	Subjects							
	1	2	3	4	5	6	7	8
Location of drawings on the page	X		X	X		X	X	
Proportionate size of drawings	X	X	X	X		X		
Clothing Used	X	X						
Angle of head							X	
Angle of figure								
Treatment of hair	X				X	X	X	X
Treatment of feet	X	X	X				X	X
Treatment of hands	X			X			X	
Type of line used	X		X	X	X	X		
Significant erasures or shading		X	X	X	X	X	X	X
Significant use of symbols	X	X		X	X	X	X	X
Total number of deviations	8	5	5	6	4	6	7	4

TABLE 4

Degree of Personal Adjustment Found Among the Twenty-Two Students Having Drawings
With Three or More Deviations From the Expected Norm

Degree of adjustment	Number of deviations from "Normal" drawings								
	0	1	2	3	4	5	6	7	8
Good					XX	X			
Fair				XX	XXX				
Average				XX	X		XX	X	
Poor									
Very Poor					XX	XX	XX	X	X

many aspects these "very poor" drawings did differ.

When drawings have three or more deviations from the expected norm where sorted from the 175, it was found that three were classified as "good" adjustment, five as "fair," and the other 13 (64 per cent) "average" or "very poor." The results of this particular analysis are shown in Table 4.

In light of the writer's experiences during this preliminary study and in view of the results reported in this paper, it was concluded that the drawing of the human figure does give meaningful information about an individual even when the drawing is done in a group situation. A tentative criterion was established for judging a "normal" drawing. Any drawing having three or more deviations from this established "norm" could indicate need for more detailed consideration of the personal adjustment of the drawer.

There did appear certain advantages to this technique of using figure drawing which need further investigation (and such research is under way). For example, it may prove to be a rapid method of screening college students to pick out the ones who are experiencing difficulties, or who may be in need of referral to a counseling center for individual consultation. Also it may help to identify tensive situations (perhaps subconscious) which may be causing (or may cause in the future) personal adjustment problems. As a teaching technique it proved to be an excellent device to arouse interest in the study of the personality and to establish rapport conducive to learning.

Harold Seashore

THE IDENTIFICATION OF THE GIFTED

There isn't a teacher or parent who has not, at some time wondered—this child must truly be gifted—but how does one know? At what age is the superior child really identifiable?

The following article deals with the problems of a faculty who were anxious to identify the gifted children in their school. It shows that the need for a standard measure of criteria is great. Psychologists will be the first to utilize it to help advise parents and schools how to handle the child who is identified as gifted. Depending on the area of the child's talent, special plans and programs should be developed to help the child make the most of his outstanding ability.

It has been suggested that giftedness should not only be recognized by society but rewarded and supported by it. Some have suggested that a special government subsidy be given to schools to allow the best possible education and nurture of a child's talents.

Naturally, a philosophical question must be raised as to what to do with gifted children who are not interested in developing and using their capabilities, and/or who have families who are not interested. Should society take the responsibility for developing talents which, through personal ambivalence, might otherwise remain dormant? These, and other questions, are presented in this descriptive story of a faculty meeting on the problem of identifying the gifted child.

Stan Devian is a counselor in a junior-senior high school. There are two counselors. Mr. Devian is senior to his enthusiastic young colleague, Norm Curve. After getting a start in training through an NDEA Institute and then completing a standard MA program in Educational Counseling, Mr. Curve returned to the university for two more courses in measurement and statistics. Mr. Devian thinks counseling is so important that he has turned down two opportunities to become a principal.

Mr. Devian has been asked to chair a series of faculty meetings to bring about "a plan for providing better education for the gifted." After using that phrase at the opening session, he continued, subvocally, "Whatever that means. This will be a real go!"

The administrators and the teachers were genuinely concerned that something be done about the gifted. They were not sure what the program should be. Enrichment, acceleration, special projects, sectioning? They were agreed that there must be many gifted students in the school. As Miss Needler wryly explained, "After all, we're a typical school, half of our students must be above average, and three per cent in the upper three per cent."

But *who* are the gifted? The teachers said they knew from daily contact and looking at previous report cards. The director of research was sure he knew how to spot them: "I've got their grade placement ratings on last year's achievement test." But this challenge sparked the home economics teacher to voice her annual complaint that Dr. Trender never includes any tests of achievement

in home economics, which exchange brought Miss Needler back into the conversation. Looking at the director of physical education she remarked, "Coach, you're the only person who has had as much as thirty years of experience in picking the best two or three per cent of talented kids and excluding all others from *your* program for your kind of gifted. What would you do?" This was met with general silence.

After a brief ploy by Dr. Trender on the centrality of achievement in the basic subjects, most of the faculty agreed that average grade placement, or stanines, on arithmetic, reading and language skills would be *one* sound basis for identifying the gifted. One violent holdout, however, was Mr. Astroblo, a young science instructor, who had won local distinction but almost lost his job last spring. His prize pupil, affectionately named Rocky the Rocketeer, with an F in French and a year lag in reading performance, had blown up half the bleachers while getting a three-pound rocket 1425 feet in the air in less than eight seconds.

The principal thought that some consideration should be given to youngsters from deprived homes. Asked for definitions, he remarked, "We'll get at that later. Perhaps," he added, "we should also adjust the ratings for these kids to allow for inborn abilities not yet flowering." This suggestion, or at least the problem from which it arose, was deemed worthy of an extended faculty discussion in November, but no one could think of a sound

Adapted from the *Test Service Bulletin* of the Psychological Corporation, No. 50, June 1956.

procedure for implementing the idea just now.

After three sessions, the faculty had not agreed on who is gifted or how he should be identified. Mr. Devian realized that this rate of progress was about par for the course. Having attended symposia on giftedness at two conventions recently, he had acquired high tolerance for non-closure on the topic.

In October, the superintendent expressed concern that the state allowance for such projects would lapse "for lack of our capacity to answer a simple question: Who are our gifted – or talented – or academically able – or high capacity children? Let's cut through the middle of the problem with an operating decision. We can't make all the decisions right, but, on the whole, we can identify these unusual students one way or another. The simpler and more automatic the procedure the better." Speaking with his most administrative inflections, he turned to Mr. Devian. "Stan, why don't you and Norm Curve carry the ball? You've got intelligence tests on all these students. Can't we, by Thursday a week, have a list of the gifted – say, those in the highest three per cent in IQ – or anything you think best?" With a quiet sigh, Mr. Curve appreciated the "out" in the superintendent's trailing phrase.

The faculty sensed difficulties, but at least here were objectivity, precision, and, all in all, a quite defensible approach. Certainly you could explain straightforward rules to the PTA. Stan groaned a bit, which the faculty took as a protest over getting the job of working extra hours to spot the bright kids. Actually, his mind was gyrating with concepts he had learned well in graduate school, terms like individual differences, multipotentiality, multi-score ability tests, standard error of measurement, reliability, significance of differences.

Stan Devian and Norm Curve agreed to go right to work. In their school the ninth graders had just taken the *Differential Aptitude Tests*. There were neat rosters, in duplicate, and press-on labels were already in the cumulative files. Last week, the two men had begun poring over these rosters, mainly studying the profiles of the forty-seven boys who had been called under-achievers by the teachers last spring, the four boys who were under out-patient psychiatric care in the community clinic, the twelve boys who had skipped more than five days so far out of twenty-five school days – and so on.* There were even a dozen students classed as over-achievers, a topic which surely called for a technical discussion with the faculty about running faster than one can, about errors of scores, and about the 12-hour school day some youngsters live.

Lighting a cigarette, Norm quipped, "Let's give the class that famous 12-minute test. A few minutes – and we can just rank the 444 kids from top to bottom, chop off the 13.32 cases who are the upper three per cent." Chewing the soft wood of his electrographic pencil for a full minute, Stan mused, "But I'm still thinking about Rocky the Rocketeer who seems so bright but we can't keep him interested in verbal things. He'd be lucky to reach the 75th percentile on your bushel-basket verbal test."

"You're right, Stan, and for every Rocky you name, I can spot another youngster with an odd profile on the DAT who would be excluded from the boss's list if we only do a quick and dirty screening with wordy tests. But we've got the DAT profiles and it looks like both of us want to give the whole staff a stiff lesson in individual differences – both up and down each scale and sidewise across the ability spectrum. Let's dig in."

"Yeah, we can't lose. If we can't convince them that the term 'top three per cent in intelligence' is mostly meaningless, we can always fall back on rank order of students on a scholastic index. The VR + NA† score on the DAT would be as reasonable as any."

*There are girls in this school, but a lot of print space can be saved by writing "boys" instead of "boys and girls."
†VR + NA is a combined score based on the Verbal Reasoning and Numerical Ability subtests of the DAT battery. The two tests and the score combining them are good predictors of academic performance.

"While we're at it," said Norm, "let's raise serious questions about what mental ability is composed of. We don't need to include push-ups and chinning or soloing on the clarinet as components of mental ability, but with the DAT we can talk about some other variables which are socially and educationally relevant. By the way, I was looking at two profiles today which might illustrate something or other. Look at these. One happens to be Rocky the Rocketeer and this one is the chap who was generally recognized as the school genius last year. No one will argue that Pete isn't a brain, an all-around brain, too. He'll show up on the nomination sheets the teachers are going to give us. Doc Trender's grade placements will probably spot him. But now, look at Rocky—he's only at the 90th percentile on VR + NA. On the boss's quickie rule we're not even supposed to mention his name to the faculty! He's verbally weak—his VR actually is near the median, and his language skills eliminate him. But how, in all good conscience, can we escape calling him a special kind of brain? Look what he has! Old Trendy will say that we're reneging on our own knowledge about what the best predictors of academic grades are. So what! Rocky's got something; and if you want to put it in terms of Red, White, and Blue, he's got something Uncle Sam needs badly."

Nodding agreement, Stan added, "He's really an upper-three-percenter by some good logic—even if it may be in abilities we don't know how to teach for in this school. Our ways of grading for classroom performance don't permit him to scintillate in his 'course of study.' Maybe his verbal score is associated with the fact that his father and mother came to America just 16 years ago. Maybe we can boost his language abilities. If we could convince someone that Rocky is talented, really gifted, sombody might latch on to his best talents and make them a motivating force for upgrading even his lagging language skills."

A week later Stan Devian and Norm Curve had studied the DAT rosters, their eyes exophoric from focussing widely across the nine-column profile of each pupil. Each came up with a working list of names. But still they were not sure of a rationale for making final nominations. Stan, the senior man on the team, set the task.

"Our first screening could be this: All students who rank in the upper tenth on VR + NA will enter our pool of candidates for nomination as mentally gifted, possessing high academic talent. These we can say are the academically superior youngsters in grade 9; but their inclusion here doesn't mean we are going to predict they'll all be in the upper brackets when they go to college or try for advanced placement. Let's remember, a percentile rank of 90 on VR + NA in grade 9 is roughly equivalent to about 500–550 on V and M on the College Board SAT in grade 12. So this step will be picking out more than we need but at least we have a chance to give Rocky with his wiggly profile a chance at being tagged as meriting consideration for, say, accelerated math this year and the special physics course a couple of years from now. Then, among those we have thus spotted for test-estimated scholastic promise, let's look at the rest of the test profiles for over-all breadth of ability or some one or two other peaks."

"I was thinking in the same direction, Stan," said Norm. "To help me I made this table last night to put the boys in a sort of logical order. Group A shows the boys with VR + NA at the 99th percentile; there are 18 of them. Group B includes boys at the 97th percentile. In each group, I have ordered them roughly by the number of tests on which they ranked above 95 and 90. To reduce the numbers in the chart and to focus on the high points, I have written a plus sign if a boy's rank was under 90, but still high (percentile rank of 75, 80, or 85) and a minus sign when the rank was under 75. (I left out the Clerical score because it may not mean much for this purpose; we can come back to it when we talk with these boys individually.) Now obviously our boy Pete is top man. There are in all 13 who rank 90 or above in at least *five* of the *seven separate* scores we are considering. These are the all-around talented chaps. I say, let's include *all the ninety-niners* on our nomination list, even the five boys who rate 90 or better on only two to four of the seven scales. As you said, let's call them the very academically superior, *most* of whom also possess *breadth* of superiority."

While obviously agreeing, Stan expressed concern about individual differences even in this group who had just been declared intellectually homogeneous at the 99th percentile. "Just for the record, I submit that Nos. 17 and 18 are not the same kind of top one-percenters as are boys 1 to 13. But, OK, they're bright in anybody's book. What about the ninety-seveners — the boys who just reach the superintendent's 'practical decision' point?"

Curve dragged out more of his homework. "Well, I plotted profiles for a couple of these — Bill Brown and Stu Strong. Their patterns don't look alike, even though we'd agree that both are generally bright, on VR+NA, and probably should be in our list for some particular curricular projects. Who knows, maybe Bill's better abilities may be less important than the greater motivations of Stu. By the way, there's a problem we haven't faced yet. How many points of elevation and breadth of profiled abilities are equal to how many points of motivation, such as we've asked the teachers to take into account in making their nominations? And, a second needle: Do we plan different programs for Stu and Bill, if, as I guess, their interests are different?"

"I do hope the teachers understand, Norm, that their nominations to the 'pool of genius' are to be taken seriously. The boss's stress on *our* spotting the upper three per cent students may stifle the teachers. Let's pass the word today that we don't want to, and won't, make the decisions from the tests alone. The best reason for not having a rigid cutoff

score for classifying brilliance is that all the test scores and all the faculty opinions have an error term. Each score and each opinion indicates a region or a probability, not a point or a certainty. Let's get going! The question before the house now is: Are those at the 95th percentile brilliant? Let me give you a loaded pair of profiles. Look at Stu again. He qualifies on academic promise; he's 97 on a good predictor. Now look at Mike Lodge: he's Number 1 in Group C. He illustrates the point that life would be easier if we could really be happy with bureaucratically or legally defined minimum scores to define giftedness. Stu is in, he's 97; Mike is out, he's 95. But all in all, Mike looks good too. We'll have to explain to the staff that even if we have no satisfactory method of profile analysis, just studying the profiles of Mike and the others will cause us to consider both *elevation* of one score and *versatility* over several abilities. I wish we could put these two dimensions into a simple formula. Five of Mike's test scores are 90 or better as against three for Stu. Look at his nonverbal abilities.

"You know," Stan continued, "I'm against any system that counts Mike out of a program for generally superior students if it includes Stu. I can't say as much for *all* those in Group C, though. Look at C-16 — his 85 and 90 on VR and NA give him 95 on the combination score, but he hasn't another up to the 75th percentile."

The discussion went on about the boys with ranks of 90 on VR+NA. Each man admitted to the temptation of biasing the profiles upwards if he knew a boy was a serious student, an easy-to-live-with conformist, or an unusually talented basketball player. Especially challenging was Percy Stone: every test 80 or above, three at 95 or better, three others at 90, and a VR+NA rank of 90. Compared to Bill, Stu, and Mike, this chap too, they agreed, was generally superior.

Stan put it this way. "Surely Percy has a breadth of abilities which he should be able to develop and mobilize for any one of many intellectually demanding careers. If we had

TABLE I

PROFILES OF STUDENTS WHOSE DAT VR + NA SCORES ARE AT THE 99TH, 97TH, 95TH, AND 90TH PERCENTILES

Group A. VR + NA is at 99th percentile

Student	VR + NA	VR	NA	AR	MR	SR	LU-I	LU-II
1 (Pete)	99	99	99	97	90	99	99	99
2	99	99	95	95	95	95	95	95
3	99	97	99	97	90	95	97	99
4	99	99	97	97	90	97	95	95
5	99	95	97	97	90	95	99	95
6	99	97	97	95	95	95	+*	97
7	99	99	99	97	90	99	90	97
8	99	99	99	99	90	97	+	99
9	99	97	97	97	90	95	90	90
10	99	97	99	99	95	99	−	90
11	99	99	97	+	97	97	−	97
12	99	97	90	99	90	95	90	+
13	99	97	90	90	90	95	+	+
14	99	97	99	97	−	+	−	95
15	99	95	99	+	+	−	97	95
16	99	97	95	+	90	+	95	−
17	99	97	90	+	−	90	+	+
18	99	99	95	+	−	+	+	−

Group B. VR + NA is at 97th percentile

Student	VR + NA	VR	NA	AR	MR	SR	LU-I	LU-II
1 (Bill)	97	90	95	99	90	99	95	97
2	97	90	97	99	−	90	95	95
3	97	95	95	95	90	99	−	+
4	97	95	97	95	90	+	+	+
5	97	97	85	97	95	+	90	+
6	97	97	90	+	95	−	+	90
7	97	95	90	90	95	+	−	90
8	97	95	97	+	+	+	+	+
9	97	90	95	+	−	−	90	97
10 (Stu)	97	95	90	−	+	−	95	+
11	97	90	99	90	−	+	+	+

*To simplify the story, percentile ranks of 75, 80, and 85 on all but VR and NA are recorded here as + signs; percentile ranks under the 75th are recorded as − signs. Percentile ranks for Clerical Speed and Accuracy are omitted because of their general irrelevance for the selection of the intellectually gifted.

Group C. VR + NA is at 95th percentile

Student	VR + NA	VR	NA	AR	MR	SR	LU-I	LU-II
1 (Mike)	95	90	90	99	−	97	+	95
2	95	85	95	97	+	+	95	90
3	95	85	95	99	−	95	+	90
4	95	70	99	−	95	95	+	90
5	95	95	85	+	95	+	+	95
6	95	97	80	99	+	97	+	+
7	95	75	99	95	−	−	95	+
8	95	95	85	+	−	+	90	97
9	95	90	90	95	−	−	−	90
10	95	95	85	+	+	−	−	90
11	95	60	99	95	−	−	+	+
12	95	97	80	+	−	−	−	90
13	95	85	90	90	+	+	−	−
14	95	95	85	+	−	−	+	+
15	95	90	85	99	−	−	−	−
16	95	85	90	−	−	−	−	−

Group D. VR + NA is at 90th percentile

1 (Percy)	90	85	80	95	90	97	97	90
2	90	90	75	99	90	97	95	+
3	90	70	95	+	99	99	−	95
4 (Rocky)	90	55	99	95	99	97	−	−
5	90	97	45	90	+	+	95	+
6	90	85	80	97	+	97	−	+
7	90	85	85	95	+	−	90	90
8	90	90	85	97	+	+	+	90
9	90	85	90	97	90	97	−	−
10	90	70	95	+	90	95	−	−
11	90	80	90	97	−	90	−	+
12	90	85	90	+	95	−	+	+
13	90	85	85	95	−	95	−	−
14	90	80	85	97	−	+	+	+
15	90	85	80	90	−	+	−	+
16	90	75	90	−	−	−	+	90
17	90	85	80	−	−	+	−	90
18	90	85	85	+	−	+	+	−
19	90	90	75	+	−	−	−	+
20	90	85	85	−	−	−	−	+

norms based on a *total score* from all the DAT components, I guess he'd be in the 99th percentile on such an eight-test combination, but you know the reasons why the authors do not provide such a single score. One of them is to make us think about each case in differential detail rather than settle for a single index number, a sort of super-IQ. Some teachers tell me they hanker for the good old days, the one-score IQ days. If we show them some of these profiles we have been explaining to ourselves, maybe they'll understand better why a single composite test score at some predetermined level is not a satisfactory basis for identifying and understanding the gifted. We must help teachers to think about bright kids as being differently versatile. To do that, *breadth* of measurement is the key. For every generally superior kid who has a flat, high-level profile there are others with peaks and valleys."

At home that night, Stan's restlessness about the issue of who is gifted drove him to his study to think. After much thinking with pipe in hand, five pipe cleanings and 45 matches, he began to think with pencil in hand. The next morning he greeted Norm. "You know, Norm, identifying bright kids doesn't make much sense unless we know why we want to know who they are and what we can do about them. You and I are only part of this team which is committed to developing a better program in our school for the 'feeding and care of bright young things.' We're the psychometric boys, others are the curriculum makers, and somebody's even got to worry about the public relations aspects of a program for the gifted. When this selection job is done, we'll be expected to swivel our chairs around and become counselors to build fires under the cold geniuses, to help the intellectual flailers direct their energies, to show parents where their pride should be. Last night I was trying to pull together what I have learned about the *role of test scores* in this problem. I ended up with what I am hoping you will agree we can call 'The Counselor's Policy on Giftedness.' I guess no one will

agree with all of it, but, give or take a little, I'll stand on this statement of principles for use of ability tests in identifying the mentally superior, or the high potentials – you choose your term. Want to talk about it?"

Stan suggested that they read each principle and then haggle about its meaning, mainly because he wanted to be ready to handle any discussion in faculty meeting.

"Point one is a fine cliché, Stan, but it's got to be point one in any outline. OK, let's assume we have good goals and the community wants us to do something special for its intellectually gifted boys and girls. And, let's also assume there will be continuous refinement of goals."

Silently they read the next few points.

"Stop squirming, Norm. Before you clobber me for merely stating the obvious in point two, let me say that I don't believe we're going to end up with a clean and neat series of *unusual* educational sequences for the gifted. Let's assume there will be some variety in what the curriculum thinkers come up with and the budget department will finance. Our first job is to hold out against narrowness and rigidity of programs. Brilliant boys and girls do not display brilliance in the same patterns; let's insist on a program which is responsive to the range of individual patterns."

After a quarter hour of trying to tease out the operational bugs in a nomination procedure, Norm proposed that Stan have these points in mind for oral clarification: "First, most schools probably have informal nominating procedures, although 'voting in' and 'vetoing out' of pupils may sometimes be dominated by one or more prestigious, or just plain vocal, persons. Then, a school like ours, with 900 boys and girls in grade 9, certainly needs a formal procedure. Third, nominations by the various specialists and the teachers may be quite contaminated since some teachers have records of grade placement and ability tests in their class books; lunchroom and corridor talk among teachers about pupils surely raises the intercorrelations among their so-called independent nominations; and the climate of the school or departments within the school may be such that even a little nonconformity is equated to irresponsible trouble-making. Fourth, granted all this, a formal nomination system still greatly increases the probability that no unusually gifted child is omitted from consideration. For example, the objective tests will protect the interests of a bright but unliked and troublesome pupil who may find himself unlisted by the faculty; since pupils can 'goof' on tests, nominations by teachers can protect them from too much objectivity. Lastly, whatever we do, let's not make a plan which even suggests that the ultimate responsibility for developing these pupils we judge to have high abilities rests anywhere else than in the classroom."

The fourth point seemed fairly clear and obvious. Perhaps relevant was Norm's general concern that too many teachers and parents still seem to be "either-or" thinkers: Artistic talent and intellectual abilities are still thought by many to be negatively correlated in spite of the mass of evidence that in the matter of aptitudes, the so-called "law of compensation" is not valid.

Elaborating on his own fifth point, Stan said, "Sure, a one- or two-score IQ-type test could give us an over-all estimate of general level of ability which might be useful if all we want is gross classification. But multi-score aptitude batteries, just like multi-subject achievement batteries, can yield reliable differential information which will enrich the descriptions of students who are candidates for special attention. Considering the range and social utility of all the various human assets, fairly extensive multi-score testing schedules are justified. I believe you will agree, Norm, that we must come up with rather precise examples of the idea that talent is a many-splendored thing. Let's look again at that list of students' percentile ranks on the DAT. Why don't we mimeograph it and, to keep the argument objective, let's omit all the names, except for the few boys for whom you have drawn profiles. Then let's put the profiles on the opaque projector so all can see the point. And, later when we are helping the faculty write out their rules for nominating pupils, let's try to convince them that they might well engage in this same kind of thinking about their pupils' classroom performances, so that they, too, will nominate not only the verbal scholars but also those superior in other abilities. We might even get some nominations of budding basement chemists with bottom quarter sociability."

"And that isn't necessarily bad," added Curve, as he gave his final consent to the list of guidelines.

"That reminds me, Norm, we may have some problems with our roster of percentile ranks. I had a little hassle at lunch yesterday with Miss Alpha. You know, she's great on Greek culture but literally fears numbers. She can't quite see how a person who ranks at the 90th percentile on Verbal Reasoning and also on Numerical Ability can possibly be ranked at the 95th percentile on the combination score, VR+NA. She insists such a person's average rank of 90 must be his rank on the combination. I think I got the idea across that a fairly good clarinet player who is also a fairly good tap dancer is a more rare entertainer than is one who is fairly good on either but not on both. Now, our problem is this: How shall we set our cutoff scores on the parts of this battery to be sure we don't pass over both the less versatile pupil who scores extremely high on one or two tests and the more versatile student who may not be in the upper one or three per cent in any test but whose scores are generally high all across the profile?

"Norm, look again at your rank order listing. Group A, as a group, seems more gifted than Group B; and so also Group C, as a whole, seems more able than the D's. We could just settle for listing the 99's, the 97's, and maybe the 95's, keeping the list of boys ranking at 90 in our pocket for quick referral if anyone else proposes any of the names.

But, if we do that, then we're saying that the narrowly bright boys, like C-15 and C-16, are more gifted than are Percy, your D-1; Rocky who is D-4; and also D-2 and D-3, for instance. It seems to me that we must avoid just setting up a simple rank order list and chopping it off somewhere."

Norm had been doodling away at various times during the past hour. Passing a sheet to Stan, he said, in his best audio-visual voice, "These blobs are my idea of what our strategy should be. We, the aptitude test specialists, nominate a fairly large blob of students. So do the teachers. Incidentally, who is going to help them agree on how to make their composite list? Dr. Trender can identify a similar cluster of students from the achievement test results and scores, and the school clerk can provide the names of the top fifteen per cent in rank order on average grades. These overlapping blobs will include some students who are on all four lists – the real dark area in my sketch. There won't be perfect correlation among the nominators' lists; some areas will overlap more than others. I suspect the aptitude test list and achievement test list will overlap most. But any pupil who appears on all four lists surely could be labelled academically gifted without much further discussion."

Thinking of his committee chairmanship, Stan suggested that Norm use this sketch to show the faculty why each nomination list must include a considerably higher percentage of the class than the percentage the faculty thought should be included finally in a group of gifted for whom special courses could be arranged. "Incidentally," he remarked, "this sketch illustrates another case of the same problem I tried to explain to Miss Alpha yesterday. Suppose I suggest that each group bring in a list including ten to fifteen per cent of the class, hoping that when we study the overlapping, maybe five per cent will be on at least two out of four lists?"

Norm, pushing hard toward arriving at a precise plan, interrupted, "I was thinking that we might define three levels of decision.

I'd like to propose something like this: (1) All students nominated three or four times are to be called gifted and set aside for whatever program assignment we find appropriate for each in the light of all the information we have. (2) A student receiving two nominations is to be called gifted *unless* someone can advance information which is so convincing that the committee decides he should be excluded from special treatment, at least for the next term. (3) A student nominated on only one list *may* be included if his sponsors can convince the committee that he is intellectually unusual and well-motivated and deserves a try at the curriculum for the gifted, perhaps some one course for which he is unusually fitted."

"OK, Norm, that about winds up our chore with regard to our own list of nominees from aptitude tests and our ideas of a good procedure for integrating the information we get from the four sources of nominations. Incidentally, I'm sure some clever fellow in an electronic data processing center will tell us he could do this job faster and better. I'll agree – with some big *ifs*, the same iffiness which has forced us to use the human computer. The big *ifs* are these: If we knew all the variables, *if* we knew how to weight all the variables, *if* we knew how the ratings on all the variables were correlated, and *if* we had precise estimates of the errors in scores and judgments, *then* we might reduce the search for talent to punched card procedures."

"Well, fortunately, Stan, our decisions need not and, indeed, must not, be irreversible. I sincerely hope the continuing faculty evaluations and our counseling work with the gifted will result in some flow of students into these programs as evidence on the performance of our chosen gifted accumulates and as new evidence of unusualness appears for some late bloomers. Once this job of selection is done, we'll put on our other hats, assume our roles as counselors for educational and career planning and as consultants to the faculty on pupil motivation and adjustment in their programs. I'm sure quite a few of these intellectually gifted will need to clarify their images of themselves as potential scholars. Some of the leather-jacket, duck-haircut boys may even resist being identified as bright. Some parents may not have realized the dormant power in their little Dennis-the-Menaces. We'll need to do a job in guiding some through remedial programs to bolster their weaker skills. Golly, Stan, our work is never done. Now just as you've relaxed and feel you have completed our departmental task and your committee chairmanship is under control, let me toss you some more homework. Just to tease you a bit, and certainly not to suggest that these three boys meet high standards of academic promise, take a gander at Joe, Hank, and Bob. They are just a few of the boys in this school who rank low on VR+NA. They aren't 'college material' by any generally accepted definition, but each one has one or more high scores on the less verbal aptitudes reflected in Abstract Reasoning, Space Relations, and Mechanical Reasoning. I ask you, Stan, are they gifted?"

"All I can say, Norm, is that our school hasn't yet recognized that for every Indian chief we need a dozen competent Indians. For every new executive in an automated plant, we need a dozen guys who can set up, monitor, and fix the automations! I suspect our next big job, Norm, is to tell the faculty, administrators, the Board of Education, and the taxpayers about Joe, Hank, and Bob. But first we'd better get the gifted scholars off the ground!"

"Sure, Stan, just remember these kids have been waiting a long time while the geniuses and the retarded get center stage and lots of subsidy!"

Walter S. Olson

SOCIOMETRY AND THE SCHOOLS

For as long as there has been formal teaching, teachers have been applying principles of sociometry without perhaps being aware of it or using them to the best possible advantage.

The general literature has been reviewed by Mr. Olson and a practical application has been tested. His research points up the use that teachers and school personnel can make of the technique developed over the past few years by such leaders as Moreno and Redl. By trying a project with school-aged children, involving a number of teachers and hundreds of children, and by measuring change with a psychological measurement, results proved to be significant, and provided insights for both teachers and students by the use of the sociometric technique.

With considerable attention directed toward groups and group dynamics today, the professional should give thought to using some modification of the sociometric test to understand the relationships that exist within his group, to aid himself in gaining experience in recognizing the interactions within a group, and in manipulating these relationships and their resulting effects once they are recognized. Surprisingly, most of the investigators find that often the leader or teacher may be very wrong in assessing the emotional tone of a group and the attitudes that exist between members of the group; apparently only the participants can really reveal the inter-dynamics which need to be understood if they are to be used in bringing about desired change.

Once the teacher has had an opportunity to study the relative positions of various members of his class, he could then analyze what change might be made for the welfare of all concerned and then develop teaching methods to make these changes and alter the feelings of one student toward another. This may involve elaborate, long-term programs as attitudes do not change easily, rapidly, nor permanently. From time to time the same sociometric technique, perhaps in modified form, could be repeated to test for changes that might be occurring and to determine modifications in emphasis that should be made.

It has been suggested that an interesting and promising alteration of the plan reported by Mr. Olson, resulting from the conference with the staff of the project, would be to work out a structured observational plan within a relatively permanent group, one which is well acquainted and apt to be together for several months. Each member of the group would concentrate on observing and judging a limited number of the group, without anyone being aware of who was observing whom, and then detailed comments would be collected and compiled on each participant, without any means of identifying the source. Trial experience has indicated that such information should not be given directly to the subject involved as it was often found to be too threatening and ego-damaging, but rather it should be interpreted by the professional leader.

This idea, developed from Mr. Olson's work, bears further investigation and no doubt teachers and related professionals will profit additionally from this added technique once it is refined and the information published.

Sociometry can provide answers to many of the problems of social development, social inter-relatedness, and mental health in a school and in a counseling relationship.

Following the work of J. L. Moreno and Fritz Redl, considerable attention has been given to techniques for measuring and analyzing the inter-dynamics within groups. Sociometry is the most developed and most systematic tool for group measurement in the social sciences. It allows an inter-comparison of different groups' potentialities for satisfying their members' psychological needs. Business, industrial, military and educational institutions are well aware of the importance of harmonious and satisfying interpersonal relations in furthering *esprit de corps* and effectiveness within small groups. Programs oriented around human relations are springing up throughout the school systems.[1]

SOCIOMETRIC INSTRUMENTS

Psychologists have a great variety of test instruments from which to choose, and those that come closest to the sociometric instruments are the rating scales and value judgement inventories. Sociometry has an advantage over other types of rating scales in that it

is not necessary to train the raters. Peer groups are asked to evaluate their own members, and certainly no one knows better how a person feels than a member of the same group.

The use of this relatively simple device is not limited exclusively to the psychologist or counselor. It can also be used profitably by the classroom teacher with a minimum of instruction in its use and interpretation. Because of the simplicity of the test, and because no elaborate equipment is involved, the test can be used with confidence and without undue cost.

"It is easy to conceive of the sociometric test as a variety of rating scale – the members of the group are asked to rate or order the members of the group in terms of their attractiveness or desirability for sharing certain activities.

"The rater is asked to apply exactly those particular, unique, and sometimes irrational criteria he has spent a lifetime developing. Everyone is an experienced or expert rater when it comes to sociometric judgements. Each of us has a vast body of experience in deciding with whom we wish to interact and

1. Eric F. Gardner and George G. Thompson, *Social Relations and Morale in Small Groups*, New York: Appleton-Century-Crofts, Inc., 1956, p. 2.

whom we wish to avoid. Liking and disliking, accepting and rejecting are part of the process of daily living."[2]

MORENO'S SOCIOMETRIC TEST

Psychologists, teachers, and group social workers have come to rely on the sociometric measure to determine the attractions and repulsions within a group of people. Sociometric tests help these professionals and others giving the test to find a variety of specific facts and information.

The most important requirements of the sociometric test generally advocated by Moreno are:

1) The limits of the group should be indicated to the subject. The sociometric test places no restrictions on the persons within the group who may be chosen or rejected, but subject should clearly understand the nature of this group.

2) The subjects should be permitted an unlimited number of choices or rejections. They should be encouraged to choose as many or as few of the group members as they wish.

3) The subjects should be asked to indicate the individuals they choose or reject in terms of specific criteria. Each sociometric choice or rejection should be made with a particular activity in mind, and the activity should be meaningful to the subjects.

4) Results of the sociometric questions should be used to restructure the group. Moreover, the subjects should be told that their choices and rejections will play a decisive role in determining with whom they will associate in this activity.

5) The subjects should be permitted to make their choices and rejections privately, without other members of the group being able to identify the responses.

6) The questions should be gauged to the level of understanding of the members of the group. With older children and adults, the questionnaire form of presentation is usually appropriate. With younger children who are not yet facile with writing, individual reports to the administrator of the sociometric test may be most appropriate. With the very young and others who do not have adequate control of language, responses to a sociometric test may be meaningless, although other instruments may function effectively.[3]

OBSERVATION SYSTEMS OF SOCIAL BEHAVIOR

Many of the pioneers in the study of social behavior used children. Subsequently, a large number of observation systems have been developed applicable to the social behavior of children.

The procedure of measurement of ascendance-submission in children was developed in connection with an attempt to modify the social behavior of pre-school children, particularly along the dimensions of ascendance-submission. To determine whether a particular training technique was effective in modifying the incidence of ascendant behavior, it was necessary to develop measures of ascendance. After considerable preliminary work, eight categories of ascendant behavior were specified:

1. Verbal attempt to secure play materials.
2. Forceful attempts to secure play materials.
3. Success in securing play materials.
4. Defending, snatching back materials taken from his possession.
5. Verbal attempts to direct behavior of companion.
6. Companion complies with direction.
7. Forbidding, criticizing, reproving companion.
8. Providing patterns of behavior which companion imitates.[4]

2. Gardner Lindzey and Edna Borgatta, "Sociometric Measurement," Chapter 11, *Handbook of Social Psychology,* ed. Gardner Lindzey, Reading, Mass.: Addison-Wesley Publishing Co., Inc., 1954, p. 406.
3. *Ibid.,* p. 407.
4. Roger W. Heyns and Ronald Lippitt, "Systematic Observational Techniques," Chapter 10, *Handbook of Social Psychology, op. cit.,* p. 391.

ANDERSON'S OBSERVATIONAL TECHNIQUES

Anderson has worked with kindergarten and young children as a basis of his research in the study of the behavior of children and teachers. The observational techniques that he developed have two concepts: domination and integration. To test and measure them, he developed an instrument for observing the interaction of children and teachers, and the dominative and integrative behavior in teachers' behavior toward children.

ANDERSON'S CATEGORIES OF DOMINATION AND INTEGRATION BEHAVIOR[5]

TEACHER SYSTEM

Domination

Determines a detail of activity or acts for the child in carrying out a detail

Direct refusal

Relocating, repeating, or placing children in different relations to each other or to property

Postponing, slowing up the child

Disapproval, blame, or obstruction

Warning, threats, or conditional promises

Calls to attention or group activity

Rations material

Lecture method (defining a problem or anticipating a question)

Questions lecture method (one answer questions)

Perfunctory questions as statements (indifference)

Integration

Approval

Accepts difference

Extends invitations to activity

Question or statement regarding child's expressed interest or activity

Build up (helps child to better definition or solution without giving final answer)

Participates in joint activity with children

Gives sympathy

Gives permission

CHILDREN SYSTEM

Integrative

Shows common purpose by word or action (includes attempts to cooperate and attempts to share or participate)

Verbal request or suggestion to direct companions' behavior or secure materials

Complies with request or suggestion

Sets pattern including gestures which companion imitates

According to Anderson, domination is that behavior which represents resistance to differences, change, and growth. A person with this pattern of behavior is rigid, stubborn, inconsiderate of others and often has preconceived ideas. He expresses fear of impending change by being authoritarian and autocratic, by bullying, threatening, shouting, and using physical force. Anderson classifies integration as behavior which indicates permissiveness, acceptance, approval, and sympathy. Integrated individuals accept children for what they are without preconceived prejudices or inhibitions.

APPLICATIONS IN SCHOOL SETTINGS

Teachers have long been looking for a technique that would help them better understand their students and the interaction within their classrooms. Group dynamics has become the focal point of much educational and psychological research and attention. Not only is the teacher often not aware of how students feel about each other, but also once the teacher becomes aware of this fact, he is not able to appraise changes that may occur within a group. Sociometrics does give the teacher a device needed to evaluate interaction among students and changes in attitudes and relationships over a period of time. Once aware, he can better provide the necessary setting and structure to bring about personal and educational growth and development.

The technique itself shows the students a sincere interest on the part of the teacher in their feelings and attitudes. It provides a

5. Anderson, H. H. "Domination and Social Integration in the Behavior of Kindergarten Children and Teachers." *Genetic Psychological Monograms*, XXI, No. 3 (1939), p. 285.

means for each student to become involved in the group structure and process.

"Not only do schools present groups that are well designed to facilitate the use of sociometric measures, but also many of the problems faced by teachers and school administrators can be approached constructively through the use of sociometric measures. Thus, formation of cohesive, smooth-working groups is facilitated by information that the sociometrist can provide. The task of sensitizing the teacher to the existence of interpersonal difficulties within her classes is facilitated by sociometric data, and efforts to combat these difficulties can be appraised through the use of sociometric measures. Further, and perhaps most important, these same techniques provide an excellent means of identifying the child whose relations with his classmates are sufficiently defective to suggest the likelihood of more serious difficulties in the future. In general, sociometric measures may serve equally well the functions of improving normal interpersonal relations within the classroom and of diagnosing failures of interpersonal adjustment which may become the psychiatric casualties of a later period.

"In a paper, Moreno discussed the results of sociometric testing in a public elementary school, indicating the possibility of reassignment and also reporting surprising inaccuracy on the part of the teachers in judgements of the choice status of the students. The fallibility of the teacher as a judge of student relations indicates the importance of sociometric techniques.

"A number of additional studies indicate that teachers' judgements, although variable in terms of the particular judge and the age of the students being evaluated, are not highly sensitive to individual differences in social acceptance. In particular, the teacher seems unable to discriminate effectively the objectives of main interest – the individual who receives a very low proportion of social choices. The teacher tends to overestimate the choice status of children they like and to underestimate that of children they dislike."[6]

AN EXPERIMENTAL APPROACH TO DETERMINE PRACTICAL APPLICATION OF SOCIOMETRICS

To determine the practicality of using sociometry, five elementary school classes and their teachers were involved over a one-year period and in addition two groups in a city park recreational program were also included. The teachers and park supervisor involved met and carefully reviewed, under supervision of the director, the general research available in the literature concerning sociometry. All of the teachers had degrees in education, psychology, sociology or recreation and many had additional graduate work in their field. All excepting one were experienced by more than 5 years; one was a new teacher.

The classroom children were either 5th or 6th graders and those in the recreation programs ranged from eleven to sixteen years with an average age of 12.2 years. At the beginning of the academic year, after about 2 weeks, during which time the teacher and our supervisor and participants became acquainted, a simple sociometric test was given. It was worded in such simple terms that even the most academically limited could understand, and it was explained orally and in detail by the adult leader. Based on these tests, the traditional sociometric diagrams were drawn, and again the leader-participants conferred and discussed the meaning of the results obtained. Based on this information, each leader worked with various individuals in his or her group so as to help the isolates and help those who had particular problems or conflicts. At the end of the first semester the same procedure was repeated with slight variations in the questions. The changes in sociometric configuration were noted and discussed in a group situation among the leaders. Again their added insight was applied to their teaching and direction of their group, and the testing procedure was

6. Lindzey and Borgatta, *op. cit.*, pp. 436–437.

repeated approximately three weeks prior to the finish of the spring semester.

Considerable movement was noted on the part of many individuals within the group structure, and a California test of Personality which was given at the beginning of the semester in September and repeated in the spring, in general, showed marked improvement in the personal adjustment of the majority of students. The greatest improvement was noted in almost every case of the individuals who were identified by the test as isolates in September. By the end of the year, they were somewhat involved in intergroup relations. It was the unanimous feeling on the part of the leaders that the insight given to them by use of the sociometric technique was one of the prime reasons for the apparent improvement in the adjustment of the individuals concerned. It is recognized that considerable subjective evaluation was made and it was suggested by the group that further measurements of adjustment and other criteria in addition to the California test be applied at the end of the semester to determine change. However, it was agreed that sociometry had made a significant contribution to the situation.

CONCLUSION

Social relations information is needed to help pupils in achieving better social interaction. Pupils who have not been socially accepted by their classmates can be found and helped by using social relations information. Frequently, teachers have to talk to the school staff or parents about their pupils' problems. If there is concrete information on pupil adjustment, it is much easier to discuss and very often help the child. The teacher can provide useful information because she is with her pupils a long period of time. This information can be useful to counseling and psychologists in helping the children.

Jerome E. Doppelt and George K. Bennett

TESTING JOB APPLICANTS FROM DISADVANTAGED GROUPS

Psychologists continue their efforts to develop more exacting and more useful instruments for the measurement of experimental data. Psychological test specialists still have a long way to go to reach a comparable advantage in statistical measurements available to those in such related professions as medicine. However, progress is rapidly being made and more time and money is constantly being directed into research aimed at producing the best possible specialized test instruments.

Some of the specific charges frequently leveled at various test instruments and their uses are discussed in the following article. Doppelt and Bennett have given particular emphasis to the problems of testing disadvantaged groups. Their points are pertinent to their experiments but also apply to much of testing in general. This study points to the pressing need to develop better testing techniques to supply meaningful and accurate measurements for the psychologist, teacher, and professional counselor.

Every day people make decisions which affect the lives of other people. When tests play a role in the decision process, considerable feeling may be engendered, not only among those directly concerned but among the "spectators" as well. Those of us who have been seriously concerned with improving the effectiveness of tests have been aware of their limitations and of circumstances which may diminish their usefulness. We have long recognized, for example, that a test of mental ability does not measure native ability but rather it measures the individual's present capability of demonstrating his skills or knowledge. From this demonstration one can then estimate the individual's likelihood of success in certain endeavors.

It would be a formidable task to discuss the pros and cons of testing in all the fields in which decisions are, or might be, influenced by tests. We will limit this discussion, therefore, to an area of importance to all of us – the use of tests in the employment of people who are members of "disadvantaged groups."

The term "disadvantaged groups," as used in this discussion, refers to the subgroups in our population who have been victims of educational, cultural, or economic disadvantages. The deprivations suffered by people in such groups are assumed to stem primarily from their membership in the groups. Several observations may be made about the term "disadvantaged groups." First, it seems to be an ethnic or national-origin classification. Negroes and Puerto Ricans are usually included among the disadvantaged; so are Mexican-Americans and Indians. Second, there are subgroups of the white majority who are economically and educationally disadvantaged, but the term is seldom applied to them. Third, the term conveys the impression of a group that is homogeneous with respect to ability and deprivation, in spite of the fact that its members usually show a range in abilities and interests. Of course, this range may be restricted when compared with that of the general population.

Employment decisions require the making of predictions, whether the latter are made from mathematical equations or by intuition. We are concerned, therefore, with problems in predicting job success from the test scores of disadvantaged persons. It has been proposed that procedures which are suitable for a majority of applicants are not appropriate for those who may be described as educationally or culturally deprived. This may possibly be so, but one must guard against oversimplified solutions to a complex problem. Naïve solutions which are applied equally to all members of a disadvantaged group (or to different groups of disadvantaged) are likely to be ineffective, and may even create new problems of undesirable discrimination. Let us consider some of the charges leveled against tests in this context, and evaluate some suggested corrective measures.

SOME OF THE CHARGES

Anxiety in the Testing Situation. A frequent criticism is that many existing tests do not adequately evaluate the capabilities of members of disadvantaged groups. It is pointed out that the disadvantaged may score poorly because of anxiety about the testing situation and because of low motivation. It is also felt that examiners from the "advantaged" population tend to inhibit the performance of the disadvantaged. This is more likely to be a problem when individual tests rather than group tests are administered, and when the examinees are children rather than job applicants. Even in employment offices, however, it is still a problem.

Unfairness of Content. It is further maintained that most existing tests, especially verbal measures, emphasize middle-class concepts and information and are therefore unfair to those who have not been exposed to

From the *Test Service Bulletin* of the Psychological Corporation, No. 57, May 1967.

Jerome E. Doppelt and George K. Bennett 313

middle-class cultural and educational influences. Consequently, the low test scores which are earned are not indicative of the "true" abilities of the disadvantaged. Predictions of job success made from such scores are therefore held to be inaccurate.

Improper Interpretation of Scores. There is the contention that scores do not have the same meaning for the disadvantaged that they do for the advantaged. Both the pattern of scores (when a battery is used) and the level of performance (on even a single test) require interpretation in the light of the background of the examinee. It is argued, however, that for interpreting the scores of disadvantaged persons the usual kinds of background evaluation are not enough. Test scores of the disadvantaged, it is held, should be compared only with test scores of others similarly disadvantaged. In this way, a score which would be considered mediocre, according to norms based on a national sample, might be considered superior when compared with the performance of a particular deprived group.

Lack of Relevance. It is charged that test items are often not related to the work required on the job for which the applicant is being considered, and that even where relationships can be shown between test scores and job success, there is no need to eliminate low-scoring disadvantaged people since they can be taught the necessary skills and knowledge in a training period after hiring. In addition, some critics feel that bias against disadvantaged groups frequently enters into the performance ratings which serve as the criteria for validating the tests, and this artificially confirms the gloomy predictions made from the scores. Thus, the picture is one of a self-fulfilling prophecy of doom for the disadvantaged.

MEETING THE CRITICISMS

In response to these charges, reasonable people generally offer suggestions which they believe will make the tests "fairer" rather than demand that all testing cease. Eliminating tests entirely would remove from the hiring process an approach which is potentially more objective, more color-blind, and more susceptible to verification as to effectiveness than most of the other techniques used in the employment procedure. As John W. Gardner, the present Secretary of Health, Education, and Welfare, wrote in the book *Excellence*[1] in reference to testing in schools: "The tests couldn't see whether the youngster was in rags or in tweeds, and they couldn't hear the accents of the slum. The tests revealed intellectual gifts at every level of the population." More is to be gained from the proper use of tests than from their exclusion; accordingly, some of the corrective measures that have been offered should be carefully scrutinized.

METHODS OF ALLEVIATING ANXIETY

To allay test anxiety it has been suggested that if an examinee has failed, he be permitted to come back for one or more retests. It is alleged that this procedure would provide the practice in taking tests which is so lacking among the disadvantaged.

Where the test requires demonstration of proficiency, as in typewriting, the test is a sample of the actual skill required for the job, and practice by the applicant between testings would only tend to improve his real skill. The administration of a form that may have been given previously would not result in distorted interpretations of his current typing skill, although it is preferable to have alternate forms available for retesting.

With a general ability test, however, permitting applicants to take it again and again, as a means of reducing anxiety, has serious consequences. Retests are sometimes sought by individuals who hope to become familiar with the nature of the specific test and, consequently, to do better on the retest. If the

1. New York: Harper & Bros., 1961. Pp. 48–49.

same form of a test is administered more than once within a short time period, practice between testings is likely to result not in improved general ability that would be pertinent to success on the job, but rather in improved scores which may simply be due to practice in remembering answers to specific questions. Furthermore, the examinee may have searched for outside help to provide answers to some items. The validity of scores obtained under such conditions is suspect.

Nevertheless, people who wish to be retested should probably be given the opportunity to take the test or tests again, but any test which is to be given to the same people more than once should have alternate forms. Although the availability of two or three forms of a test is not uncommon, the preparation of a large number of forms is a time-consuming and expensive process. In addition to alternate forms of the *same* test, it would be desirable to have *different* tests, each with several forms, available for testing and retesting. Of course, studies which establish the comparability of scores on the different tests used would be essential.

It is apparent from the discussion above that the successive administration of "real tests" over a short time interval is not always a practical procedure for allaying test anxiety. Rather, it is preferable to provide a practice or demonstration period in which different kinds of tests and answer media are discussed. This kind of activity can alleviate the unfamiliarity and dispel some of the fear of the unknown about the testing situation without compromising any "real tests." In response to this need, The Psychological Corporation has been developing a presentation on tape, accompanied by a practice booklet,[2] to acquaint students and others who might soon be applying for jobs with some of the common types of employment tests. If this approach proves useful, schools and employment offices may find it an economical way to eliminate one source of concern.

As a means of reducing the role of the live examiner in the testing situation, the use of recorded directions to administer actual tests, with both the reading of directions and the timing included on the tape or record, has been suggested. The advantages of such uniform administration are obvious. Moreover, the use of tapes may be more acceptable to those who tend to feel uncomfortable when the examiner is a member of a different group.

Diminishing Cultural Bias

Either because of their content or style, there are some types of test questions which provoke charges of cultural bias from well-meaning persons even when such charges may have little basis in fact. If it is possible to achieve the purpose of the testing by using measures which do not contain such provocative items, it is manifestly desirable to do so, regardless of the merits of the charges. Many of those who feel that existing tests are too loaded with "middle-class" items to be fair to disadvantaged groups propose "culture-free" or "culture-fair" tests as substitutes. The term "culture-free" is misleading; no instrument which measures behavior can be free of cultural influences. What is sought are "culture-fair" or "cross-cultural" or "culture-common" tests which are measures based on experiences equally familiar or unfamiliar to advantaged and disadvantaged groups. It is often suggested that verbal tests should be replaced by nonverbal measures in order to eliminate cultural bias. However, the preponderant weight of research evidence indicates that nonverbal tests do not measurably benefit disadvantaged groups. In most instances, the disadvantaged score no better on nonverbal or so-called "culture-fair" tests than they do on conventional tests.

Perhaps the answer lies in trying to obtain the "culture-laden" rather than the "culture-free" test. The purpose of employment test-

2. *Test Orientation Procedure (TOP).* See page 8.

ing is to select people who ultimately will be successful in one or more jobs. The jobs are inevitably embedded in some cultural matrix, and the criteria of success will undoubtedly be influenced by cultural factors. Thus the abilities to understand oral and perhaps written instructions, to go from one place to another in a reasonable manner, and to cope with simple arithmetic, are activities which are "culture-laden" but which are also likely to be criterion-related. Such behaviors have their parallels in everyday living and can be translated into test questions which are not unfair to disadvantaged applicants.

Prompted by such considerations, a series of tests entitled *Fundamental Achievement Series* is being developed by The Psychological Corporation. The series includes verbal and numerical tests, with many of the items in each test based on "culture-laden" experiences assumed to be quite common in the population.

Investigation of Bonuses and Separate Norms

To compensate the disadvantaged for the effects of deprivation they have experienced, various devices have been proposed to adjust their test scores. One suggestion is that raw score points be given as a bonus, a procedure apparently similar, though not truly comparable, to the awarding of bonus points to veterans taking a civil service examination. Aside from the problems of determining who should be given a bonus and how much bonus, making the award is a discriminatory act which adds nothing to the essential predictive value of the test.

The position that test scores of the disadvantaged should be compared only with the scores of others similarly disadvantaged can become, in some circumstances, a special case of awarding a bonus. Norms based on the disadvantaged provide useful descriptive information and, together with norms for the majority group, the data could be helpful to counselors and psychologists who are advis-

ing individuals. But if a separate cutoff score is established for each norm's group, in order to yield the same percentage of acceptable cases from the different groups, we have essentially the situation of giving bonus points to the lower-scoring groups.

These approaches to the problem of employing the disadvantaged have little value in selection. Adoption of such procedures would place a burden on the civilian employer which is not undertaken by either the civil service or the military agencies of the United States. It is clearly the obligation of an employer not to discriminate among persons on the grounds of race, religion, or national origin, but it is clearly not the obligation of an employer to hire or to promote the less qualified in an attempt to compensate for some injustice of society in general.

When there is adequate evidence that test scores have different meanings for different groups, an improvement in accuracy of prediction may result from the use of weightings which would be optimum for each group. Experience to date has not revealed frequent occasions for such differential weighting.

Appropriate Use of Test Scores

All of us recognize the importance of the training or apprenticeship period in developing the skills needed for certain kinds of jobs. Some have maintained that during the training period conducted by a company for newly hired people, the disadvantaged can be taught what they need to know, regardless of their scores on the employment tests. Therefore, it is argued, the administration of tests which include questions that have little to do with the job is unjustified. This argument deserves serious examination. Certainly, skills and knowledge can be imparted to motivated people during a training period, and efforts in this direction should be encouraged. Usually such training is more successful for relatively simple jobs which require few skills and operations than for higher level jobs which call for a broader spectrum of previously developed talents. But even in training situations, tests will ordinarily predict the ability to learn *about* the job while on the job, or the ability to complete the necessary training. Many companies would like to hire people who can be promoted to better jobs after they have mastered the entry job. Tests which measure general ability—as reflected in verbal and numerical aptitude—are helpful in identifying applicants who would be suitable for promotion in the future. It is important to remember that tests which seem unrelated to immediate jobs might be useful in identifying those who could advance to higher levels.

Tests, like other predictive instruments, must be evaluated in terms of how well predictions made from them conform with reality as represented by measures of success on the job (criteria). Without an adequate criterion, meaningful and free of bias, it will be difficult for anyone to know what predictors are effective. It is obvious to professional users of tests that criteria must be studied and refined; others may occasionally need a reminder not to forget the criteria while they are busy attacking the predictors.

SUMMING UP

Companies have been accused of using tests as a means of maintaining unfair discrimination against groups which have already suffered from many forms of discrimination. Such practices are a distortion of the proper function of tests and deserve condemnation. It does not follow, however, that tests themselves merit condemnation. Most users in industry expect the tests to help them identify the people best suited for the jobs to be filled.

From the standpoint of corporate management, the employment function can legitimately be viewed as a type of purchasing operation. It then is the duty of the employment manager to hire those candidates who offer the best promise of contributing to the success of the enterprise. The reason that tests have been used for many years by many employers is that, in management's opinion, the information furnished by tests is valuable in making hiring decisions. If the employer sets his minimum scores too high he does not fill the available jobs. If he sets his minimum scores too low he hires persons difficult to train, low in productivity, and high in liability to error. Sophisticated personnel officers realize that predictors such as interviews, reference investigations, and tests are part of a total evaluation problem, that of obtaining better workers or of matching workers and jobs more precisely.

Whenever the number of applicants exceeds the number of job openings, some applicants will be rejected. This is one of the hard facts of life. It is not surprising that those who are rejected sometimes attack the selection procedures on the grounds that these are invalid or unfair. Although testing is not free from defect or beyond criticism, appropriately chosen and properly administered ability tests are superior to most available alternatives.

Some of the problems which stem from the testing of disadvantaged groups are of a technical nature and are not related to the issue of discrimination. Reduced reliability is often due to the fact that score distributions obtained from disadvantaged groups are compressed. The same compression (and reduced reliability) is also found when only highly capable individuals are being tested. These problems require technical study and, in some instances, may call for the use of different measures or the development of new and more appropriate tests. The basic issue is not necessarily one of discrimination against a particular subgroup.

Many of the issues in the testing of disadvantaged groups have both psychometric and social aspects. Some of the current testing procedures should be changed to reduce the fear and hostility that may be engendered by materials felt to be biased or unfair. More attention must be devoted to research with actual score and performance data in order to improve the predictive efficiency of tests. Such changes in employment and research procedures will increase the likelihood of employment tests fulfilling their primary mission of helping the employer select the people best able to do the jobs. These approaches are basically psychometric steps.

Discrimination against disadvantaged groups, which is at the root of the concern of many who attack tests, will not be resolved by improved psychometrics alone. Discrimination in the world of work is a social ailment. Although poor showings on tests may be a symptom of the ailment, the use of tests in employee selection is inherently a friendly rather than a hostile act to those who come to the job market from backgrounds of limited opportunity. Society may well have the responsibility of providing effective remedial instruction for those who have been culturally deprived. The rejection of measuring instruments which register the consequence of such deprivation is merely a modern version of killing the messenger who brings bad news.

SELECTED BIBLIOGRAPHY

"Creativity and Children," by Keith Bailey

Anderson, Harold H. *Creativity and Its Cultivation*. New York: Harper & Row, Inc., 1959, 279.

Arieti, Silvano. "The Rise of Creativity: From Primary to Tertiary Process," *Contemporary Psychoanalysis*, I, no. 51 (1964), 58–64.

Arieti, Silvano. "Creativity and Its Cultivation: Relation to Psychopathology and Mental Health," in *American Handbook of Psychiatry*, vol. 3. Edited by S. Arieti. New York: Basic Books, Inc., 1966. 722–741.

Freud, Sigmund. *The Interpretation of Dreams*. New York: Basic Books, Inc., 1960.

Freud, Sigmund. "The Unconscious," *Collected Papers of Sigmund Freud*, vol. IV, no. 84. New York: Basic Books, Inc., 1959, 92–105.

Freud, Sigmund. "Wit and Its Relation to the Unconscious," *The Basic Writings of Sigmund Freud*. Edited by A. A. Brill. New York: Modern Library, 1938.

Freud, Sigmund. "Psychopathology of Everyday Life," *The Basic Writings of Sigmund Freud*. Edited by A. A. Brill. New York: Modern Library, 1938.

Jung, Carl G. "The Archetypes and the Collective Unconscious," *Collected Works*. New York: Pantheon Books, 1959.

Maslow, Abraham H. *Motivation and Personality*. New York: Harper & Row, Inc., 1954.

Peters, R. S. *The Concept of Motivation*. New York: Humanities Press, Inc., 1958.

Piaget, Jean. *The Origins of Intelligence in Children*. New York: International Universities Press, Inc., 1956.

Schachtel, Ernest G. "The Development of Focal Attention and the Emergence of Reality," *Psychiatry*, XVII, no. 309 (1954), 309–324.

Schachtel, Ernest G. *Metamorphosis: On the Development of Affect, Perception, Attention, and Memory*. New York: Basic Books, Inc., 1959.

Scheler, Max. *Man's Place in Nature*. Boston: Beacon Press, 1961.

Simon, Alexander, Herbert, C. C., and Strauss, R., eds. *The Physiology of Emotions*. Springfield, Illinois: Charles C. Thomas, Publisher, 1961.

Stolnitz, J. "On the Origins of 'Aesthetic Disinterestedness,'" *Journal of Aesthetics and Art Criticism*, XX, no. 131 (1961), 18–106.

Taylor, Calvin W., and Barron, Frank. *Scientific Creativity: Its Recognition and Development*. New York: John Wiley & Sons, Inc., 1963.

"Psychology and Musical Talent," by Leonard Simutis

Bentley, Arnold. *Measures of Musical Ability.* New York: October House, Inc., 1966.

Diserens, C. N., and Fine, H. *A Psychology of Music: The Influence of Music on Behavior.* Cincinnati: The College of Music, 1939.

Drake, Raleigh. *Drake Musical Aptitude Tests.* Chicago: Science Research Associates, 1954.

Farnsworth, Paul R. *The Social Psychology of Music.* New York: The Dryden Press, 1958.

Gaston, E. Thayer. *Test of Musicality.* Lawrence, Kansas: Odell's Instrumental Service, 1942. Rev. ed., 1957.

Gordon, Edwin. *Musical Aptitude Profile.* Boston: Houghton Mifflin Company, 1965.

Kwalwasser, Jacob. *Kwalwasser Music Talent Test.* New York: Mills Music, Inc., 1953.

Kwalwasser, Jacob, and Dykema, Peter W. *Kwalwasser-Dykema Music Tests.* New York: Carl Fischer, Inc., 1930.

Lundin, Robert W. *An Objective Psychology of Music.* New York: Ronald Press Company, 1953. 2nd rev. ed., 1967.

Mursell, James L. *The Psychology of Music.* New York: W. W. Norton & Co., Inc., 1937.

Revesz, Geza. *Introduction to the Psychology of Music.* Translated from the German by G. I. C. de Courcy. Norman: University of Oklahoma Press, 1954.

Schoen, Max. *The Psychology of Music.* New York: Ronald Press Company, 1940.

Seashore, Carl E. *Psychology of Music.* New York: McGraw-Hill Book Company, 1938. New York: Dover Publications, Inc., 1967.

Seashore, Carl E. *Seashore Measures of Musical Talent.* Chicago: C. H. Stoelting & Co., 1919. Rev. ed., 1960.

Seashore, Carl E. *The Psychology of Musical Talent.* New York: Silver Burdett Company, 1919.

Tilson, Lowell. *Tilson-Gretsch Musical Aptitude Test.* Chicago: Fred Gretsch Mfg. Co., 1941.

Wing, Herbert D. *Wing Musical Aptitude Test.* London: National Foundation for Educational Research, 1939. Rev. ed., 1961.

"Effects of Maternal Deprivation," by Rudolph Deyle

Bakwin, H. "Loneliness in Infants," *American Journal of Diseases of Children,* LXIII (1942), 30–40.

Bettelheim, B., and Sylvester, E. "A Therapeutic Milieu," *American Journal of Ortho-psychiatry*, XVIII (1948), 191–206.

Bowlby, J. "Maternal Care and Mental Health," *World Health Organization*, Monograph series, no. 2 (1952), 66–68.

Crow, L., and Crow, A. *Child Development and Adjustment*. New York: The Macmillan Company, 1962.

Fisher, L. "Psychological Appraisal of the Unattached Preschool Child," *American Journal of Orthopsychiatry*, XXIII (1953), 803–814.

Goldfarb, H. "The Effects of Early Institutional Care on Adolescent Personality," *Child Development*, XIV (1943), 213–223.

Goldfarb, H. "Infant Rearing and Problem Behavior," *American Journal of Orthopsychiatry*, XIII (1943), 249–265.

Harlow, H., and Harlow, M. "The Effect of Rearing Conditions on Behavior," *Bulletin of the Menninger Clinic*, XXVI (1962), 213–224.

McClelland, D., Atkinson, J., Clark, R., and Lowell, E. *The Achievement Motive*. New York: Appleton-Century-Crofts, 1953.

Rheingold, H. "The Modification of Social Responsiveness in Institutional Babies," *Monograph, Society for Research in Child Development*, XXI, no. 63 (1956).

Rheingold, H., and Bayley, N. "The Later Effects of an Experimental Modification of Mothering," *Child Development*, XXX (1959), 363–372.

Rhodes, W., and Matthews, P. "Combatting Maternal Deprivation," *Children*, IV, no. 2 (1957), 54–60.

Rogers, C. *On Becoming A Person*. New York: Houghton Mifflin Company, 1961.

Sears, R., MacCoby, E., and Levin, H. *Patterns in Child Rearing*. New York: Harper & Row, Inc., 1957.

Senn, Milton J. E. "Fads and Facts as the Bases of Child-Care Practices," *Children*, IV, no. 2 (1957), 43–47.

Spitz, R. "Hospitalism," in *Psychoanalytic Study of the Child*, vol. 1. Edited by O. Fenichel. New York: International University Press, 1945, 53–74. vol. 2, 1946, 113–117.

Witmer, H. L., Yarrow, L. J., Ainsworth, M. D., and Glaser, K. *Maternal Deprivation*. New York: Child Welfare League of America, 1962.

"Crisis in the Education of the Handicapped," by Frances Mullen

Baller, W. *Antecedents of Change in Mentally Retarded Persons at Mid Life*. Washington: Vocational Rehabilitation Administration, 1965.

Dunn, L. M. "A Comparison of the Reading Processes of Mentally Retarded Boys of the Same Mental Age" in L. M. Dunn and R. J. Capobianco, *Studies of Reading and Arithmetic in Mentally Retarded Boys.* Monograph, Society for Research in Child Development, XIX, no. 1 (1954), 7–99.

Frazee, Vernon. "Implementation of House Bill 1407," in *Community Day Centers for the Mentally Retarded,* Proceedings, Third Annual Meeting of Executive Directors. Springfield: Illinois Department of Mental Health, 1966.

Jordan, T. E. *The Mentally Retarded.* 2nd ed. Columbus, Ohio: Charles E. Merrill Books, Inc., 1966.

Kennedy, R. J. R. *A Connecticut Community Revisited: A Study of the Social Adjustment of a Group of Mentally Deficient Adults in 1948 and 1960.* Washington: U.S. Office of Vocational Rehabilitation, 1962.

Kirk, Samuel A. *Early Education of the Mentally Retarded.* Urbana: University of Illinois Press, 1958.

Kirk, Samuel A. "Research in Education," in Stevens and Heber, *Mental Retardation: A Review of Research.* Chicago: University of Chicago Press, 1964.

Mackie, Romaine. "Spotlighting Advances in Special Education," *Exceptional Children,* (October 1965), 77–81.

Mackie, Romaine. *Special Education Enrollments and Number of Teachers.* Washington, D.C.: Office of Education Leaflet OE 35066, April 1965.

President's Panel on Mental Retardation: A Proposed Program for National Action to Combat Mental Retardation. Washington, D.C.: Government Printing Office, 1962.

Skeels, H. M. "A Study of the Effects of Differential Stimulation," *Proceedings: American Association on Mental Deficiency,* XLIV (1939), 114–136.

Skeels, H. M. "A Study of the Effects of Differential Stimulation on Mentally Retarded Children," *American Journal Mental Deficiency,* XLVI (1942), 340–355.

"The Fallacy of the Superego," by Father Francis Chiaramonte

Davis, Rev. Henry. *Moral and Pastoral Theology,* vol. 1. London: Sheed & Ward Ltd., 1946. 64–79.

Hall, Calvin S., and Lindzey, Gardner. *Theories of Personality.* New York: John Wiley & Sons, Inc., 1962. 29–75.

Haring, Rev. Bernard. *The Law of Christ,* vol. 1. Glen Rock, New Jersey: Newman Press, 1961. 120–164.

Healy, Edwin F. *Moral Guidance.* Chicago: Loyola University Press, 1960. 24–27.

Knox, Msgr. Ronald. *Translation of the Bible* (Old and New Testament), vols. 1–3. New York: Sheed & Ward Inc., 1950.

Rogers, Carl R. *Client-Centered Therapy*. Boston: Houghton Mifflin Company, 1951.

Stoats, Arthur W., and Stoats, Carolyn K. *Complex Human Behavior*. New York: Holt, Rinehart and Winston, Inc., 1963. 270–274.

Thorpe, Louis P. *The Psychology of Mental Health*. New York: Ronald Press Company, 1960. 33–48.

Van der Veldt, Rev. James H., and Odenwald, Robert P. *Psychiatry and Catholicism*. New York: McGraw-Hill Book Company, 1957. 108–154.

"The Effects of Increased Rewards on Reading Achievement and School Attitudes of Potential Dropouts," by Carl A. Clark and Herbert J. Walberg

Brown, Jo Ann. "The Effect of Varying Amounts of Praise on Aspiration Level and Achievement of Elementary School Children," Thesis, Chicago Teachers College, 1964.

Dawson, Grace, and Dawson, J. G. "The Effect of an Exceptional Amount of Praise on the Spelling Habits of Educable Mentally Handicapped Children," *Special Report*, Chicago Teachers College, 1961.

Harris, Leola G. "A Study of Competition in Motivating Achievement of Educable Mentally Handicapped Children." Thesis, Chicago Teachers College, 1958.

"Behavior Modification of an Adjustment Class," by Wesley C. Becker and K. Daniel O'Leary

Birnbrauer, J. S., Bijou, S. W., Wolf, M. M., and Kidder, J. D. "Programmed Instruction in the Classroom," in *Case Studies in Behavior Modification*. Edited by L. Ullman and L. Krasner. New York: Holt, Rinehart and Winston, Inc., 1965.

Birnbrauer, J. S., Wolf, M. M., Kidder, J. D., and Tague, Cecilia E. "Classroom Behavior of Retarded Pupils with Token Reinforcement," *Journal of Experimental Child Psychology*, II (1965), 219–235.

Birnbrauer, J. S., and Lawler, Julia. "Token Reinforcement for Learning," *Mental Retardation*, II (1964), 275–279.

Quay, H. C., Werry, J. S., McQueen, Marjorie, and Sprague, R. L. "Remediation of the Conduct Problem Child in the Special Class Setting," *Exceptional Children*, XXXII (1966), 509–515.

Sidman, M. *Tactics of Scientific Research*. New York: Basic Books, Inc., 1960.

Wolf, M. M., Risley, T. R., and Mees, H. L. "Application of Operant Conditioning Procedures to the Behavioral Problems of an Autistic Child," *Behaviour Research and Therapy,* I (1964), 305–312.

"Adolescence: Between Home and Society," by Laurence A. Flaherty

Aichorn, August. *Wayward Youth.* New York: Viking Press, Inc., 1935.

Bateson, Gregory, Jackson, Don D., Haley, Jay, and Weakland, John. "Toward a Theory of Schizophrenia," *Behavioral Science,* I (1956), 251–264.

Diagnostic and Statistical Manual: Mental Disorders. Washington, D.C.: American Psychiatric Association, 1965.

Johnson, Adelaide M. "Juvenile Delinquency," in *American Handbook of Psychiatry,* vol. 1. Edited by S. Arieti. New York: Basic Books, Inc., 1959. 840–856.

Masters, W. H., and Johnson, V. E. *Human Sexual Response.* Boston: Little, Brown and Company, 1966.

Masterson, J. F., Jr. "The Symptomatic Adolescent Five Years Later: He Didn't Grow Out of It," *Journal of the American Psychiatric Association,* CXXIII (May 1967), 1338–1345.

"An Exploratory Study in the Use of Figure Drawings," by Bryant Feather

Burton, A., and Harris, R. *Case Histories in Clinical and Abnormal Psychology.* New York: Harper & Brothers, 1947.

Ferdern, P. "Narcissism in the Structure of the Ego," *International Journal of Psycho-Analysis,* IX (1928), 401.

Freud, S. *New Introductory Lectures in Psychoanalysis.* New York: W. W. Norton & Co., Inc., 1933.

Goodenough, F. *Measurement of Intelligence by Drawings.* New York: World Book Company, 1926.

Harms, E. "Child Art as Aid in the Diagnosis of Juvenile Neurosis," *American Journal of Orthopsychiatry,* IX (1941), 191–209.

Machover, K. *Personality Projection in the Drawings of the Human Figure.* Springfield, Illinois: Charles C. Thomas, Publisher, 1949.

Meyer, A. "Spontaneity," *Sociometry,* IV (1941), 159–167.

Namburg, M. "Children's Art Expression and War," *Nervous Child,* II (1943), 360–373.

Namburg, M. *Studies of the Free Art Expression of Behavior of Problem Children and Adolescents as a Means of Diagnosis and Therapy.* New York: Coolidge Foundation, 1947.

Prudhommeau, M. *Le Dessin de l'Enfant.* Paris: Presses Universitaires de France, 1947.

Rapaport, D. "Principles Underlying Projective Techniques," *Charac. & Personal.*, X (1942), 213–220.

Schmidl, W. T. "Formal Criteria for the Analysis of Children's Drawings," *American Journal of Orthopsychiatry*, XII (1942), 95–104.

"Sociometry and the Schools," by Walter S. Olson

Anderson, H. H. "Domination and Social Integration in the Behavior of Kindergarten Children and Teachers," *Genetic Psychological Monograms*, XXI, no. 3 (1939), 285–385.

Gardner, E. F., and Thompson, G. G. *Social Relations and Morale in Small Groups.* New York: Appleton-Century-Crofts, 1956. 78–171.

Heyns, Roger W., and Lippitt, Ronald. "Systematic Observational Techniques," *Handbook of Social Psychology.* Edited by Gardner Lindzey. Reading, Massachusetts: Addison-Wesley Publishing Company, Inc., 1954. Chapter 10.

Lindzey, Gardner, and Borgatta, Edna. "Sociometric Measurement," *Handbook of Social Psychology.* Edited by Gardner Lindzey. Reading, Massachusetts: Addison-Wesley Publishing Company, Inc., 1954.

Moreno, J. L. "Who Shall Survive?" *Nervous and Mental Disease Monograph*, no. 58, Washington, D.C., 1934.

Moreno, J. L. "Sociometry in Action," *Sociometry*, V (1942), 298–315.

Moreno, J. L. "Sociometry in the Classroom," *Sociometry*, VI (1943), 299–344.

Moreno, J. L. "The Sociometry Reader," *Sociometry*, XXIII (1960), 3–15, 401–490.

BIOGRAPHICAL NOTES

Carole Revelle Arnold is an Assistant Professor of Child Development at Iowa State.

Richard Armour is Professor Emeritus of English at Scripps College, Claremont, California, and the author of numerous books, including *American Lit Relit.*

Keith Bailey, M.S., is Supervisor of Art Instruction at Western Michigan University.

Wesley C. Becker, Ph.D., is Professor of Psychology at the University of Illinois.

George K. Bennett received his Ph.D. from Yale University and is President of the Psychological Corporation in New York.

Helen Bradley, M.S., has been Director of the Head Start Program for the Chicago Board of Education since 1965. The program has serviced over 23,000 students a year. A former teacher, principal, and director of experimental programs for nursery and preschool children, she has been working with problems of deprived urban areas since 1962.

Marvin G. Brook, M.D., is a member of the Psychiatry Department of Western Reserve University Hospitals in Cleveland. He is also President of the Cleveland Society of Neurology and Psychiatry.

Father Francis Chiaramonte is a lecturer in the Department of Psychology at Chicago State College. Previously, he was Professor of Theology at St. Mary's Seminary in Norwalk, Connecticut. He also has served as a chaplain at Harlem Hospital and Assistant Pastor at St. Mark the Evangelist Church in the Harlem district of New York City.

Carl A. Clark, Ph.D., is Chairman of the Department of Psychology at Chicago State College. Dr. Clark is a renowned psychological statistician and has served as a consultant to several government projects.

Juan S. Cruz, M.A., has served as a teacher in the elementary schools and has taught classes for the socially maladjusted. Currently, he is Human Relations Coordinator for the Chicago Board of Education.

Gilbert Derr, M.A., is coordinator of the training and transition phase of the Urban Youth Program in Chicago. He is responsible for the development of a program for dropouts. He has also served as a Vocational Guidance Counselor for the government's Great Cities Program.

Rudolph R. Deyle, Ph.D., is currently Clinical Psychologist for the mental health program in Englewood, Colorado, and a Psychological Consultant to the Lookout Mountain School for Boys, Golden, Colorado.

Lillian Dimitroff, Ph.D., is Professor of Education at Chicago State College, supervising student teaching in culturally deprived areas.

Jerome E. Doppelt, Ph.D., is Assistant Director of the Testing Division of the Psychological Corporation in New York.

Ralph G. Eckert, formerly Coordinator of Counseling and Guidance, Riverside County Schools, California, has joined the faculty of California State College at Long Beach, California.

Bryant Feather, Ph.D., is presently Associate Professor of Psychology at Chicago State College and a private psychological consultant and counselor. He has presented a series for educational TV in Chicago and has been doing research in penology and counseling at the Illinois State Penitentiary for the past four years. Affiliated with many civic groups, he is also Psychological Consultant to the Chicago Urban Youth Development Program.

Francis L. Filas, S.J., is Professor of Theology at Loyola University of Chicago. He introduced the Cana Conference movement to encourage healthy family life, has authored ten books, and has made many radio and television appearances on the subject of sex and family living.

Laurence A. Flaherty, M.D., has served as a psychiatrist in the United States Air Force Mental Hygiene Division and is presently Staff Psychiatrist at the Hines Veterans Hospital in Chicago. He is on the teaching staff of the School of Medicine at Loyola University, Chicago, and is consultant to the Alcohol Treatment Center at Elgin State Hospital.

Paul Friggens is a noted educational journalist and lecturer. He is presently a roving editor for *Reader's Digest*.

Robert Jemilo, M.A., is Director of Supportive Services for the Youth Action Program in Chicago. Mr. Jemilo has taught in the public schools in Chicago, at St. Joseph's College, and for the Chicago Police Department.

Amelia John is an educational editor and free-lance writer.

Philip M. Katz, M.A., is Principal of the Lewis-Champlin Elementary School in Chicago. He has contributed numerous articles to professional journals, and his case-conference approach has been widely accepted in both elementary and high schools.

Charles H. Madsen, Jr., is an Assistant Professor of Psychology at Florida State University.

William C. Morse, Ph.D., is Professor of Education at the University of Michigan and author of many texts, including *Psychology and Teaching*. His work with leaders in the field of mental health and child psychiatry is known nationally.

Frances A. Mullen, Ph.D., was formerly Assistant Superintendent of Special Education in the Chicago Public Schools and a Director of the Bureau of Mentally Handicapped Children. Dr. Mullen is presently a consultant for the education of the handicapped.

John Naisbitt, of Science Research Associates, Chicago, was formerly an aide to former HEW Secretary John Gardner.

John P. O'Brien, M.S.W., is Director of Court Services for the Juvenile Court of Cook County, Chicago.

K. Daniel O'Leary is an Assistant Professor of Psychology at the State University of New York at Stoney Brook.

Walter S. Olson, M.S., teacher and counselor, is at present with the Bureau of Child Study, the Chicago Board of Education, and Assistant Director of Family Counseling Service, a private counseling group. He has developed instructional materials, background information, and research data for educational television.

Lawrence B. Perkins is a senior partner in The Perkins & Will Partnership, Architects, Chicago. Mr. Perkins is a Fellow of the American Institute of Architects and has been guest lecturer at more than forty colleges.

Margaret Hall Powers, Ph.D., is Director of the Division of the Blind and Partially Seeing, Bureau of the Physically Handicapped Children, Chicago Board of Education. Samuel M. Schall is Consulting Ophthalmologist, and Rosemary Welsch is Supervisor of the bureau.

Wilma J. Pyle, Ph.D., is Professor of Education at State University, Fredonia, New York. Dr. Pyle was a former elementary school teacher and coordinator of student teaching at Wayne State University in Detroit.

George R. Ricks, Ph.D., is the Director of the Department of Human Relations for the Chicago Board of Education.

James H. Ricks, Jr. Ph.D., is Assistant Director of the Testing Division of the Psychological Corporation, New York.

John E. Roberts, M.A., is Director of the Urban Youth Program of Chicago and has served as consultant to educators in various cities across the nation.

Concetta V. Romanow, Ph.D., is visiting lecturer in the Department of Psychology at Chicago State College.

Samuel M. Schall, M.D., is the Consulting Ophthalmologist for the Division of Blind and Partially Seeing, Bureau of Physically Handicapped, Chicago Board of Education.

Ben N. Schuman, M.D., is Staff Psychiatrist at Hines Veterans Hospital in Chicago and Consultant to the Mental Health Division of the Chicago Board of Health.

Jane Schwertfeger, Ph.D., is Associate Professor of Education at the University of Michigan and consultant to the Hawthorne Center, Northville, Michigan, and to the Office of Economic Opportunity in Washington, D.C.

Harold Seashore is Director of the Testing Division of the Psychological Corporation in New York and editor of the *Test Service Bulletin.*

Ray H. Simpson, Ph.D., is Professor of Educational Psychology at the University of Illinois. He is author and co-author of five books and over sixty articles.

Leonard J. Simutis, Ph.D., is Professor of Music at Chicago State College and lecturer at Loyola University.

Helen F. Southard is Director of the Bureau of Research and Program Resources of the National YWCA. Her latest book is entitled *Sex Before Twenty.*

Herbert A. Thelen, Ph.D., is Professor of Educational Psychology at the University of Chicago and is author of *Education and the Human Quest* and *Dynamics of Groups at Work.*

Don R. Thomas is a graduate student in the Department of Psychology at the University of Illinois.

William Clark Trow, Ph.D., is Professor Emeritus of Education and Psychology at the University of Michigan. Dr. Trow's extensive publications have made him internationally known, and his text in the field of educational psychology is still in use in many of the major colleges.

Herbert J. Walberg, Ph.D., was formerly consultant to the Great Cities School Improvement Project in Chicago and is now an Assistant Professor of Education at Harvard University.

David P. Weikart, M.A., has been a school psychologist for the Ypsilanti Public Schools since 1960.

Rosemary A. Welsch, M.A., is a Supervisor in the Division of Blind and Partially Seeing, Bureau of Physically Handicapped, Chicago Board of Education.

James J. Zigerell, Ph.D., is Dean of Television Instruction at Chicago State College and former Professor of English at Loyola University of Chicago. He has authored articles on uses of television in education and served as a consultant to various groups involved in teaching by television.